The Economic Consequences of Demographic Change in East Asia

NBER—East Asia Seminar on Economics
Volume 19

The Economic Consequences of Demographic Change in East Asia

Edited by **Takatoshi Ito and Andrew K. Rose**

The University of Chicago Press

Chicago and London

TAKATOSHI ITO is a professor in the graduate schools of public policy and of economics at the University of Tokyo, and a research associate of the National Bureau of Economic Research. ANDREW K. ROSE is the B. T. Rocca Professor of Economic Analysis and Policy at the Haas School of Business, University of California, Berkeley, and a research associate of the National Bureau of Economic Research.

The University of Chicago Press, Chicago 60637
The University of Chicago Press, Ltd., London
© 2010 by the National Bureau of Economic Research
All rights reserved. Published 2010
Printed in the United States of America

19 18 17 16 15 14 13 12 11 10   1 2 3 4 5
ISBN-13: 978-0-226-38685-0 (cloth)
ISBN-10: 0-226-38685-6 (cloth)

Library of Congress Cataloging-in-Publication Data

The economic consequences of demographic change in East Asia /
  edited by Takatoshi Ito and Andrew K. Rose.
    p. cm.
  Selection of papers presented at the 19th annual East Asian
Seminar on Economics (EASE-19) on June 19–21, 2009 in Seoul,
Korea.
  Includes bibliographical references and index.
  ISBN-13: 978-0-226-38685-0 (cloth : alk. paper)
  ISBN-10: 0-226-38685-6 (cloth : alk. paper)   1. Demographic
transition—Economic aspects—East Asia—Congresses. 2. East
Asia—Population—Economic aspects—Congresses. 3. Economic
development—East Asia—Congresses. 4. Population aging—
Economic aspects—East Asia—Congresses. I. Ito, Takatoshi,
1950– II. Rose, Andrew, 1959– III. NBER-East Asia Seminar on
Economics (19th : 2009 : Seoul, Korea)
  HB3650.5.A3E36 2010
  330.95—dc22
                                                          2009045172

Relation of the Directors to the
Work and Publications of the
National Bureau of Economic Research

1. The object of the NBER is to ascertain and present to the economics profession, and to the public more generally, important economic facts and their interpretation in a scientific manner without policy recommendations. The Board of Directors is charged with the responsibility of ensuring that the work of the NBER is carried on in strict conformity with this object.

2. The President shall establish an internal review process to ensure that book manuscripts proposed for publication DO NOT contain policy recommendations. This shall apply both to the proceedings of conferences and to manuscripts by a single author or by one or more co-authors but shall not apply to authors of comments at NBER conferences who are not NBER affiliates.

3. No book manuscript reporting research shall be published by the NBER until the President has sent to each member of the Board a notice that a manuscript is recommended for publication and that in the President's opinion it is suitable for publication in accordance with the above principles of the NBER. Such notification will include a table of contents and an abstract or summary of the manuscript's content, a list of contributors if applicable, and a response form for use by Directors who desire a copy of the manuscript for review. Each manuscript shall contain a summary drawing attention to the nature and treatment of the problem studied and the main conclusions reached.

4. No volume shall be published until forty-five days have elapsed from the above notification of intention to publish it. During this period a copy shall be sent to any Director requesting it, and if any Director objects to publication on the grounds that the manuscript contains policy recommendations, the objection will be presented to the author(s) or editor(s). In case of dispute, all members of the Board shall be notified, and the President shall appoint an ad hoc committee of the Board to decide the matter; thirty days additional shall be granted for this purpose.

5. The President shall present annually to the Board a report describing the internal manuscript review process, any objections made by Directors before publication or by anyone after publication, any disputes about such matters, and how they were handled.

6. Publications of the NBER issued for informational purposes concerning the work of the Bureau, or issued to inform the public of the activities at the Bureau, including but not limited to the NBER Digest and Reporter, shall be consistent with the object stated in paragraph 1. They shall contain a specific disclaimer noting that they have not passed through the review procedures required in this resolution. The Executive Committee of the Board is charged with the review of all such publications from time to time.

7. NBER working papers and manuscripts distributed on the Bureau's web site are not deemed to be publications for the purpose of this resolution, but they shall be consistent with the object stated in paragraph 1. Working papers shall contain a specific disclaimer noting that they have not passed through the review procedures required in this resolution. The NBER's web site shall contain a similar disclaimer. The President shall establish an internal review process to ensure that the working papers and the web site do not contain policy recommendations, and shall report annually to the Board on this process and any concerns raised in connection with it.

8. Unless otherwise determined by the Board or exempted by the terms of paragraphs 6 and 7, a copy of this resolution shall be printed in each NBER publication as described in paragraph 2 above.

Contents

Acknowledgments

This volume is a collection of papers that were presented at the nineteenth annual East Asian Seminar in Economics (EASE). EASE is co-organized by the National Bureau of Economic Research (NBER) in Cambridge, MA; the Productivity Commission of Australia; the Hong Kong University of Science and Technology; the Korea Development Institute (KDI) in Seoul; Singapore Management University; the Chung-Hua Institution for Economic Research in Taipei; the Tokyo Center for Economic Research; and the Chinese Center for Economic Research in Beijing. EASE-19 was held in Seoul, Korea, June 19–21, 2007; the Korea Development Institute was the local organizer.

We thank all our sponsors—the NBER, All Nippon Airways, and KDI—for making EASE-19 possible. The conference department of the NBER led by Carl Beck with support by Brett Maranjian for this conference, and the publication department led by Helena Fitz-Patrick, as usual, made the organization and publication process run smoothly. The local team led by Chin-Hee Hahn at KDI deserves special mention for ensuring that the conference and all local arrangements ran as smoothly as they did.

Introduction

Takatoshi Ito and Andrew K. Rose

The world currently faces dramatic short-term economic problems like the ongoing global financial crises. But a number of long-term economic problems also exist. Of these, only one is both hugely important and reasonably predictable: the long-run demographic issue. Many advanced countries have followed a similar pattern of change in their demographic composition, and are now reaching a final stage of aging. A predictable crisis, due to the adverse effects of the aging population, is looming in many advanced countries. The situation is perhaps most acutely in East Asia, where particularly rapid demographic change is occurring now.

Over the past decades, almost all industrial countries have experienced large decreases in the fertility rate. Their populations have simply become older and older. Since women are having fewer babies, and people are living longer, populations across the industrial world are aging; Japan is one the most extreme examples of high life expectancy and low fertility. Most rich countries now have fertility rates below the replacement rate of 2.1 children per woman; if this effect continues, their population will actually begin to shrink. This will not occur any time soon for most countries, but it is already happening in Japan and will soon be the case for Korea. This aging of the population has already had enormous economic and social consequences, and these consequences are likely only to rise in importance over time.

A number of economic consequences of an aging society have been inves-

Takatoshi Ito is a professor in the graduate schools of public policy and of economics at the University of Tokyo, and a research associate of the National Bureau of Economic Research. Andrew K. Rose is the B. T. Rocca Professor of Economic Analysis and Policy at the Haas School of Business, University of California, Berkeley, and a research associate of the National Bureau of Economic Research.

tigated by many authors.[1] First, an aging population is expected to lower the (total and per-capita) growth rate, as the working population (in absolute number and as the ratio of total population) declines. Thus an aging society is expected to be a drag on economic growth. The second feature stems from the fact that many countries use a Pay-As-You-Go (PAYGO) feature to finance their pension systems; that is, they use the current young's premium payments for the current retired pension benefits. The pension system is thus an income transfer from working generations to retired generations, often using fiscal deficits to mitigate the transfer problem. In many countries, the Pay-As-You-Go pension system is about to run into a problem as the baby boomers are about to retire and drastically change the support ratio. This is happening not only in Japan but also in Korea, Hong Kong, and in the near future, China (which has adopted a one-child policy). Third, as most health care costs are publicly provided in almost all countries, the aging population is expected to increase government spending on health considerably. As society ages, such expenditures have to be covered from a smaller tax base of the working population, and the aged have higher health care expenditures. It is no surprise that many countries have shifted to fund government expenditures by indirect value-added-taxes rather than personal income tax, as population ages. Fourth, the ratio of savers and dissavers changes as the ratio of working to retired population changes. Thus a demographic change has impacts on saving and asset holding behavior of the aggregate household sector, thus affecting asset prices (such as housing, stock, and bond prices), unless the supply side adjust to this change.

This volume consists of a selection of papers presented at the nineteenth annual East Asian Seminar on Economics (EASE-19) on June 19–21, 2008, in Seoul, Korea. The main theme of the conference was the economic consequences of the demographic transition in East Asia, an area of the world currently experiencing a dramatic demographic transition.

The conference for this book took place in June 2008, a few months before the rapid global financial meltdown which took place in the wake of the Lehman Brothers collapse. Many workers close to or in retirement lost a sizable portion of their savings as a result. For young workers, the 2008 financial shock may turn out to be a short-term (though deep) financial cycle, and its consequences may be dominated by long demographic trends. The financial shocks of 2008 and its consequences on saving and consumption are not treated in the chapters in this volume.

1. For the last two decades, the NBER "Aging" group has been active in publishing various lines of work related to aging. See their website, http://www.nber.org/programs/ag/ for a guide to a summary of activities as well as the past papers and books. The NBER group on Aging and Health has been issuing quarterly bulletin since 2002; see http://www.nber.org/aginghealth/2009no1/2009no1.pdf. The most recent conference volume in the 20-year long series is Wise (2009). The NBER group also produced the two volumes on the U.S.–Japan comparison in aging. See Noguchi and Wise (1994) and Hurd and Yashiro (1997).

In the rest of this introduction, we first highlight several themes that run through several chapters in this volume, and weave those themes into several relevant questions. We then give summaries of the chapters, linking them to our themes.

Demographic Transition

It is easy to understand the demographic transition from a low-income developing state to a high-income advanced state. Health and family behaviors across countries and time have a number of common features in economic development. There are four phases. Poor undeveloped states have fertility and mortality rates which are both high. There are many children per family, but people tend to die young, sometimes very young. During the second phase of development, the mortality rate begins to decline due to better nutrition and sanitary conditions, but the fertility rate remains high. As a consequence, the population grows, with a higher child dependency ratio as more children survive. As development continues, the country enters a third phase where the fertility begins to fall and eventually catches up to the falling mortality rate; this leads to a drop in the child and total (child plus elderly) dependency ratios. The drop in the dependency ratios implies an increase in gross domestic product (GDP) per capita, since the share of working-age people in the total population grows. In short, even if the GDP *per worker* had remained the same, the GDP *per capita* (population) would increase in this state. Thus, the first demographic dividend can be reaped. There is little controversy in the literature about the certainty of events and economic benefits about this dividend. However, longer life expectancy and lower fertility eventually causes population aging.

In the fourth and last phase, both the fertility and mortality rates become low. In this stage, the elderly and total dependency ratios rise due to the shrinking number of workers (resulting from the lower fertility rate) and the rising number of elderly (resulting from the lower mortality rate). The first dividend disappears. There is a controversy, both theoretically and empirically, whether there is the second demographic dividend at the final stage. The second demographic dividend occurs if individuals do more lifecycle saving to prepare for a longer stretch of retirement, funded either by private savings or a fully funded pension scheme. If much of the wealth remains at home (as opposed to flowing out of the country), this accumulated wealth for retirement increases the capital/labor ratio. The higher capital/labor ratio, due to accumulated life-cycle saving, promotes growth. However, the second dividend will not materialize if the pension scheme is of the PAYGO type.

The East Asian countries are at various stages of the demographic transition. Japan is in the final phase of demographic transition; Korea and China are in the third phase (the latter due in part to the one-child policy); and the

Association of Southeast Asian Nations (ASEAN) countries (except Singapore) are in the second phase. This volume studies East Asian countries, and will attempt to give some insights concerning the demographic transition that the rest of the world may experience in the future. This book covers topics such as economic growth, economic security of the elderly, national saving and external assets, female labor participation, and expenditures of public education.

In this volume, most papers explain the economic consequences, such as economic growth, of demographic transition. They do not study the other direction of causality, how the fertility rate is affected by economic growth. Therefore, an interesting question of an interaction between economic growth and the fertility rate is not dealt with squarely. However, that topic is amply covered in the literature of demography.

Throughout the volume, an assumption is typically maintained that the retirement age is sixty-five. In the pension systems of most advanced countries, a full pension requires delaying the start of benefits until the age of sixty-five. An option of having pension benefits start at a younger age is an option, but the total benefits are then reduced. Of course, as the general health level and work aspirations of older people is rising in many countries including those in East Asia, a revision of the retirement age may be desirable for the sustainability of the pension system. However, this is beyond our scope in this volume.

Economic Growth

Although the demographic transition has many effects, economic growth is among the most important of all implications. The first three chapters of the volume examine prospects of economic growth among Asian countries based on demographic changes that have occurred and that are projected to occur.[2]

Mason, Lee, and Lee (chap. 1 in this volume) provide a fine overview of the common patterns of demographic transition in the major countries of East Asia. First, they show dramatic change in the support ratios between 2008 and 2050: The population ratio of the old (age sixty-five and older) increases in Japan from 17 percent to 38 percent, Hong Kong from 11 percent to 33 percent, Korea from 7 percent to 35 percent, Singapore from 7 percent to 33 percent, China from 7 percent to 24 percent, Thailand from 7 percent to 23 percent, and Taiwan from 8 percent to 26 percent.

The authors are particularly concerned with the methods through which resources (not only income, but also healthcare) can be provided for the needs of the elderly. This question is relevant in predicting whether or not there is

2. Kelley and Schmidt (2005) provide a comprehensive survey of the literature on this topic.

a second demographic dividend. They contrast PAYGO systems with fully funded systems. In PAYGO systems, no extra capital (in the form of reserves) is accumulated during the period of the first demographic dividend, whether the transfers are provided by the state or through more informal family arrangements. On the other hand, if transfers are provided by fully funded savings from the workers themselves, there is extra capital accumulation. The latter (but not the former) can give rise to a second demographic dividend of economic growth. The authors show the inverse relationship between the fertility rate and educational and health expenditures (a proxy for human capital formation) per child in the region. Taiwan, Japan, and Korea are a group of countries with a very low fertility rate accompanied by very high health care and education expenditure in relation to average labor income of ages thirty through forty-nine. India, the Philippines, and Indonesia are just the opposite. Although the authors emphasize the relation between higher human capital investment and the fertility decline, they admit that the direction of causality direction is unclear. Japan and Taiwan are shown to rely more on public transfers and family transfers, thus effects of raising capital is not clear. Through a simulation model for ASEAN countries, based on Mason and Lee (2007), the authors show that asset accumulation patterns would be very different depending on the assumption on intergenerational transfers. In the case of low transfers (35 percent of old age consumption by transfers), the amount of assets would rise to seven times labor income in 2050; while in the case of high transfers (65 percent of old age consumption by transfers), assets would rise to two times labor income in 2050. The model assumes that open capital markets, so that some assets may take the form of foreign assets, so it is not straightforward to make inference from assets accumulation to the domestic capital-labor ratio. The result is suggestive of the possibility of second demographic dividend.

Bloom, Canning, and Finlay (chap. 2 in this volume) also focus on the shifting age structure in Asia. The authors examine how much effect the aging would affect economic growth in the process of dissolving the first demographic dividend. The authors employ reduced-form regressions, explaining per capita growth by demographic factors, in addition to a standard set from the convergence growth model, such as the real GDP per capital at the initial year. The demographic factors include young-age share (in population) and old-age share at the initial year of regression, the five-year changes in the young-age share and old-age share. The long run effect of demographic composition is estimated from the coefficients of the young-age share and old-age share at the initial year. The old-age share turns out to be insignificant in affecting the per capita growth, while the young-age share at the initial year turns out to affect growth negatively. The magnitude of the long-run effect is estimated as follows: a 10 percentage point decrease in the youth-age share will increase the economic growth per capita by 2.2 percentage points, leading to a higher steady state income per capita in the long run. The short-run effects of the changes in the young-age and old-age shares are estimated from coefficients of five year changes in those shares: a one percentage point decrease in the youth-age share over a five year period increases per capita economic growth by 0.7 percentage points. A 1.0 percentage point increase in the old age share over a five year period decreases per capital economic growth by 1.5 percentage points. The positive impact of a decline in youth age share and the neutrality of the old age share on economic growth per capita are consistent with Kelley and Schmidt (2005).

The authors infer that the difference between the short and long run effects of the old-age share comes from various behavioral responses of people to demographic change. The authors emphasize an increase in female labor participation rate, the quantity-quality trade-off for children, a change in saving behavior and a change in social security (such as postponement of retirement age), with literature survey of these behavioral responses. These behavioral responses to aging may partially, if not totally, mitigate the adverse effect of aging on growth. The authors conclude that that population aging may not significantly impede economic performance in Asia in the long run.

Mason, Lee, and Lee (chap. 1 in this volume) and Bloom, Canning, and Finlay (chap. 2 in this volume) are complementary in that they provide two different sets of explanations concerning why Asian growth may not slow down due to the disappearing first demographic dividend—certainly not as much as a naïve model would predict. The former emphasize a possible second dividend (higher capital labor ratio due to higher life-cycle saving), while the latter emphasize behavioral change of people in response to changing fertility and life expectancy.

Hahn and Park (chap. 3 in this volume) investigate the relationships between: (a) the speed of demographic transition and per capita income growth, and (b) the speed of demographic transition and human capital accumulation. They employ both cross-country regression and micro-level household survey data of Korea. Although the authors motivate the study by invoking an endogenous growth model with endogenous fertility, an empirical part of the study is not explicitly derived from the theory, as the authors admit. The contribution of this chapter thus lies in its empirical undertaking.

In this cross-country (141 countries) study, Hahn and Park specify a growth regression, which is essentially common with that of the two preceding chapters; it includes a speed of demographic transition. Three sets of regressions are examined, each having standard variables of convergence growth model along with one of the three demographic variables: (a) the change in fertility rate (an average yearly change); (b) the change in the working-age population ratio; and (c) the change in population growth rate. They find that an increase in the speed of fertility decline increases the growth rate of per capita income; a faster increase in working-age population ratio also increases the growth rate of per capital income. Finally, a higher population growth rate increases the growth rate of per capita income. Although the authors do not directly examine it, the regression is quite close to testing the degree of first dividend, which is directly specified in Bloom, Canning, and Finlay (chap. 2 in this volume).

Next, Hahn and Park examine the relationship between the speed of demographic transition of a country and the speed of its human capital accumulation. They find that countries with faster changes in working-age population ratio or faster decline in population growth rate, also experience a faster increase in years of schooling at all levels.

In the second half of the chapter, Hahn and Park examine a different data set. The household level survey in Korea is used to test the quality-quantity trade-off. Educating a child requires considerable resources in terms of both time and money. Indeed, a standard explanation for the decline in fertility is the trade-off between child quality and the quantity of children; this states that richer parents tend to prefer fewer "high quality" children in whom they invest their resources rather than more but "lower quality" children. This commonly heard hypothesis is rarely tested directly. Hahn and Park make use of a Korean micro data to investigate investment in human capital and take the quality-quantity trade-off seriously. It is found that with many reasonable control variables, the per-child expenditure on education is negatively influenced by the number of children. Reassuringly, their empirics are quite consistent with the quality-quantity trade-off, a rare but important feat in this mostly theoretical area of work.

Japan

Japan is a large open economy that stands out as the most rapidly aging country in the world. It has the longest life expectancy as well as one of the lowest fertility rates. This means that Japan's soon-to-retire baby boomers will enter the final phase of the demographic transition (with a shrinking population), something that has not been experienced by any other society. The Japanese population peaked in 2004, and Japan is now in the phase of declining population. By 2080, the population is estimated to be half its current size. In 2004, the Japanese total fertility rate was 1.26, one of the lowest in the world. The aging of Japanese society is very rapid; the proportion of the elderly (sixty-five years and above) will rise from 20.2 percent in 2005 to 30 percent by 2023, rising further to more than 40 percent by 2052.

Accordingly, three chapters in this volume focus on Japan. Ogawa, Mason, Chawla, and Matsukura (chap. 4 in this volume) describe the past, present, and future of the demographic transition, using many indicators. Takayama (chap. 5 in this volume) focuses on the Japanese social security system that is mostly a PAYGO system. The rapid aging is expected to cause great stress on the PAYGO pension system. Ohtake and Sano (chap. 6 in this volume) will examine the political economy of education support for the young.

Ogawa, Mason, Chawla, and Matsukura provide an overview of Japan's truly unprecedented demographic transition. Compared with other countries, Japan experienced a very short baby boom; the fertility rate rapidly rose and then dramatically fell after World War II. A large number of Japanese women have become, and are projected to remain, unmarried and childless. Some of this low fertility may be involuntary, since the ideal number of children (as expressed by mature Japanese) remains higher than the actual fertility rate. Nevertheless, the decrease in fertility is only part of the larger picture. Even more important is the fact that the expected Japanese lifespan has increased quickly. Mortality is becoming an increasingly important demographic feature, and Japan correspondingly has a low fraction of lifetime devoted to work. Few of the elderly are now living with married children, and expect to depend on care provided by children. The authors provide a fascinating and compelling portrait of these stylized facts with a terrific visual display of quantitative information. They show that Japan benefited from the first dividend in the 1950s and 1960s, reaching 1 percentage point of economic growth rate at the peak. However, the first dividend turned negative in the 2000s, and is projected to remain negative for a long time. The second dividend was large in the 1980s, reaching 1.5 percent at the peak, but this has gradually declined to less than 0.5 percent in the 2000s. Since the current retired and the soon-to-retire baby boomers have accumulated large private wealth, how these elderly utilize or spend their wealth has impacts on the future course of the economy.

The authors examine the mix of public and private transfers as well as private wealth reallocation in life cycle. A number of interesting findings are highlighted. They find that the impact of the rapid growth of the elderly population on transfers has been remarkable. Transfers to the old (sixty-five years and older) increased three-fold between 1984 and 2004, in which public transfers increased 4.4 times, while the amount of net familial transfers declined by 75 percent. Conversely, net public transfers are negative for the working population (ages twenty to fifty-nine). In 2004, the peak of negative transfers occurred approximately at age fifty-seven. The authors find that the Japanese relatively young elderly (in their sixties and seventies) provided more assistance to adult children and /or grandchildren than financial transfers they receive. This is quite an interesting finding.

The authors suggest that the second dividend is still a possibility, given that large private wealth has been accumulated, and conclude, "the Japanese elderly represent a powerful asset to keep the country on a sound and steady growth path in the years to come. Furthermore, over the past decade or so, they have been informally playing the role of the society's safety net by providing financial assistance to their adult children and grandchildren suffering from financial difficulties."

Takayama provides a comprehensive survey of the past, present, and future of the Japanese pension system. He describes the original pension system, the 2004 reforms, and related problems such as the incentives problem stemming from high rates of social security contribution (higher than taxes), and worsening demographic support ratio. He uses the "balance sheet" approach to analyzing pensions throughout, and focuses on inter- and intragenerational equity. The Japanese system is quite generous; many of the elderly are better off than most workers. There have been many implementation problems associated with Japanese pensions, especially and most visibly in recent years (most infamously when fifty million social security files were discovered to be unmatched to people). However, these short-term problems pale in comparison to the more serious long-term problems. There are two such problems. First, as a PAYGO system, Japan has to pay benefits to retirees that have been promised in the past. This phenomenon is known as the "legacy debt" problem. More importantly, the Japanese population is shrinking and projected to decline for the foreseeable future; creating a sustainable system for the future is a second and separate problem, apart from that of legacy debt. As the demographic transition makes it harder and harder to keep benefit level (replacement ratio) from falling and keep contribution rate from rising, the current younger generation necessarily is worse off than the current retired in their life-time net benefit from the pension system.[3]

In 2004, the Japanese system was changed so as to become more sustainable, since it was, and remains, currently underfunded (unless the economy suddenly begins to grow at a much higher rate than a rate commonly believed to be possible). The 2004 reform includes: a new system of indexation that depends on wage growth rate; increased but also capped contributions; a reduced replacement rate; and increased government subsidies to the basic pension scheme from the general budget. Takayama shows that this reform makes the system substantially less desirable for the young generation. The higher contribution rates hurt the young to the benefit of the elderly. The present value of future benefits is only around 80 percent of contributions, which seems unfair to younger generations to come. Takayama reviews five policy options that have been proposed in Japan: privatizing the second-tier proportional-to-earning portion; move to a fully funded pension; switch to universal pension; move to notional defined contribution; and introducing minimum guaranteed pension. Either proposal has benefits and shortcomings. We are left with a depressing picture indeed, though of an important critical assessment of an important Japanese public policy.

Ohtake and Sano (chap. 6 in this volume) poses an interesting political economy question on the relationship between aging and public education support. Do the elderly support government expenditure on education? If

---

3. For those who think the issue in a broader intergenerational transfers, a generational accounting may be a better way of examining the issue. See Takayama, Kitamura, and Yoshida (1999).

the elderly are median voters, one would theoretically expect the elderly not to support education, since they receive no direct benefits from public education. Indeed, transfers to the elderly may come at the expense of education, given that they compete in the municipal government budgets.

However, the elderly may be supportive of public education, if they are altruistic vis-à-vis the younger generation. Alternatively, the elderly may be self-interested, if the extra human capital provided by education provides an indirect benefit to the elderly. The literature has a large number of mixed empirical results linking the importance of the elderly and their support for public spending. But there has been relatively little empirical analysis covering Japan, and this chapter fills the gap.

Ohtake and Sano use a panel data set covering Japan's 47 prefectures between 1975 and 2005. The authors use panel data analysis with fixed effect; divide the sample into two periods: between 1975 and 1985, and from 1990 to 2009. They find that a higher share of the elderly increased the expenditure on compulsory education per student by local governments in the 1970s–1980s. However, the reverse became true in the 1990s–2000s. Then Ohtake and Sano also ask *why* there was a change in attitudes of the elderly towards educational spending after 1990. They examine four possible reasons. First, it is possible that the elderly suddenly became selfish rather than altruistic around 1990 (though this is hardly an explanation). Second, the young became uninterested in politics and thus increasingly absent from the voting booth. Simultaneously the elderly continue to faithfully participate in elections. Combined with demographic gravity (which is tilting toward the elderly), the elderly have thus seized political power and now control the local governments, which duly implement policies that are beneficial to the elderly. A third hypothesis is that the change in the household structure has caused the decline in support of public education. The ratio of the elderly living alone (as opposed to living with children and grandchildren), has increased and this might gradually reduce the altruism of the elderly. Fourth, the change in the sign of coefficient may have been caused by the change in the public finance system of local governments.

There were fewer three-generation families by the end of the sample, but the authors show that this explanation does not explain the patterns observed. The same negative result is obtained in a specification that includes different living arrangements of the elderly in the regression. The authors then speculate that the change arose from the switch in the public subsidy system, where discretionary power and burden of the local government in public education spending has increased since 1985. For example, the subsidy from the national government for the salary of public school teachers has been gradually reduced.

Ohtake and Sano provide evidence suggestive of generational conflict in terms of support for public education. As admitted by the authors, going to municipal data rather than prefectural data would sharpen the results, as most public education decisions are done at the municipal level.

Korea

Two chapters examine issues in Korea. Publicly-provided pensions are a relatively new phenomenon in Korea, where intergenerational transfers within family have been the norm historically. What is the relationship between these different types of transfers? Do public transfers crowd out those from family members? Kim (chap. 7 in this volume) pursues this fascinating issue empirically with the four data sets: Korean Labor and Income Panel Study, the Korean Longitudinal Study of Ageing, and the Korean Retirement and Income Study. Moreover, Kim compares the result with a comparable data set from the United States.

First, Kim describes notable features from the three Korean data sets. For example, he finds that Koreans have given to their parents much more than comparable Americans. About 62 percent of Korean households give some transfers to their parents or parents-in-law; in contrast, only 16.5 percent of American households make transfers to their parents or parents-in-law. Recall Ogawa et al.; while Japanese (relatively young) elderly give transfers to their adult children, the Korean elderly are on the receiving end of transfers.

Second, Kim shows that some of the transfers are motivated by altruism, since an increase in public support negatively affects private transfers. In 1980, three-quarters of elderly income took the form of transfers; in 2003, the ratio had fallen to just quarter. This has happened in part because of public policy; Kim finds evidence that expectations of public pensions have crowded out private transfers. Transfers are also motivated by exchange motive, as more care for grandchildren is rewarded by more transfers to the elderly by their adult children.

Third, the eldest takes on the heavy burden of supporting the parents. In return, Koreans also differ from Americans since they give concentrated bequests, often to their eldest son (in America, by way of contrast, bequests tend to be spread evenly). Fourth, investing in an additional year of education into child tends to result in higher transfers to the parent (when they become old), by an equivalent of ninety U.S. dollars. Kim concludes that investment in child's education is not worthwhile as an investment vehicle for retirement, at least measured in purely pecuniary terms.

Kim concludes that the current trend towards deteriorating familial support mechanisms in Korea is thereby shifting burdens to the public sector and the elderly themselves. Perhaps though future generations may become more self-reliant and accumulate wealth, possibly giving rise to a second demographic dividend.

Lee (chap. 8 in this volume) investigates the labor force participation

(LFP) of older males (sixty and above) in Korea over the past fifty years, taking advantage of the availability of a long span of data through the Population and Housing Census. The author is interested in understanding the increase in LFP for Korean men from the 1960s to the mid-1990s, while in other OECD countries, the LFP tends to have declined. Lee shows that there was a substantial decline in LFP from 1997 to 2000, most likely due to the East Asian financial crisis. He shows that the increase in LFP from 1965 to 1995 is largely due to an increase in LFP in rural areas, from 46 percent in 1965 to 70 percent in 1995. Population aging in rural areas is produced by the mass-migration of younger people to urban areas, which contributed to an increase in LFP among older males. The average size of farm households decreased from 6.4 persons in 1963 to 2.8 persons in 2006.

Lee uses an econometric model of LFP using data that are pooled over time, and links it to education, marital status, family size, and various regional characteristics. Age, as expected, is negatively correlated with labor participation. Among city dwellers, college graduates tend to stay in the labor market, but among rural dwellers, all levels of education have a negative impact on labor market participation. Married men were much more likely to be in the labor force than single men. The family size is negatively correlated with the labor market participation. Older men in rural areas were much more likely to be active in the labor force than their counterparts in the city. Being a farmer has strong impact on the labor participation rate, and the coefficient is much higher in rural areas than in city. From these, Lee concludes that losing family labor in rural households owning to rural-urban migrations was a major cause of the rise in the LFP of older males between 1980 and 1997.

The author pursues empirical analysis using a relatively untouched micro data set concerning housing and population. Unfortunately, the data set has a number of disadvantages, including an absence of income data. Thus, all the data set allows one to observe is whether a given participant is working (or working occasionally). Reassuringly, those data line up well with those from other surveys. With help of different sources, Lee observes that the ratio of the income of farm households to the income of urban households shows a long-term declining trend, except for the late 1960s. People living in rural areas are much less prepared financially for old-age security than city dwellers. The average amount of net savings of rural households was only 76 percent of the net wealth held by urban households.

Lee concludes that older males in rural areas tend to stay in the labor force longer involuntarily because of insufficient savings. Lee hypothesizes that this results from the shrinking size of the families located on farms (as the young leave the farms for the cities); rural income and wealth are both low, and farmers may find it difficult to save for retirement.

The Kim and Lee chapters are complementary in understanding the status and behavior of the elderly in Korea: Kim focuses on intergenerational (monetary and in-kind) transfers without distinguishing rural and city dwellers; Lee focuses on the difference in labor market participation among the rural and city dwellers based on micro survey, but without income information. Ideally, comprehensive micro information on income, labor participation, and asset holding, with rural-city distinction, would be desirable in such an analysis.

China

While the demographic transition probably has its most visible effects on growth and transfers to the elderly, it also has a large number of other effects. The consequences for health and fertility decision are among the most important.

Almond, Edmund, and Lee (chap. 9 in this volume) ask the important question "What are the long-term effects of maternal malnutrition?" History matters if there are important effects, since even short-term deprivation during pregnancy can affect up to two subsequent generations.[4] But are health and labor productivity really be affected by conditions in the distant past? This chapter provides persuasive evidence that the answer is clearly positive. The authors use the awful Chinese famine of 1959–1961 associated with the "Great Leap Forward." This famine is a natural experiment which seems independent of education, labor market, and other such phenomena that might otherwise be confounding issues (i.e., it is plausibly exogenous). The authors examine people born during this period of time examined using data from the 2000 census, for example, some forty years later. Because weaker people are more likely to die in a famine, any estimated effects are likely to be conservative (because of selection bias). The authors find that those in gestation during the famine were disproportionately on leave from work in 2000, were supported disproportionately by other household members, and have smaller houses. They also have less human capital, are less likely to be married, are more disabled, are more likely to be female, and are less likely to work. Further, there is also an "echo effect" for subsequent generations. These strong and persuasive negative consequences are basically the same, independent of whether one relies on time-series or cross-sectional variation in the data set. Also, comparable features are *not* apparent in those born in Hong Kong during the same period of time. While this is a clever use of a natural but narrow experiment, it has potentially broad implications, since there continues to be tremendous inequality in nutrition access in developing countries.

As discussed in the Mason, Lee, and Lee (chap. 1 in this volume) and Bloom, Canning, and Finlay (chap. 2 in this volume), one possible response of low fertility is higher educational investment into child(ren)—the quantity-

---

4. Females are born with their eggs, so malnutrition during pregnancy can affect grandchildren as well as children.

quality trade-off. However, if a woman has no children, the trade-off cannot be taken advantage of. Indeed, low fertility means that many women will never have children, while others have multiple children. With no children, human capital investment disappears. This poses an important problem to models of endogenous economic growth as well as to society; the possibility of childless woman is often neglected in the literature.

In the literature, many studies have examined the determinants of the fertility rate, and it is well known that the fertility rate is negatively correlated with woman's educational attainment and income level. It is true that that a higher proportion of women in East Asia have recently gained higher education and mainstream jobs, but the speed of the decline in fertility rate in Japan, Korea, Taiwan, and Hong Kong is remarkable. Lui (chap. 10 in this volume) tackles this problem along three innovative lines. First, the variable to be explained is the *desired* number of children rather than the *actual* number of children at the time of data collection, since women bear children in different ages. The author takes advantage of a survey that asks women for their desired number of children (the sum of existing children and "the number of additional children the respondent plans to have") as well as other information that affects the decision. Second, the childless phenomenon is seriously examined. An ordinary least squares (OLS) regression to explain the fertility rate might produce a fitted value of *negative* children (at least for some combination of right-hand-side variables). In order to fix this problem, Lui uses alternative techniques: Tobit, the generalized Poisson regression, and a binary dummy variable approach. Third, Lui utilizes interesting questions on the survey of controls to sharpen the results.

Lui (chap. 10 in this volume) shows that the status of being married, having siblings, and living in a larger house all have positive impacts on the number of desired children. Further, schooling, age, experience (number of years) of work, and commuting time all have negative impacts on the number of desired children. Both the squared schooling and the squared experience of work have positive coefficient, so that the negative effect of very high education attainment is mitigated. Interestingly, income is statistically insignificant in Tobit and Probit regressions, and has a positive coefficient in the generalized Poisson regression. The dummy variables that are unique from the survey also give interesting insights. Factors lowering desired fertility include (a) a perceived negative impact on job and career; (b) lack of confidence in the education system; (c) ignorance concerning how to raise children; (d) distaste for children; and (e) a lack of confidence in the existing marriage. Although the number of respondents who evinced the distaste for children (d) is small, 4.5 percent, it has the largest magnitude of coefficient. There are also positive factors for desired fertility, including (f) a taste for children; (g) a perceived social responsibility to have children; and (h) a desire to have children in order to secure old-age support. Putting the results all together, Lui contributes to the literature of fertility decisions in an innovative way. This type of work is very much needed in other East Asian countries with very low fertility rates.

References

Hurd, M., and N. Yashiro, eds. 1997. *The economic effects of aging in the United States and Japan.* Chicago: University of Chicago Press.

Kelley, A. C., and R. M. Schmidt. 2005. Evolution of recent economic-demographic modeling: A synthesis. *Journal of Population Economics.* 18: 275–300.

Mason, A., and R. Lee. 2007. Transfers, Capital, and Consumption over the Demographic Transition, R. Clark, N. Ogawa and A. Mason (eds.), In *Population Aging, Intergenerational Transfers, and the Macroeconomy,* eds. R. Clark, N. Ogawa, and A. Mason. Gloucestershire, United Kingdom: Elgar Press.

Noguchi, Y., and D. A. Wise. 1994. *Aging in the United States and Japan.* Chicago: University of Chicago Press.

Takayama, N., Y. Kitamura, and H. Yoshida. 1999. Generational accounting in Japan. In *Generational Accounting around the World,* eds. Auerbach, Alan J., Laurence J. Kotlikoff, and Willi Leibfritz, 447–69. NBER: University of Chicago Press.

Wise, D., ed. 2009. *Developments in the economics of aging.* Chicago: University of Chicago Press.

I

Economic Growth

1

The Demographic Transition and Economic Growth in the Pacific Rim

Andrew Mason, Ronald Lee, and Sang-Hyop Lee

Asian countries, like other countries around the world, are in the midst of a systematic series of demographic changes known as the demographic transition, driven by declining fertility and mortality. In addition to declining fertility and mortality, the demographic transition involves changes in population size, growth rate and age distribution. Populations start and end with similar total dependency ratios, but before the transition the dependents are primarily children and at the end they are primarily the elderly.

Although children and the elderly are both referred to as *dependents,* they differ in a very important way. Children rely almost exclusively on transfers to fill the large gap between what they consume and what they earn. The elderly, in contrast, rely on a combination of transfers and life-cycle saving to fill the gap between what they consume and what they earn. Thus, aging—and the anticipation of aging—can lead to an enormous increase in transfers and/or assets.

For this reason, the shift in the structure of dependency from children to the elderly has large potential consequences for the accumulation of physical capital and human capital, as we shall consider in some detail as our

Andrew Mason is a professor of economics at the University of Hawaii at Manoa, and senior fellow of the East-West Center. Ronald Lee is a professor of demography and economics at the University of California, Berkeley, and a research associate of the National Bureau of Economic Research. Sang-Hyop Lee is an associate professor of economics at the University of Hawaii at Manoa and a fellow of the East-West Center.

This chapter was prepared for the East Asian Seminar on Economics (EASE), held in Seoul, Korea, June 19–21, 2008. Research was supported in part by two grants from the National Institutes of Health, NIA R01-AG025488 and NIA R37-AG025247, and by MEXT Academic Frontier Project (2006–2010). Diana Wongkaren provided excellent assistance with many of the calculations. This chapter draws on Mason, Lee, and Lee (2008), prepared for the Asian Development Bank.

main theme. Closely related to this theme is the important role of institutional arrangements governing intergenerational transfers which interact with changing population age distributions and motivation for old-age support. Depending on these institutions, population aging may either drive a vast accumulation of implicit debt in public transfer systems for health and retirement, or it may generate a greater accumulation of assets raising incomes and perhaps labor productivity depending on whether assets are accumulated domestically or abroad.

This is not the place to discuss the causes of changing fertility and mortality, but it will be helpful to begin by considering the general form of changes over a classic demographic transition, as done in figure 1.1. The figure shows actual historical and projected data for India from 1890 to 2100, along with simulated outcomes based on parameterized curves for fertility and mortality. The purpose of the simulated outcomes is to emphasize the systematic and regular aspect of the changes shown which result from the broad qualitative features of the transition and are not special to the Indian context. This stylized transition will then serve as a template for placing the transitions in Asia into a broader context.

We see in figure 1.1 that the mortality decline in India began early in the twentieth century while fertility did not begin to decline until around 1960. A lag of this sort between the inception of mortality and fertility decline is typical of demographic transitions, although the length of the lag is often shorter and there have been some exceptions. During the lag period the rate of population growth accelerates, here from less than a half percent per year to over 2 percent per year, and then decelerates after fertility begins its decline. Population size rises markedly, here by a factor of five or six from 1900 to the present, with substantially more increase yet to come.

The last panel in the figure summarizes the changes in the age distributions by plotting the youth and old age dependency ratios, defined conventionally as the ratio of the populations aged zero to fourteen years, or sixty-five and over, to the working age population aged fifteen to sixty-five. The first notable change is the rise in the child dependency ratio as mortality declines while fertility remains high. As mortality declines, more children survive raising the ratio, much as would happen if fertility were to rise. The increase is evidently quite substantial. Only when fertility begins to decline after 1960 does the youth dependency and total dependency begin to fall, and this decline continues for fifty to sixty years. This phase of declining total dependency corresponds to a rising proportion of the population in the working ages that raises per capita income, other things equal, as we will discuss at length later. This boost to per capita income is called the first demographic dividend. Around 2015 this phase comes to an end as rising old age dependency first offsets and then outweighs the decline in child dependency. Population aging now raises total dependency, which continues its ascent until 2060 or so in this simulation, which assumes that fertility declines until

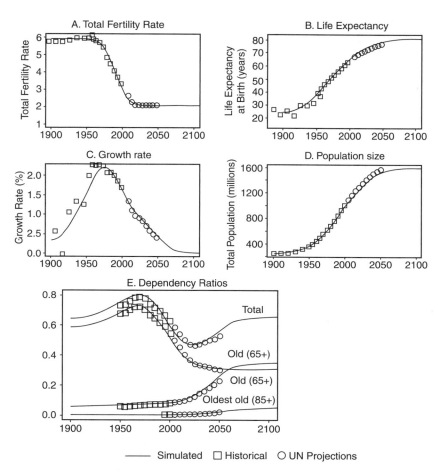

Fig. 1.1   A classic demographic transition, India 1890 to 2100, historical, projected and simulated

Notes: The simulation is based on a fertility transition in which the total fertility rate follows a quintic path declining from 5.9 in 1953 to 2.1 in 2025 and a mortality transition in which a Lee-Carter mortality index follows a sinusoidal path as e(0) increases from 24.7 in 1900 to 80.0 in 2100. Actual India data for the period 1891–1901 to 1941–1951 are taken from Bhat (1989). Actual and projected data are taken from UN (2001).

replacement level at 2.1 births per woman and assumes that mortality decline ceases when a life expectancy of eighty is reached. It is entirely possible that fertility might continue to decline to the lower levels seen throughout much of East Asia, and that life expectancy may continue to rise, so that population aging continues to rise to higher levels more similar to those expected for Japan and Korea.

We will be considering some of the consequences of this series of demographic changes for economic growth. To summarize, the first dividend stage presents an opportunity to convert the transient gains into long term progress through investment. Low and declining fertility has been widely associated with increased investments in human capital, which is one such investment. In various ways, the demographic changes driving the transition should greatly increase the aggregate demand for wealth, raising saving rates and leading to increased capital intensity in the aggregate economy. However, this response is not automatic. To the extent that old age consumption is funded through intergenerational transfers—either private, through the family, or public, through pension and health care systems—this boost to capital accumulation will be diminished. Each of these points provides leverage for policy intervention.

Whether countries will rely on transfers or assets to fund the needs of a growing elderly population will depend on policies, culture, and institutions. As compared with European and Latin American countries, Asia has relied less on public Pay-As-You-Go (PAYGO) pension programs, although the situation is somewhat different in Japan (Ogawa, Mason, Chawla, and Matsukura, chap. 4 in this volume). But health care for the elderly is a large and increasing cost that is often heavily subsidized by the public sector. Moreover, familial transfers to the elderly may be very important in Asia, and these are similar to PAYGO pension programs in some important respects. Thus, aging in Asia may lead to large implicit debts that are shared by taxpayers and the adult children of elderly.

If the needs of a growing elderly population are met through greater reliance on life-cycle saving, population aging will lead to an increase both in assets and income. Previous studies and the subsequent analysis show that through this mechanism, changes in age structure can lead to a second demographic dividend—higher standards of living that persist long after the favorable effects of the first dividend have ended.

The economic effects are not confined by national borders. Divergent demographic trends in the region are likely to generate international capital flows from those countries experiencing the most rapid increase in saving rates to countries that are aging more slowly (but have rapidly growing labor forces).

Some countries in Asia have experienced very rapid transitions. Japan, Korea, China and some members of the Association of Southeast Asian Nations (ASEAN) are examples of countries in which changes in age structure are particularly dramatic. Moreover, the timing of the demographic transitions varies across the region. Japan is furthest along, while India and some ASEAN countries are relatively early in the transition. As a consequence, the impact of age structure for any particular decade varies considerably from country to country. Moreover, the differences in the transition create the demographic divergence that leads to differences in factor ratios with implications for trade, foreign investment, and immigration.

The remainder of this chapter addresses these issues in more detail. In keeping with the approach of this study, we contrast the experiences and prospects in Japan, Korea, India, ASEAN, and greater China—consisting of the People's Republic of China (PRC), Hong Kong, and Taiwan (also referred to as "China+" in the tables and figures). Demographic trends are discussed in section 1.1.

The economic implications of demographic changes are addressed in section 1.2 following the broad outlines discussed in the introduction. We discuss research on the relationship between population and economics and we present a new analysis of how demographic change will influence key macroeconomic variables in ASEAN, greater China, India, Japan, and Korea.

1.1   Demographic Change in Asia

1.1.1   Demographic Transition and Population Growth

In the middle of the twentieth century birth rates were high in every Asian country but Japan. Death rates had begun to decline in a number of Asian countries, leading to more rapid population growth and to increasing proportions of children because the declines in mortality were concentrated at young ages. In terms of the transition shown in figure 1.1, some of these countries in 1950 were in the late stages of rising youth dependency, and others were in the stage of fertility decline and the first dividend.

Except in Japan, birth rates were generally around forty births per 1,000 population between 1950 and 1955, while death rates were as low as ten per 1,000 population in Japan, and as high as twenty-five per 1,000 in China and India (United Nations 2007). The rate of natural increase (RNI), the difference between the birth rate and the death rate, is the rate at which the population would grow with no net immigration. The RNI was high between 1950 and 1955, varying from around 20 to 25; that is, 2 to 2.5 percent per year (see figure 1.2).

During the next fifty years death rates declined very substantially. By the period from 2000 to 2005, the death rate was near or below ten per 1,000 in every country, while birth rates also declined. In some countries the birth rate declined by more than the death rate, slowing population growth, but growth rates remained near 2 percent per year or more in many countries between 1975 and 1980. Between 2000 and 2005, however, further declines in the birth rate are apparent in figure 1.2. In Japan, births and deaths were nearly equal during this period. In other countries, population growth ranged from near 0 to almost 2 percent per year.

Figure 1.2 also shows United Nations (UN) medium projections through 2050, which assume that in countries with very low fertility—for example, Japan, Korea, Taiwan, Hong Kong, China, and Singapore—it will rise in the future, and that in countries with relatively high fertility, such as the

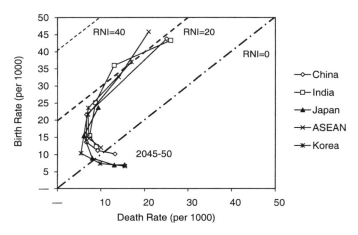

Fig. 1.2   Birth rates and death rates for ASEAN and selected Asian countries, 1950–1955, 1975–1980, 2000–2005, 2025–2030, and 2045–2050

Source: Based on data from United Nations Population Division (2007).

Notes: The RNI is rate of natural increase per 1,000 persons. ASEAN is a simple average of country values.

Philippines and India, it will decline further (UN 2007). The implied variation in population growth rates lies between minus and plus 1 percent per year. Death rates will rise moderately in many countries as their populations age.

The broad outlines of the demographic transition are similar across Asia, but speed and timing vary. The transition began first in Japan, then in other East and Southeast Asian countries, and more recently in some ASEAN countries and India. It has been very rapid in Korea and China as compared with countries elsewhere in Asia, other parts of the developing world, or in Western countries.

Population growth rates are reported for ASEAN, greater China, India, Japan, and Korea in table 1.1. Between 2000 and 2005, Japan's population growth was almost zero. The PRC and Taiwan had population growth rates well below 1 percent per annum. Among the ASEAN countries, only Thailand and Myanmar were growing at less than 1 percent per annum. Two Asian countries had growth rates that would have been well below 10 were it not for substantial rates of immigration—Singapore and Hong Kong, China. The population growth rates between the years 2000 and 2005 of other ASEAN countries vary from 1.3 percent in Indonesia to 2.3 percent in Brunei. India's growth rate is moderately high at 1.6 percent per year for the period from 2000 to 2005.

Because of differences in population growth rates, the populations of ASEAN and India are increasing relative to China, Japan, and Korea.

Table 1.1   **Population growth rates (%), 1950–2050**

	1950–1955	1975–1980	2000–2005	2025–2010	2045–2050
ASEAN	2.10	2.14	1.39	0.69	0.19
Brunei Darussalam	5.56	3.65	2.29	1.28	0.78
Cambodia	2.15	−1.01	1.76	1.26	0.77
Indonesia	1.67	2.20	1.31	0.61	0.10
Lao PDR	2.73	1.30	1.62	1.08	0.50
Malaysia	2.72	2.32	1.95	0.87	0.41
Myanmar	1.96	2.19	0.89	0.47	0.01
Philippines	2.99	2.70	2.08	1.09	0.50
Singapore	4.90	1.30	1.49	0.38	−0.37
Thailand	2.84	2.08	0.76	0.12	−0.27
Viet Nam	1.87	1.99	1.45	0.75	0.21
CHINA +	1.90	1.49	0.67	0.17	−0.32
China, People's Rep. of	1.87	1.48	0.67	0.17	−0.32
Hong Kong, China	4.64	2.73	1.15	0.54	0.11
Taiwan	3.63	1.95	0.54	−0.06	−0.89
India	1.73	2.30	1.62	0.79	0.32
Japan	1.43	0.93	0.14	−0.56	−0.78
Korea, Rep. of	2.55	1.55	0.46	−0.25	−0.89

Source: United Nations Population Prospects, 2006. Taiwan: Council for Economic Planning and Development, China, "Population Projections for Taiwan Areas: 2008–2056."

Notes: Values for ASEAN and China + are for the combined populations, not simple average across the group members.

India's population is projected to exceed greater China's population by 2030 (figures 1.3 and 1.4).

1.1.2   Population Age Structure

Population age structure changes in a very predictable way over the demographic transition. Early in the transition, the percent of children increases as infant and child mortality declines, as we saw in figure 1.1. Later, the child share declines and the percent in the working ages increases. In the final stages, the share of the working age population declines while the share at old ages increases.

The rise in the child share of the population occurred in ASEAN, China, and India between 1950 and 1975. In ASEAN, for example, the percent under age twenty increased from 49.0 percent to 53.0 percent (table 1.2). The decline in the proportion under age twenty has been extraordinarily rapid in some Asian countries such as greater China and Korea. In 1975, just over 50 percent of Korea's population consisted of children under the age of twenty. The projected value for 2025 is 16.8 percent.

The low level reflects the fact that Korea has among the lowest total fertility rates of any country in the world. Other countries in which the child share

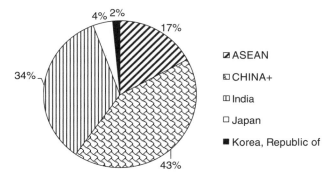

Fig. 1.3   Regional distribution of population for major country groupings, 2000
Source: See text.

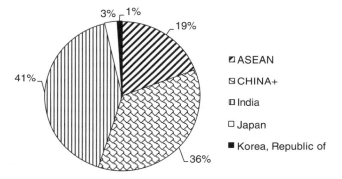

Fig. 1.4   Regional distribution of population for major country groupings, 2050
Source: See text.

is expected to drop to very low levels over the coming decades are Singapore, China, Hong Kong, China, Taiwan, and Japan.

The percentage of the population in the working ages, defined here as those between ages twenty and sixty-four inclusive, increased between 1975 and 2000 in every member of greater China, India, Japan, Korea, and every ASEAN country but Cambodia and Lao People's Democratic Republic (PDR). The percentage reached 60 percent or more in Singapore, Thailand, greater China, Japan, and Korea. These countries are at or near the peak and will not experience any substantial change in the share of their working-age population between 2000 and 2025. Japan is an exception and it will experience a significant decline in the working-age share and size (table 1.3).

The largest increases in the working-age populations are occurring in ASEAN and India. Between 2000 and 2025 the working-age share will increase 7 percentage points in ASEAN and almost 9 percentage points in

Table 1.2   Percentage of population under age twenty, 1950–2050

	1950	1975	2000	2025	2050
ASEAN	49.0	53.0	41.8	30.3	24.1
Brunei Darussalam	46.0	50.5	40.0	29.6	24.7
Cambodia	52.6	52.8	54.3	39.0	29.4
Indonesia	50.0	52.3	40.6	28.9	23.6
Lao PDR	49.5	54.3	54.1	38.7	26.9
Malaysia	50.4	53.2	43.6	31.7	24.5
Myanmar	44.3	51.7	40.4	27.9	23.0
Philippines	53.7	55.4	48.4	37.3	26.6
Singapore	50.0	45.7	28.1	16.4	15.5
Thailand	53.0	53.3	32.1	24.4	21.4
Viet Nam	41.9	53.8	44.1	29.4	23.1
CHINA +	43.4	48.8	32.8	23.7	20.5
China, People's Rep. of	43.3	48.9	32.9	23.8	20.5
Hong Kong, China	41.2	42.3	23.7	15.7	15.2
Taiwan	52.5	47.4	29.7	20.6	18.6
India	47.7	50.6	45.1	33.3	24.4
Japan	45.8	31.5	20.5	15.5	15.3
Korea, Rep. of	51.7	50.3	28.9	16.8	14.2

Source: United Nations Population Prospects, 2006. Taiwan: Council for Economic Planning and Development, "Population Projections for Taiwan Areas: 2008–2056."

Table 1.3   Percentage of population aged twenty to sixty-four, 1950–2050

	1950	1975	2000	2025	2050
ASEAN	47.2	43.4	53.3	60.6	58.3
Brunei Darussalam	49.2	46.0	57.0	62.8	60.5
Cambodia	44.7	44.4	42.7	56.0	60.9
Indonesia	46.1	44.4	54.5	62.1	57.8
Lao PDR	48.4	42.7	42.5	56.5	62.5
Malaysia	44.6	43.0	52.5	59.6	59.2
Myanmar	52.3	44.0	54.1	62.9	58.1
Philippines	42.7	41.6	48.0	56.3	60.4
Singapore	47.6	50.1	64.8	60.8	51.7
Thailand	43.8	43.1	61.2	60.7	55.3
Viet Nam	53.9	41.3	50.5	61.9	57.7
CHINA +	52.1	46.8	60.3	62.5	55.7
China, People's Rep. of	52.2	46.7	60.3	62.5	55.8
Hong Kong, China	56.3	52.3	65.4	62.6	52.1
Taiwan	45.0	49.2	62.1	62.3	55.5
India	49.2	46.0	50.3	58.9	61.1
Japan	49.3	60.6	62.2	55.1	47.0
Korea, Rep. of	45.2	46.1	63.7	63.6	50.6

Source: United Nations Population Prospects, 2006. Taiwan: Council for Economic Planning and Development, "Population Projections for Taiwan Areas: 2008–2056."

India. Within ASEAN, the gains will be dramatic in Cambodia (13 points), Lao PDR (14 points), and Vietnam (11 points).

Population aging is coming very rapidly to the countries of East Asia. Japan, with the percentage of people aged sixty-five and older increasing from 17.2 in 2000 to 29.5 in 2025, has the oldest population in the world. The percentage sixty-five and older will double between 2000 and 2025 in greater China, from 6.9 percent to 13.8 percent, and in Thailand, from 6.7 percent to 14.9 percent. Even more rapid aging will occur in Singapore and Korea where 22.8 percent and 19.6 percent of the populations are projected to be sixty-five and older by 2025 (table 1.4).

Elsewhere, the share of the population aged sixty-five and older will not reach 10 percent until after 2025. By 2050, however, the ASEAN share is projected to reach 17.7 percent and India's share 14.5 percent. At first glance demographic characteristics in 2050 may appear to be remote to the economic concerns of today. Nothing could be further from the truth, however. The elderly population of 2050 is the working population of today. The prospect of old-age and retirement will influence current behavior—with respect to saving, for example. Moreover, policies implemented by governments today will determine the success with which the working population of today can adequately prepare for an extended period of old age, and the ways in which they prepare.

Table 1.4   **Percentage of population sixty-five and older, 1950–2050**

	1950	1975	2000	2025	2050
ASEAN	3.8	3.6	4.9	9.1	17.7
Brunei Darussalam	4.9	3.5	2.9	7.6	14.8
Cambodia	2.7	2.8	2.9	5.0	9.8
Indonesia	4.0	3.3	4.9	9.0	18.6
Lao PDR	2.2	3.1	3.4	4.7	10.6
Malaysia	5.1	3.7	3.9	8.7	16.3
Myanmar	3.4	4.2	5.5	9.3	18.9
Philippines	3.6	3.1	3.5	6.5	12.9
Singapore	2.4	4.1	7.2	22.8	32.8
Thailand	3.2	3.6	6.7	14.9	23.3
Viet Nam	4.2	4.9	5.5	8.7	19.2
CHINA +	4.4	4.4	6.9	13.8	23.8
China, People's Rep. of	4.5	4.4	6.8	13.7	23.7
Hong Kong, China	2.5	5.4	11.0	21.7	32.6
Taiwan	2.4	3.4	8.1	17.2	25.9
India	3.1	3.4	4.6	7.7	14.5
Japan	4.9	7.9	17.2	29.5	37.7
Korea, Rep. of	3.0	3.6	7.4	19.6	35.1

Source: United Nations Population Prospects, 2006. Taiwan: Council for Economic Planning and Development, "Population Projections for Taiwan Areas: 2008–2056."

1.1.3   Role of Immigration

Immigration plays a relatively modest role in determining population growth and age structure in Asia as compared with births and deaths. Immigrant flows are heavily regulated and limited—mostly by receiving countries. With a few exceptions, the countries of Asia have not opened their borders to immigrants, and there is little to suggest that will change soon irrespective of economic or demographic pressures that may emerge in the coming years.[1]

Asia's largest countries are net sending countries. Net migration from India, China, Indonesia, and the Philippines has consistently been negative (outward). The rate of net migration is quite small in India and China and, thus, has little effect on the size of their national populations. Between 2000 and 2005, for example, China lost 0.03 percent per year of its population, and India lost 0.02 percent per year of its population due to immigration. The rate of out-migration from Indonesia and the Philippines is relatively great as compared with most other countries, at –0.09 percent per year in Indonesia and –0.22 percent per year in the Philippines. But even in these two countries, the impact on the growth of the population in any year is modest (table 1.5).

These four countries do contribute relatively large shares to global migration flows because their populations are so large. For 2000 to 2005 the annual net numbers of immigrants were 390,000 from China, 280,000 from India, 200,000 from Indonesia, and 180,000 from the Philippines. Combined, they contributed just over one million net immigrants a year to the global flow. This compares with a total outflow of 2.6 million per year from the less developed regions to the more developed regions of the world during the same period.

For the most part these immigrants were not moving to other Asian countries. Total net inflows, including immigrants from outside Asia, were approximately 100,000 immigrants per year to the net receiving countries of ASEAN, 60,000 per year for Hong Kong, and only 54,000 per year for Japan.

For a few countries in the region migration is significant relative to their domestic populations. The Philippines has sustained immigrant outflows at a significant level for many years. As a consequence, remittances are currently about 13 percent of gross domestic product (GDP). Hong Kong, Brunei, and Singapore have actively encouraged immigration to their countries. Over 40 percent of Hong Kong's and Singapore's populations, and one-third of Brunei's population are immigrants.

Japan falls at the other end of the immigration spectrum with its relatively closed borders. Given the high wages of its workers relative to those

---

1. Estimates presented in this section are all drawn from two sources: United Nations (2006, 2007).

Table 1.5   Annual net migration rate (net migrants per thousand population)

	1950–1955	1955–1960	1960–1965	1965–1970	1970–1975	1975–1980	1980–1985	1985–1990	1990–1995	1995–2000	2000–2005
ASEAN											
Brunei Darussalam	18.0	13.6	11.0	17.3	13.6	10.9	2.5	4.7	2.6	2.2	2.0
Cambodia	-0.0	-0.0	-0.0	-0.1	-12.8	-3.6	—	3.4	2.8	1.3	0.2
Indonesia	-0.0	-0.0	-0.1	-0.1	-0.0	-0.1	-0.1	-0.5	-0.8	-0.9	-0.9
Lao PDR	-0.0	0.0	0.0	0.0	0.0	-13.2	-2.1	0.0	-1.4	-3.5	-4.2
Malaysia	1.9	1.3	1.0	-1.5	-1.6	1.5	-0.3	1.8	3.0	4.5	1.2
Myanmar	—	—	—	—	—	—	-0.3	-0.7	-0.6	0.0	-0.4
Philippines	—	—	—	-0.7	-1.1	-1.6	-3.0	-2.7	-2.8	-2.5	-2.2
Singapore	15.0	11.6	1.1	0.4	1.3	0.9	11.7	9.7	15.4	19.6	9.6
Thailand	—	—	—	—	0.4	0.9	0.0	0.0	0.6	1.7	0.7
Viet Nam	—	—	—	—	—	-3.2	-0.9	-0.8	-0.7	-0.5	-0.5
China +											
China	-0.1	-0.1	-0.2	—	-0.2	-0.1	-0.0	-0.1	-0.2	-0.2	-0.3
China, Hong Kong SAR	17.4	13.0	9.5	-5.0	7.3	15.1	5.1	0.9	10.1	9.3	8.7
Taiwan	—	—	0.1	-0.0	-0.5	-0.4	-0.4	-0.3	-0.2	-0.2	-0.2
Japan	-0.0	-0.1	-0.0	-0.1	-0.1	-0.0	0.0	0.3	0.4	0.4	0.4
Korea, Rep. of	5.4	-0.0	-0.2	-0.2	-0.8	-1.0	-1.0	-0.9	-0.5	-0.3	-0.3
India	-0.0	-0.0	-0.0	-0.1	-0.1	-0.1	-0.1	-0.1	-0.2	-0.3	-0.2

Sources: UN 2007 World Population Prospects; Taiwan–Fuchien Demographic Fact Book, various years.

Note: Dashed cells indicate that data not available.

of its neighbors and the declining numbers in the working ages, one might well expect substantial immigration into Japan. Currently about two million immigrants live in Japan or, 1.6 percent of its population. This compares with an immigrant share for the more developed regions of the world of 9.5 percent and a figure of 12.9 percent for the U.S. population.

1.2   Economic and Social Implications

Demographic change in general, and the demographic transition in particular, has three broad kinds of economic consequence. First, the support ratio is altered, such that output produced by the working age population must be shared with differing numbers of children and elderly. During the phase of the transition when fertility is falling, rising support ratios boost the growth rate of per capita income or consumption, other things equal, and this is called the "first demographic dividend." Second, the process of capital accumulation is affected, since both longer life and fewer children lead to higher savings in preparation for retirement, while population aging increases the relative number of wealth-holding elderly in the population. The combined effect raises the aggregate capital-labor ratio and therefore labor productivity, generating the so-called "second demographic dividend." However, the extent to which this happens depends on the extent to which income of the elderly is derived from public or familial transfers, rather than private saving, and the degree of openness of the economy influences the extent to which labor productivity is raised domestically or in other countries. In any event, although the capital-labor ratio increases, the rate of saving out of GDP may decrease as populations age. Third, both lower fertility and higher survival lead to increased human capital investment per child. While the support ratio falls, rises, and then falls again over the demographic transition, the accumulation of physical and human capital per capita rises permanently, at least once fertility begins to fall. We will consider each of these three kinds of effects in more detail, drawing on information about the economic life cycle for various Asian countries from the National Transfer Accounts (NTA) project.[2]

Population change has important implications for individual countries, but also for regional economies and regional integration. First, national and regional populations are growing at very different rates, with India and ASEAN increasing relative to greater China, Japan, and Korea. Inevitably changes in the size of populations influence the size of regional economies. More people means more consumers, more workers, and more savers and

---

2. The National Transfer Accounts (NTA) project uses new methods to construct measures of the flows of resources across ages through the public sector and through the private sector, including within families. Estimates are consistent with National Income and Product Accounts. Currently, twenty-eight countries in Asia, the Americas, Europe, and Africa are participating in the project. More information is available at www.ntaccounts.org.

investors. The extent to which larger populations result in greater aggregate consumption, aggregate earners, aggregate saving, and investment will be influenced by a host of factors beyond the size of national and regional populations. Nonetheless, population size is an important consideration.

National and regional differences in the growth of consumer demand, labor forces, and aggregate saving and investment will influence international flows of workers, goods and services, and capital. The classic approach to this issue is that international flows arise in response to international differences in relative factor endowments (Deardorff 1987). In this context a key issue is whether divergent population trends lead to divergent factor endowments.

The impact of divergent factor endowments will depend to a great extent on the institutional context. Divergent capital-labor ratios can lead to immigration, capital flows, and/or trade depending on the policy context. As should be clear from the brief description in the preceding section, international labor flows are relatively limited in Asia. In the absence of radical changes in policy, population aging is more likely to influence international capital flows and trade than immigration.

1.2.1   The Economic Life Cycle

The economic life cycle is fundamental to understanding the relationship between population age structure and the economy. In all populations there are extended periods of dependency. Children consume more resources than they produce through their own labor and must rely heavily on intergenerational transfers from their parents (and grandparents), and from taxpayers. The elderly also consume more than they produce. They rely on intergenerational familial and public transfers, but also on personal assets to fill the gap between what they consume and what they produce through their own labors.

Figure 1.5 is an estimate of the economic life cycle based on analysis of consumption and labor income data for four developing economies. The figure is a cross-sectional profile constructed from per capita measures of labor income and consumption by single year of age. The values are normalized on average labor income of adults aged thirty through forty-nine. Labor income includes all pretax returns to labor: earnings, benefits, and self-employment income estimated as a proportion of the operating surplus or mixed income of the household sector. The age profiles are based on nationally representative household surveys of income and adjusted to match National Income Account data.

Labor income is a composite. It includes the labor income of both men and women. It is influenced by labor force participation rates, by variation in hours worked, and by variation in wages for employees and productivity for the self-employed. Earnings, which can be measured with relative accuracy, is a dominant share of labor income in developed countries. However,

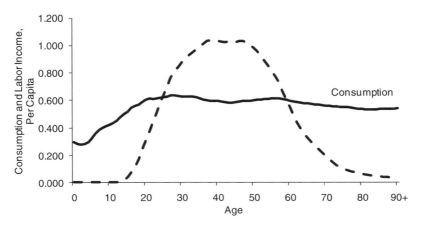

Fig. 1.5   The economic life cycle, developing world profile
Source: Lee and Mason (2007).

self-employment income, which is poorly measured, is a substantially large share of labor income in low-income countries.

Consumption includes both public and private consumption. Private consumption of health, education, and other goods and services has been estimated separately using nationally representative surveys of consumption. Public consumption has also been estimated separately for education, health, and other publicly provided goods and services. Private and public consumption have also been adjusted to match National Income and Product Accounts (NIPA) values.[3]

One must avoid interpreting these figures as longitudinal or cohort profiles rather than as cross-sectional profiles. In a growing economy with these cross-sectional profiles, labor income will rise more steeply for young cohorts, peak at a later age, and decline more slowly for the elderly. Consumption will not be flat for a cohort—rather it will rise with age at a rate roughly equal to the rate of aggregate per capita consumption growth.

The age at which children become economically independent is surprisingly old. Children under age twenty-five are producing less than they consume. Likewise, old age dependency occurs at a surprisingly early age. Those aged sixty and older are producing less from their labor than they consume. The life-cycle surplus is confined to thirty-four years—from ages twenty-five to fifty-nine.

The extent of dependency varies across the dependent ages, however. Those in their early twenties are producing almost as much as they consume; as are those in their early sixties. Young children produce nothing, but they also consume much less than a teenager or someone over the age of sixty.

3. Detailed information about the methodology is available in Lee, Lee, and Mason (2008).

An important issue is whether the economic life cycle is changing over time, how it is changing, and whether it is susceptible to policy. The potential for policy intervention is discussed in the conclusion to the chapter. An important possibility that is widely discussed is that the age at retirement will increase as health improves and life expectancy rises. This may happen, and in a few industrial countries—including the United States—labor force participation rates have risen slightly at older ages in recent years. For the most part, however, the age at retirement has declined dramatically around the world, although Japan has been different. The labor income profile for the United States and Taiwan have become increasingly concentrated, declining for both the young and the old relative to prime age adults. Another possibility is that the consumption side of the economic life cycle will change. Our preliminary analysis suggests that this may be occurring—consumption is rising most steeply at older ages in the industrial countries and particularly in the United States, consumption of the elderly has increased very sharply. In the following analysis we abstract from these changes. If we were to incorporate them, however, they would reinforce our conclusions.

The subsequent sections will make extensive use of the economic life cycle to provide a more refined measure of how changes in population age structure will influence trends in consumption, labor, and their magnitudes relative to one another.

1.2.2   The First Dividend

Recent studies on the macroeconomic effects of population age structure are based on growth models that explicitly incorporate population age structure. The simplest form for these models distinguishes two components of per capita income:

$$(1) \qquad \frac{Y}{N} = \frac{L}{N} \frac{Y}{L}.$$

The exact definitions of the terms vary across studies, but broadly speaking Y/N is per capita income, L/N is the share of the population in the working ages—also called the support ratio, and Y/L is income per worker or working age person. Letting gr represent the growth rate, equation (1) can also be expressed as:

$$(2) \qquad gr\left[\frac{Y}{N}\right] = gr\left[\frac{L}{N}\right] + gr\left[\frac{Y}{L}\right].$$

Equation (2) identifies two channels through which population can influence per capita income. First, the support ratio varies with changes in the population age structure. Given the rate of growth in Y/L, a 1 percentage point increase in the support ratio yields a 1 percentage point increase in per capita income. This effect is referred to as the accounting effect or the first dividend. Note that equation (2) is an identity and, hence, given output per effective producer, changes in the support ratio must produce point-for-point changes in output per effective consumer. A comprehensive understanding requires that we explore the second channel, as well: how changes in population age structure, other population changes, and nondemographic factors influence productivity growth, in other words, the growth of Y/L.

Elaborations on this simple formulation have been used to study population and economic growth using three approaches. First, aggregate panel data have been used to estimate growth models, usually adapting equation (2) to a Barro-type growth framework (Kelley and Schmidt 1995; Bloom and Williamson 1998; Bloom and Canning 2001; Kelley and Schmidt 2001; Kelley and Schmidt 2007). A second approach relies on growth accounting methods (Mason 2001). A third method uses simulation modeling (Cutler et al. 1990; Mason 2005; Attanasio et al. 2006; Mason and Lee 2006; Mason 2007).

A simple refinement of this formulation incorporates the age variation in the economic life cycle into the calculation of the support ratio. In this formulation, L is the effective labor force calculated using the age-profile of labor income to weight the population age distribution. The effective labor force then incorporates age variation in labor force participation, hours worked, and productivity. The denominator N should also incorporate age variation in consumption to measure the effective number of consumers. Thus, if income per effective consumer, Y/N, increases by 1 percent, the per capita age profile of consumption in figure 1.5 can increase by 1 percent holding the consumption ratio (the ratio of aggregate consumption to national income) constant. To be explicit, the effective number of producers, L, and the effective number of consumers, N, are defined to be:

(3)
$$L(t) = \sum_x \gamma(x)P(x, t)$$
$$N(t) = \sum_x \alpha(x)P(x, t),$$

where $P(x, t)$ is the population aged x in year t, $\gamma(x)$ is the age-profile of labor income, and $\alpha(x)$ is the age-profile of consumption. Both age-profiles are held constant over time.[4] The support ratio is defined as the ratio $L(t)/N(t)$.

The economic support ratio for five countries/groups from 1950 to 2050 is plotted in figure 1.6. Japan's support ratio has peaked and is beginning to decline, but for all others in Asia the economic support ratio is rising and thus contributing to more rapid growth in income per effective consumer. The impact of the economic support ratio does not depend on its level; its effect on income per effective consumer—the first dividend—is equal to the growth rate of the support ratio (figure 1.7).

Figure 1.7 presents the first dividend for 1990 to 2025. In the early 1990s

4. An interesting and important question is how the economic life-cycle changes over time and how that will influence the analysis presented here.

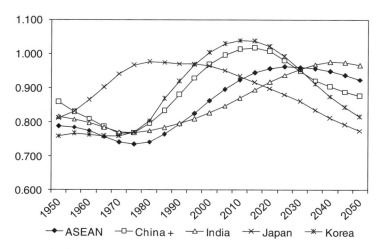

Fig. 1.6   Economic support ratio, country groupings, 1950–2050
Source: Calculated by authors.

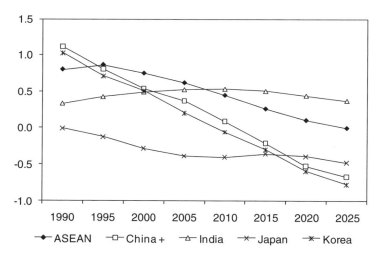

Fig. 1.7   The first demographic dividend (%), 1990–2025, country groupings
Source: Calculated by authors.

the first dividend was turning negative in Japan, increasingly so as time progressed. By 2025 the decline in the economic support ratio will be depressing growth in income per effective consumer by 0.5 percent per year.

The experiences of greater China and Korea are similar with the first dividend, marginally larger in greater China in each year. In the early 1990s, the first dividend added about 1 percent per year to growth in income per effective consumer. The impact has declined steadily. It is still positive, but will soon disappear and after 2020 will depress growth by 0.5 percent per year. In India and ASEAN the dividend is positive for the entire thirty-five year period. Currently, the increase in the economic support ratio is adding approximately 0.5 percent per year to growth in income per effective consumer. Over the period 1990 to 2025, the first dividend has raised income per effective consumer in total by 21 percent in ASEAN and by 18 percent in India.

Changes in the economic support ratio emphasize the implications of population age structure for per capita values. The changes in total number of effective consumers and producers are also of interest because of their implications for trade, capital flows, and immigration. The most rapid growth in the effective number of consumers is in ASEAN and India. For the period from 2005 to 2010, the annual growth rate in the effective number of consumers is 1.4 percent per annum in ASEAN and 1.7 percent per annum in India. The effective number of consumers is growing much more slowly in China and Korea and declining slowly in Japan (table 1.6).

Currently, the effective number of producers is growing more rapidly than the effective number of consumers except in Japan. The growth rate is about 2 percent per annum in ASEAN and India, 1 percent in greater China, 0.7 percent per annum in Korea, and declining by 0.4 percent per annum in Japan.

The regional differences in growth rates may seem small but their cumulative effect is not because they are persistent. The coming decades will see a significant shift to the West and to the South. India will supplant China as the largest country in terms of effective number of consumers and effective number of producers. The ASEAN's share will grow to approach about 20 percent by 2050. Japan and Korea will shrink relative to their neighbors. Korea's share of effective producers will be cut in half by 2050, and Japan's by over 60 percent (table 1.7).

Table 1.6   **Annual growth rates (%), effective numbers of consumers and producers**

	1990	1995	2000	2005	2010	2015	2020
Effective consumers							
ASEAN	2.0	1.8	1.6	1.4	1.2	1.1	0.9
China +	1.3	1.1	0.9	0.7	0.6	0.5	0.3
India	2.2	2.0	1.8	1.7	1.5	1.3	1.1
Japan	0.5	0.3	0.1	−0.1	−0.2	−0.3	−0.5
Korea, Rep. of	1.1	0.9	0.7	0.5	0.3	0.1	−0.1
Effective producers							
ASEAN	2.8	2.7	2.3	2.1	1.7	1.3	1.0
China +	2.4	1.9	1.4	1.1	0.7	0.3	−0.2
India	2.5	2.4	2.3	2.2	2.0	1.8	1.6
Japan	0.5	0.2	−0.1	−0.4	−0.6	−0.7	−0.8
Korea, Rep. of	2.2	1.6	1.2	0.7	0.2	−0.2	−0.7

Table 1.7   **Distribution of effective consumers and producers**

	1990	2025	2050
Effective consumers			
ASEAN	16.4	18.0	19.0
China +	45.3	39.5	36.0
India	31.7	37.8	41.4
Japan	4.9	3.3	2.6
Korea, Rep. of	1.7	1.3	1.1
Total	100.0	100.0	100.0
Effective producers			
ASEAN	15.4	18.1	19.1
China +	47.2	40.5	34.3
India	29.9	37.0	43.5
Japan	5.7	3.0	2.2
Korea, Rep. of	1.8	1.4	0.9
Total	100.0	100.0	100.0

The first dividend depends entirely on changes in the size of the effective workforce relative to the population (or the effective number of consumers). Output and income per working-age adult are held constant and, hence, the possible effects of population growth or changing age structure on the second component in the basic growth identity, equation (2), are set aside. In the next sections we explore the possibility that demographic trends are influencing income per effective worker.

There are many potentially important channels through which productivity may be influenced by population. We will consider two important ones: the accumulation of human capital and the accumulation of physical capital, with our emphasis on the latter.

Human Capital Formation

In Becker's quantity-quality trade-off theory (1991), one possible explanation for fertility decline is that rising incomes lead couples to choose to invest so much more per child that they also choose to have fewer children. But within that theory there are also other possibilities. Newly available contraceptives raise the price of quantity by disconnecting fertility from sex, and could thereby reduce fertility and raise investments per child through a complex interaction. New public education or cheaper transportation to existing schools could reduce the price of quality, raising investments and reducing numbers of children. Mortality decline or economic development would both raise rates of return to education and thereby could lead couples to choose quality over quantity. In all these cases we would expect to observe an inverse relationship between quantity and quality reflecting movements along the hyperbolic budget constraint, although the causal forces at work would be quite different.

Some theories assign a central role to human capital. For example, Becker, Murphy, and Tamura (1990) make output of consumption goods proportional to the stock of human capital (constant returns), and human capital per child proportional to the human capital of the parent generation. If this growth model escapes a Malthusian trap, then it converges to a steady state growth path with constant fertility, growing human capital per person, and a growing rate of return to human capital.

Using data from National Transfer Accounts, we have constructed a measure of investment in children's human capital. We begin with measures of public and private spending on children's health and education at each age. We then sum these across age up to eighteen years for health and up to twenty-six years for education. This sum measures total human capital investment per child, in a cross-sectional synthetic cohort sense. To normalize these measures to facilitate comparison across countries, we then divide by the average level of labor income from ages thirty to forty-nine, as before. The natural logarithm of this ratio is then compared to the logarithm of the Total Fertility Rate, which is also a cross-sectional synthetic cohort measure.

The result is plotted in figure 1.8, which shows a strong inverse association across countries between human capital investment per child and the level of fertility. The elasticity is −1.3, indicating that couples in countries with lower fertility actually spend a higher proportion of their labor income on human capital investments than do couples in the countries with higher fer-

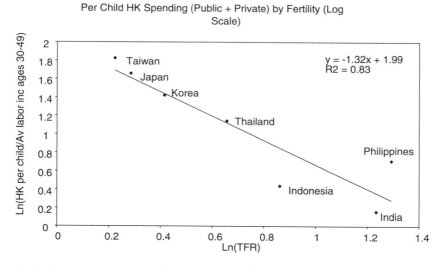

Fig. 1.8   Total human capital spending per child on health up to age eighteen and education up to age twenty-six, public and private, divided by average labor income ages 30–49

tility. When countries outside of Asia are included, however, this elasticity is indistinguishable from unity (Lee and Mason 2009). The inverse association displayed in figure 1.8 can be viewed as a kind of meta budget constraint for quantity-quality, an interpretation developed in Lee and Mason (2009).

Although figure 1.8 shows a cross-sectional rather than a longitudinal relationship, it suggests that fertility decline in Asia has been accompanied by a sharp increase in investment per child relative to family resources. We would expect an increase of this sort to raise labor productivity and contribute powerfully to economic growth, a process that is modeled and explored in Lee and Mason (2009). Here, however, we will simply note that this rising level of investment may have been rooted in declining fertility and must surely have contributed importantly to rising labor productivity and economic growth.

Physical Capital Accumulation and the Second Dividend

A fundamental result that follows from the neoclassical growth model is that for a given saving rate, slower population growth or slower growth in the effective labor force leads to capital deepening and an increase in output per worker (Solow 1956). When the workforce grows more rapidly, a larger share of current investment must be devoted to providing capital to new workers (capital widening). Less is available for increasing capital per worker (capital deepening). The steady state capital output ratio (K/Y) depends only on the saving rate (s), the rate of population growth (n), and technological change (λ) (if we ignore depreciation): $K/Y = s/(n + \lambda)$. Any decline in the population growth rate leads to a rise in the capital output ratio.

This is an important point because the decline in the economic support ratio at the end of the demographic transition is a direct result of slower growth in the labor force. The first dividend turns negative, but, given a constant saving rate, output per worker will rise. Hence, population aging may lead to higher—not lower—per capita income. Indeed, this was the conclusion reached by Cutler et al. (1990) in their analysis of U.S. aging.

Given the objective of this analysis, two assumptions underlying the simple neoclassical growth model are unattractive: that the saving rate is exogenous and that the economy is closed.

The life cycle saving model is widely used to analyze the effects of population and other factors on saving (Modigliani and Brumberg 1954; Modigliani 1988) and capital (Tobin 1967). In the classic life cycle model, individuals save when they are young and dissave during their retirement years. Thus, given the age profile of saving, an increase in the old-age population leads to lower aggregate saving. A lower saving rate does not unambiguously lead to a decline in capital because of the capital deepening effect. If n and s both decline, K/Y may increase or fall.

The validity of the life cycle model is widely debated. Factors other than the desire to provide for old age may motivate saving. The bequest motive may influence saving, in addition to life cycle saving, but neither we nor others know how the motivation to bequeath varies with fertility or other demographic factors. Hurd (1987) finds that the bequest behavior of individuals with and without children is similar, suggesting either that bequests are mainly unintended or that saving for bequests may be motivated by others besides one's own children (Kuehlwein 1993). Old age support may be provided through public or through familial support. Models estimated using aggregate data support very large effects of age structure (Kelley and Schmidt 1996; Higgins and Williamson 1997; Williamson and Higgins 2001). Models based on survey data suggest more modest influences from age structure (Deaton and Paxson 2000). Simulation models imply that age structure has an important effect, but one that is smaller than found in aggregate empirical work (Lee et al. 2000).

A potentially important elaboration on the life cycle model incorporates the effects of life expectancy on the age profile of saving in addition to the composition of the population. People are living longer and, hence, the duration of their retirement is longer. Although a possible response would be to retire at a later age, this has not occurred for reasons that are not entirely understood. Several recent studies have found support for a strong positive life expectancy effect on aggregate saving rates (Bloom et al. 2003; Kinugasa 2004; Kinugasa and Mason 2007). Fertility decline may also have a significant effect on saving. A number of studies have concluded that populations with high child dependency have lower saving rates (Mason 1987; Higgins 1994; Kelley and Schmidt 1996).

Transfers also play an important role. In principal, old age consumption can be financed entirely through intergenerational transfers, as in Samuelson's consumption-loan economy (Samuelson 1958). More realistically, intergenerational transfers vary in their importance from country to country. Some countries rely heavily on PAYGO public pension programs. Other countries rely heavily on familial support systems, although much less is known about this form of intergenerational transfer and its implication for saving.

A high percentage of elderly and adult children live together in most Asian countries. In Japan and Korea the extent of coresidence has declined substantially in recent decades. Moreover, young adults have much lower expectations about receiving old-age support in the future than was previously the case (Ogawa and Retherford 1993). Coresidence, however, does not provide a clear guide to the magnitude or direction of familial transfers.

National Transfer Accounts provide comprehensive estimates of the importance of assets and intergenerational transfers, both public and familial, for a few countries. Figure 1.9 provides estimates for Japan, Taiwan, Thailand and the United States of the fraction of the life cycle deficit (consumption less labor income) of those sixty-five and older funded by familial transfers, public transfers, and assets (asset income and dissaving combined). The

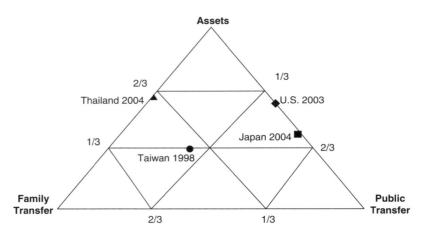

Fig. 1.9   Proportion of life cycle deficit of those sixty-five and older funded through familial transfers, public transfers, and asset-based reallocations (asset income and dis-saving)

Notes: Selected Asian countries and the United States. Computational details available at www.ntaccounts.org. Estimates from the National Transfer Accounts Project. Japan estimates constructed by Naohiro Ogawa, Rikiya Matsukura, and Amonthep Chawla. Thai estimates constructed by Chawla. Information about Taiwan and U.S. estimates available in Mason et al. (2009).

elderly in Taiwan and Japan both depend heavily on transfers—covering almost two-thirds of their life cycle deficits. Taiwan is much more heavily dependent on family transfers and Japan on public transfers, but in total they rely heavily on combined transfers. They rely on assets to cover roughly one-third of their life cycle deficits. In contrast, the United States and Thailand depend on transfers for roughly one-third of their life cycle deficit. Thailand depends more on family transfers and the United States on public transfers, but their total dependence on combined transfers is similar. Thailand and the United States rely much more on assets to cover their life cycle deficits than do Japan and Taiwan.

That U.S. elderly depend more on assets for their retirement than Japanese elderly may seem surprising given that Japanese saving rates are higher than U.S. saving rates. The estimates are constructed to insure consistency with NIPA estimates of saving. There are many possible explanations of the seeming inconsistency, however. This is a snapshot of the use of assets to support retirement by the elderly. Aggregate saving rates also depend on the saving behavior of nonelderly adults. Moreover, the estimates presented in figure 1.9 address only the life cycle use of saving and not other motives; for example, the bequest motive.

Because comprehensive measures of familial transfers are just becoming available, there are no empirical studies of their effect on aggregate saving rates. But Lee, Mason, and Miller (2000, 2002, 2003) use a simulation model to explore their potential effect on aggregate saving. In their analysis of Taiwan, they find that changes in age structure and life expectancy alone can account for only a portion of the rise in aggregate saving rates that accompanied its demographic transition. However, demographic change combined with a widespread abandonment of familial support systems can explain the boom in saving that occurred there.

The results presented here make use of a similar simulation model to assess the implications of population change for wealth and income. The details of the model are described in Mason and Lee (2007) and only its key features are sketched out here.

The economy is assumed to be completely open to international capital flows and interest rates, so domestic wages and interest rates are unaffected by the supply of capital by residents. The age profile of labor income is fixed; for example, relative productivity and labor force participation rates do not change over time, but the labor income profile shifts upward in response to technological growth, which is exogenously determined. These aspects of the model are relatively conventional. However, the treatment of consumption and saving in the model is distinctive.

The model used here implicitly assumes that intergenerational altruism is a pervasive feature of the society. We assume that the cross-sectional age-consumption profile incorporates those preferences for the well-being, for example, of children and the elderly. The shape of this age profile is assumed not to change over time but it shifts upward (or downward) depending on the accumulation of assets, technological progress, and changes in the support ratio driven by changing population age structure. Individual consumption is determined only indirectly by the individual's economic success, since there is extensive sharing of income through public and private intergenerational transfers. Likewise, total consumption by a cohort at each age is only indirectly influenced by the lifetime economic success of that cohort. This approach is far more consistent with the consumption patterns observed in Asia, which in each year are quite constant across all adult ages, regardless of the income histories of each generation.[5]

Consumption at older ages is realized through a combination of intergenerational transfers and life cycle saving. The importance of transfers relative to life cycle saving is exogenously determined and treated in this model as a policy variable or a feature of each society. The economy is subject to an aggregate budget constraint on flows that, along with other features of the model, determines the time path of assets, transfer wealth and implicit debt, and income.

In each period, t aggregate wealth is equal to the present value of current and future consumption of all individuals who are adults in year t, less the

5. Models based on the standard life-cycle theory or the Ramsey approach produce broadly similar results.

present value of current and future labor income of all individuals who are adults in year t. Wealth (W) defined in this way is a broad measure of wealth that includes both real assets (A) and the present value of current and future net transfers to year t adults, called transfer wealth (T). Transfer wealth consists of two components: child transfer wealth and pension transfer wealth. Child transfer wealth is the present value of transfers from year t adults to living dependent children and to children who will be born in the future. Child transfer wealth is negative and it is equal to the present value of the future cost of children to those who are adults in year t.

Pension transfer wealth is the present value of net transfers that year t adults will receive from year t children and from future generations. These transfers may be familial transfers or public transfers. Pension transfer wealth is the counterpart of implicit debt—the transfer wealth of those who are adults today is equal in magnitude to the implicit debt of future generations. Implicit debt as calculated here is not limited to public transfers programs; for example, PAYGO pension programs. It includes all intergenerational transfers whether public or private (familial).

The impact of demographic change on capital accumulation and economic growth depends on the extent to which the economy in question relies on pension transfer wealth versus capital accumulation to support consumption in old age. We treat this as an exogenous variable rooted in each country's institutions, but changeable through policy. Thus we specify the relative shares of assets and pension transfer wealth. Two sets of results are presented following. In one, a very low percentage of pension wealth is transfer wealth (35 percent) with assets accounting for the other 65 percent. In the alternative simulation, transfer wealth is 65 percent of pension wealth and assets are 35 percent.

Before we turn to the results it should be clearly stated that the model is not intended to be a complete and comprehensive model of the economy. Its purpose is quite specific to showing how demographic changes are likely to influence wealth and assets, and with what implication for economic growth. There are three ways in which demographic change will influence wealth in our model. First, changes in the support ratio influence consumption at each age. If the support ratio is high, perhaps due to low fertility, then higher consumption at every age is possible. Anticipated higher consumption at old age means that more wealth (assets plus pension transfer wealth) must be held at every age to finance that consumption. Second, people are living longer. To support consumption over an extended period of retirement, they must accumulate more wealth during their working years. Third, given the age profile of wealth holdings, changes in the population age structure influence aggregate wealth. Up to a point, wealth rises with age and, hence, a population concentrated in the late working years and early retirement years has greater wealth, in one form or the other.

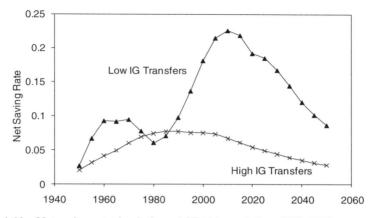

Fig. 1.10   Net saving rate simulations, ASEAN population, 1950–2050
Note: Low (high) IG transfer assumes that transfer wealth is 35 percent (65 percent) of pension wealth.

1.2.3   Simulation Results for ASEAN

Simulated net saving rates in ASEAN for 1950 to 2050 are shown in figure 1.10. Comparative results will be presented in the next section. Productivity growth is assumed to be 2 percent per annum here and in all other results presented. The high intergenerational (IG) transfer simulation gives the saving rate if 65 percent of the wealth required to support consumption in old age is provided through public and familial transfer programs. The low intergenerational (IG) transfer simulation gives the saving rate if intergenerational transfers cover only 35 percent of the consumption needed during retirement.

Changes in age structure lead to a rise and then to a decline in net saving rates. One might incorrectly infer from the pattern that population aging is leading to a decline in saving rates, but this is not correct. Saving rates are rising in anticipation of population aging. The change in saving rates is transitory, however. As the population stabilizes at an older age structure, saving rates decline to levels closer to their pretransition level.

Saving rates are strongly influenced by the size of intergenerational transfers. If transfers play a modest role in supporting the consumption of older adults, changes in age structure have a very substantial effect on net saving rates, which rise from about 3 percent of national income in 1950 to peak at 23 percent of national income in 2010.

If intergenerational transfers play a dominant role in providing support to the elderly, then the effect of age structure on saving is moderate. Net national saving rates rise from 2 percent in 1950 to peak at around 8 percent in 1985 before gradually declining.

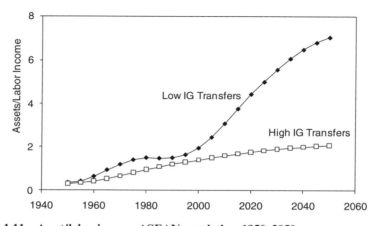

Fig. 1.11   Asset/labor income, ASEAN population, 1950–2050

Note: Low (high) IG transfer assumes that transfer wealth is 35 percent (65 percent) of life cycle pension wealth.

The impact of age structure on assets is substantial (figure 1.11). In 1950 the ratio of total assets to total labor income is about 0.3 for both intergenerational transfer systems. By 1990 assets have increased to 1.5 times labor income for the low IG transfer case and to 1.2 times labor income in the high IG transfer case. After 1990, the systems diverge with assets relative to labor income increasing to 7 in 2050 for the low IG transfer case, but only to 2 in 2050 for the high IG transfer case. Total wealth in 2050 in the low IG transfer case is also 350 percent greater than in the high IG transfer case in 2050.[6]

As compared with 1950, changes in age structure lead to about a 30 percent increase in consumption per equivalent consumer in 2030 given the high IG transfer policy (figure 1.12). Using the low IG transfer policy, changes in age structure lead to an increase in consumption per equivalent consumer of about 50 percent in 2050. Note that the higher consumption after 2025 for the low IG transfer policy comes with a cost. The higher saving rates and lower consumption rates necessary lead to lower consumption between 1995 and 2020 under the low IG transfer policy than under the high IG transfer policy. Consumption remains permanently higher under the low IG transfer policy. Over the next 100 years (not shown) consumption is 20 percent higher on average given the low IG transfer policy. In a closed economy these differences would be larger.

The simulations presume that the economic life cycle itself does not respond to changes in age structure and, hence, the gains (or losses) in consumption are equally shared by all age groups. Of course, other outcomes are

---

6. Because a small open economy assumption is used, labor income growth is the same in either case. The greater wealth is accumulated as foreign assets in the low IG transfer economy.

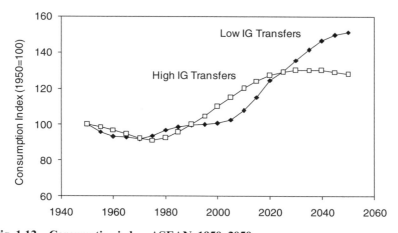

Fig. 1.12   Consumption index, ASEAN, 1950–2050

Notes: Low (high) IG transfer assumes that transfer wealth is 35 percent (65 percent) of life cycle pension wealth. Consumption index equals 100 in 1950. Effect of age structure only; effect of productivity increases not included.

possible. The elderly might flex its political power and increase its consumption relative to younger generations. Or young generations may rebel if IG transfers are too burdensome to the detriment of the elderly.

1.2.4   Comparative Results

The results presented in this section focus more narrowly on two periods: from 1995 to 2005, and from 2005 to 2020. The effects of changes in age structure on saving rates depend on the importance of intergenerational transfers to the elderly (table 1.8). Given low reliance on intergenerational transfers, net national saving rates reach very high peaks in 1995 in greater China, Japan, and Korea. In these countries saving rates decline to intermediate levels in 2005, and to much lower levels in 2025. In India and ASEAN, the saving effects are somewhat more modest and are delayed reflecting the slower and later changes in age structure.

If intergenerational transfers play a very important role, the effects of age structure on saving are muted.

Accumulated assets are reported in table 1.9. Age structure has a substantial influence on the life cycle demand for assets if intergenerational transfers are low. In this case, the ratio of assets to labor income in 1995 ranges from 1.1 given the demography of India, to 10.2 given the demography of Japan. The demand for life cycle assets grows in all cases between 1995 and 2005, and between 2005 and 2025. By 2025, Korea is approaching the simulated level of assets for Japan. Percentage growth rates are very strong in ASEAN and India. Between 1995 and 2025, assets relative to labor income increase threefold in both cases.

Table 1.8   Net saving/national income (%), country groupings

	IG trans share low (0.35)			IG trans share high (0.65)		
	1995	2005	2025	1995	2005	2025
ASEAN	13.6	21.5	18.5	7.5	7.3	4.9
China +	32.4	21.6	6.5	7.6	5.3	2.8
India	7.0	15.0	21.6	7.1	7.6	5.7
Japan	38.6	15.9	3.5	4.5	2.9	1.4
Korea, Rep. of	52.9	32.4	2.6	7.9	4.7	1.4

Note: IG = intergenerational.

Table 1.9   Assets/labor income, country groupings

	IG trans share low (0.35)			IG trans share high (0.65)		
	1995	2005	2025	1995	2005	2025
ASEAN	1.6	2.4	5.0	1.3	1.5	1.8
China +	2.6	4.4	7.1	1.5	1.7	2.0
India	1.1	1.5	3.9	1.0	1.2	1.7
Japan	10.2	13.6	14.9	2.5	2.6	2.8
Korea, Rep. of	5.2	8.9	12.7	2.1	2.2	2.3

The complexities of the relationship between age structure and consumption growth are apparent in table 1.10. Consumption growth changes because of changes in income per effective consumer and changes in the ratio of consumption to national income that underlie the second dividend. If the consumption ratio changes very little, the trend in consumption is dominated by changes in the support ratio; for example, the first dividend. Thus, consumption per equivalent consumer will grow more rapidly during the dividend period and then decline as population aging dominates the support ratio.

However, if there is a strong response in the consumption ratio the outcome is more complex. Rapid accumulation of capital is realized through a decline in the consumption ratio and slow growth in consumption per effective consumer. As the consumption ratio rises from low levels, however, consumption growth can be very rapid.

Consumption growth in ASEAN shows this pattern. Given a strong saving response (low intergenerational transfers), consumption growth is slow from 1995 until 2005, but very substantial from 2005 to 2025. In contrast, given a modest saving response (high intergenerational transfers), consumption growth is more rapid from 1995 to 2005, and dissipates between 2005 and 2025.

The situation in India is somewhat different. From 1995 to 2005, con-

Table 1.10   **Annual growth in consumption due to age structure (%), country groupings**

	IG trans share low (0.35)		IG trans share high (0.65)	
	1995–2005	2005–2025	1995–2005	2005–2025
ASEAN	0.3	1.2	0.9	0.6
China +	3.0	1.4	1.0	0.1
India	−0.2	0.7	0.6	0.7
Japan	4.1	0.5	0.0	−0.3
Korea, Rep. of	5.9	2.6	1.0	0.0

sumption is actually declining modestly (relative to productivity gains) as a result of a decline in the share of national income consumed. Consumption rebounds after 2005. For the two decades taken as a whole, consumption growth rates are the same given either policy, but more detailed results show that consumption growth is substantially more rapid given the high saving scenario after 2015.

Greater China, Japan, and Korea are in similar situations given a low level of intergenerational transfers. For the period from 1995 to 2005, consumption growth is very rapid—ranging from 3 percent to nearly 6 percent above the assumed rate of productivity growth of 2 percent per year. During this period saving rates are declining from the high levels of 1995 and earlier, and income growth is strong leading to rapid growth in consumption. After 2005, consumption growth rates are well above those possible in the absence of a strong saving response.

A note of caution is in order here. The very large simulated effects are conditioned on low intergenerational transfers. The evidence from Japan, Taiwan, and preliminary estimates for Korea not presented here indicates that intergenerational transfers to the elderly were closer to the high IG transfer scenario than the low IG transfer scenario. Hence, the second dividends realized in East Asia were probably well below the possible gains that could have been realized. Estimates of the contribution of changes in age structure to growth in per capita income in East Asia range from about one-third to one-quarter of actual growth (Bloom and Williamson 1998; Mason 2001). The simulated impact on consumption is substantially greater than the simulated effect on per capita income, because of the rapid increase in consumption rates for Korea, Japan, and greater China.

1.3   Discussion and Conclusions

Declining mortality followed by declining fertility leads to a roller coaster of changes in dependency with initial increases in child dependency, then a period of improving support ratios spanning about fifty years and generating the first dividend, and finally population aging. Asian countries have all entered the first dividend phase, with India and ASEAN midway through it, China and Korea near its end, and Japan well past it and into population aging.

Population aging is the inevitable last stage of the demographic transition, and the costs of supporting the consumption of a large dependent elderly population, reflected in falling support ratios, lead to concerns by policymakers, the media, and the public. The declining support ratios due to population aging are a predictable and very concrete aspect of the complex constellation of economically important changes occurring over the course of the demographic transition, and it is therefore tempting to view population aging separately from these other changes that result from the same basic causes. Earlier we have highlighted the relation of the demographic transition and population aging to increased investment in human capital and physical capital. Both raise productivity and incomes far more significantly than declining support ratios diminish them.

The changes in age structure that accompany the demographic transition are emphasized here because of their importance particularly in countries that have experienced rapid fertility decline in East Asia and elsewhere. The post-World War II baby booms of the United States and other Western countries have also produced significant changes in age structure and demographic dividends. These are qualitatively similar to those experienced in East Asia but are smaller in scale. Although Japan experienced its own postwar baby boom, it was short-lived with little discernable effect.

We will now briefly consider some policy issues related to these themes.

As noted, population aging will lead to substantial declines in support ratios from their peaks at the culmination of the first dividend phase of the transition. Assuming that the shapes of the age profiles of consumption and labor income do not change, we can calculate the size of these declines. In Japan, the support ratio will decline by 25 percent between 2008 and 2050, or at 0.7 percent per year. In Korea, the decline will be by 22 percent, or 0.6 percent per year. In China, the decline will be only 14 percent, and in India and ASEAN the support ratio will rise.

The projected declines in support ratios have occasioned deep concerns in many countries, since they imply an increased dependency burden on the working age population and threaten fiscal instability. They depend on both demographic trends and on the age patterns of consumption and labor income. Some governments have considered policies to reduce the pace and depth of future population aging by raising fertility. The past experience of European nations with pronatalist policies has not been encouraging in this regard, however. Another possibility is immigration, but this seems unlikely to play a significant role in ameliorating population aging in the Asian context, since Asia is a major net supplier of migrants to other parts of the world, and the more highly industrialized countries like Japan and

Korea have a history of highly restrictive immigration policies (Mason and Lee 2008).

Another way to reduce the projected declines in support ratios is to modify the age patterns of consumption and labor income in a way that raises support ratios for a given demographic structure. Policies to encourage later retirement have not drawn much attention in Asia; indeed many countries have mandatory retirement laws (see Mason and Lee 2008), but later retirement could moderate the decline in support ratios, as could increases in female labor supply. The incentive structure created by public pension programs can have an important effect on retirement behavior (Gruber and Wise 1999) and the design of any new pension programs could be shaped accordingly. Turning to the consumption age profiles, Japan (Ogawa et al., chap. 4 in this volume) and Western industrial countries have experienced disproportional increases in consumption by the elderly relative to younger adults in recent decades, and such changes exacerbate the costs of population aging and its effects on support ratios. Some of this increase in old age consumption appears to be driven directly by the structure of public transfers to the elderly for pensions and health care. It is possible that declines in elder coresidence with adult children are in part an indirect consequence of these public transfers, and this decline may also have contributed to the increases in old age consumption by reducing family level income pooling.

The great increase in human capital investment over the course of the demographic transition has surely played an important role in economic development. Both theory and empirical analysis suggest that the increased human capital investment is closely tied to fertility decline and, to a lesser degree, mortality decline. However, the direction of causality is not entirely clear, leaving some uncertainty about whether policy driven changes in fertility, for example through pronatalist policies, would lead to opposite changes in human capital.

In the global context, East Asia stands out as investing particularly heavily in children's human capital, but in our analysis (Lee and Mason 2009) the level of investment is to be expected, given the exceptionally low fertility in East Asia. The strong role for private spending on education, complementing public education, is also distinctive in East Asia. Given this already strong pattern of human capital investment, the main policy concern appears to be that new policies not interfere with this existing tendency. It is also possible that the demand for a high level of human capital investment is itself a driving force behind the very low levels of fertility in East Asia.

Our final point is the need for governments and societies to consider carefully the arrangements supporting consumption by the elderly, and potential changes in these arrangements. Should continuation of familial support for the elderly be encouraged by policy? Or should governments move toward public pension programs, and should any new pension programs be funded or PAYGO?

A switch from familial support to public PAYGO pensions may entail less change than it appears, since both accumulate implicit debt as the population ages, and both entail increasing dependency burdens on the working age adult. However, public sector pension programs spread the support costs more evenly across the population while altering the incentives of the elderly and adult children in various ways. In either case, it should be kept in mind that the transfer wealth generated by familial support or PAYGO pensions is likely to substitute for capital in individual's retirement plans. Transfer programs of these kinds likely diminish the promotion of capital accumulation by population aging, the second dividend. Policies that encourage life-cycle saving and personal retirement accounts, whether public or private, would enable countries to harness the power of population aging to generate increased capital per worker.

There are trade-offs between the benefits and drawbacks of familial, PAYGO, and funded old age support programs, and each society may choose a different mix. The key point is that most but not all of the countries of Asia are still at an early enough stage in the transition that they have options that are no longer open to Japan and the other industrial nations. For these countries to transit from their PAYGO programs to funded programs would entail very heavy costs amounting to a year or several years' worth of GDP. For countries earlier in the transition that do not yet have comprehensive PAYGO programs, steps to encourage individual responsibility for own retirement are much more feasible and less painful.

Population aging and the forces leading to it produce not only frightening declines in support ratios, but also very substantial increases in productivity and per capita income. Low fertility and low mortality are associated with large increases in human capital investment in children, and they also cause large increases in the accumulation of physical capital. Together, these positive changes will likely outweigh the problems of declining support ratios. Population aging brings economic benefits as well as costs, and we should view this package of consequences as a whole, while developing policies to minimize the costs and amplify the benefits.

References

Attanasio, O. P., S. Kitao, et al. 2006. Quantifying the effects of the demographic transition in developing economies. *Advances in Macroeconomics* 6 (1): Article 2.

Becker, G. 1991. *A treatise on the family: Enlarged edition.* Cambridge: Harvard University Press.

Becker, G. S., K. M. Murphy, and R. Tamura. 1990. "Human capital, fertility, and economic growth." *Journal of Political Economy* 98 (5[2]): S12–S37.

Bhat, P. N. Mari. 1989. Mortality and fertility in India, 1881–1961: A reassessment.

In *India's historical demography: Studies in famine, disease, and society,* ed. T. Dyson, 73–118. London: Curzon Press.

Bloom, D. E., and D. Canning. 2001. Cumulative causality, economic growth, and the demographic transition. In *Population matters: Demographic change, economic growth, and poverty in the developing world,* eds. N. Birdsall, A. C. Kelley, and S. W. Sinding, 165–200. Oxford: Oxford University Press.

Bloom, D. E., D. Canning, and B. Graham. 2003. Longevity and life-cycle savings. *Scandinavian Journal of Economics* 105 (3): 319–38.

Bloom, D. E., and J. G. Williamson. 1998. "Demographic transitions and economic miracles in emerging Asia." *World Bank Economic Review* 12 (3): 419–56.

Cutler, D. M., J. M. Poterba, L. M. Sheiner, and L. H. Summers. 1990. An aging society: Opportunity or challenge? *Brookings Papers on Economic Activity,* Issue no. 1: 1–56.

Deardorff, A. V. 1987. Trade and capital mobility in a world of diverging populations. In *Population growth and economic development: Issues and evidence,* eds. D.-G. Johnson, and R.-D. Lee, 523–60. Social Demography series, Madison, WI: University of Wisconsin Press.

Deaton, A., and C. H. Paxson. 2000. Growth, demographic structure, and national saving in Taiwan. In *Population and economic change in East Asia, a supplement to Population and Development Review,* eds. R. Lee and C. Y. Chu, volume 26: 141–73. New York: Population Council.

Gruber, J., and D. A. Wise. 1999. Introduction and summary. In *Social Security and retirement around the world,* eds. J. Gruber and D. A. Wise, 437–74. Chicago: The University of Chicago Press.

Higgins, M. 1994. *The demographic determinants of savings, investment, and international capital flows.* PhD diss., Harvard University, Cambridge, MA.

Higgins, M., and J. G. Williamson. 1997. Age structure dynamics in Asia and dependence on foreign capital. *Population and Development Review* 23 (2): 261–93.

Hurd, M. 1987. Savings of the elderly and desired bequests. *American Economic Review* 77 (3): 298–312.

Kelley, A. C., and R. M. Schmidt. 1995. Aggregate population and economic growth correlations: The role of the components of demographic change. *Demography* 32 (4): 543–55.

———. 1996. Saving, dependency, and development. *Journal of Population Economics* 9 (4): 365–86.

———. 2001. Economic and demographic change: A synthesis of models, findings, and perspectives. In *Population matters: Demographic change, economic growth, and poverty in the developing world,* eds. N. Birdsall, A. C. Kelley, and S. W. Sinding, 67–105. Oxford: Oxford University Press.

———. 2007. Evolution of recent economic-demographic modeling: A synthesis. In *Population change, labor markets, and sustainable growth: Towards a new economic paradigm,* eds. A. Mason, and M. Yamaguchi, 5–38. Amsterdam: Elsevier.

Kinugasa, T. 2004. *Life expectancy, labor force, and saving.* PhD diss. Manoa: University of Hawaii at Manoa.

Kinugasa, T., and A. Mason. 2007. Why nations become wealthy: The effects of adult longevity on saving. *World Development* 35 (1): 1–23.

Kuehlwein, M. 1993. Life-cycle and altruistic theories of saving with lifetime uncertainty. *The Review of Economics and Statistics* 75 (1): 38–47.

Lee, R., and A. Mason. 2007. Population aging, wealth, and economic growth: Demographic dividends and public policy. UN World Economic and Social Survey Background Paper.

———. 2009. Fertility, human capital, and economic growth over the demographic transition. *European Journal of Population* (June 19).

Lee, R., S.-H. Lee, and A. Mason. 2008. Charting the economic lifecycle. In *Population aging, human capital accumulation, and productivity growth. Population and Development Review* 34 (Supplement): 208-37, eds. A. Prskawetz, D. E. Bloom, and W. Lutz. New York: Population Council.

Lee, R., A. Mason, and T. Miller. 2000. Life cycle saving and the demographic transition in East Asia. *Population and Development Review* 26 (Supplement): S194–219.

———. 2002. Saving, wealth, and the transition from transfers to individual responsibility: The cases of Taiwan and the United States. The Swedish Journal of Economics 105 (3): 339–57.

———. 2003. From transfers to individual responsibility: Implications for savings and capital accumulation in Taiwan and the United States. *Scandinavian Journal of Economics* 105 (3): 339–57.

Mason, A. 1987. National saving rates and population growth: A new model and new evidence. In *Population growth and economic development: Issues and evidence,* eds. D. G. Johnson and R. D. Lee, 523–60. Social Demography series, Madison, WI: University of Wisconsin Press.

———. 2001. Population and economic growth in East Asia. In *Population change and economic development in East Asia: Challenges met, opportunities seized,* ed. A. Mason, 1–30. Stanford: Stanford University Press.

———. 2005. *Demographic transition and demographic dividends in developed and developing countries.* United Nations Expert Group Meeting on Social and Economic Implications of Changing Population Age Structures, Mexico City.

———. 2007. Demographic dividends: The past, the present, and the future. In *Population change, labor markets and sustainable growth: Towards a new economic paradigm,* eds. A. Mason and M. Yamaguchi, 75–98. Oxford: Elsevier Press.

Mason, A., and R. Lee. 2006. Reform and support systems for the elderly in developing countries: Capturing the second demographic dividend. *GENUS* LXII (2): 11–35.

———. 2007. Transfers, capital, and consumption over the demographic transition. In *Population Aging, Intergenerational Transfers and the Macroeconomy,* eds. R. Clark, N. Ogawa, and A. Mason, 128–162. Northampton, MA: Elgar Press.

Mason, A., R. Lee, A.-C. Tung, M. S. Lai, and T. Miller. 2009. Population aging and intergenerational transfers: Introducing age into national income accounts. In *Developments in the economics of aging,* ed. David Wise, 89–122. Chicago: University of Chicago Press.

Mason, A., S.-H. Lee, and R. Lee. 2008. Asian demographic change: Its economic and social implications written for a volume: Emerging Asian regionalism: Ten Years after the crisis—*A Study by the Asian Development Bank.*

Modigliani, F. 1988. Measuring the contribution of intergenerational transfers to total wealth: Conceptual issues and empirical findings. In *Modeling the accumulation and distribution of wealth,* eds. D. Kessler and A. Masson, 21–52. Oxford: Oxford University Press.

Modigliani, F., and R. Brumberg. 1954. Utility analysis and the consumption function: An interpretation of cross-section data. In *Post-Keynesian economics,* eds. K. K. Kurihara, 388–435. New Brunswick, N.J.: Rutgers University Press.

Ogawa, N., and R. D. Retherford. 1993. Care of the elderly in Japan: Changing norms and expectations. *Journal of Marriage and the Family* 55 (3): 585–97.

Samuelson, P. 1958. An exact consumption loan model of interest with or without the social contrivance of money. *Journal of Political Economy* 66: 467–82.

Solow, R. M. 1956. A contribution to the theory of economic growth. *Quarterly Journal of Economics* 70 (1): 65–94.

Tobin, J. 1967. Life cycle saving and balanced economic growth. In *Ten Economic Studies in the Tradition of Irving Fisher,* ed. W. Fellner, 231–56. New York: Wiley.

United Nations, Population Division. 2001. World population prospects: The 2000 Revision. Disk 2: Extensive Set. CDROM. New York, February.

———. 2006. *International migration 2006.* New York: United Nations.

———. 2007. *World Population Prospects: The 2006 Revision.* New York, United Nations.

Williamson, J. G., and M. Higgins. 2001. The accumulation and demography connection in East Asia. In *Population Change and Economic Development in East Asia: Challenges Met, Opportunities Seized,* ed. A. Mason, 123–54. Stanford: Stanford University Press.

Comment   Jocelyn E. Finlay

In their chapter, Mason, Lee, and Lee explore the macroeconomic implications of the decline in fertility and mortality over the past fifty years with a particular focus on the Asian region.

During the demographic transition there is a decline in the mortality rate followed (often much later, as in the case of India) by the decline in the fertility rate. In the early stages of the demographic transition when mortality rates fall but the fertility rate remains high, population growth is very strong. In India, during this window of time the population growth rate hiked from 0.3 in 1900 to 2.2 around 1980.

The economic implications of the demographic transition have long been an avenue of enquiry. It was the work by Kelley and Schmidt (1995) which showed that population growth as a single variable did not have a significant effect on economic growth, but rather the components behind population growth were considered empirically important and theoretically interesting.

In addition to their effect on population growth, changes in mortality and fertility rates also have an effect on age structure of the population. With people living longer, the number of people in the older age groups increases. Couple this with the decline in fertility and the proportion of youth relative to the elderly declines.

One striking demographic feature that has come about during the demographic transition is the rise in the working-age share. When the fertility rate declines, the number of youth-age individuals declines relative to the number of working-age individuals. The working-age share increases. The

Jocelyn E. Finlay is a Research Associate in the Department of Global Health and Population at the Harvard School of Public Health.

number of workers relative to the number of dependents increases (assuming little or no change in the number of old-age dependents), and income per capita increases through this accounting measure. Mason, Lee, and Lee define this as the first demographic dividend as explained in this chapter and by others (Bloom, Canning, and Sevilla 2003).

Throughout the second half of the twentieth century, as the fertility rate fell in many countries the working-age share increased. The effects of the rapid decline in fertility dominated the effects of the increase in life expectancy so that the working-age share increased. Lowering the number of births and lowering the number of deaths per thousand in the population have an equal effect on population growth (the Rate of Natural Increase, NRI). However, births have a more dramatic effect on age structure than deaths as the injection of births is concentrated at the first age group, while deaths are spread over the entire age distribution. The working-age share will increase with a decline in the fertility rate as the number of individuals entering the youth age-group instantaneously declines.

Presently, many countries are entering a period where we observe a stabilizing of the fertility rate decline. Thus the upward pressure on the working-age share from the declining youth-age end of the age spectrum will weaken, and the downward force on the working-age share from an increasing proportion of old-age individuals will become stronger. With stabilizing fertility rates and an ever increasing life expectancy in many Asian countries the working-age share is set to decline.

Approaching the issues of population change from the age-structure perspective, Mason, Lee, and Lee then explore the economic implications of the demographic transition. The authors look at past trends in the relationship between age structure and economic growth, but consider the role of the second demographic dividend in offsetting the negative effects of the decline in the working-age share. The second demographic dividend comes about as the rise in life expectancy encourages greater savings. With higher savings and lower population growth, the capital-output ratio defined through the Solow-Swan model increases.

Population numbers in the future are not all based on predictions; cohorts alive today will survive into future age groups probabilistically and make up the population stock in the future. The combination of certainty over the current stock and observed prior serial correlation in fertility and mortality trends means that we can predict the future population level with a degree of confidence. An epidemic that unexpectedly kills a large number of people or an unexpected rebound of the fertility rate to 1960 rates could, of course, make the predictions over population growth and levels inaccurate.

What is less predictable in the course of the demographic transition is the behavioral change that comes with the shift in the age structure of the population. In the second half of the twentieth century, the rise in the working-age share was largely driven by the decline in the fertility rate. The rise in the working-age share brought with it a rise in female labor force participation (Bloom, Canning, Fink, and Finlay 2007) and an increase in human capital accumulation (Galor and Weil 1996)—factors that are predominantly backed by the decline in the fertility rate.

The reason for caution regarding predications over behavioral change into the future is that the decline in the working-age share in the years to come will be backed by the rise in life expectancy and an increasing proportion of elderly dependents. Trends in the past that came with the decline in fertility may not translate to the scenario of an increase in life expectancy. Thus behavioral patterns we observed with the increase in the working-age share in the past may not be reversed as the working-age share is set to decline in the future.

The two behavioral responses to the demographic transition Mason, Lee, and Lee focus on are the change human capital accumulation and physical capital accumulation, with particular attention on the latter. Changes in the savings rate are subject to unknown behavioral responses. Population growth rate decline is understood with a degree of confidence. Thus predictions over future capital-output ratios depend on predictions over savings behavior change.

Mason, Lee, and Lee, too, are careful with these assumptions over predicted behavioral change and draw on our understanding of behavioral responses in an aging society. In particular for this article they draw on the savings rate implications. Asia is a particularly interesting example in terms of savings and capital flows across time and generations. For while many Asian countries do not have a formal Pay-As-You-Go system (PAYGO), they have a strong culture of intergenerational transfers which are in effect very similar to the pay-as-you-go system. Asian countries have also been typically known as high saving countries, but these rates are declining.

In a simulation exercise, Mason, Lee, and Lee plot out projections through 2050 over net savings rate, asset/labor income ratios, and consumption index under two scenarios: a high savings/low intergenerational transfers; and, a low savings/high intergenerational transfers. The assumption is that those in old-age will fund the gap between income and expenditure with either savings or intergenerational transfers. The authors show that, relatively, Thailand in 2004 was of the high savings/low transfer category, and Japan in 2004 was a low savings/high transfer country. Thus within Asia, either scenario is possible.

Some of the simulation results are not surprising: a high savings environment will lead to stronger net savings and stronger asset/labor income. Interestingly, the low intergenerational transfer scenario will lead to higher consumption in the future. It is not clear why high savings will lead to higher consumption than high intergenerational transfers. Assumptions over the interest earned on savings will certainly affect this result.

The simulation results in this chapter would suggest that savings over intergenerational transfers may be more effective. The authors do caution the reader with regard to existing trends indicating that many Asian countries comply more strongly to the high transfers/low savings scenario (Japan, Korea, Rep., Philippines, Sri Lanka, Taiwan, and Vietnam each have a Pay-As-You-Go social security system). However, there are many Asian countries that have low intergenerational transfers and also within the formal social security setting adopt the fully funded pension scheme (Hong Kong, India, Indonesia, Malaysia, and Singapore have fully funded social security schemes) (Bloom, Canning, Mansfield, and Moore 2007) thus comply with the low transfers/high savings scenario.

Throughout the Asian region the demographic transition will lead to an increasing proportion of the population aged over sixty years—the aging of the population. In many Asian countries, significant aging will not begin to occur until after 2025, and many individuals due to retire in 2025 are currently in the workforce. Current savings patterns and transfer policies will affect aging societies in the future.

This chapter by Mason, Lee, and Lee provides a cautionary note. Pay-As-You-Go social security systems and the promotion of familial transfers may lead to lower welfare outcomes than fully funded systems, and private savings to fund retirement years. But in these discussions the uncertainty lies in the behavioral changes and future policy changes that will come as a society ages. Labor force participation behavior of men and women of various ages, savings patterns at the various ages, education choices and its returns are just some fundamental factors that remain unknown. Pronatalist policies, mandated age of retirement increasing, and immigration policies could also shift the age structure, the working-age share, and its implications dramatically. We observed behavioral changes and policy shifts as the fertility rate declined over the past fifty years, but as societies become aging societies over the next fifty years, what behavioral and policy changes will this bring and what will be the implications of these changes? A contribution of the Mason, Lee, and Lee chapter is that it brings knowledge to this question.

References

Bloom, D. E., D. Canning, G. Fink, and J. E. Finlay. 2007. Fertility, female labor force participation, and the demographic dividend. NBER Working Paper no. 13583. Cambridge, MA: National Bureau of Economic Research, November.

Bloom, D. E., D. Canning, R. Mansfield, and M. Moore. 2007. Demographic change, social security systems, and savings. *Journal of Monetary Economics* 54 (1): 92–114.

Bloom, D. E., D. Canning, and J. Sevilla. 2003. The demographic dividend: A new perspective on the economic consequences of population change. Population Matters Monograph MR–1274. Santa Monica: RAND.

Galor, O., and D. N. Weil. 1996. The gender gap, fertility, and growth. *American Economic Review* 86 (3): 374–87.

Kelley, A. C., and R. M. Schmidt. 1995. Aggregate population and economic growth correlations: The role of the components of demographic change. *Demography* 32 (4): 543–55.

Comment   Jong-Wha Lee

The Mason, Lee, and Lee chapter summarizes the main features of demographic transition in Asia since 1960—characterized by fertility decline, population aging, and decrease in working-age population. The chapter highlights three important channels by which demographic transition influences economic growth in Asia. They include (a) the change in working-age population (first demographic dividend), (b) the change in savings rate and capital accumulation (second demographic dividend), and (c) human capital investment.

This chapter addresses an important issue: fertility decline and population aging are becoming increasingly important in the region, especially in Northeast Asia. This chapter addresses the economic and social implications of demographic transition and discusses the role of an intergenerational transfer system for supporting the growing number of elderly population. While I agree on most of the chapter's findings, I have a few questions.

The first concerns the second demographic dividend in Asia. The estimation of the first dividend is straightforward. The estimates show that the first dividend has become negative in several Asian economies with rapidly expanding elderly populations. The critical question concerns the size of the second dividend, which is important for the aggregate growth effect of demographic dividends. The chapter claims that longer life leads to higher savings, which raises the capital-labor ratio and thus labor productivity. Hence, if the second dividend is large, an aging population could lead to higher—not lower—per capita income. However, it is not clear how strong leaving bequest or any other motives are to support increased elderly savings. Uncertainty surrounding the timing of retirement and death may have a strong influence on the pace of dissaving among the elderly and retirees. But it is not clear to what extent a motive of building inheritance can dampen the decline in savings during retirement. The chapter needs to discuss more empirical evidence of elderly savings in Asia.

Second, the chapter emphasizes the role of intergenerational transfers from the young to the old on net savings and financial asset accumulation. The impact of demographic change on capital accumulation and economic growth hinges on the extent to which the population accumulates pension-transfer wealth versus physical capital accumulation over the lifetime.

Jong-Wha Lee is chief economist of the Asian Development Bank, and professor of economics at Korea University.

Higher reliance on intergenerational (IG) pension transfer wealth would lead to significantly lower levels of lifetime savings. The simulation results for selected Asian economies support the contention that the effect of aging on savings critically depends on the assumption of the relative share of assets and pension-transfer wealth. However, it is not clear how accurate the estimates are. For example, the figures in table 1.8 show that in 1995 net savings for the Republic of Korea (Korea) was estimated to be 52.9 percent of national income with the low IG transfer share assumed, and 7.9 percent with the high IG transfer share. It seems the range of estimates is too wide. The details of the simulation model are not presented, so it is difficult to know the assumptions on critical parameters. The chapter can explain first how the model can simulate the behavior of savings rates in an economy like Korea or in ASEAN, and then show how the predicted savings rates can change depending on the value of the IG transfer share.

In addition, in a small open economy with perfect capital mobility, a change in savings rate does not necessarily lead to a change in investment rate, as the savings-investment imbalance is adjusted by external transactions. Demographic change is expected to negatively influence investment demand as slower labor force growth and lower expected output growth reduce the rates-of-return on investment. If an aging population causes national savings to rise and domestic investment to fall, it will lead to an improvement in the current account, but not necessarily to an increase in capital accumulation and output growth rate.

Finally, while the title of the chapter emphasizes the impact of population change in economic growth, the authors do not address other important channels by which demographic change influences economic growth. For example, population aging can influence education and training, and technological progress. Also, new technology and better health care can alter the effects of population aging—by leading to extension of retirement age, for example. Human capital investment will also induce new technological development in the economy.

Population Aging and Economic Growth in Asia

David E. Bloom, David Canning, and Jocelyn E. Finlay

2.1 Introduction

The demographic transition and evolution of past birth and death rates in Asia have brought about dramatic shifts in the age structure between 1960 and 2005 (Bloom, Canning, and Fink 2008). The combined forces of declining fertility, increasing life expectancy, and the transitional dynamics of varying cohort sizes moving through the age distribution have led to the rapid aging of societies across much of Asia.[1] From 1960 to 2005, China experienced the largest absolute increase in life expectancy in the world. During the same period, the total fertility rate in the Republic of Korea plummeted from 5.7 to 1.1—a change that only a handful of countries have experienced. Japan boasts the highest life expectancy in the world at 85.6 for women and 78.7 for men, and it continues to rise.

With a decline in fertility, in the short run the youth-age population share declines and the working-age share increases. Working-age people contribute to the labor force more than youth-age, and if these individuals are gainfully employed (Bloom, Canning, Fink, and Finlay 2007), then while income per worker can remain the same, income per capita increases. In Asia, the decline in the total fertility rate from a regional average of 6.05 (see table 2.1) in 1960, to a regional average of 2.63 has brought with it an

David E. Bloom is Clarence James Gamble Professor of Economics and Demography and chair of the Department of Global Health and Population at the Harvard School of Public Health. David Canning is a Professor of Economics and International Health in the Department of Global Health and Population at the Harvard School of Public Health. Jocelyn E. Finlay is a Research Associate in the Department of Global Health and Population at the Harvard School of Public Health.

1. Aging in Asia has been particularly dramatic, but it is also taking place in nearly all other regions of the world.

Table 2.1   Summary statistics

	GDP per capita		Total fertility rate		Life expectancy (female)		WA/dependents	
	1960	2005	1960	2005	1960	2005	1960	2005
World (average)	3,821	9,887	5.51	3.03	55.22	68.60	1.32	1.68
World (standard deviation)	3,567	10,221	1.78	1.65	12.71	13.37	0.30	0.43
Asia (average)	2,254	10,529	6.05	2.63	52.89	72.67	1.24	1.80
Asia (standard deviation)	1,720	11,118	1.34	1.23	10.99	7.04	0.17	0.45
Afghanistan		581	7.70		34.4		1.20	1.03
Armenia		4,765	4.47	1.37	69.2	76.4	1.30	2.14
Azerbaijan		3,671	5.55	2.33	68.2	75.1	1.33	2.09
Bahrain		19,561	7.09	2.34	57.5	76.3	1.03	1.91
Bangladesh		2,155	6.81	2.98	39.9	64.8	1.16	1.55
Bhutan		933	5.90	2.50	38.5	65.2	1.32	1.32
Brunei Darussalam		26,239	6.83	2.38	62.9	79.4	1.11	2.07
Cambodia		580	6.29	3.89	44.1	60.6	1.21	1.52
China	445	5,333	3.39	1.81	37.6	73.7	1.26	2.42
Cyprus		22,383	3.44	1.42	70.6	81.7	1.41	2.13
Georgia		5,788	2.95	1.39	67.5	74.9	1.75	1.97
China, Hong Kong Special Administrative Region	3,264	29,644	5.06	0.97	69.8	84.5	1.25	2.91
India	870	2,990	6.57	2.84	43.5	64.3	1.31	1.65
Indonesia	1,099	4,064	5.52	2.27	42.3	69.7	1.32	1.95
Iran (Islamic Republic of)	3,269	6,398	7.00	2.07	48.5	72.8	1.09	2.04
Iraq		1,230	7.27		51.2		1.05	1.28
Israel	6,526	21,242	3.87	2.82	73.2	81.8	1.46	1.61
Japan	4,632	24,660	2.00	1.26	70.1	85.6	1.82	1.81
Jordan	4,187	3,742	7.75	3.29	48.5	73.6	1.09	1.43
Kazakhstan		10,169		1.75		71.9	1.48	2.10
Democratic People's Republic of Korea		1,429	4.37	1.96	56.8	66.9	1.52	2.09

Republic of Korea	1,544	18,421	5.67	1.08	55.8	81.1	1.24	2.46
Kuwait		26,098	7.27	2.39	61.5	79.7	1.06	2.16
Kyrgyzstan				2.41		72.4	1.37	1.65
Lao People's Democratic Republic		1,412	6.15	4.50	41.8	57	1.23	1.27
Lebanon		6,085	5.70	2.25	63	74.8	1.16	1.83
China, Macao Special Administrative Region		37,956	5.02	0.88	61.9	82.4	1.20	3.14
Malaysia	1,829	12,131	6.81	2.74	55.9	76.1	1.03	1.70
Maldives		5,086	7.00	4.00	42.6	67.3	1.19	1.24
Mongolia		1,597	6.00	2.33	48.3	68.5	1.18	1.93
Myanmar			6.00	2.23	45.4	64.1	1.25	1.92
Nepal	818	1,441	6.06	3.46	38.4	63.1	1.29	1.40
Oman		16,273	7.20	3.44	42.9	76.3	1.08	1.43
Pakistan	803	2,685	6.92	4.12	43.1	65.5	1.20	1.36
Philippines		3,938	6.96	3.20	55.3	73.2	1.05	1.57
Qatar	2,037	36,183	6.97	2.89	55	76.6	1.22	1.93
Saudi Arabia		16,010	7.22	3.83	45.8	74.6	1.14	1.34
Singapore	4,211	29,419	5.45	1.24	65.7	81.6	1.14	2.54
Sri Lanka	865	4,274	5.35	1.91	56.8	77.4	1.15	2.11
Syrian Arab Republic	829	2,016	7.48	3.24	51	75.7	1.03	1.51
Tajikistan		1,942	6.26	3.53	58.9	66.7	1.29	1.36
Thailand	1,086	7,275	6.40	1.89	58.3	74.5	1.11	2.24
Democratic Republic of Timor-Leste			6.36	7.47	34.6	57.8	1.23	1.23
Turkey	2,264	5,982	6.28	2.19	52.1	73.8	1.18	1.86
Turkmenistan		7,342	6.46	2.60	58.3	67.2	1.31	1.74
United Arab Emirates		35,676	6.91	2.43	55	81.6	1.15	1.84
Uzbekistan		3,915		2.22	62.7	70.7	1.32	1.64
Viet Nam		2,561	6.05	1.78	46.3	73.2	1.28	1.87
Yemen		1,076	8.36	5.87	34.9	63.2	1.05	1.06

Sources: Penn World Tables 6.2 (Heston, Summers, and Aten 2006); (World Bank 2007).

Note: Blank cells indicate missing data.

increase in the working-age share. However, as the total fertility rate falls below the replacement rate in many Asian countries, the working-age share will decrease in the long run (Bloom, Canning, Fink, and Finlay 2009b) and old-age shares will increase.

As reviewed in Bloom, Canning, and Fink (2008), a popular view of the negative effects of aging is born of the growth accounting calculation. If labor supply and savings behavior remain unchanged, then labor supply, as well as savings (and thus income) per capita would decline as old-age shares increase and working-age shares decline. However, the dramatic change in family structure creates avenues for behavioral change. With fewer children to care for and the support of elderly parents to care for children and contribute to household expenses, individuals who are of working age may be able to work more than they could previously. Savings patterns may change as life expectancy, income potential, and expenditure requirements change. Furthermore, incentives to invest in one's own and one's children's education may change as life expectancy increases and earning opportunities expand. These behavioral effects may add up to offset the negative accounting effects of aging.

There are three key drivers of population aging: fertility decline, increase in life expectancy, and age-structure dynamics. When we factor in the behavioral responses to the changes in the various demographic variables, we find that these different demographic forces have different effects on economic growth. The decline in fertility causes an increase in the female labor supply (Bloom, Canning, Fink, and Finlay 2009a), an increase in life expectancy will alter savings incentives (Bloom, Canning, and Moore 2007), and a combination of factors leads to increased investment in education per person. The accounting effects of aging, combined with these behavioral responses, mean that aging has an ambiguous effect on economic growth.

Changing institutional settings compound the complexity of analyzing the effects of aging on economic growth. Reforms in social security and diminished adherence to filial piety make for a transformative situation for identifying the responsible agent for elder support and care: adult children, the state, own savings or labor supply, or a company pension.

Will aging have a negative effect on economic growth in Asia? This is the key question that we explore in this chapter. In the next section we break down what we actually mean by aging and illustrate the role of fertility decline and mortality improvements on shifts in age structure. In section 2.3 we use regression analysis to identify the statistical relationship between age structure and economic growth in Asia, and discuss the various behavioral responses to aging in the Asian context. A summary follows.

2.2   Population Aging in Asia

We classify a population with an increasing share of old-age persons as one that is aging. This shift in the age structure is brought about by a decline in fertility that reduces the number of youth, and thus with no change in the size of the elderly population, the elderly share increases. An increase in this share can also come about by a disproportionate increase in the survival of individuals aged sixty-five and older relative to the improvement in survival rates of other age groups. An increasing share of old-age individuals can also result from past variation in birth and death rates. These three forces all contribute to the trend in most Asian countries of an increasing proportion of individuals aged sixty-five and older (figure 2.6).

The reason for the fertility decline is a contentious issue debated among economists and demographers. Bongaarts (1984; 1994; 1999) argues that the improvements in contraceptive access have aided the decrease in fertility rates. But Pritchett asserts that access to contraception cannot explain why fertility rates have fallen by so much, so quickly, and that a shift in preferences explains most of the plummet in fertility rates (Pritchett 1994). Deciphering why the total fertility rate has fallen in Asia is not the focus of this chapter; we analyze the economic consequences of the observed decline in the total fertility rate and the associated increase in old-age population shares.

Improvements in life expectancy in many Asian countries between 1960 and 2005 in large part reflect declines in child mortality. Improvements in mortality can be attributed to public health interventions (for example, improvements in nutrition and the provision of water and sanitation) and to medical interventions such as vaccine coverage and the use of antibiotics (Cutler, Deaton, and Lleras-Muney 2006). But health disparities within Asia remain broad: childhood mortality remains high in Laos and Cambodia, for example; life expectancy is the highest in the world in Japan, and survival to sixty is close to certain; and adult mortality is high in West Asian countries relative to East Asia. Despite the disparities, life expectancy has increased in all Asian countries (see table 2.1) between 1960 and 2005.

Aging is also a consequence of the dynamic evolution of past fertility and mortality rates. Cohorts move through the age groups of the population age distribution. The size of the eighty to eighty-five age group in 2000 will depend on births between 1915 and 1920 and the mortality rates this cohort experienced as it aged. When the total fertility rate falls below replacement, the birth cohort will be smaller than the parent cohort (excluding migration effects).

In this section, we examine the effect of fertility and mortality changes between 1960 and 2005 on age structure. This exercise illustrates the dominant role of the fertility decline in shaping the increase in the proportion of old-age individuals. We illustrate how age structure will change between 2005 and 2050 as a consequence of fertility and mortality changes during that period. We also discuss the effects of the dynamic evolution of changes from 1960 to 2005 in mortality and fertility rates on age structure changes between 2005 and 2050.

2.2.1   The Effects of Mortality and Fertility Changes on Age Structure

In figure 2.1, we illustrate the effect of fertility and mortality changes on age structure between 1960 and 2005. As an example of how to interpret these graphs, consider India and the zero to five age group. The fertility effect of approximately 0.07 indicates that if fertility rates had remained at 1960 rates, then in 2005 the fraction of individuals aged zero to five years old would be seven percentage points higher. The mortality effect of approximately –0.001 indicates that if age-specific mortality rates had remained at 1960 rates then the fraction of individuals in the zero to five age group would be 0.1 percentage points lower than it actually is today. For each of the represented Asian countries (India, Indonesia, Vietnam, China, Japan, Republic of Korea), we see that the fertility changes have had a much greater effect on age structure than the mortality changes. In figure 2.1, we see that the fertility decline in the six example countries has had a similar effect on the respective country's age structure (though the effect in Japan is minimal). If fertility rates had remained at 1960 rates, youth population shares would be higher, working-age shares would be lower, and old-age shares would be lower[2]. Figure 2.1 illustrates the accounting effect of a decline in fertility leading to an increase in the working-age share (or, as the graph represents: if the fertility rate had not fallen from 1960 rates, the working-age share would be lower). As to the mortality effect, we see that in four of the six example countries[3] if mortality rates had remained at 1960 rates then the youth population share would be lower (as more of the children would have died). With the exception of Vietnam and possibly China, working-age shares would be higher (as improvements in mortality have been concentrated in the childhood age groups).

The cohorts born in the 1960 to 2005 period do not reach the sixty-five and older age group until 2025 to 2070. Even so, the fertility decline between 1960 and 2005 has an effect on the sixty-five and older age group share. In the case of India in 2005, figure 2.1 illustrates that if the total fertility rate had remained at the 1960 rate then the sixty-five and older age-group population shares would be lower. Changes in the total fertility rate in the present do not affect old-age population *sizes* in the present, but they do affect old-age population *shares* in the present.

For the age structure of a population to change (with zero migration), either (a) the fertility rate must change, (b) there must be heterogeneous change in the age-specific mortality rates, or (c) there must have been past variation in mortality and fertility rates.

2. Old-age shares would be lower in all example countries except for the case of Japan, where the fertility decline between 1960 and 2005 has been very small relative to the other example countries.
3. Japan is different as in 1960 child mortality rates were already very low compared to the other example countries.

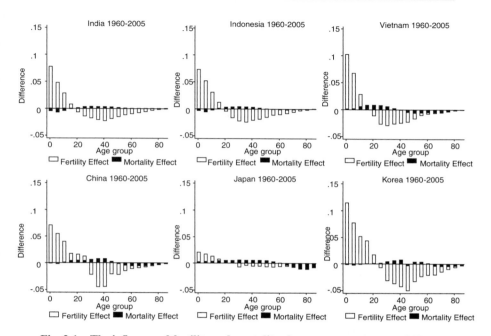

Fig. 2.1   The influence of fertility and mortality change on age structure shifts, 1960–2005

Source: Authors' own calculations using United Nations (2007), World Bank (2007), and ModMatch in Stata 9.

As shown in figure 2.1, the effect of fertility changes on age structure in the selected Asian countries has been much more dramatic than mortality changes (even for China, where female life expectancy climbed from 37.6 to 73.7). As the improvements in life expectancy are a result of improvements in mortality rates across all of the age groups, the proportion of individuals in each age group does not change much even in the face of such steep life expectancy improvements. However, fertility improvements are concentrated in the 0 to 1 age group, which leads to an immediate effect on age structure.

A change in fertility or a heterogeneous change in mortality has a cohort effect that will have an instantaneous effect on age structure. Importantly, this effect will persist through the age distribution as cohorts move through the different age groups. These population dynamics imply that changes in the 1960 to 2005 period will continue to affect the age structure through the 2005 to 2050 period (as discussed in section 2.2.3).

2.2.2   The Problem of Aging Societies

The problem with an aging society is that the number of old-age dependents will increase relative to the number of working-age individuals. With-

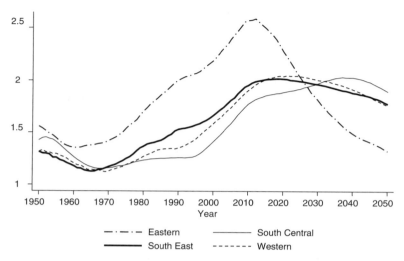

Fig. 2.2   Ratio of working-age population to dependent population, by Asian region
Source: United Nations (2007).

out deep analysis, it seems obvious that if people of working age are the workers and people in old age are retired, and that if changes in the age structure of the population bring about no change in behavior (an increase in savings, for example), then there will be a rising number of old-age people dependent on the support of working-age individuals.

We show in figure 2.2 that the working-age to dependents ratio will eventually decline throughout Asia, and comparing figure 2.3 and figure 2.4 we can see that this will be due to the declining ratio of working-age people to old-age dependents. In all Asian regions the ratio of working-age people to old-age dependents will decline (figure 2.4); however, the ratio of working-age to youth-age dependents will increase in all Asian regions except East Asia (figure 2.3). In the past, the rise in the working-age share was backed by a decrease in youth-age shares. In the future, the decline in the working-age share will be backed by an increase in the old-age shares.

The major reason population aging matters is that human productivity and human consumption have different time profiles. Children consume more than they produce. This phase now lasts into the late twenties in many countries as they continue in advanced education. Between twenty-five and roughly sixty-five are the prime working years, in which production exceeds consumption. After age sixty-five, consumption exceeds labor income. In most cases the young are supported by intra-family transfers. Support for the elderly, who have normal consumption and require medical care, is more complex, coming from family support, personal savings, pensions, and social security transfers. The mix of these support systems for the elderly differs greatly across countries. The coping ability of transfer systems (whether

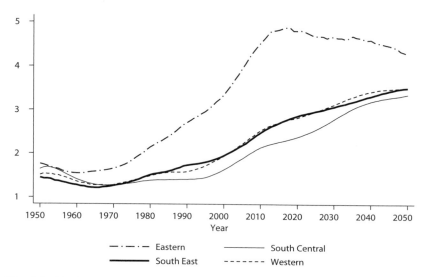

Fig. 2.3   Ratio of working-age population to youth population, by Asian region
Source: United Nations (2007).

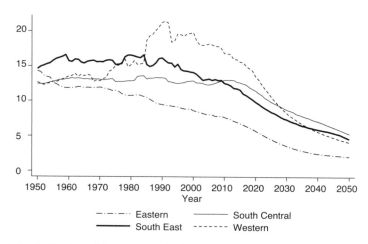

Fig. 2.4   Ratio of working-age population to old-age population, by Asian region
Source: United Nations (2007).

mediated by the family or the state) is limited by the rising proportion of the elderly and the consequent high burden on the working-age population.

2.2.3   Aging in the Future

In section 2.2.1 we showed that much of the aging of a society is driven by the decline in fertility. Sharp declines in the fertility rate decrease the number of youth and increase the proportion of individuals in old age, even though

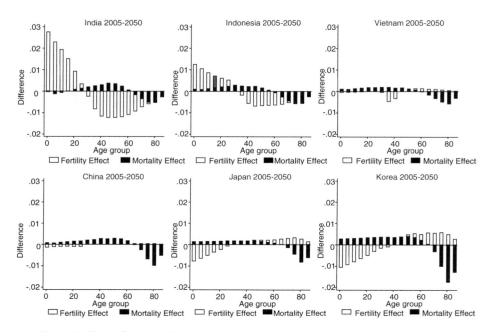

Fig. 2.5   The influence of fertility and mortality change on age structure shifts 2005–2050

the population of old people remains unchanged. Largely as a consequence of the fertility decline, age structure shifted sharply between 1960 and 2005. Changes in the age structure between 2005 and 2050 also appear to be steep in figure 2.6. However, by comparing figure 2.5 with 2005 and 2050 age structure in figure 2.6, we see that changes in age structure between 2005 and 2050 are not fully consequent on changes over that period—in particular the age structure changes for the fifty and older age groups. This is due to the fact that, in addition to the 2005 to 2050 fertility and mortality effects on age structure, shifts in the age structure between 2005 and 2050 will be a result of changes in cohort sizes stemming from steep changes in fertility and mortality rates between 1960 and 2005, as these cohorts move through the age distribution.

As the fertility rate is already below replacement in many Asian countries, and the mortality improvements are diminishing, changes in age structure as a result of changes in fertility and mortality changes over the next forty-five years will not be as dramatic as they were between 1960 and 2005.[4] With fertility and mortality rates stabilizing at low levels, the changes in the age structure over the next forty-five years will largely reflect dynamic evolu-

4. India is an exception to this.

tion of past birth and death rates, and the age structure will move toward stability.

To illustrate the dynamic evolution effects of past birth and death rates on the age structure, consider the case of Indonesia in figure 2.5. The graph indicates that if fertility and mortality rates remain at 2005 rates, then by 2050 the share of sixty-five to seventy year olds would be 0.5 percentage points less than what the predicted 2050 sixty-five to seventy year old age share is, as represented in figure 2.6. From figure 2.6, we see that the share of sixty-five to seventy-year-olds increased by 0.035 (3.5 percent); 0.005 of that is explained by fertility and mortality changes between 2005 and 2050, but the remainder (0.03) is explained by past variation in birth and death rates. Thus aging, the increase in the proportion of individuals, aged sixty-five and older between 2005 and 2050 is largely consequent on fertility and mortality rate changes prior to 2005.

2.3 Population Aging and Economic Growth in Asia

Asia's, and in particular East Asia's, macroeconomic performance is tracked very closely by its demographic transition and resulting changes in age structure. Estimates indicate that as much as one-third of its "economic miracle" can be attributed to a demographic dividend (Bloom and Williamson 1998; Bloom, Canning, and Malaney 2000; Bloom, Canning, and Sevilla 2001; Bloom, Craig, and Malaney 2001; Bloom, Canning, and Sevilla 2003). Another set, due to Kelley and Schmidt (2005) indicates that demographic change accounts for 44 percent of income per capita growth from 1960 to 1990. The first demographic dividend comes about as an accounting effect of a decline in fertility and the resultant rise in the working-age share. When the fertility rate declines, the working-age share increases as the number of individuals of working age increases relative to the number in the youth age groups. With an increase in the working-age share, countries stand to benefit from the proportional increase in the pool of potential workers in the economy, and income per capita can increase. By contrast, the absence of demographic change also accounts for a large portion of Africa's economic debacle (Bloom and Sachs 1998; Bloom, Canning, and Sevilla 2003). In addition, the introduction of demographic factors has reduced the need for the argument that there was something exceptional about East Asia or idiosyncratic to Africa. Most models of economic growth have significant region dummies, usually negative for Sub-Saharan Africa and positive for East Asia, indicating that the poor performance of Africa and the exceptionally good growth performance of East Asia cannot be explained within the models. Once age structure dynamics are introduced into an economic growth model, these regions are much closer to reflecting widely understood drivers of economic growth (Bloom, Canning, and Malaney 2000) and the statistical significance of the region dummy variables disappears.

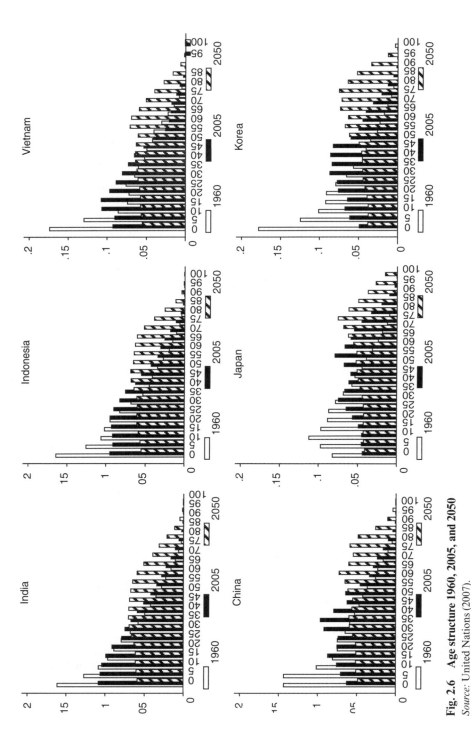

Fig. 2.6   Age structure 1960, 2005, and 2050

Source: United Nations (2007).

Note: The proportion of individuals in the five-year age group (0 on the *x*-axis is the 0–4 age group, 5 is the 5–9 age group).

The effect of changes in the working-age share on economic growth is well-documented. We now turn our focus to the effect of old-age share on economic growth. This analysis is not independent of the relationship between working-age share and economic growth. However, when considering the working-age share affecting economic growth, the downward forces of youth- and old-age shares is considered symmetric. In this chapter, we treat youth- and old-age shares separately so as not to impose this symmetry assumption.

2.3.1   Channels by Which Aging Affects Economic Growth

In section 2.2 of this chapter we illustrated in detail the process of aging in Asia. Sharp declines in fertility between 1960 and 2005 had dramatic effects on the age structure of the population. Moreover, we showed how the age structure will continue to evolve as population cohorts age between now and 2050.

In this section, we analyze the effect of this shift in age structure on economic growth, with a particular focus on Asia. There are many channels by which the shift in age structure affects economic growth. In the first instance we illustrate the empirical relationship between age-structure shifts and economic growth. Secondly, we discuss the behavioral response to a rapid shift in the age distribution: household-level life-cycle decisions may be influenced by society-level age structure composition. The third channel we examine is the role of institutional settings in the face of rapid changes in age structure. In particular, we look at the role of old-age social security and the incentives created by slow-changing laws.

2.3.2   Economic Growth and Age Structure

When analyzing the effects of age structure on economic growth, typically the working-age share is isolated as the age group of interest. In the coming years, however, concern over the potentially depressing effects of old-age dependency on economic growth and the differing effects of youth- and old-age dependency has increased interest in directly observing the partial effect of these latter variables on economic growth.

We take the convergence model framework outlined in Bloom and Canning (2008), and dissect population into youth, C, working age, WA, and old, O.

Growth of gross domestic product (GDP) per worker is characterized by the distance from steady state,

$$(1) \qquad\qquad g_z = \lambda(z^* - z_0)$$

and a vector of variables, X, can affect the steady-state level of labor productivity. Following the discrete time models in Barro and Sala-i-Martin (2004), there is a log-linearization around the steady state. Thus $z = \log(Y/L)$, and the steady-state level of income per worker is summarized as,

(2) $$g_z = \lambda(X\beta - z_0).$$

To then utilize this theory of convergence in an income per capita model, consider the relationship used in Bloom and Canning (2008) that highlights the inclusion of age structure in the form of working-age share,

(3) $$\frac{Y}{N} = \frac{Y}{L}\frac{L}{WA}\frac{WA}{N}.$$

If age structure is represented by working-age share, and the participation rate is constant, then,

(4) $$g_{Y/N} = g_{Y/L} + g_{WA/N}$$

Growth of income per worker is explained by the convergence term in (2). As for the growth of the working-age share, we wish to observe the separate effects of youth- and old-age dependency on the growth of income per capita and not just the growth of the working-age share. Thus we want to identify,

(5) $$g_{Y/N} = g_{Y/L} + g_{(N-C-O)/N}.$$

To isolate the growth of the youth- and old-age we can draw on rules of approximation. Firstly, the difference in logs is an approximation for the growth of the working-age share,

(6) $$g_{WA/N} \approx \ln\left(\frac{WA}{N}\right)_t - \ln\left(\frac{WA}{N}\right)_0.$$

Then, the working-age is the population less the youth- and old-age populations, so growth of the working age can be redefined as

(7) $$g_{(N-C-O)/N} = \ln\left(\frac{N-C-O}{N}\right)_t - \ln\left(\frac{N-C-O}{N}\right)_0.$$

The approximation accuracy of $\ln(1-x) \approx x$ is increasing in the working-age share, and we use this approximation to assert that,

(8) $$g_{(N-C-O)/N} = -\left(\frac{C+O}{N}\right)_t + \left(\frac{C+O}{N}\right)_0.$$

$$g_{(N-C-O)/N} = \frac{C}{N_0} - \frac{C}{N_t} + \frac{O}{N_0} - \frac{O}{N_t}.$$

Using the following substitutions,

(9) $$y = \log\left(\frac{Y}{N}\right), z = \log\left(\frac{Y}{L}\right), w = \log\left(\frac{WA}{N}\right),$$

and the fact that taking the logs of both sides of equation (3) gives,

(10) $$y = z + w.$$

Then,

(11) $g_{y/N} = \lambda(X\beta - z_0) + \dfrac{C}{N_0} - \dfrac{C}{N_t} + \dfrac{O}{N_0} - \dfrac{O}{N_t}$

$g_{y/N} = \lambda(X\beta + w_0 - y_0) + \dfrac{C}{N_0} - \dfrac{C}{N_t} + \dfrac{O}{N_0} - \dfrac{O}{N_t}$

$g_{y/N} = \lambda\left(X_0\beta - \dfrac{C}{N_0} - \dfrac{O}{N_0} - y_0\right) - \left[\dfrac{C}{N_t} - \dfrac{C}{N_0}\right] - \left[\dfrac{O}{N_t} - \dfrac{O}{N_0}\right]$

$g_{y/N} = \left(X_0\beta_0 + \beta_1\dfrac{C}{N_0} + \beta_2\dfrac{O}{N_0} + \beta_3 y_0\right) + \beta_4\Delta\dfrac{C}{N_t} + \beta_5\Delta\dfrac{O}{N_t}.$

Thus the effects of youth- and old-age dependency on growth of income per capita can be estimated using the specification outlined in equation (11).

An implication of equation (5) is that the coefficients on the change in youth- and old-age shares are minus one. Any deviation from this coefficient is brought about by misspecification. That is, the youth-age and old-age will have heterogeneous effects on income per capita as changes in the youth- and old-age shares incite different behavioral responses. High youth-age dependency will cause women to exit the workforce to care for children. Higher old-age shares, in part brought about by higher life expectancies, may reflect lower morbidity thus extending the time which people stay in the workforce. Moreover, the older individuals may accumulate capital (we control for this in our regression analysis) for a longer period before they draw down on savings.

Included in the vector of explanatory variables describing the steady state level of GDP per worker, X, are capital stock, education, and institutional quality, and other factors that may affect labor productivity. We also include a global time trend and a random error term in this vector. To measure the growth of income per capita we take the difference in logs. Thus, the estimated equation is,

(12) $\ln(y_t) - \ln(y_{t-1}) = \beta_1 y_{t-1} + \beta_2 edu_{t-1} + \beta_3 cap_{t-1} + \beta_4 inst_{t-1}$
$+ \beta_5 c_{t-1} + \beta_6 o_{t-1}\beta_6\Delta c_t + \beta_6\Delta o_t + \delta_i + \delta_t + \varepsilon_{it}.$

Fixed effects with a lagged dependent variable introduce a Nickell (1981) bias. Thus, we do not estimate a fixed effects model and instead we control for some potential country fixed effects with time invariant country specific geographic variables such as fraction of land in the tropics, and whether the country is landlocked or not. We also control for regional dummies.

It is reasonable to be concerned about possible endogeneity of the age structure variables in the economic growth equation. Periods of high growth may increase the working-age share through migration effects, or have an effect on fertility and thus the youth-age population shares (Bloom and Canning 2008). To control for this issue of reverse causality, we use five-year lags of the age structure variables (and an alternative instrument set using five-year-lag fertility and life expectancy).

Using data from the Penn World Tables 6.2 (Heston, Summers, and Aten 2006) for GDP per capita and Penn World Tables 5.6 for capital stock, and demographic data from the World Population Prospects (United Nations 2007), we estimate the effect of changes in age structure on economic growth. In the appendix we detail the data sources with citations.

In table 2.2 we present the descriptive statistics of all of the variables, including the instrumental variables, in the regression analysis. We see from these statistics that a range of countries are represented in the sample: high to low income, low to high fertility rates, low to high infant mortality rates. In table 2.3 we detail the country lists of the country dummies used. The sample of countries is larger than this, and the country lists only detail those of the continent dummies included.

In table 2.4, we present the regression results. In column (1), we present the ordinary least squares (OLS) results for the long run demographic model. In column (2) we introduce the short run effects of youth- and old-age share changes. For these latter variables, a change in the youth- or old-age share will have an impact in the short run on the annual average five year economic growth rate. The initial level of the youth- and old-age shares will affect the long run growth rate. In column (3) we present the two-stage-least-squares results for the demographic model. We use the five year lag of the youth- and old-age change in population share, and the initial year fertility rate and initial year infant mortality rate. In columns (4) and (5) we introduce the Asian and African continent dummies.

Table 2.2   **Descriptive statistics**

Variable	Mean	Standard deviation	Min	Max
Five-year growth rate of income per capita	1.35	3.36	−23.48	20.38
Log real GDP per capita	8.44	1.15	5.14	10.49
Capital stock	0.63	1.96	0.00	22.88
Average years of secondary schooling	5.45	2.83	0.35	12.05
Trade openness	65.23	46.14	3.78	462.93
Freedom House Polity Index	6.14	3.30	0.19	10.00
Life expectancy	64.06	11.84	31.20	82.10
Tropical location	0.53	0.48	0.00	1.00
Landlocked	0.18	0.38	0.00	1.00
Youth-age share	0.35	0.10	0.14	0.51
Old-age share	0.06	0.05	0.01	0.20
Youth-age share change	−0.01	0.01	−0.07	0.02
Old-age share change	0.003	0.005	−0.012	0.026
Total fertility rate	3.88	1.96	1.08	8.50
Infant mortality rate	53	46	3	199

Note: $N = 616$

Table 2.3   **Country dummy lists**

East Asia	South Central Asia	South East Asia	Sub-saharan Africa	Latin America
China	Bangladesh	Indonesia	Benin	Argentina
Japan	India	Malaysia	Botswana	Bolivia
Republic of Korea	Iran (Islamic Republic of)	Philippines	Cameroon	Brazil
	Nepal	Singapore	Central African Republic	Chile
	Pakistan	Thailand	Democratic Republic of the Congo	Colombia
	Sri Lanka		Congo	Costa Rica
			Gambia	Dominican Republic
			Ghana	Ecuador
			Guinea-Bissau	El Salvador
			Kenya	Guatemala
			Lesotho	Haiti
			Liberia	Honduras
			Malawi	Jamaica
			Mali	Mexico
			Mauritius	Nicaragua
			Mozambique	Panama
			Niger	Paraguay
			Rwanda	Peru
			Senegal	Trinidad and Tobago
			Sierra Leone	Uruguay
			South Africa	Venezuela
			Sudan	
			United Republic of Tanzania	
			Togo	
			Uganda	
			Zambia	
			Zimbabwe	

Table 2.4　　　　　**Regression results**

	OLS (1)	OLS (2)	IV (3)	OLS (4)	IV (5)
Log real GDP per capita in the base year	−2.184*** (0.35)	−2.077*** (0.34)	−2.153*** (0.36)	−2.037*** (0.39)	−2.111*** (0.41)
Capital stock in the base year	0.140*** (0.041)	0.168*** (0.040)	0.171*** (0.044)	0.112** (0.045)	0.120*** (0.041)
Average years of secondary schooling in the base year	−0.0114 (0.080)	−0.0577 (0.079)	−0.0246 (0.081)	−0.0909 (0.078)	−0.0641 (0.081)
Trade openness in the base year	0.0137*** (0.0032)	0.0143*** (0.0030)	0.0110*** (0.0025)	0.0149*** (0.0033)	0.0105*** (0.0027)
Freedom House Polity Index in the base year	0.152*** (0.050)	0.140*** (0.048)	0.155*** (0.051)	0.167*** (0.051)	0.187*** (0.054)
Life expectancy in the base year	0.146*** (0.027)	0.0943*** (0.028)	0.0748** (0.032)	0.0606** (0.030)	0.0497 (0.034)
Youth-age share in the base year	−19.53*** (3.30)	−21.44*** (3.57)	−24.68*** (4.41)	−18.37*** (3.95)	−21.95*** (4.62)
Old-age share in the base year	−29.46*** (6.93)	−18.38*** (6.77)	−18.76** (7.52)	−8.902 (7.36)	−10.87 (8.19)
Youth-age share change		−57.73*** (10.5)	−75.70*** (14.8)	−53.57*** (10.8)	−70.38*** (14.3)
Old-age share change		−57.18** (23.0)	−125.2*** (46.6)	−64.44** (25.0)	−149.5*** (48.9)
Tropical location	−1.103*** (0.35)	−0.928*** (0.33)	−0.879** (0.35)	−1.104** (0.43)	−1.135** (0.44)
Landlocked	0.389 (0.37)	0.506 (0.37)	0.692* (0.39)	0.606* (0.37)	0.754* (0.39)
Latin America Dummy				0.300 (0.44)	0.259 (0.46)
Sub-saharan Africa				−0.773 (0.56)	−0.568 (0.59)
East Asia Dummy				2.038*** (0.63)	1.895*** (0.63)
South Central Asia Dummy				−0.307 (0.59)	−0.389 (0.59)
South East Asia Dummy				1.305** (0.58)	1.554*** (0.58)
Constant	20.40*** (3.15)	22.78*** (3.24)	21.58*** (3.80)	19.14*** (4.14)	21.80*** (4.58)
Year dummies	Yes	Yes	Yes	Yes	Yes
Observations	722	720	649	714	643
R^2	0.27	0.31	0.26	0.32	0.28
Cragg-Donald F-stat			45.70		40.51
Hansen J p-value			0.411		0.500

Notes: Robust standard errors in parentheses. Instruments: five-year lag of the change in the youth- and old-age shares, five-year lag of fertility rates and infant mortality rates.

***Significant at the 1 percent level.

**Significant at the 5 percent level.

*Significant at the 10 percent level.

We see from the regression results that changes in both youth- and old-age shares over a five-year period have a negative effect on the short run (five year) growth rate. This effect is negative and significant even in the two-stage-least-squares specifications in columns (3) and (5). Once we control for the continent dummies, however, the results indicate that the long run effect of the level of old-age population share is negative but not significant. The long run effect of the level of the youth-age population share is, how-ever, negative and significant.

Capital stock, trade openness, and institutional quality each have a posi-tive and significant effect on the five-year growth rate. The significance of these control variables is consistent with other studies: even when controlling for these core variables that explain cross-country differences in economic growth, the level and change in the age structure of the population have an effect on economic growth. Highlighting the importance of demographic change in explaining economic growth is a feature of Bloom, Canning, and Sevilla (2003) but in this chapter, we treat youth-age and old-age population shares as heterogeneous. The positive and significant East Asian dummy indicates that on average, over the 1960 to 2005 period, East Asia's economic growth rate was higher than the global average.

Taking the results in column (5) of table 2.4, we can interpret the magni-tude of the coefficients on the demographic variables. A 10 percentage point decrease in the youth-age share, will increase the economic growth rate by 2.2 percentage points leading to a higher steady state income per capita in the long run. From the results, we see that a change in the old-age share does not have a significant effect on economic performance in the long run. In the short run, if the change in the youth-age share decreases by 1 percent point over a five-year period, then the average annual economic growth rate will increase by 0.7 percentage points. If the change in the old-age share increase by 1.0 percentage point then the average annual economic growth rate in that five year period will decline by 1.5 percentage points. Thus, the increasing old-age shares we observe throughout Asia will have a negative effect on economic growth in the short run, but in the long run it does not appear that the rising old-age shares will impede economic performance. The positive impact of a decline in youth-age shares and the neutrality of the old-age shares on economic growth are consistent with the findings of Kelley and Schmidt (2005).

In past studies, the positive influence of an increase in working-age share may, in part, have been a proxy for the decline in youth-age dependents. The decline in the working-age share that is to come in East Asia over the next forty-five years is coupled with an increase in old-age, and not youth-age, dependency. The observed partial effect of changes in the growth of the working-age share on economic growth may differ in the future, as declines in the working-age share will be coupled with increases in the old-age share, and not increases in the youth-age share. From the regression results in table

2.4, however, we see that for East Asia, the heterogeneity of the effect of youth- and old-age shares on economic growth is evident in the long run, but not in the short run. In the short run, changes in either youth- and old-age shares have a similar magnitude of effect on economic growth. However, the long run effect differs: in the long run low youth-age shares will have a positive effect on economic growth, but high old-age shares may have an insignificant effect on economic growth.

The results indicate that in the short run both high youth- and old-age dependency will have a negative effect on the growth of income per capita. But in the long run, when the population age distribution stabilizes, higher youth-age dependency will have, for a given working-age share, a negative effect on economic growth, whereas higher old-age dependency will have no effect on economic growth. This difference presumably reflects the inherently greater capacity of economies to adapt to changes in old-age population shares than to changes in youth shares.

Old-age dependency is not a given. The compression of morbidity means that a significant portion of this population can continue to work, if they so desire. By working longer they can save more than in the past for their retirement. But rising income means greater demand for leisure and retirement, and this effect may dominate, leading to early retirement (Costa 1995). However, if retirement is voluntary and older people have saved enough for their old age, they are not dependents. Dependency means financing old-age consumption through transfers. If retirement is funded by productive savings or own labor supply, then the elderly should not be considered dependent. The case of youth dependency is clearer. Born into the world with no financial assets, the young do not have the savings or work-effort potential that the elderly have, and they are clearly dependent.

Our results suggest that high youth-age shares are negatively associated with economic performance in the long run, and high old-age shares may not have a significant effect the long run steady-state level of income per capita. This stands to be potentially good news for those Asian countries that are about to experience a decline in working-age share coupled with an increase in the old-age shares. The increase in income in the past, in part boosted by the increase in the working-age share, was backed by the decline in the youth-age shares. In the future, the decline in working-age share will not necessarily bring with it a decline in income, as this demographic trend will be backed by an increase in old-age population shares and not an increase in youth-age shares.

2.3.3   Behavioral Change: Labor Supply, Savings, and Education

Although the model we proposed in the previous section implies age structure variables have coefficients of -1 in the growth equation, the estimation revealed otherwise. This indicates that there is some kind of measurement error in age structure effects. This measurement error can be explained by accounting and behavioral responses to age structure shifts.

Given well-established life-cycle variations in behavior, it is reasonable to suppose that changes in age structure will have effects on aggregate outcomes. Changes in age structure bring with them changes in labor supply, savings, and education as the number of people engaging in the various life-cycle decisions changes. For example, since labor supply tends to follow an inverted U-shaped pattern with respect to age, changes in the age composition of the population are likely to have effects on aggregate labor supply. Savings rates also vary with age, with the highest rates occurring for forty- to seventy-year-olds, implying that changes in the age structure will affect aggregate savings rates. Furthermore, increases in life expectancy mean that more people survive through the school ages, and the average number of years of education increases.

However, in addition to these accounting effects there are also behavioral effects of aging. Generational crowding (i.e., being born into a large cohort) may have effects on relative wages and individual labor supply (Easterlin 1980; Bloom, Freeman, and Korenman 1988; Korenman and Neumark 2000). In addition, falling fertility and youth dependency rates may be linked to increased labor market participation, particularly among women, as found in Bloom et al. (2009b).

Improvements in life expectancy (which is a proxy for better health) that are inherent to an aging society can invoke behavioral responses that have a positive effect on economic growth. Better health may improve worker productivity (Bloom, Canning, and Sevilla 2004). However, there may also be a demographic effect as a longer prospective life span can change life-cycle behavior, leading to a longer working life and higher saving for retirement (Bloom, Canning, and Moore 2005; Bloom et al. 2007; Bloom, Canning, and Moore 2007). Moreover, a higher life expectancy may increase the incentive to invest in education, as the years over which returns can be amortized are extended (Finlay 2006).

Labor Supply

In Bloom et al. (2009b), the authors show that the decline in total fertility rate has had a significant effect on the increase in female labor force participation. They show that a reduction in the fertility rate of one child is associated with an increase in labor force participation of four years. With fewer children, women have more opportunities to stay in, or reenter, the workforce as the time required by child care declines. Increased child care services, and the decline in the stigma of a working mother, have helped to make the option of women staying in (or reentering) the workforce more attractive.

In Bloom et al. (2009b), the Republic of Korea is used as an example to illustrate the effect of fertility decline on economic growth. The authors show that in Korea, demographic effects explain about 14 percent of the increase in income per capita. The decline in population growth, the increase in the working-age share, and then the positive female labor force participation response to the decline in the fertility rate all contribute to the rapid rise in income per capita in the Republic of Korea.

The behavioral female labor supply response contributes about 25 percent of the 14 percent increase in income per capita. This is only one of the behavioral responses that can occur during the demographic transition. Further analysis of the savings and education responses may find compounded effects compared with those found in Bloom et al. (2007) and may thus yield even higher estimates of the income effects of demographic change.

Savings

Central to our understanding of the East Asian "miracle" has been Alwyn Young's work (1994, 1995) showing that rapid economic growth in the region was mainly due to increases in factor inputs—notably labor, capital, and education—and not to improvements in total factor productivity.[5] In order to understand the rise in income levels in East Asia we must therefore understand the driving forces behind the growth in these inputs. All of the Asian "Tiger" economies enjoyed a surge in savings and investment during their period of rapid economic growth. We focus here on Taiwan, for which there are fairly good data on household savings. The private savings rate in Taiwan rose from around 5 percent in the 1950s to well over 20 percent in the 1980s and 1990s. Savings rates vary by age, being highest in Taiwan for households with heads in the fifty- to sixty-year-old range. We would therefore expect changing age structure to be a possible explanation for this increase in aggregate saving. Studies that examine the link between demographic structure and national savings rates do find a strong connection (Leff 1969; Fry and Mason 1982; Mason 1987; Mason 1988; Kelley and Schmidt 1995; Kelley and Schmidt 1996; Higgins and Williamson 1997; Higgins 1998) and suggest that a large part of the savings boom in East Asia can be explained by the changing age structure of the population.

However, Deaton and Paxson (2000) show that, based on household savings data for Taiwan, changes in age structure account for only a modest increase in the overall savings rate, perhaps 4 percentage points. They show that the rise in the aggregate savings rate has not been mainly due to changes in the age composition of the population but, rather, to a secular rise in the savings rates of all age groups.

The question then arises as to why savings rates rose at each age. One possible explanation, proposed by Lee, Mason, and Miller (2000) is that increased savings rates are due to rising life expectancy and a subsequent

5. This argument is controversial, as discussed in Krugman (1994).

need to fund retirement income. Tsai, Chu, and Chung (2000) show that the timing of the rise in household savings rates matches the increases in life expectancy of the population.

With a fixed retirement age we would expect such a savings effect. However, Deaton and Paxson (2000) argue that in a flexible economy, without mandatory retirement, the main effect of a rise in longevity will be on the span of the working life, with no obvious prediction for the rate of saving. Bloom, Canning, and Moore (2005) formalize this argument to show that under reasonable assumptions the optimal response to an improvement in health and a rise in life expectancy is to increase the length of working life, though less than proportionately, with no need to raise saving rates at all (due to the gains from enjoying compound interest over a longer life span).

The effect of savings on investment and domestic production depends on the nature of the capital market. With perfect capital mobility, demographic change may have an impact on international capital flows (Higgins 1998). In this case, effects on domestic interest rates and investment may be minimal (Poterba 2004). However, if capital markets are imperfect, the demographic transition can lead to a mismatch between the investment needs of a large, young, working-age population and the retirement savings of older workers (Higgins and Williamson 1997).

Education

Demography can affect educational investments through several mechanisms. Perhaps the most important is the quantity-quality trade-off whereby fertility choices and human capital investment decisions are jointly made. This framework points to lower fertility rates being both a cause and a consequence of increased educational investments, with both fertility and schooling determined by a common set of factors that affect families' incentives.

Notwithstanding families' desired fertility, actual fertility in the absence of contraception may be much higher. The provision of family planning services to populations in which desired fertility is low can both lower fertility outcomes and increase schooling levels. This effect may be particularly pronounced for girls' schooling because with high fertility, girls are frequently kept out of school to help care for their younger siblings. Foster and Roy (1997) show how a randomized trial providing family planning services in Bangladesh affected both fertility outcomes and children's schooling levels.

The quantity-quality trade-off can also appear to some extent at the national level if schooling is publicly funded. Smaller youth cohorts can increase the availability of educational funding per child and can lead to an expansion of public education (Kelley 1996; Lee and Mason 2008).

One reason for an increased incentive to invest in education may be the rise in life expectancy. A longer life increases the time over which education investments can be recouped. Kalemli-Ozcan, Ryder, and Weil (2000) argue that the effect of improved health and longevity on educational investments has played a large role in economic growth over the last 150 years. This incentive effect, however, is clearly linked to the prospective working life rather than total lifespan, suggesting that education levels may be linked to planned retirement ages and social security incentives.

2.3.4   Institutional Settings: Social Security

With health improvements and longer life expectancies, the optimal response for workers with perfect markets may be to have a longer working life. However, mandatory or conventional retirement ages, coupled with the strong financial incentives to retire that are inherent in many social security systems, seem to result in early retirement and increased needs for saving for old age (Bloom et al. 2007).

Generous state transfer systems not only have financing problems, they undermine and reduce labor supply of the elderly, increasing effective dependency rates. Many social security systems impose a very high effective tax rate on older workers by withholding or reducing benefits if they continue to work.

Singapore, Malaysia, and Hong Kong (China) have fully funded universal systems. These systems consist of personal accounts so an older worker who continues working benefits from a larger sum to retire on. These systems should not discourage work at older ages and should be associated with high savings rates. Taiwan, China, India, Vietnam, and Indonesia do not have universal systems. In these countries planning for retirement has historically been rare. However, they do have systems for the formal sector and public sector that can generate large future liabilities.

Specific social security systems were designed for existing demographic situations and may not be appropriate as the proportion of elderly continues to rise. However, transforming these systems once established is very difficult politically, as entitlements under the systems are difficult to reduce. In countries without universal systems, population aging will put pressure on governments to provide more coverage, given the difficulties experienced by families trying to cope with the issue. The systems put in place will have a large impact on how aging affects those economies.

2.4   Summary

In this chapter we have illustrated the effects of aging on economic growth in Asia. Aging is driven by a decline in fertility, an increase in life expectancy, or the dynamic evolution of past variation in birth and death rates. In the first part of the chapter we illustrate these driving forces of aging. We show that between 1960 and 2005 the shift in age structure of the population has been predominantly driven by the rapid decline in fertility, and between 2005 and 2050 the dynamic evolution of fertility and mortality changes in the period from 1960 to 2005 will continue to shape the age distribution. In the second part of the chapter, we estimated the statistical relationship between the youth-age, and old-age population shares and economic growth, both in the long run and in the short run. Regression analysis indicates that in the long run, old-age shares may not have a significant impact on economic growth. A change in the old-age shares has a negative effect on economic growth in the short run, but not in the long run. The level of youth-age shares (and the change) has a negative effect on long-run economic performance. This result is good news for Asian countries in the long run as the old-age population share increases.

We discuss that population aging has more than a simple accounting effect on economic growth and we discuss the various behavioral responses that come with the shift in age structure: an increase in female labor force participation as fertility declines, an increase in savings, and an increase in education. These factors act together and may offset any negative accounting effects of a shift in the age structure, thus in the regression analysis we observe an insignificant effect of rising old-age shares on economic performance in the long run. Overall, the effect of aging on economic growth will be ambiguous, as the various behavioral responses may impose economic growth effects of differing magnitudes across different countries.

Appendix

Table 2A.1   Data sources

Variable	Source
Five-year growth rate of income per capita	Penn World Tables 6.2, (log(Real GDP per capita)(t) – log(Real GDP per capita)(t – 5))/5 × 100
Log real GDP per capita	Penn World Tables 6.2, log(Real GDP per capita) PPP constant 2000 prices
Capital stock	Penn World Tables 5.6, interpolated
Average years of secondary schooling	Barro and Lee (2001), Average years of schooling for people ages 15 years of age or older
Trade openness	Penn World Tables 6.2, Exports plus Imports divided by GDP per capita, constant prices
Freedom House Polity Index	http://www.freedomhouse.org/template.cfm?page=1, degree of democracy less degree of autocracy
Life expectancy	World Development Indicators 2007, Life Expectancy at Birth
Tropical location	Sala-i-Martin, Doppelhofer, Miller (2004), Proportion of land in tropical area
Landlocked	Sala-i-Martin, Doppelhofer, Miller (2004), Landlocked country dummy
Youth-age share	World Development Indicators 2007, Fraction of Population 0–14 years old
Old-age share	World Development Indicators 2007, Fraction of Population 65+ years old
Youth-age share change	World Development Indicators 2007, Youth age share (t) – Youth age share (t – 1)
Old-age share change	World Development Indicators 2007, Old-age share (t) – Old-age share (t – 1)
Total fertility rate	World Development Indicators 2007, Total Fertility Rate
Infant mortality rate	World Development Indicators 2007, Infant (< 1 year) mortality rate per 1,000 live births

References

Barro, R. J., and J. W. Lee. 2001. International data on education attainment: Updates and implications. *Oxford Economic Papers* 53 (3): 541–63.

Barro, R. J., and X. Sala-i-Martin. 2004. *Economic growth.* Cambridge, MA: MIT Press.

Bloom, D. E., and D. Canning. 2008. Global demographic change: Dimensions and economic significance. *Population and Development Review* 34 (Supplement): 17–51.

Bloom, D. E., D. Canning, and G. Fink. 2008. Population aging and economic growth. PGDA working paper no. 31. Boston: Program on the Global Demography of Aging, April.

Bloom, D. E., D. Canning, G. Fink, and J. E. Finlay. 2007. Realizing the demographic dividend: Is Africa any different? PGDA working paper no. 23. Boston: Program on the Global Demography of Aging, May.

———. 2009a. Fertility, female labor force participation, and the demographic dividend. *Journal of Economic Growth* 14: 79–101.

———. 2009b. The cost of low fertility in Europe. *European Journal of Population,* forthcoming.

Bloom, D. E., D. Canning, and P. Malaney. 2000. Population dynamics and economic growth in Asia. *Population and Development Review* 26 (Supplement): 257–90.

Bloom, D. E., D. Canning, R. K. Mansfield, and M. Moore. 2007. Demographic change, social security systems, and savings. *Journal of Monetary Economics* 54:92–114.

Bloom, D. E., D. Canning, and M. Moore. 2005. The effect of improvements in health and longevity on optimal retirement and savings. PGDA working paper no. 2. Boston: Program on the Global Demography of Aging, April.

———. 2007. A Theory of Retirement. PGDA working paper no. 26. Boston: Program on the Global Demography of Aging, November.

Bloom, D. E., D. Canning, and J. Sevilla. 2001. Economic growth and the demographic transition. NBER Working Paper no. 8685. Cambridge, MA: National Bureau of Economic Research, December.

———. 2003. The demographic dividend: A new perspective on the economic consequences of population change. Population Matters Monograph MR–1274. Santa Monica: RAND.

———. 2004. The effect of health on economic growth: A production function approach. *World Development* 32 (1): 1–13.

Bloom, D. E., P. H. Craig, and P. N. Malaney. 2001. *The quality of life in rural Asia.* Hong Kong: Oxford University Press.

Bloom, D. E., R. Freeman, and S. Korenman. 1988. The labor market consequences of generational crowding. *European Journal of Population* 3 (2): 131–76.

Bloom, D. E., and J. Sachs. 1998. Geography, demography, and economic growth in Africa. *Brookings Papers on Economic Activity,* Issue no. 2: 207–73.

Bloom, D. E., and J. G. Williamson. 1998. Demographic transitions and economic miracles in emerging Asia. *World Bank Economic Review* 12 (3): 419–55.

Bongaarts, J. 1984. Implications for future fertility trends for contraceptive practice. *Population and Development Review* 10 (2): 341–52.

———. 1994. The impact of population policies: Comment. *Population and Development Review* 20 (3): 616–20.

———. 1999. Fertility decline in the developed world: Where will it end? *The*

American Economic Review. Papers and Proceedings of the One Hundred Eleventh Annual Meeting of the American Economic Association 89 (2): 256–60.

Costa, D. 1995. Pensions and retirement: Evidence from Union Army Veterans. *Quarterly Journal of Economics* 110 (2): 297–320.

Cutler, D., A. Deaton, and A. Lleras-Muney. 2006. The determinants of mortality. *Journal of Economic Perspectives* 20 (3): 97–120.

Deaton, A., and C. Paxson. 2000. Growth, demographic structure, and national savings in Taiwan. *Population and Development Review* 26 (Supplement): 141–73.

Easterlin, R. 1980. *Birth and fortune: The impact of numbers on personal welfare.* New York: Basic Books.

Finlay, J. 2006. Endogenous longevity and economic growth. Harvard University Program on the Global Demography of Aging, Working Paper no. 7.

Foster, A., and N. Roy. 1997. The dynamics of education and fertility: Evidence from a family planning experiment. Philadelphia: The University of Pennsylvania.

Fry, M., and A. Mason. 1982. The variable rate-of-growth effect in the life-cycle saving model. *Economic Inquiry* 20 (3): 426–42.

Heston, A., R. Summers, and B. Aten. 2006. Penn World Table Version 6.2. Center for International Comparisons of Production, Income and Prices at the University of Pennsylvania, September.

Higgins, M. 1998. Demography, national savings, and international capital flows. *International Economic Review* 39 (2): 343–69.

Higgins, M., and J. G. Williamson. 1997. Age structure dynamics in Asia and dependence on foreign capital. *Population and Development Review* 23 (2): 261–93.

Kalemli-Ozcan, S., H. E. Ryder, and D. N. Weil. 2000. Mortality decline, human capital investment, and economic growth. *Journal of Development Economics* 62 (1): 1–23.

Kelley, A. C. 1996. The consequences of population growth for human resource development: The case of education. In *The impact of population growth on wellbeing in developing countries,* eds. D. A. Ahlburg, A. C. Kelley, and K. Oppenheim-Mason, 67–137. Berlin: Springer-Verlag.

Kelley, A. C., and R. M. Schmidt. 1995. Aggregate population and economic growth correlations: The role of the components of demographic change. *Demography* 32 (4): 543–55.

———. 1996. Saving, dependency, and development. *Journal of Population Economics* 9: 365–86.

———. 2005. Evolution of recent economic-demographic modeling: A synthesis. *Journal of Population Economics* 18: 275–300.

Korenman, S., and D. Neumark. 2000. Cohort crowding and youth labor markets: A cross-national analysis. In *Youth employment and joblessness in advanced countries,* eds. D. G. Blanchflower and R. B. Freeman, 57–105. Chicago: University of Chicago Press.

Krugman, P. 1994. The myth of Asia's economic miracle. *Foreign Affairs* 73:62–78.

Lee, R., and A. Mason. 2008. Fertility, human capital, and economic growth over the demographic transition. Paper presented at the 2008 Annual Meetings of the Population Association of America. April 17–19, New Orleans, LA.

Lee, R., A. Mason, and T. Miller. 2000. Life cycle saving and demographic transition: The case of Taiwan. *Population and Development Review* 26 (Supplement) 194–219.

Leff, N. H. 1969. Dependency rates and savings rates. *American Economic Review* 59 (5): 886–96.

Mason, A. 1987. National saving rates and population growth: A new model and new evidence. In *Consequences of population growth in developing countries,* eds. G. Johnson and R. D. Lee, 523–60. Madison, WI: University of Wisconsin Press.

———. 1988. Population growth, aggregate saving, and economic development. In *World population trends and their impact on economic development,* ed. D. Salvatore, 45–58. London: Greenwood Press.

Nickell, S. 1981. Biases in dynamic models with fixed effects. *Econometrica* 49 (6): 1417–26.

Poterba, J. 2004. The impact of population aging on financial markets. NBER Working Paper no. 10851. Cambridge, MA: National Bureau of Economic Research, October.

Pritchett, L. 1994. Desired fertility and the impact of population policies. *Population and Development Review* 20 (1): 1–55.

Sala-i-Martin, X., G. Doppelhofer, and R. I. Miller. 2004. Determinants of long-term growth: A Bayesian averaging of classical estimates (BACE) approach. *American Economic Review* 94 (4): 813–35.

Tsai, I.-J., C. Y. C. Chu, and C.-F. Chung. 2000. Demographic transition and household savings in Taiwan. *Population and Development Review* 26 (Supplement): 174–93.

United Nations. 2007. World population prospects: The 2006 revision. Comprehensive Dataset (CD-ROM). United Nations, Department of Economic and Social Affairs.

World Bank (2007). World Bank Development Indicators CD-ROM.

Young, A. 1994. Lessons from the East Asian NICs: A contrarian view. *European Economic Review* 38:964–73.

———. 1995. The tyranny of numbers: Confronting the statistical realities of the East Asian growth experience. *Quarterly Journal of Economics* 110:641–80.

Comment   Roberto S. Mariano

In light of declining total fertility rate (TFR), increasing life expectancy, dynamically evolving birth and death patterns, and increasing share of old-age population in the age distribution in Asia, this chapter addresses the big question: "What are the economic consequences of population aging?"

The methodology used in the chapter uses both qualitative and quantitative approaches. The qualitative analysis in the chapter is structural and this part of the chapter brings up interesting research issues which I will not get into. Rather, I will focus my comments on the quantitative part of the chapter.

The main message in the chapter is that the economic impact of population aging depends on behavioral responses, in various dimensions, to the shift in the population age distribution. The major factors are:

Roberto S. Mariano is a professor of economics and statistics, and dean of the School of Economics at Singapore Management University, and Professor Emeritus of Economics and Statistics at the University of Pennsylvania.

- Response of the female labor force participation to the decline in fertility
- Adjustments in savings and retirement decisions to the increase in life expectancy
- Ability of policy adjustments and financial market developments to keep pace with life expectancy improvements.

There is a wide disparity across Asian countries vis-à-vis the stage of development of financial markets for retirement security in Asia. One question that comes to mind is what products financial markets should promote in Asia to enhance retirement security and financial well-being—annuities, reverse mortgages, longevity risk bonds, long-term care insurance, to mention a few—and how these would impact the economic growth in the region.

The regression analysis in the chapter is a "reduced-form" analysis that quantifies the dependence of growth in per capita income in Asia on population age structure as well as the various behavioral responses to aging. Technically, for the zero mean assumption for the error term in the regression equation to be valid, $(C + O)/P$ must be small (as the authors point out in their footnote). Is this really the case—is $(C + O)/P$ really small?

The estimation procedure uses ten-year lags of age structure (alternatively, lags of fertility and lags of life expectancy) as instruments for the age structure variables to get two-stage least squares (2SLS) estimates. The difference between the ordinary least squares (OLS) and 2SLS estimates can be used to test the endogeneity of the age structure variables. If the difference turns out to be statistically significant, then use the 2SLS estimates, not OLS. (This assumes the instruments used are valid instruments.)

There may be bias in the regression estimates due to omitted variables in the equation. The chapter talks about the behavioral responses (to the shift in age structure) that should be included in the regression equation. Financial market developments may be another set. These variables can be incorporated in the regression equation to extend the analysis, and perhaps get a sharper conclusion than "The effect of aging on economic growth will be ambiguous as the various behavioral responses may impose economic growth effects of differing magnitudes across different countries."

Comment   Kwanho Shin

Age structure is significantly changing in Asia. This change is driven by many factors such as decline in total fertility rate, increase in life expec-

Kwanho Shin is a professor of economics at Korea University.

tancy, and dynamic evolution of past variation. In shaping the demography structure, however, the decline in total fertility plays a dominant role. In the chapter, the authors attempt to empirically estimate the impact of aging on growth. They find that while the impact of youth-age population share is negative, the impact of old-age population share, especially in the long run, is not. They conclude that population aging may not impede growth prospective in Asia.

The most intriguing finding of the authors' is that while youth-age population share decreases economic growth, old-age population share does not. They argue that, even if the economy is aging, increased labor force participation of aged workers as well as female workers may help increase growth. They also argue that savings rate may also rise as the life expectancy increases, and hence a subsequent need to fund retirement income increase. They further point out that as the fertility rate decreases, the quantity-quality trade-off kicks in so that investment in human capital increases, leading to higher productivity of labor.

While rising life expectancy may increase saving, this is true as long as those who save belong to the working population. Once they become old, they have to dissave. Most empirical studies actually find that as the economy is aged, the saving rate decreases. See among others, Leff (1969), Mason (1987), Horioka (1989), Higgins (1998), and Bosworth and Chodorow-Reich (2006).

The equation adopted to empirically estimate the impact of youth- and aging-population shares may subject to an endogeneity problem. The authors regress the growth rate of output on youth- and old-age dependency rates and other control variables that determine the steady state level of per capita gross domestic product (GDP). While they have used a reasonable set of control variables, there may remain other unobserved country fixed effects. For example, if some unobserved country fixed effects generate faster TFR growth and at the same time lead to longer life expectancy, higher growth and larger old-age population share can be spuriously correlated.

I believe that how an aging economy affects growth potential is an important question. However aging is expected to influence the economy through a number of channels, which cannot be completely comprehended by estimating a reduced-form, single equation. In order to answer the question, we need more structure of the model and each channel through which aging affects growth potential should be investigated.

References

Bosworth, B. P., and G. Chodorow-Reich. 2006. Saving and demographic change: The global dimension. Population Aging Working Paper. Washington, DC: Brookings Institution.

Higgins, M. 1998. Demography, national savings, and international capital flows. *International Economic Review* 39 (2): 343–69.

Horioka, C. Y. 1989. Why is Japan's private saving rate so high? In *Developments in Japanese economics,* ed. R. Sato and T. Negishi, 145–178. Tokyo: Academic Press/Harcourt Brace Jovanovich Japan, Inc.

Leff, N. H. 1969. Dependency rates and savings rates. *The American Economic Review* 59 (5): 886–96.

Mason, A. 1987. National saving rates and population growth: A new model and new evidence. In *Population growth in developing countries,* ed. D. G. Johnson and R. D. Lee, 523–60. Madison, WI: University of Wisconsin Press.

Demographic Transition, Human Capital Accumulation, and Economic Growth
Some Evidence from Cross-Country and Korean Microdata

Chin Hee Hahn and Chang-Gyun Park

3.1 Introduction and Background

It is well known that Korea has sustained remarkably fast catch-up growth since the 1960s. Another salient but less well-noted aspect of the Korean economy is its fast demographic transition. Total fertility rate, which was 5.67 in 1960, has declined very fast to hit alarmingly low level of 1.16 in 2004. Meanwhile, death rate measured by the number of death per 1,000 people also declined from 13.46 in 1960 to 5.30 in 1995, and roughly remained at that level since then. With rapid decline in both fertility and death rates, population growth rate and working age population ratio went through rapid changes as well.[1]

From an international perspective, what distinguishes Korea from other countries is her fast *speed* of demographic transition (figures 3.1 through 3.4). Compared with other countries, various indicators of demographic structure such as fertility rate, working-age population ratio, and population growth rate in Korea went through the most dramatic changes since the 1960s.[2] In the early 1960s, the levels of these demographic indicators in Korea and other high-performing East Asian countries were similar to the average levels of Sub-Saharan African countries. By the early 1990s,

---

Chin Hee Hahn is a Senior Research Fellow at the Korea Development Institute. Chang-Gyun Park is an assistant professor in the College of Business Administration at Chung-Ang University.

1. Population growth rate registered 3.09 percent in 1960 but has declined since then to reach 0.49 percent in 2004. The number of working-age population per dependent population (working-age population ratio) was as low as 1.21 in 1960. After a brief decline, it increased continuously to reach 2.6 in 2004. See appendix table 3A.1.

2. Fast demographic transition is not confined to Korean case. The same kind of phenomenon is also observed in many high performing Asian countries.

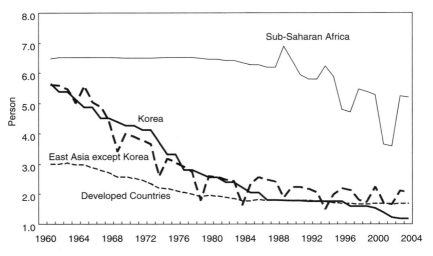

Fig. 3.1   Trends of the fertility rates in major regions

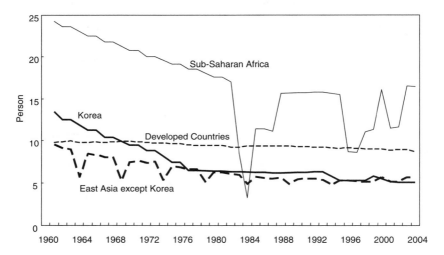

Fig. 3.2   Trends of the death rates in major regions

however, they were roughly comparable to those of developed countries. By contrast, averaged over the whole period, levels of the demographic indicators in Korea and other East Asian countries do not stand out and are placed between those of developed and Sub-Saharan African countries. The above observation that Korea and other East Asian countries simultaneously experienced fast economic growth and fast speed of demographic transition motivates our study.

In this chapter, we explore whether similar patterns can be found in a more

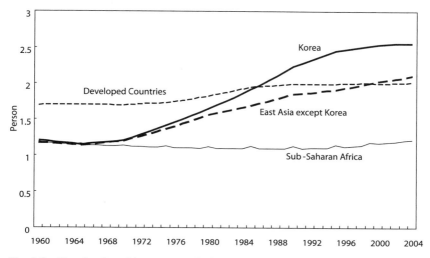

Fig. 3.3   Trends of working-age population ratios in major regions

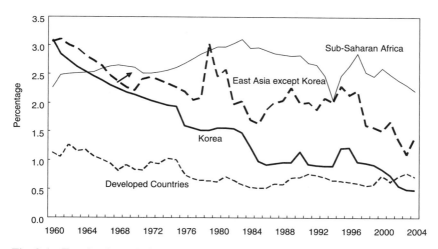

Fig. 3.4   Trends of population growth rates in major regions

broad set of countries. We cast two specific questions. "Is faster speed of demographic transition associated with faster growth of per capita income?" and "Does faster speed of demographic transition imply faster speed of human capital accumulation?" We try to tackle these questions utilizing both cross-country data and micro-level household survey data from Korea. In cross-country analysis, first of all, we suggest several measures of the *speed* of demographic transition of a country. Then we relate these measures to per capita income growth of countries relying on traditional growth regression framework, and to measures of human capital accumulation. As a complement to the cross-country analysis, we also use household survey data in Korea to examine whether families with fewer children invest more on their education. In our opinion, empirical evidence from Korea is particularly interesting in that Korea has gone through remarkably fast economic growth and, at the same time, remarkably fast changes in demographic structure.

There are many micro-level empirical studies on the Beckerian trade-off between number and quality of children.[3] Also, there are many cross-country studies relating demographic indicators or demographic structure to per capita income growth.[4] However, in the case of cross-country studies, most of them do not take seriously either the theoretical implications of endogenous growth with endogenous fertility choice or the possibility that demographic transition is endogenously triggered by the conscious choice of between quality and quantity of children.

Meanwhile, some recent endogenous growth theories with endogenous fertility choice demonstrate the possible existence of multiple equilibria and try to explain the transition from high-fertility no-growth Malthusian equilibrium to low-fertility sustained-growth modern growth equilibrium (e.g., Becker, Murphy, and Tamura 1990; Tamura 1996; Lucas 2002). According to these theories, the transition from no-growth equilibrium to sustained growth equilibrium is triggered by the rise of return to human capital investment and the resulting changes in household choice favoring the quality over the quantity of children—for example, lower fertility and more investment on human capital per child.[5] In other words, these theories suggest that economic growth, human capital accumulation, and demographic transition are all simultaneously triggered by changes in fertility pattern stemming from increased rate of return to human capital investment. However, to the best of our knowledge, it is hard to find empirical studies which take the body of growth literature with endogenous fertility choice as an empirical framework to examine the relationship between demographic transition and per capita income growth.

Although this study could be regarded as an empirical examination of broad implications of the above class of theories, strictly speaking, the spe-

3. Empirical studies employing micro-level data to test the significance of quality-quantity trade-off hypotheses include, among many, Rosenzweig and Wolpin (1980), Hanushek (1992), and Grawe (2005).

4. Examples of cross-countries on the relationship between demographic indicators and economic growth are Romer (1990), Brander and Dowrick (1994), Kelly and Schmidt (1995), and Bloom and Williamson (1998). There are also many country-level studies examining demography and economic growth, such as Cutler et al. (1990), Fougere and Merette (1999). Meanwhile, there are some cross-country studies examining the relationship between fertility rate and income level. For example, Barro and Sala-i-Martin (1995) shows that there exists an inverted U relationship between fertility and income level.

5. There could be many factors raising the rate of return to investment in human capital which triggers the transition.

cific questions asked in this study are not explicitly derived from these theories. That is, the above theoretical models do not have an explicit analysis on the relationship between the speed of demographic transition on one hand and per capita income growth as well as human capital accumulation on the other. Thus, this chapter is a fact finding exercise broadly guided by a class of theories, rather than a formal test of existing theories, motivated by the casual observation that Korea and other high-performing countries also experienced fast speed of demographic transition.

Our chapter contributes empirically not only to the better understanding of the process of economic growth, but also to understanding the nature of population aging. It is often suggested that a country experiencing faster increase in working-age population ratio is likely to experience faster growth of per capita gross domestic product (GDP). This argument seems to be based on the presumption that increase in working-age population ratio contributes to growth primarily through increased supply of labor input per capita. For example, Bloom and Williamson (1998) argue that much of the miraculous per capita income growth of East Asian countries are attributable to the favorable demographic changes in those countries, such as the rapid increase in working-age population relative to population. They argue that as the East Asian countries are expected to experience rapid population aging or a decrease in working-age population ratio, these countries will face significant slow down in per capita income growth in near future. In sum, Bloom and Williamson (1998) suggest that the *direction* of change in working-age population ratio matters for per capita income growth.

Not denying the possibility that directional change has significant implications on economic growth, we suggest that the *speed* of demographic transition may matter for economic growth. In this chapter, we suggest several measures of the speed of demographic transition, and examine whether those measures are systematically related to per capita income growth and human capital accumulation.

Finally, by providing empirical evidence on the relationship between demographic transition and human capital accumulation, we believe that the results from our chapter also help understand the role of human capital in economic growth. Despite the important role of human capital as the engine of growth as repeatedly pointed out by endogenous growth theories, it is also true that it is quite difficult to find empirical studies documenting the importance of human capital in economic development at the comparable level suggested by theoretical studies. In so far as the changes in fertility behavior and, hence, the demographic transition are systematically related in theory to the human capital investment decision by households, the empirical relationship between demographic transition and economic growth or human capital accumulation could be presented as an indirect evidence on the role of human capital in economic growth.

The organization of this chapter is as follows. In the following section, we briefly overview related theoretical studies. Section 3.3 explains the data, specification of the basic regression model, and measurement of the speed of demographic transition. Section 3.4 provides our cross-country regression results. We first provide per capita GDP growth regressions with the speed of demographic transition as the key explanatory variable. Then, we examine whether measures of human capital growth are related to the speed of demographic transition. Also, we discuss whether our measures of the speed of demographic transition reflect indeed the speed of demographic transition. Section 3.5 provides our empirical results for the household behavior on quality-quantity choice, based on micro data of Korea. The final section offers a conclusion of our findings.

3.2   A Brief Overview of Related Theoretical Studies

Dating back to early pioneering works by Becker (1960), the effort to explain child-bearing and fertility pattern as results of deliberate economic decision by rational economic agents has a long tradition in economics. Especially, the negative correlation between the number (quantity) of children and quality of children within a family had long been a well-noted statistical regularity, and several authors had tried to construct theoretical models to predict trade-off between quality and quantity of children within a family. It was Becker and Lewis (1973) who first derived the quantity-quality trade-off under a general setting of utility maximization by a household without ad hoc assumption to induce quality and quantity trade-off.[6]

Upon repeatedly observing declining fertility along with increasing per capita income, researchers had tried to explicitly introduce the Beckerain quality-quantity trade-off into the growing growth literature. Becker, Murphy, and Tamura (1990) constructed one of the studies that reinterpreted the implications of earlier researches on fertility decision and human capital investment in the context of economic growth. They developed a dynamic general equilibrium model with two steady state development regimes: a Malthusian regime with high fertility, no human capital accumulation, and no growth; and an economic growth regime with low fertility, high human capital investment per child, and positive growth. Although they provided an integrated explanation of the fertility behavior, human capital investment, and divergent economic growth performances, they did not explain endogenously how a country starts to make the demographic and economic transition from one development regime to another. Tamura (1996) introduces a conditional external effect of human capital in the human capital

6. The key feature of the model that derives the trade-off relationship is the fact that the shadow price of children depends on the quality as well as the number of the children in the family. The shadow price of children with respect to the number of children is greater the higher their quality is. Similarly, the shadow price of children with respect to their quality is greater, the greater the number of children.

investment sector or international knowledge or human capital spillovers from the advanced rest of the world and shows the possibility of an endogenous transition from the Malthusian regime to the economic growth regime. Tamura (1996) also shows that, among the set of countries that make the transition, there is a convergence. Here, the conditional convergence arises from the existence of international knowledge spillovers, combined with the existence of multiple equilibria. Thus, with ever-growing world human capital stock which raises the rate of return to human capital investment in follower countries, one of Tamura's main propositions is an accelerating growth: late transitioners grow faster.[7]

In line with Tamura's theory, Lucas (2002) views sustained economic growth of countries since the late nineteenth century—that is, industrialization—as a process of diffusion of the Western industrial revolution to other regions of the world. He further suggests that countries with open trading regime and private property right protection went through changes in a household's decision in the direction of favoring quality, rather than quantity of children, and experienced *both demographic transition and sustained increase in per capita income.* Under the perspectives of the theories we just discussed, demographic transition, human capital accumulation, and sustained per capita income growth could be understood as different manifestations of one phenomenon, in as much as all are triggered by changes in fertility decisions of households in response to the changes in the rate of return to human capital investment.

3.3   Data and Specification of Cross-Country Regressions

3.3.1   Measurement of Speed of Demographic Transition

Construction of the Measure

Our measures of the speed of demographic transition are based on the assumption that the speed of demographic transition is fixed for a country, and are basically the magnitudes of changes in certain demographic indicators during a given time interval. We consider three alternative demographic indicators—fertility rate, working-age population ratio, and population growth rate—and, for each of these indicators, construct the measure of the speed of demographic transition. Our measure of the speed of demographic transition is devised to capture how much on average certain demographic indicator has changed for a country during one unit of time interval. SFERTIL is defined as the estimated coefficient on linear time trend when

---

7. As mentioned at introduction, Tamura (1996) does not try to link the speed of demographic transition to economic growth and human capital accumulation. Nevertheless, as we will subsequently discuss, the positive association between the speed of demographic transition and per capita income growth is found to be a fairly robust feature of the cross-country data.

fertility rate is regressed on a constant and linear time trend from 1960 to 2004. SWRATIO and SPOPGR are similarly defined for working age population ratio and population growth rate.[8]

In fact, measuring the speed of demographic transition for a country for a given time period is not as obvious a task as it might seem, even with the assumption of fixed speed. Above all, it is more likely that the demographic indicators move in a nonlinear pattern rather than change linearly over time as we assumed in deriving the second type of measures. It is well known that the time profile of a country's working-age population ratio exhibits a nonlinear pattern. During one cycle of a typical demographic transition, as exemplified in figure 3.5,[9] both working-age population ratio and population growth rate follow roughly inversely U-shaped pattern. The working-age population ratio, for example, mildly declines for a short time and then continues to increase with the decline in fertility rate during the early stage of a demographic transition. In later stages, it begins to decline until it finally levels off. Therefore, it is possible that the linearity assumption produces two different estimates for two countries that are experiencing the same of speed of demographic transition, depending on which phase of the transition each country is located.

Even with these limitations of our measure of demographic transition, we chose to maintain the linearity assumption primarily because it is a simple and easy way to start. More importantly, as suggested by figure 3.1, even in the case of working-age population ratio for which the linearity assumption could potentially be most problematic, most countries are located to the left half of the inversely U-shaped curve at least during the period of our analysis, which seems to make the linearity assumption less problematic.[10]

Preliminary Analysis

Table 3.1 shows summary statistics of our measure of speed of demographic transition. First of all, the average estimated speed of change in fertility rate in the whole sample is about −0.06, which means that it took about seventeen years on average for fertility rate to decline by one, say, from three to two persons per woman. However, we can note that there is a large variation across countries in the measure as suggested by the large standard

8. In an earlier version of this chapter, we also considered a simpler measure of the speed of demographic transition, which is the difference between the time averages of the corresponding demographic indicator for the two roughly evenly divided sub-periods. Specifically, for each country, DFERTIL was defined as the difference in mean fertility rates for the two adjacent sub-periods: 1960 to 1984 and 1985 to 2004. The DWRATIO and DPOPGR were defined correspondingly for working-age population ratio and population growth rate. Since the regression results using this alternative measure were not qualitatively different from tables 3.4 through 3.6, we do not report them separately here.

9. Figure 3.2 is taken from Bloom and Williamson (1998).

10. In the case of working-age population ratio, there is also the problem of whether the measured speed of change truly reflects the speed of demographic transition or the direction of change. This issue will be discussed later in the chapter.

Fertility Rate and Death Rate

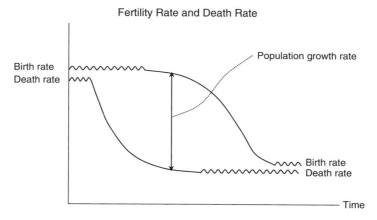

Population Growth and Working-Age Population Ratio

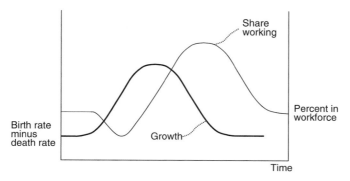

Fig. 3.5   Patterns of demographic indicators in a demographic transition
Source: Bloom and Williamson (1998).

deviation (about 0.04). So, the estimated speed of change in fertility rate of a country at one standard deviation above the sample mean is about –0.02, which suggests that it takes about fifty years for this country to experience 1 percentage point decline in fertility rate. Next, the average estimated speed of change in working-age population ratio defined as the number of working-age population per dependent population, is about 0.01, which suggests that it takes about one hundred years on average for working-age population ratio to rise, say, from one to two. Again, there is a large variation of this measure across countries. Lastly, the average estimated speed of change in population growth rate is about –0.017, which means that it takes about sixty years on average for population growth rate to drop by one percentage point, say, from 2 percent to 1 percent per annum.

The estimated speed of demographic transition also shows large variation

Table 3.1   **Measures of speed of demographic transition: Summary statistics**

Region	Mean	Standard deviation	Min	Max	N
		A SFERTIL			
EASIA	−0.09	0.01	−0.12	−0.08	7
SASIA	−0.07	0.03	−0.11	−0.01	8
SUBSAHA	−0.03	0.04	−0.11	0.04	43
MENA	−0.10	0.04	−0.15	−0.03	16
LAMERICA	−0.08	0.03	−0.12	−0.02	30
INDUSTRY	−0.04	0.02	−0.10	−0.01	23
PACIFIC	−0.07	0.03	−0.11	−0.03	10
EURCASIA	−0.03	0.01	−0.03	−0.02	3
CHINA	−0.11		−0.11	−0.11	1
Total	−0.06	0.04	−0.15	0.04	141
		B SWRATIO			
EASIA	0.03	0.01	0.01	0.04	7
SASIA	0.01	0.01	0.00	0.02	8
SUBSAHA	0.000	0.01	−0.01	0.03	43
MENA	0.01	0.01	0.00	0.03	16
LAMERICA	0.01	0.01	0.00	0.04	30
INDUSTRY	0.01	0.01	0.00	0.02	23
PACIFIC	0.02	0.02	0.00	0.06	10
EURCASIA	0.01	0.004	0.00	0.01	3
CHINA	0.03		0.03	0.03	1
Total	0.01	0.01	−0.01	0.06	141
		C SPOPGR			
EASIA	−0.03	0.02	−0.07	0.00	7
SASIA	−0.01	0.03	−0.04	0.05	8
SUBSAHA	−0.001	0.03	−0.14	0.08	43
MENA	−0.04	0.06	−0.22	0.02	16
LAMERICA	−0.02	0.02	−0.07	0.01	30
INDUSTRY	−0.01	0.01	−0.03	0.01	23
PACIFIC	−0.02	0.03	−0.07	0.02	10
EURCASIA	−0.03	0.01	−0.04	−0.02	3
CHINA	−0.03		−0.03	−0.03	1
Total	−0.02	0.03	−0.22	0.08	141

across regions. Overall, East Asia and China stand out from other regions in all of the three measures. For example, the speed of changes in fertility rate in East Asia and China are −0.09 and −0.11 respectively, which are about three times as large as developed countries or Sub-Saharan African countries. The estimated speed of changes in fertility rate for most other developing regions falls in between East Asia and Sub-Saharan African countries.[11]

11. However, MENA (Middle East and North Africa) region experienced somewhat faster decline in fertility rate than East Asia and Europe and Central Asia slower decline than Sub-Saharan African region.

Similar phenomenon is observed for the speed of changes in working-age population ratio. It was highest in China followed by East Asia, which are fast growers, and lowest in Sub-Saharan Africa followed by Europe and Central Asia and developed countries. The speeds of change in working-age population ratio in East Asia and China are also about three times as large as developed countries.

Although many, if not most, countries experienced decline in fertility rate, increase in working-age population ratio, and decline in population growth rate during the sample period we examine, there were some countries that do not follow this general pattern. Table 3.2 shows the number of countries according to the estimated sign of each measured speed of demographic transition. In the case of SFERTIL, negative coefficient values were obtained for 133 countries out of 141, among which 128 cases were significant at the 1 percent level. There were eight countries where the coefficient was negative, and five of them were significant at the 5 percent level. Meanwhile, in the case of SWRATIO and SPOPGR, thirty-six and thirty-four out of 141 countries, respectively, exhibited negative coefficient most of which are significant at the 10 percent level.

Particularly in the case of working-age population, the existence of negative coefficients may be problematic especially if these are for mature economies that have already passed the peak of the inverted U-shaped curve. This is so because we are trying to examine whether the speed, rather than the direction, of demographic transition matters for growth and, hence, want to get a positive estimate of the speed of changes in working-age population ratio for a country located at the declining phase of the inverted U-shaped curve. However, among the thirty-six countries where negative values of SWRATIO were obtained, only one country (Sweden) belongs to the developed region, and twenty-eight countries belongs to Sub-Saharan Africa. Nevertheless, we take this phenomenon into account and consider

Table 3.2	Sign distributions of measures of speed of demographic transition		
	Number of countries with positive coefficient	Number of countries with negative coefficient	Total number of countries
SFERTIL	8	133	141
	(3, 2, 0)	(128, 0, 1)	
SWRATIO	105	36	141
	(98, 0, 0)	(29, 1, 2)	
SPOPGR	34	107	141
	(19, 3, 3)	(81, 4, 4)	

Notes: The speed of demographic transition using, for example, fertility rate (SFERTIL), is the slope of the simple regressions of fertility rate on year variable. Numbers in parentheses are number of countries that have estimated coefficient significant at the 1 percent, 5 percent, and 10 percent level, respectively.

Table 3.3   Correlations between speed of demographic transition and per capita GDP growth

	GRGDPL	SFERTIL	SWRATIO	SPOPGR
GRGDPL	1.00	−0.22	0.45	−0.01
	(0.0000)	(0.0078)	(0.0001)	(0.9247)
SFERTIL	−0.22	1.00	−0.64	0.61
	(0.0078)	(0.0000)	(0.0001)	(0.0001)
SWRATIO	0.45	−0.64	1.00	−0.54
	(0.0001)	(0.0001)	(0.0000)	(0.0001)
SPOPGR	−0.01	0.61	−0.54	1.00
	(0.9247)	(0.0001)	(0.0001)	(0.0000)

Notes: Numbers in parentheses are *p*-values. Measures of speed of demographic transition are for the period from 1960 to 2004. The GRGDPL is annual average real per capita GDP growth rate for the same period.

alternative measures of the speed of changes in working-age population ratio later in this paper.

As the last preliminary analysis, we present simple correlations of various measures of the speed of demographic transition and per capita GDP growth of countries for the period from 1960 to 2004. As shown in table 3.3, per capita GDP growth of countries are negatively correlated with SFERTIL and positively correlated with SWRATIO at conventional significance level, although it is not significantly correlated with SPOPGR. Also, there are strong correlations among the three measures of speed of demographic transition. That is, countries under fast demographic transition by one measure, SFERTIL for example, also exhibit fast demographic transition by other measures, such as SWRATIO and SPOPGR. The existence of strong correlations among these variables suggests that these variables indeed are likely to be three different ways to measure the speed of demographic transition of a country. One can also infer that it is useful to take into account all three of these variables in examining the relationship between demographic transition and per capita GDP growth.

3.3.2   Specification of the Empirical Models and Data

Equipped with three different measures of speed of demographic transition, we are now ready to embark on examining the hypotheses presented in previous section.

In testing the first hypothesis on the positive relationship between economic growth and speed of demographic transition, we follow the typical strategy found in empirical growth literature; that is, including the key variable of interest as an additional explanatory variable into a reduced-form "standard" growth regression specification and testing the statistical validity of the variable of interest:

$$GI_i = \gamma DT_i + \beta' X_i + \varepsilon_i,$$

where GI_i is country i's growth rate of per capita GDP and DT_i is the variable of key interest in our study and represents one of the measures of speed of demographic transition defined earlier. The vector of usual suspect variables recognized as having certain explanatory power as the determinants of economic growth is X_i.

In this chapter, we consider three specifications as the standard regression models: two of them suggested by Levine and Renelt (1992), and one with additional explanatory variables taking subsequent development in literature into account. Then we examine whether our measure of demographic transition has additional explanatory power.[12] The first regression from Levine and Renelt (1992) includes—as explanatory variables—initial real GDP per capita in 1960, investment share of GDP, initial secondary school enrollment rate and the average annual rate of population growth. The second regression from Levine and Renelt (1992) has almost equivalent structure to Barro (1991), which, in addition to the first specification, includes primary school enrolment rate, average rate of government consumption expenditure to GDP, a dummy variable for socialist economic systems, indicators for revolutions and coups, and dummy variables for countries in Latin America and Sub-Saharan Africa. The third regression includes, in addition to the explanatory variables in the second regression, institutional quality, openness, natural resource abundance, and terms of trade growth.

To test the second hypothesis that relates speed of demographic transition to human capital accumulation, we examine the simple correlation between various measures of speed of demographic transition and measures of changes in human capital investment by estimating simple regression model.

The data sources for this chapter are as follows. We use real GDP per capita (RGDPL) from Penn World Table (PWT) 6.2 to measure growth rate of per capita GDP for each country. Fertility rate, death rate, population growth rate, and working-age population ratio are taken from the World Development Indicator (WDI) (World Bank 2006). The control variables in the first and the second regression equations are from the data set provided by Levine and Renelt (1992). The data sources for other control variables are as follows. Openness—the average years a country is open between 1950 and 1990—and natural resource abundance, the share of primary product exports in GDP in 1970, are from Sachs and Warner (1995). Institutional quality is from Knack and Keefer (1995). Terms of trade is the average terms of trade growth rate between 1960 and 1990 from Barro and Lee (1994).

In regressions of human capital accumulation, human capital investment is measured with years of schooling. Barro and Lee (2000) provide estimates of the number of years of schooling achieved by the average person at various levels and at all levels of schooling combined. We use total years of schooling (TYR), primary years of schooling (PYR), secondary years of

---

12. These are the regression equations (i) and (ii) in table 5 from Levine and Renelt (1992).

schooling (SYR), and years of higher schooling (HYR) for population aged twenty-five years or above from Barro and Lee's data set.

We tried to construct as large a sample of countries as possible for which the data on real GDP and several key demographic indicators are available. Our sample consists of 141 countries.[13]

3.4   Cross-Country Regression Results

3.4.1   Per Capita GDP Growth

Tables 3.4–3.6 show our cross-country regressions of per capita GDP growth with measures of speed of demographic transition as the explanatory variables of main interest. We use ordinary least squares (OLS), as well as the generalized method of moments (GMM) estimation technique to address the endogeneity problem that might exist in measures of speed of demographic transition. Along with all explanatory variables in the original regressions except for the speed measure, we include as the instruments measures of human capital of a country relative to the frontier country in 1960, TYR of each country divided by total years of schooling of the frontier country (the United States) in 1960, and the difference between average educational attainment of a country and that of the United States in 1960.[14] Other instruments included are working-age population ration in 1960, fertility rate in 1960, population growth rate in 1960, life expectancy at birth in 1960, and female labor participation rate in 1960, which are available from WDI.[15]

Overall, the regression results strongly support our first hypothesis that faster speed of demographic transition is associated with faster growth of per capita GDP.[16] The comparison between OLS and GMM results tells us

13. However, the number of observations in the regressions below can be smaller than 141 due to missing values for some of the variables. For more detailed description of the construction of our sample countries, see appendix A.

14. We calculated average educational attainment of a country simply as the sum of educational attainment of population aged twenty-five or above at six levels of schooling from Barro and Lee (2000)—primary school attained, primary school completed, secondary school attained, secondary school completed, higher school attained, and higher school completed.

15. The way we choose instruments for the measure of speed of demographic transition reflects the difficulty of finding "smart" instruments. One possible justification for the strategy adopted in the chapter is that those initial values, especially the initial human capital stock, are likely to be correlated with the speed measure but not with the error term in the regression equation. Another justification is purely a statistical one. It is not unusual to include all lagged variables as instruments in GMM estimation if we have a time series data set. Surely, one should worry about the problems associated with weak instruments. However, we ended up with fairly accurate GMM estimates. We believe that not too much concern on weak instruments is called for in interpreting the estimation result.

16. Taking logarithms of our measures of speed of demographic transition hardly affected the results qualitatively. In the case of the speed of changes in fertility rate, we considered an alternative measure—the number of years it takes for fertility rate to decline from five to replacement level (about two)—and observed qualitatively similar results, which we do not report here.

that endogeneity issue may not be a major concern at least in our specifications.[17]

Most of all, table 3.4 shows that estimated coefficients on SFERTIL are mostly negative and highly significant, suggesting that countries with rapidly declining fertility rate experienced higher growth rate of per capita income. The result is robust to the inclusion of some of the conventional determinants of growth. Next, SWRATIO also enters the regressions with positive and highly significant coefficients, suggesting that countries with rapidly changing working-age population ratio exhibited faster growth (table 3.5).[18] Table 3.6 shows that the estimated coefficient on SPOPGR is also negative, as expected, although it lost significance with the inclusion of additional controls.

Thus, as discussed in section 3.2, the regression results are broadly consistent with the implications of several growth theories with endogenous fertility choice. Also, the fact that we could obtain qualitatively similar results using all three alternative measures of the speed of demographic transition is strongly supportive of our first hypothesis.

3.4.2   Human Capital Accumulation: Growth of Years in Schooling

Now, we turn to our second hypothesis: the faster the speed of demographic transition of a country, the faster the speed of its human capital accumulation. So, we ran simple regressions with the speed of accumulation of human capital as dependent variable and our measure of speed of demographic transition as independent variable. As the measure of the speed of human capital accumulation, we use each country's annualized difference in years of schooling for the period from 1960 to 2000. Table 3.7 shows twelve regression results. The first row of the table shows the four dependent variables—annualized differences in TYR, PYR, SYR, and HYR—and the first column shows three measures of the speed of demographic transition.

The regression results are fairly strongly supportive of our hypothesis that a country experiencing fast demographic transition also experiences fast accumulation of human capital. That is, all three measures of the speed of demographic transition successfully explain variations of annualized differences in TYR and PYR. Specifically, the coefficients of SFERTIL are significantly negative in regressions of (annualized differences in) TYR and PYR. Although insignificant in regressions of SYR and HYR, they are still estimated to be negative. Both SWRATIO and SPOPGR, respectively, enter the four regressions significantly with positive coefficients. So, countries with faster changes in working-age population ratio or faster decline in population growth rate also experienced faster increase in years of schooling at all levels.

---

17. According to the *J*-statistic reported in the last row of table 3.4, we cannot reject the null hypothesis of overidentifying restrictions.
18. In section 3.4.3, we discuss whether the speed of change or the direction of change in working-age population ratio, in particular, matters for growth.

Table 3.4   Per capita GDP growth: Changes in fertility rate

	(1)	(2)		(3)		(4)	
	OLS	OLS	GMM	OLS	GMM	OLS	GMM
SFERTIL		−19.128***	−11.016	−15.675***	−10.212*	−14.365***	−14.155***
		(−5.10)	(−1.59)	(−3.22)	(−1.87)	(−2.84)	(−2.47)
Initial GDP per capita	−0.245*	−0.208*	−0.312***	−0.248**	−0.442***	−0.518***	−0.593***
	(−1.85)	(−1.75)	(−3.01)	(−2.00)	(−5.18)	(−3.29)	(−5.37)
Investment share	10.120***	6.640***	18.343***	3.876	7.250*	1.048	−1.409
	(3.83)	(2.70)	(5.14)	(1.40)	(1.92)	(0.34)	(−0.42)
Population growth	−0.514**	−0.932***	−0.612***	−0.656***	−0.298	−0.247	0.324
	(−2.37)	(−4.42)	(−2.92)	(−2.75)	(−1.48)	(−0.88)	(1.62)
Secondary school enrollment	2.455*	1.549	1.799*	0.127	1.117	−0.084	1.904**
	(1.81)	(1.26)	(1.79)	(0.10)	(1.42)	(−0.06)	(2.22)
Primary school enrollment				1.161*	1.563**	0.909	1.348*
				(1.67)	(2.08)	(1.17)	(1.64)
Government share				−1.475	3.882*	−0.993	−0.244
				(−0.47)	(1.83)	(−0.28)	(−0.09)
Socialist economy				−0.114	−0.501	−0.396	0.666
				(−0.25)	(−0.82)	(−0.77)	(1.42)
Revolution/coups				−0.610	−0.768*	−0.295	−0.720
				(−0.97)	(−1.67)	(−0.39)	(−1.19)

Africa dummy				−0.868*	−1.374***	−1.139**	−0.959
				(−1.85)	(−3.62)	(−2.02)	(−1.61)
Latin America dummy				−1.209***	−1.036***	−0.708*	−0.599*
				(−3.13)	(−3.41)	(−1.70)	(−1.85)
Quality of institutions						0.397***	0.365***
						(2.84)	(3.11)
Openness						0.246	1.237**
						(0.37)	(2.61)
Natural resource abundance						−3.178*	−5.484***
						(−1.90)	(−3.20)
Terms of trade						0.112	0.011
						(1.48)	(0.15)
Number of observations	107	107	86	103	83	86	75
Adjusted R^2	0.292	0.431	0.368	0.479	0.485	0.590	0.582
J-statistic			0.105		0.096		0.083

Notes: The SFERTIL is the estimated speed measure for fertility rate. Numbers in parentheses are t-statistics. The J-statistic is the test statistic for overidentifying restrictions for GMM estimates. The test statistic is distributed as χ^2 with the degrees of freedom 7.

***Significant at the 1 percent level.

**Significant at the 5 percent level.

*Significant at the 10 percent level.

Table 3.5 Per capita GDP growth: Changes in working-age population ratio

	(1)	(2)		(3)		(4)	
	OLS	OLS	GMM	OLS	GMM	OLS	GMM
SWRATIO		82.416***	56.436***	72.406***	57.736***	66.979***	102.29***
		(6.33)	(3.03)	(4.49)	(3.38)	(3.76)	(4.85)
Initial GDP per capita	-0.245*	-0.212*	-0.371***	-0.270**	-0.377***	-0.536***	-0.482***
	(-1.85)	(-1.88)	(-5.41)	(-2.32)	(-5.65)	(-3.56)	(-5.15)
Investment share	10.120***	5.467**	9.098**	2.774	4.642	0.473	-2.874
	(3.83)	(2.32)	(2.14)	(1.04)	(1.15)	(0.16)	(-0.67)
Population growth	-0.514**	-0.543***	-0.622***	-0.389**	-0.308**	-0.126	-0.265
	(-2.37)	(-2.95)	(-4.33)	(-2.00)	(-2.09)	(-0.51)	(-1.45)
Secondary school enrollment	2.455*	1.302	2.058***	-0.126	0.208	-0.106	0.652
	(1.81)	(1.12)	(2.86)	(-0.10)	(0.29)	(-0.08)	(0.69)
Primary school enrollment				1.075	1.155*	0.802	1.044
				(1.63)	(1.86)	(1.07)	(1.36)
Government share				2.558	5.631**	3.169	3.673
				(0.81)	(2.47)	(0.90)	(1.20)
Socialist economy				-0.059	-0.231	-0.425	0.517
				(-0.14)	(-0.42)	(-0.86)	(1.18)
Revolution/coups				-0.207	-0.466	0.110	-0.175
				(-0.34)	(-1.26)	(0.15)	(-0.34)

Africa dummy				-0.849**	-1.418***	-1.078**	-0.800
				(-2.00)	(-3.89)	(-2.04)	(-1.46)
Latin America dummy				-1.011***	-0.955***	-0.552	-0.554*
				(-2.73)	(-3.44)	(-1.37)	(-1.75)
Quality of institutions						0.357**	0.174
						(2.64)	(1.52)
Openness						-0.107	0.350
						(-0.16)	(0.81)
Natural resource abundance						-3.197**	-3.935*
						(-2.01)	(-1.88)
Terms of trade						0.123*	0.036
						(1.69)	(0.57)
Number of observations	107	107	86	103	93	86	75
Adjusted R^2	0.292	0.488	0.458	0.526	0.517	0.620	0.616
J-statistic			0.079		0.019		0.029

Notes: The SWRATIO is the estimated speed measure for working-age population rate. Numbers in parentheses are *t*-statistics. The *J*-statistic is the test statistic for overidentifying restrictions for GMM estimates. The test statistic is distributed as χ^2 with the degrees of freedom 7.

***Significant at the 1 percent level.

**Significant at the 5 percent level.

*Significant at the 10 percent level.

Table 3.6   Per capita GDP growth: Changes in population growth rate

	(1)	(2)		(3)		(4)	
	OLS	OLS	GMM	OLS	GMM	OLS	GMM
SPOPGR		−25.730***	−34.356***	−13.530*	−20.131	−13.717	−9.373
		(−3.74)	(−2.80)	(−1.68)	(−1.23)	(−1.45)	(−0.65)
Initial GDP per capita	−0.245*	−0.283**	−0.420***	−0.333***	−0.430***	−0.615***	−0.559***
	(−1.85)	(−2.26)	(−4.00)	(−2.65)	(−4.71)	(−3.71)	(−4.44)
Investment share	10.120***	8.303***	14.333***	4.516	11.165***	1.007	0.443
	(3.83)	(3.28)	(4.08)	(1.57)	(2.89)	(0.31)	(0.11)
Population growth	−0.514**	−0.893***	−0.903***	−0.490*	−0.485	−0.133	0.389
	(−2.37)	(−3.92)	(−3.45)	(−1.92)	(−1.46)	(−0.42)	(1.09)
Secondary school enrollment	2.455*	1.142	1.267	−0.374	0.294	−0.656	1.055
	(1.81)	(0.86)	(1.19)	(−0.28)	(0.36)	(−0.46)	(1.09)
Primary school enrollment				1.401*	0.628	1.131	0.906
				(1.92)	(0.76)	(1.41)	(0.99)
Government share				−1.199	3.055	−0.062	−1.049
				(−0.36)	(1.34)	(−0.02)	(−0.40)
Socialist economy				0.012	−0.284	−0.321	0.771
				(0.03)	(−0.43)	(−0.60)	(1.43)
Revolution/coups				−0.694	−0.647	−0.455	−0.614
				(−1.07)	(−1.55)	(−0.57)	(−1.12)

Africa dummy			−1.380***	−1.399***	−1.551***	−1.988***
			(−3.09)	(−3.43)	(−2.77)	(−3.23)
Latin America dummy			−1.188***	−0.909***	−0.680	−0.738**
			(−2.96)	(−3.10)	(−1.57)	(−2.36)
Quality of Institutions					0.384**	0.345**
					(2.64)	(2.53)
Openness					0.320	1.011**
					(0.46)	(2.26)
Natural resource abundance					−3.657**	−3.206
					(−2.09)	(−1.52)
Terms of trade					0.156*	−0.021
					(1.90)	(−0.25)
Number of observations	107	107	86	103	83	86	75
Adjusted R^2	0.292	0.372	0.369	0.438	0.416	0.557	0.490
J-statistic			0.073	0.088	0.088		0.106

Notes: The **SPOPGR** is the estimated speed measure for population growth rate. Numbers in parentheses are *t*-statistics. The *J*-statistic is the test statistic for overidentifying restrictions for GMM estimates. The test statistic is distributed as χ^2 with the degrees of freedom 7.

***Significant at the 1 percent level.
**Significant at the 5 percent level.
*Significant at the 10 percent level.

Table 3.7   **Regressions of human capital accumulation**

	TYR	PYR	SYR	HYR
SFERTIL	−0.373***	−0.291***	−0.080	−0.014
	(−4.78)	(−6.15)	(−1.50)	(−0.91)
	[0.18]	[0.27]	[0.01]	[−0.001]
SPOPGR	−0.421***	−0.158**	−0.228***	−0.049***
	(−3.89)	(−2.18)	(−3.37)	(−2.38)
	[0.13]	[0.04]	[0.09]	[0.04]
SWRATIO	1.563***	0.487**	0.919***	0.201***
	(5.57)	(2.44)	(5.25)	(3.70)
	[0.23]	[0.02]	[0.21]	[0.11]

Notes: Numbers in parentheses are *t*-statistics and numbers in bracket are Adjusted R^2. The number of observations is 100.
***Significant at the 1 percent level.
**Significant at the 5 percent level.
*Significant at the 10 percent level.

In order to see whether the regression results reflect cross-regional differences, rather than cross-country differences, we also ran the same regressions with the inclusion of dummy variables for Latin America and Sub-Saharan Africa (not reported). However, the regressions results with the two region dummy variables were not much different from the simple regression results above, except that the coefficients of SWRATIO and SPOPGR became insignificant in HYR regressions.[19]

3.4.3   Speed of Change Versus Direction of Change

Up to now, we have tried to come up with various measures of the speed of demographic transition of a country and provided empirical evidence suggesting that a country with faster speed of demographic transition experienced not only faster growth of GDP per capita but also faster accumulation of human capital. In the case of working-age population ratio, for example, it was shown above that a country with faster changes in working-age population ratio not only grew faster but also accumulated human capital more rapidly.

However, one could raise the question whether our measure of speed of demographic transition reflect indeed the speed of change, not the direction of change. For example, do the positive coefficients on SWRATIO in regressions of per capita GDP growth and human capital accumulation capture the effect of "the speed of demographic transition" or "the increase" in

---

19. Meanwhile, the dummy variables for Latin America and Sub-Saharan Africa were significant in many cases. We do not report the results of these regressions to save the space. The regression results are available upon request.

working-age population relative to population? As noted in our introduction, there does exists a view holding that a significant part of the miraculous growth of East Asian countries are due to rapid increase in working-age population (labor supply) relative to population (Bloom and Williamson 1998). Although assessing the validity of the above view is not a main objective of this chapter, we think this issue needs further examination regarding interpretation of our empirical results.

Thus, we tried to perform additional regressions which, we hope, can shed light on this issue, focusing on the speed of changes in working-age population ratio for which interpretation of our results could be most controversial. In the previous regressions, we tried to relate per capita GDP growth from 1960 to 2004 to measured speed of change in working-age population ratio for the same period. However, the existence of contemporaneous positive relationship between per capita GDP growth and speed of changes could be compatible with both views: speed of change and direction of change.

So, firstly, we ran again previous regressions with some modification of the time period in such a way that there is no overlap of time periods for which dependent variables and measures of speed of demographic transition are constructed. Specifically, in this subsection, the speed of changes in working-age population ratio is measured for the period from 1960 to 1980, and the per capita GDP growth rate and human capital accumulation are measured for the period from 1980 to 2004. The idea is to cut the channel where the changes in working-age population ratio affect per capita GDP growth by increasing per capita labor supply, and see whether our main results are preserved. Secondly, we ran regressions with SWRATIO replaced by absolute value of SWRATIO. Given the existence thirty-six countries with the estimated values of SWRATIO as negative, this procedure will reduce the direction nature of the measure.

The first column of table 3.8 is the reproduction of regression (3)(OLS) of table 3.5, the second column is the regression result with the overlap of time periods minimized, and the third column is the regression results which is the same as the first column except that SWRATIO is replaced with absolute value of SWRATIO. The table shows that our main results are still preserved in these additional regressions. That is, column (2) shows that the speed of changes in working-age population ratio is still strongly correlated with growth of per capita GDP in subsequent nonoverlapping period, and the size of the coefficient became even larger. Also, the absolute value of SWRATIO performed equally well. Thus, our main regression results seem to capture the relationship between the *speed* of demographic transition and growth.[20]

---

20. As mentioned already, the fact that all three measures of speed of demographic transition are significantly related with growth is also conducive to our proposition.

Table 3.8   **Per capita GDP growth: Changes in working-age population ratio**

	(1)	(2)	(3)
SWRATIO	72.406***	91.720***	56.996***
	(4.49)	(4.85)	(3.06)
Initial GDP per capita	−0.270**	−0.278**	−0.296**
	(−2.32)	(−2.03)	(−2.43)
Investment share	2.774	−1.754	1.953
	(1.04)	(−0.56)	(0.67)
Population growth	−0.389**	−0.631***	−0.257
	(−2.00)	(−2.75)	(−1.27)
Secondary school enrollment	−0.126	0.153	0.072
	(−0.10)	(0.11)	(0.06)
Primary school enrollment	1.075	0.796	1.440**
	(1.63)	(1.02)	(2.11)
Government share	2.558	3.378	1.112
	(0.81)	(0.90)	(0.34)
Socialist economy	−0.059	−0.032	0.084
	(−0.14)	(−0.06)	(0.18)
Revolution/coups	−0.207	0.058	−0.611
	(−0.34)	(0.08)	(−0.97)
Africa dummy	−0.849**	−0.440	−1.280***
	(−2.00)	(−0.88)	(−3.02)
Latin America dummy	−1.011***	−1.157***	−1.125***
	(−2.73)	(−2.66)	(−2.89)
Number of observations	103	102	103
Adjusted R^2	0.526	0.446	0.474

Note: Numbers in parentheses are *t*-statistics.
***Significant at the 1 percent level.
**Significant at the 5 percent level.
*Significant at the 10 percent level.

3.5   Quality-Quantity Choice in Korea: Evidence from Household Survey

In the previous section, we have shown that change in demographic structure is closely related to both human capital accumulation and economic growth. As already discussed in section 3.2 in detail, the main factor that derives the linkage between demographic structure and economic performance is the decision by households facing trade-off between quality and quantity of children in response to changing rate of return to human capital. Therefore, it seems to be quite an interesting exercise to examine whether the quality-quantity trade-off channel in a household's fertility and human capital investment decisions is actually working at household level.

In this section, we present some evidence that explicit choice between quality and quantity of children is deliberately made by Korean households. There are already many studies that confirm the validity of quality-quantity trade-off hypotheses both in developed and developing countries.[21] However, we believe that it would be very interesting to reexamine the hypotheses in Korean context considering the fact that Korea has experienced one of the fastest economic growth as well as demographic transition.[22]

The National Statistical Office of Korea has been conducting a household survey on income and expenditure, National Household Survey, since 1963. The Survey started with the sample of wage earners residing in urban areas and later extended the coverage to include both the self-employed and nonurban residents. The survey conveys detailed information on both sides of cash flow, income and expenditure as well as demographic information such as number of children. The Survey consists of five segments of rotating panels that each segment stays at the sample for five years. Samples from the surveys conducted in 1998 and 2007 are used. Since we are interested on human capital investment on children, we include households with dependents under age thirty.[23]

We suggest the following regression specification;

$$lave\_ex_i = \alpha N_i + \beta' X_i + \varepsilon_i,$$

where $lave\_ex_i$ is the log of per child expenditure on education[24] by household i, N_i is the number of children in household i, and X_i is the vector of covariates. We include as explanatory variables average age of children and its square, educational achievement of household head and, if any, his or her partner measured by the number of schooling years, sex of household heads, log of total debt repayment, and log of disposable income. Average age of children and its square term are included to account for possible differences in educational expenditure by level of schooling. We expect per capital educational expenditure to be inverted U-shaped reflecting the fact that educational expenditure increases as children advance to higher level of schooling at a decreasing rate. Parental educational levels are expected to exert positive impacts on average educational expenditure of their children.

---

21. See Hanushek (1992) or Grawe (2005), among others.

22. There are some, if not many, studies that examine the hypotheses in Korean context such as Lee (2007). We do not claim that our study presents new evidence on the topic but that a new regression specification and an innovative approach to instrumental variables in our study may provide more solid empirical evidence supporting quantity-quality trade-off hypotheses.

23. It is generally observed in Korea that children do not leave their parents' house until they graduate college—almost 80 percent of high school graduates go to college in Korea—and get a job or get married. For male children, they are typically between twenty-seven and thirty years old when they leave their parents' house. Therefore, expenditures on education appear in the cash flow of households with dependents aged younger than, say, thirty.

24. As properly pointed out by one commentator, educational expenditure reported in the National Household Survey includes expenditure on education of household member(s) other than children, which implies that our dependent variable may be plagued with measurement error. However, if the measurement error in dependent variable is not correlated with other variables and across observational units, we still obtain a consistent estimator without taking further remedial measures.

The reason we included the sex of household head as an explanatory variable is that women are known to put more emphasis on children's education than men do in Korea. So, the households headed by women are more likely to allocate more resources to children's education than the ones headed by men. Log of total debt repayment defined as the total debt service including the principal and interest payments is thought to have negative impact on educational expenditure and log of disposable income positive impact.

Negative estimated coefficient on the number of children N_i implies that as more children are born, the family responds by reducing the size of resources devoted to each child's education. As long as the price for one unit of education quality does not vary across household,[25] one can interpret a statistically significant negative estimate of the coefficient on N_i as a supporting evidence for quality-quantity trade-off hypothesis. Note that a household's total expenditure on education tot_ex_i can be decomposed into three different components: quality of education q_i, price for one unit of education quality p_q, and the number of children N_i:

$$tot\_ex_i = p_q \times q_i \times N_i.$$

Therefore,

$$lave\_ex_i = \ln\left(\frac{tot\_ex_i}{N_i} \right) = \ln(p_q \times q).$$

Then,

$$\alpha = \frac{\partial(lavg\_ex)}{\partial N_i} = \frac{\partial(\ln(p_q q))}{\partial N_i} = \frac{1}{q} \frac{\partial q}{\partial N_i}.$$

A fundamental difficulty with the specification suggested above is that the key explanatory variable N_i suffers from an econometric problem, endogeniety bias. The key presumption in the theoretical literature that we pay close attention to in the chapter is that fertility is the result of deliberate choice of a family and decisions on fertility cannot be separated from the ones on human capital investment. In other words, the number of children, the explanatory variable of our primary concern, is determined jointly with the dependent variable, quality of education and hence orthogonality condition crucial for the consistency of ordinary least squares estimator cannot be maintained. In order to cope with the problem, we need to find proper instruments required for GMM estimation. Along with all explanatory variables in the regression except for N_i, we use two instrumental variables; dummy for the sex of the first child and age difference between the first child and mother. Some researchers argue that the sex of the first child is strongly correlated with the number of children in the family, especially in East Asian countries such as Korea and China where preference for male child is still strong due to

25. The assumption will hold if households are "price takers" in the market for education.

Confucius tradition (Lee 2007). The family whose first child happens to be male is less likely to have another child than the family with female child as the first child. The other instrument we propose, age difference between the first child and the mother, could be also strongly correlated with the number of children in a family. That is, larger age difference implies that the mother got married and then bore the first child at relatively old age and the number of children she eventually delivers is more likely to be small. On the other hand, there is no particular reason to believe that the age gap between the first child and the mother is correlated with the average educational expenditure. It is highly unlikely that a woman postpones marriage for the concern on fertility decision.

For comparison's sake, we report the results of both OLS and GMM in table 3.5. The OLS estimate for the coefficient on the number of children shows a downward bias compared to GMM estimate. Households with higher educational achievement by parents, especially household head and

Table 3.9	Quality-quantity trade-off: Korean case		
		OLS	GMM
Number of children		−0.0237*	−0.0113*
		(−1.77)	(−1.69)
Average age of children		0.3081***	0.2873**
		(5.22)	(3.21)
Average age of children squared		−0.0233***	−0.0258**
		(−2.33)	(−3.01)
Household head's years of schooling		0.1063***	0.0953***
		(4.49)	(4.03)
Sex of household head		−0.1083**	−0.0992*
		(−2.02)	(−1.81)
Partner's years of schooling		0.0523***	0.0456**
		(3.53)	(2.02)
Debt repayment		−0.2001***	−0.1692***
		(−3.00)	(−2.99)
Disposable income		−0.0263**	−0.1210*
		(−2.19)	(−1.77)
Constant		10.0854***	11.8321***
		(3.68)	(3.91)
Number of observations		3,184	3,184
R^2		0.1026	—
J-Statistic		—	2.56E-4

Notes: Dependent variable is log of per-child expenditure on education. Dummy for the sex of the first and age difference between the first two children are used as instruments in GMM estimation. The J-statistic is under the null of non-overidentifying restrictions, and is distributed as chi-squared with the degrees of freedom 2. Numbers in parentheses are t-statistics.

***Significant at the 1 percent level.
**Significant at the 5 percent level.
*Significant at the 10 percent level.

lower debt burden, show the tendency to spend more on the education of each child. Interestingly and as expected, female-headed households spend more on education. The inverted U relationship between average educational expenditure and children's average age is also confirmed by the result. According to the estimates, it seems that average expenditure on education increases with increasing rate after children reach age five. One result that cannot be intuitively understood is the relationship between household's income and educational expenditure per child. Households with less income show the tendency to spend more on education for each child. Statistically significant negative estimate of the key explanatory variable confirms the hypothesis that the quality-quantity trade-off channel is working in fertility and human capital investment decisions among Korean households.

3.6   Summary and Concluding Remarks

We provide some empirical evidence both at macro and micro levels for possible linkage between demographic transition and long-term economic performance. Our empirical results from cross-country regressions show that countries that experienced faster economic growth also exhibited faster speed of demographic transition. It is also found that countries with faster speed of demographic transition also exhibited faster accumulation of human capital. These results are fairly robust to various measures of the speed of demographic transition. We also provide an empirical evidence for the quality-quantity trade-off hypothesis with micro-level household survey data from Korea which experienced both outstanding economic growth and one of the fastest speed of demographic change. Our empirical results seem broadly consistent with previous theoretical studies, such as Becker, Murphy, and Tamura (1990), Tamura (1996), and Lucas (2002), which try to explain simultaneously demographic transition, human capital accumulation, economic growth, and convergence. In our view, however, one of our main empirical results, the positive association between the speed of demographic transition and per capita income growth as well as human capital accumulation, seems to be a neglected feature of cross-country data set that deserves more attention by future theoretical and empirical studies.

Appendix A

Table 3A.1   **Trends in demographic indicators of Korea: 1960–2004**

Year	Fertility rate (person)	Death rate (person/1,000)	Life expectancy (age)	Population growth rate (%)	Working-age population ratio (person)
1960	5.67	13.46	54.15	3.09	1.21
1965	4.87	11.24	56.68	2.46	1.15
1970	4.27	9.44	59.93	2.13	1.20
1975	3.32	7.42	63.89	1.93	1.42
1980	2.56	6.38	66.84	1.56	1.64
1985	2.04	6.24	68.65	0.99	1.92
1990	1.77	6.26	70.28	1.15	2.24
1995	1.75	5.30	71.77	1.21	2.46
2000	1.47	5.20	75.86	0.84	2.55
2004	1.16	5.10	77.14	0.49	2.56

Source: World Bank (2006).

Notes: The fertility rate is the number of babies that one woman gives birth to throughout her life. The death rate is the number of the deceased per 1,000 people. The working-age population ratio is the reciprocal of dependency ratio, which is the number of working age people aged fifteen to sixty-four per one dependent person aged under fifteen or over sixty-five.

Appendix B

Country Sample and Country Names

Among 185 countries which are included in both PWT 6.2 and WDI, we discarded forty-four countries for which we think there are not enough observations to measure the speed of demographic transition and growth of GDP per capita for the period from 1960 to 2004. To be more specific, there were many missing observations for fertility rate for some of the years during the sample period. Since measuring the speed of demographic transition is important in our chapter, we tried to minimize the possibility that only a few observations dictate our measure. Also, mostly for transition economies, real GDP variable were not available before the 1990s. Thus, we first divided our sample period into two subperiods—1960 to 1984 and 1985 to 2004—and threw away forty-four countries that had less than five nonmissing entries for real GDP or fertility rate. Table 3A.2 shows the country names of our sample by region.

Table 3A.2   Country sample (141 countries)

East Asia (7 countries)	Sub-Saharan Africa (cont.)		Latin America (30 countries)	Industrial Countries (23 countries)
Hong Kong, China	Burkina Faso	Swaziland	Antigua and Barbuda	Australia
Indonesia	Burundi	Sudan	Argentina	Austria
Korea	Cameroon	Tanzania	Bahamas	Belgium
Malaysia	Cape Verde	Togo	Barbados	Canada
Philippines	Central Africa Rep.	Uganda	Belize	Denmark
Singapore	Chad	Zambia	Bolivia	Finland
Thailand	Cote d'Ivoire	Zimbabwe	Brazil	France
	Equatorial Guinea		Channel Islands	Greece
South Asia (8 countries)	Ethiopia	East Europe and Middle Asia (3 countries)	Colombia	Iceland
Afghanistan	Gabon	Hungary	Costa Rica	Ireland
Bangladesh	Gambia	Poland	Cuba	Italy
India	Ghana	Romania	Dominican Rep.	Japan
Maldives	Guinea		Ecuador	Luxembourg
Nepal	Guinea-Bissau	Middle East and North Africa (16 countries)	El Salvador	Netherlands
Oman	Kenya	Algeria	Guatemala	New Zealand
Pakistan	Lebanon	Bahrain	Haiti	Norway
Sri Lanka	Lesotho	Cyprus	Honduras	Portugal
	Madagascar	Djibouti	Jamaica	Spain
Pacific (10 countries)	Malawi	Egypt	Mexico	Sweden
Brunei	Mali	Iran	Netherlands Antilles	Switzerland
Cambodia	Mauritania	Iraq	Nicaragua	Turkey
Fiji	Mauritius	Israel	Panama	United Kingdom
Kiribati	Mozambique	Jordan	Paraguay	United States
Korea, Dem. Rep.	Namibia	Kuwait	Peru	
Lao PDR	Niger	Malta	Puerto Rico	China
Macao, China	Nigeria	Morocco	St. Lucia	
Mongolia	Qatar	Saudi Arabia	Suriname	
Papua New Guinea	Rwanda	Syrian Arab Rep.	Trinidad and Tobago	
Solomon Islands	Senegal	Tunisia	Uruguay	
	Sierra Leone	United Arab Emirates	Venezuela	
Sub-Saharan Africa (43 countries)	Somalia			
Benin	South Africa			
Botswana				

References

Barro, R. J. 1991. Economic growth in a cross section of countries. *Quarterly Journal of Economics* 106 (2): 407–44.

———. 1994. Sources of economic growth, Carnegie-Rochester Conference Series on Public Policy 40 (1): 1–46. Amsterdam: North Holland.

Barro, R. J., and J. W. Lee. 2000. International data on educational attainment: Updates and implications, *Oxford Economic Papers* 53 (3): 541–63. Special Issue on Skills Measurement and Economic Analysis.

Barro, R. J., and X. Sala-i-Martin. 1995. *Economic growth.* New York: McGraw-Hill.

Becker, G. S. 1960. An economic analysis of fertility. In *Demographic and economic change in developed countries.* Universities-National Bureau Conference Series, no. 11. Princeton, NJ: Princeton University Press.

Becker, G. S., and H. G. Lewis. 1973. On the interaction between the quantity and quality of children. *The Journal of Political Economy* 81:279–88.

Becker, G. S., K. M. Murphy, and R. Tamura. 1990. Human capital, fertility, and economic growth. *Journal of Political Economy* 98 (5): S12–S37.

Bloom, D. E., and J. G. Williamson. 1998. Demographic transitions and economic miracles in emerging Asia. *The World Bank Economic Review* 12 (3): 419–55.

Brander, J. A., and S. Dowrick. 1994. The role of fertility and population in economic growth: Empirical results from aggregate cross-national data. *Journal of Population Economics* 7 (1): 1–25.

Cutler, D. M., J. M. Poterba, L. M. Sheiner, and L. H. Summers. 1990. An aging society: Opportunity or challenge? *Brookings Papers on Economic Activity,* Issue no. 1: 1–56 and 71–73. Washington, DC.

Duraisamy, P., E. James, J. Lane, and J. P. Tan. 1998. Is there a quantity–quality trade-off as pupil–teacher ratios increase? Evidence from Tamil Nadu, India? *International Journal of Educational Development* 18 (5): 367–83.

Fougere, M., and M. Merette. 1999. Population ageing and economic growth in seven OECD countries. *Economic Modelling* 16 (3): 411–27.

Grawe, N. D. 2005. Family size and child achievement. In *Research on economic inequality,* vol. 13, ed. J. Creedy and G. Kalb, 189–215. Amsterdam: Elsevier.

Hanushek, E. A. 1992. The trade-off between child quantity and quality. *Journal of Political Economy* 100 (1): 84–117.

Kelly, A. C., and R. M. Schmitt. 1995. Aggregate population and economic growth correlations: The role of components of demographic change. *Demography* 32 (4): 543–55.

Knack, S., and P. Keefer. 1995. Institutions and economic performance: Cross-country tests using alternative institutional measures. *Economics and Politics* 7 (November): 207–28.

Lee, J. 2007. Sibling size and investment in children's education: An Asian instrument. *Journal of Population Economics* 21 (4): 855–75.

Levine, R., and D. Renelt. 1992. A sensitivity analysis of cross-country growth regressions. *American Economic Review* 82 (4): 942–63.

Lucas, R. E. 2002. *Lectures on economic growth.* Massachusetts: Harvard University Press.

Romer, P. M. 1990. Capital, labor, and productivity, *Brookings Papers on Economic Activity, Microeconomics:* 337–67.

Rosenzweig, M., and K. I. Wolpin. 1980. Testing the quantity-quality fertility model: The use of twins as a natural experiment. *Econometrica* 48 (1): 227–40.

Sachs, J. D., and A. Warner. 1995. Economic reform and the process of global integration. *Brookings Papers on Economic Activity,* Issue no. 1: 1–118.
Tamura, R. 1996. From decay to growth: A demographic transition to economic growth. *Journal of Economic Dynamics and Control* 20 (6–7): 1237–61.
World Bank. 2006. *World Development Indicator,* CD-ROM. Washington, DC: World Bank.

Comment   Meng-chun Liu

Motivation

Most previous articles on the subject argued that the economic growth, human capital accumulation, and demographic transition are all triggered by changes in fertility pattern. This is because the increase in working-age population ratio contributes to economic growth mainly by the increase in the labor supply. However, few empirical studies look at the issue based on endogenous economic growth theories with fertility choice based on the change in the returns to human capital. In order to bridge the gap, Hahn and Park intend to examine the issue with the evidence from cross-country data and Korea household data.

Contributions

As the main question asked by this chapter, will the higher speed of demographic transition of a country speed up both per capita income growth and human capital accumulation? This chapter suggests that the speed of demographic transition may matter for economic growth. In general, Hahn and Park's chapter provides some interesting arguments and ideas. I enjoyed reading this chapter, and have some comments at the same time.

First of all, similar to the direction of demographic transition, its speed has the significant role in driving economic growth. As argued in the chapter, fast demographic transition can speed up the accumulation in human capital, which enables developing countries to get out of the trap of "Malthusian equilibrium." Are there any other possible explanations? Suppose that the fast increase in working-age population ratio may enable an economy to accumulate physical capital stock soon. There is a higher saving ratio because of lower fertility and elder population.

Second, the speeds of change in working-age population ratio in East Asia and China are about three times as large as in developed countries. The authors provide the positive perspective on economic growth with high speed of democratic transition. However, can an economy with a low fertility

Meng-chun Liu is a research fellow and deputy director at Chung-Hua Institution for Economic Research (CIER).

rate sustain the higher economic growth, especially considering that the working-age population ratio will decrease soon?

Methodology

Hahn and Park perform empirical studies by adopting the cross-country data for two sub-periods: 1960 to 1984 (twenty-four years) and 1985 to 2004 (nineteen years). Are there any reasons why the authors choose such data of these two particular periods?

The study proposes three demographic indicators for measuring speed of demographic transition: fertility rate (SFRTIL), working-age population ratio (SWRATIO), and population growth rate (SPOPGR). However, are there any alternatives to capture the speed of demographic transition? We may consider two alternatives to measure the speed of demographic transition: the year average of difference in demographic indicator for a given time interval, and the estimated coefficient on linear time trend by a regression model.

In table 3.8, absolute value of SWRATIO is adopted to replace the original variable which may jointly proxy direction and speed of demographic transition. Is it possible to add a dummy variable for referring to the direction in the equation? In some way, we are able to measure both the direct effect and the speed effect in driving economic growth.

In models of per capita GDP growth, three variables, namely "initial GDP per capita," "openness," and "quality of institutions" are treated as the exogenous variables. However, argued by some studies, an economy's institutional quality and openness usually significantly determines its per capita income. That is, the regression model may have an endogeneity problem, more or less. Even in this chapter, such a problem may be minor or has been solved. The authors may need to mention how to solve such a problem.

Finally, as mainly argued in the chapter, the high speed of demographic transition features a country associated with economic growth. In some way, the authors may consider the existence of bidirectional causality between variables, economic growth, and demographic transition. In addition to regression analyses, a suitable quantitative approach to classify their Granger causality may be helpful, and their empirical evidence will be inspiring.

Comment   Chulhee Lee

Hahn and Park's chapter offers two types of empirical evidence as to the interrelationship among demographic transition, human capital accumulation, and economic growth. Firstly, based on cross-country regression analyses, it suggests that measures of the speed of demographic transition

Chulhee Lee is a professor of economics at Seoul National University.

between 1960 and 2004 were positively related to the growth rate during the same period. It also provides that measures of the speed of demographic transition between 1960 and 2000 were positively associated with a measure of the speed of human capital accumulation. The second type of evidence comes from the micro Korean Household Survey, from which the authors found a negative relationship between the number of children and the per capita expenditure on education. This result was taken as evidence of "quality-quantity trade-off." This is an ambitious study offering a big picture that encompasses a half century in time horizon and nearly the entire world in geographic coverage. Although I am not an expert in studies of economic growth, this work looks like a highly useful contribution to the literature that attempts to explain economic growth, focusing on the roles played by demographic transition and human capital accumulation.

A major shortcoming of the study an outsider to the field can point out is a somewhat wide gap between the endogenous growth theory this study is based upon and the empirical evidence offered in the chapter. It is not too difficult to be convinced that the theory leads to the two hypotheses tested by the paper: first, a country with a faster demographic transition experiences a higher rate of per capital income growth; and second, a country with a faster demographic transition experiences a faster human capital accumulation. And the empirical results are consistent with the predictions of the theory. However, it is unclear whether the results were indeed generated by the mechanisms explained in the theoretical model. It is perhaps a limitation arising from a reduced-form analysis. And providing empirical evidence that is consistent with a theory would be an important contribution in its own right. However, paying more attention to what really produced the results would have greatly raised the quality of the chapter. More importantly, some attempts could have been made to do so using the same data and empirical framework.

Let me take an example. A decline in fertility in the course of demographic transition could affect the growth rate through two different pathways: by encouraging human capital accumulation, and by increasing the share of the working-age population. It looks like the relationship between demographic change and human capital accumulation is a more critical element of economic growth emphasized in the theoretical model, rather than the effect of population composition. In the current regression analyses of GDP growth rate, reported in table 3.4, measures of fertility change (denoted as SFERTIL in the chapter) and schooling are included in the set of independent variables, whereas no variable is included pertaining to the share of working-age population (denoted as SWRATIO in the chapter). Given that the measures of schooling represent the magnitude of human capital accumulation, the estimated regression coefficient of SFERTIL captures the following two effects combined: first, the effect of changing human capital accumulation not explained by rising school enrolment, and second, the effect of change in SWRATIO. It would have been a better test of the theory if SFERTIL and SWRATIO were included simultaneously, and the measures of education were excluded from the regressions. This alternative specification would have helped determine the pure effect of fertility change through human capital accumulation in all forms, including schooling.

The empirical analyses are conducted carefully in general, but there are rooms for further improvements. A cross-country growth regression, as in the case of this study, often confronts a problem of potential endogeneity bias, because economic growth and other social transformations associated with it, such as urbanization and changing social norms, are major causes of fertility decline. This chapter addresses this endogeneity issue by employing GMM estimations. However, it is not fully discussed in the chapter whether the instrumental variables (IVs) used in the estimations, such as working-age population ratio in 1960, life expectancy in 1960, and female labor force participation rate in 1960, are valid IVs. More detailed discussions as to how the IVs were chosen would have made the results more convincing. An alternative approach to this problem would be to allow a time lag between demographic change and economic growth by dividing the period under study into two sub-periods.

I would also like to make several points regarding the analyses of the Korean Household Survey given in the chapter. First, the number of family members other than children should have been included in the regression model. If higher-income families have more dependents to support, the omission of this variable could produce the strange negative relationship between income and per-child educational expenditure, admitted as an unexplainable result in the paper. Second, employment status of the mother should have been taken into account. If working women tend to have fewer children, the number of children may capture the effect of mothers' labor market status. In this case, the negative effect of the number of children on educational expenditure could be explained differently. Given that mothers' time and money are substitutes in children's human capital accumulation, a working mother may replace her time by spending more money. Finally, the negative relationship between the number of children and per-child spending on education could be explained to some extent by economies of scale in educational expenditure.

Overall, this chapter is a good study tackling big questions regarding economic growth. I hope that this work will be developed into a larger research project that provides more detailed discussions of the mechanisms that produced the observed interrelationship among demographic changes, human capital accumulation, and economic growth. Looking into the cases of particular countries would also be a promising direction of extension.

II

Japan

4

Japan's Unprecedented Aging and Changing Intergenerational Transfers

Naohiro Ogawa, Andrew Mason, Amonthep Chawla, and Rikiya Matsukura

4.1 Introduction

In 2005 the total world population exceeded 6.5 billion people, which is almost double the size observed in 1965 (United Nations 2007). The annual growth rate of the world population, however, has been declining continuously during the past four decades; as opposed to its peak value of 2.02 percent during 1965 to 1970, the current annual growth rate is estimated at 1.17 percent. With the emergence of slower population growth in the latter half of the twentieth century, the world demographic outlook of today is substantially different from the one of only a few decades ago.

Slowing global population growth has been induced primarily by a significant decline in fertility over the past few decades. From 1965 to 1970, there were only eight countries with below-replacement fertility (a total fertility rate [TFR] of less than 2.1 children per woman), a number that increased to sixty-eight by the period of 2000 to 2005. Moreover, in terms of the population share, as shown in figure 4.1, only 8.4 percent of the world's population

Naohiro Ogawa is a professor of economics at the Nihon University and its Population Research Institute. Andrew Mason is a professor of economics at the University of Hawaii at Manoa, and senior fellow of the East-West Center. Amonthep Chawla is a research specialist at the Thailand Development Research Institute (TDRI). Rikiya Matsukura is a researcher at the Nihon University Population Research Institute.

Research for this chapter was funded by two grants from the National Institute of Health, NIA R01-AG025488 and AG025247. This work was also supported by a grant obtained by the Nihon University Population Research Institute from the Academic Frontier Project for Private Universities, a matching fund subsidy from the Ministry of Education, Culture, Sports, Science and Technology (MEXT), 2006–2010. Furthermore, the authors are grateful to the UNFPA (RAS5P203) and the Japan Medical Association for their financial assistance. An earlier version of this chapter was presented at the NBER-TCER-KDI Conference on the Demographic Transition in the Pacific Rim, held during June 19–21, 2008, in Seoul, Republic of Korea.

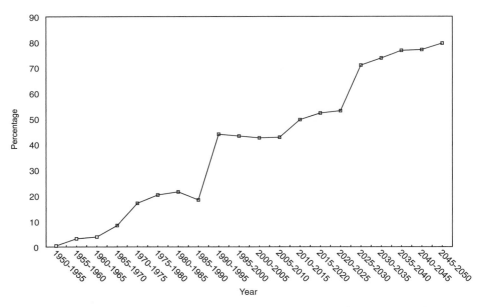

Fig. 4.1   Proportion of population with below-replacement fertility in the world population: 1950–2050

Source: United Nations (2007).

lived in countries with below-replacement fertility between 1965 and 1970, as compared to 42.7 percent from 2005 to 2010. It is projected that more than half of the world population will live in countries with a fertility rate below the replacement level in the second half of the 2010s (United Nations 2007).

At present, the majority of these low-fertility countries are in the developed regions. It should be emphasized, however, that the number of countries in developing regions with below-replacement fertility has also been increasing at a phenomenal rate in recent years. It grew from nil to twenty-four developing countries/areas over the past four decades under consideration. Fourteen of these twenty-four countries/areas belong to Asia. Three Asian countries/areas with below-replacement fertility (Hong Kong, Macao, and the Republic of Korea) are currently classified in the category of lowest-low fertility (i.e., those with a TFR below 1.3). In fact, East Asia's fertility is now the lowest in the entire world (McDonald 2009).

Parallel to the worldwide decline in fertility, marked mortality improvements have been achieved in most of the world. Approximately half of the world's population succeeded in meeting the International Conference on Population and Development (ICPD) Program of Action goal of reaching a higher-than-seventy-years life expectancy at birth for both sexes from 2000 to 2005. In many industrialized nations, life expectancy at birth is rapidly approaching eighty years. East Asia, Hong Kong, Macao, and Japan have already surpassed the eighty-year level.

As a result of these rapid fertility and mortality transformations, population age distributions are being transformed, with a relative increase in the numbers of elderly and a relative decrease in the numbers of young. Thus, the twenty-first century is likely to become the century of population aging (Lutz, Sanderson, and Scherbov 2004).

In many countries, both developed and developing, the age structure shifts are generating a wide range of disruptions at both societal and familial levels. At the societal level, many governments, mainly in developed regions, are concerned about adverse effects of population aging on various socioeconomic dimensions, ranging from their national productivity, labor supply and its quality, savings and capital formation, to the financial sustainability of their pension schemes and health care programs. At the familial level, couples are having fewer children later in their lives. Marriage is delayed, more may never marry, and divorce is on the rise. More people are living alone, and more elderly couples are living independently from their children. These family-level demographic developments are affecting the ways in which family members interact with each other, especially in providing support to their elderly parents and children (Ermisch 2003).

By and large, these general observations apply to contemporary Japan. Its postwar fertility decline was the earliest to occur in the nonWestern world, and was also the most rapid among all industrialized nations. Japan's longevity is currently at the highest level in the contemporary world. As a consequence, Japan's population has been aging extremely fast over the past several decades, and its proportion aged sixty-five and over is currently the highest in the world. Japan's social structure and family organization differ substantially from those in developed nations in the West (Hodge and Ogawa 1991; Ogawa and Retherford 1993, 1997; MacKellar 2003; Ogawa, Retherford, and Matsukura 2009). For these reasons, Japan has already faced, and most likely will continue to encounter a variety of problems, both serious and unique, as it adjusts to population aging and adjusts resources allocated to a rapidly growing elderly population.

After reviewing some key features of Japan's demographic dynamics during the postwar period, we discuss the impact of population aging on both public and familial intergenerational transfers in Japan during the last few decades. We then describe some vital features of Japan's socioeconomic system that have been affected by rapid population aging with important implications for the welfare of the elderly over the foreseeable future. Japan's ability to cope with population aging will be governed by public and familial systems of intergenerational transfers. We will rely on new estimates for Japan from 1984 to 2004, generated as part of an international project called National Transfer Accounts (NTA). In the final section, we consider some policy options available to twenty-first-century Japan for coping with its unprecedented population aging.

We confine the scope of this chapter specifically to the Japanese context. However, Japan's experiences in population aging and its policy development may provide a useful base for analyzing important policy issues related to population aging in a number of developing countries, particularly those in Asia, which are currently undergoing rapid age structural transformations. Moreover, in the face of its fast postwar economic development, Japan still retains some of its traditional cultural values, which is why the Japanese model may be of relevance to policy makers in the developing regions who are interested in establishing a comprehensive approach by combining the best of traditional and modern values in providing care and support to the elderly.

4.2   Rapid Demographic Transition in Postwar Japan

4.2.1   Falling Fertility and Mortality

Japan's fertility transition began in the early part of the twentieth century with gradual fertility reduction (Hodge and Ogawa 1991). After World War II, however, the tempo of the reduction became extremely rapid. Following a short baby boom period (1947 to 1949), Japan's TFR declined by more than 50 percent from 4.54 to 2.04 children per woman between 1947 and 1957. This 50 percent reduction of fertility over the ten-year period is the first such experience in documented history.

Thereafter, there were only minor fluctuations around the replacement level until the first oil crisis occurred in 1973, triggering a series of restructuring in the Japanese economy, which, in turn, slowed down the pace of Japan's economic growth. Parallel to this, Japan's fertility level started to fall again, as presented in figure 4.2. By the mid-1990s, Japan's TFR declined below 1.5 children per woman. In 2005 it further plummeted to 1.26, lowest in postwar time, before a rebound to 1.32 in 2006, and 1.34 in 2007. This post-1973 decline is referred to by some demographers as "Japan's second demographic transition" (Ogawa and Retherford 1993; Retherford and Ogawa 2006; Ogawa, Retherford, and Matsukura 2009).

In line with these changes in TFR, the birth cohort size varied considerably over time, as depicted in figure 4.2. During the baby boom period, there were, on average, approximately 2.7 million births per year, but by 1957, the number of births decreased to 1.6 million. In the early 1970s, however, despite the low fertility rate, the number of births increased to more than 2 million, as an "echo" effect of the baby boom, or the often called "second-generation baby boomers." Since then, births have again trended downward, reaching slightly less than 1.1 million in 2007. This represents a 60 percent decline in the annual number of births from record levels reached in the late 1940s.

Japan's fertility has attracted a great deal of attention both at home and abroad. In contrast, relatively limited attention has been paid to the speed of Japan's postwar mortality transition. From 1950 to 1952, life expectancy at birth was 59.6 years for men and 63.0 years for women. In 2007, male

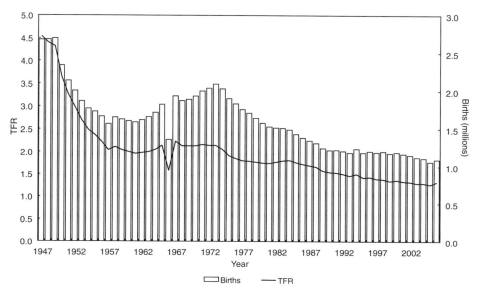

Fig. 4.2   Trends in number of births and TFR: Japan, 1947–2006
Source: Ministry of Health, Labour, and Welfare, *Vital Statistics,* various years.

life expectancy at birth reached 79.2 years to become the third highest in the world, following Iceland (79.4 years) and Hong Kong (79.3 years), and female life expectancy rose to 86.0 years, the highest in the world, followed by Hong Kong (85.4 years) and France (84.1 years). Moreover, between 1950 and 2007, life expectancy at age sixty-five grew to a substantial extent, from 11.4 to 18.6 years for men, and from 13.4 to 23.6 years for women, which implies a marked increase in the retirement period and in the joint survival to older ages for both husbands and wives.

The remarkable increase in longevity has influenced many aspects of Japan's economy. In 2007, insurance companies reduced premiums substantially for the first time in eleven years (The Asahi Shimbun 2007). The composition of sales by Japanese life insurance companies have shifted in response to longer life expectancy, lower childbearing, and rising divorce. In 2008, for the first time ever, outstanding annuity and medical insurance policies, rather than life insurance contracts, constituted more than half of the products sold by Japanese life insurance companies (The Nikkei 2008a).

A remarkable feature of aging is rapid growth in the number of centenarians. The average annual growth rate, 13 percent over the period from 1963 to 2007, exceeds that of any other age group in Japan.

In figure 4.3, the data on the average age of the thirty oldest deaths in each year over the period from 1950 to 2006 are plotted separately for men and women. The average age of the thirty oldest deaths increased substantially

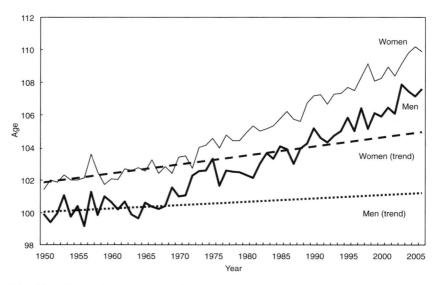

Fig. 4.3   Change in average age of death among thirty oldest persons by sex: Japan, 1950–2006

Source: Ministry of Health, Labour, and Welfare, *Vital Statistics,* various years.

Note: The trend lines for men and women have been estimated on the data from 1950 to 1968.

over the second half of the twentieth century for both sexes; in 2006 the average age of the thirty oldest deaths was 107.6 years for men and 109.9 years for women. More importantly, the plotted trends of the thirty oldest deaths indicate that the tempo of life prolongation accelerated for both sexes since the mid-1960s, a few years after the implementation of universal health coverage.

4.2.2   Population Decline and Aging

Although the number of elderly in Japan has been increasing rapidly, the number of children, those under age fifteen, has been declining for twenty-seven consecutive years; Japan now has fewer children than at any time since 1908 (*Washington Post* 2008). The overall size of Japan's population began declining from the end of 2005. According to a population projection based on the most recent version of the population-economic-social security model constructed by the Nihon University Population Research Institute (Ogawa et al. 2003), the total population is expected to decrease to 121.1 million persons in 2025, a 5.2 percent reduction from 2005.

Changes in age structure and other important demographic data are reported in table 4.1. The proportion of the population aged sixty-five and older increased from 4.9 percent in 1950 to 20.2 percent in 2005, and is projected to increase to 31.0 percent in 2025. Japan's population will likely con-

Table 4.1   **Population change in Japan: 1950–2025**

Year	Total population (1,000 persons)	0–14 (%)	65+ (%)	Total fertility rate	Total dependency ratio	75+/65+ (%)	Women 40–59/65–84
1950	83,200	35.4	4.9	3.65	67.5	25.7	1.82
1955	89,276	33.4	5.3	2.37	63.1	29.2	1.81
1960	93,419	33.0	5.7	2.00	60.4	30.4	1.80
1965	98,275	25.6	6.3	2.14	46.8	30.3	1.77
1970	103,720	23.9	7.1	2.13	44.9	30.2	1.69
1975	111,940	24.3	7.9	1.91	47.6	32.0	1.60
1980	117,060	23.5	9.1	1.75	48.4	34.4	1.48
1985	121,049	21.5	10.3	1.76	46.7	37.8	1.40
1990	123,611	18.2	12.1	1.54	43.5	40.1	1.30
1995	125,570	16.0	14.6	1.42	50.4	39.3	1.10
2000	126,926	14.6	17.4	1.36	46.9	40.9	0.91
2005	127,449	13.8	20.2	1.25	50.6	45.1	0.77
2010	127,013	13.0	23.0	1.24	55.6	48.0	0.65
2015	125,603	12.1	26.9	1.24	63.2	48.4	0.59
2020	123,235	11.0	29.5	1.24	67.6	52.1	0.57
2025	120,094	10.2	31.0	1.28	70.0	60.0	0.56

Sources: Statistics Bureau, *Population Census,* various years. Nihon University Population Research Institute, *Population Projection,* 2003.

tinue to be the world's oldest national population for the next twenty years. More importantly, the Japanese population will reach the world's highest level of aging at an unprecedented rate, as discussed elsewhere (Ogawa and Retherford 1997; Ogawa et al. 2003). Compared with such European countries as Sweden and Norway, the tempo of aging in Japan is approximately three times as fast. Furthermore, the percentage of the population aged seventy-five and older among those aged sixty-five and older is projected to increase from 45.1 percent in 2005 to 60.0 percent in 2025. Comparing NUPRI projections and recent United Nations (2007) projections reveals that Japan's concentration in the seventy-five and older age group is likely to be by far the highest in the world in 2025, followed by Sweden (52.1 percent) and Italy (51.8 percent).

4.3   Changing Economic Growth Performance and Public Transfer Programs

4.3.1   Macroeconomic Growth

During World War II, Japan's productive capacity was utterly shattered. In 1959, Japan's per capita gross national product (GNP) was only U.S. $153, lower than that of Mexico (U.S. $181) or the Philippines (U.S. $172). By the end of the 1950s, however, Japan's real per capita income had recovered to prewar levels. During the 1960s, Japan's real GDP grew at a phenomenal rate of about 11 percent per annum. After the oil crisis of 1973, as mentioned earlier, Japan's economic growth performance became significantly less impressive. In the mid-1980s, the Japanese economy entered the bubble economy phase. Its investment boom ended abruptly in the second half of 1990 and a number of leading banks and other financial institutions became insolvent. Government debt has been accumulating at an alarming rate, reaching U.S. $8.49 trillion in 2008. Debt has more than doubled during the last ten years, and its relative size to GDP is by far the worst among industrialized nations. Japan's international competitiveness has deteriorated very quickly. In the early 1990s its economy ranked first in terms of international competitiveness, but it fell to the twenty-second place in 2008 (IMD 2008). In view of these prolonged economic problems, some economists call the 1990s "Japan's lost decade" (Yoshikawa 2001).

Japan has undertaken many important structural reforms of its economy, but its mandatory retirement policy still remains an extreme case as compared with other industrialized nations (Clark et al. 2008). The proportion of firms having mandatory retirement rules has been increasing, not decreasing. The Japanese government is currently attempting to encourage firms to increase the mandatory retirement age to sixty-five. The Law Concerning Stabilization of Employment of Older Persons, passed in 2004, requires firms to increase the age of mandatory retirement to sixty-five. However, no penalties are imposed for noncompliance (Japan Institute of Labour Policy and Training 2004).

Despite these mandatory retirement policies, the elderly have high labor participation rates by international standards (Ogawa, Lee, and Matsukura 2005; Matsukura, Ogawa, and Clark 2007). In 2000, the labor force participation rate for elderly Japanese men aged sixty-five and over was greater than 30 percent. In sharp contrast, the corresponding figure for developed countries in Europe was below 10 percent, and was 18 percent for the United States. Similarly, Japanese women are more likely to continue working than older women in Europe and the United States.

4.3.2   Old-Age Pension and Medical Care Plans

As Japan recovered from the shambles of World War II, it established universal pension and medical care schemes in 1961. Since then, Japan's social security system has grown remarkably. Between 1961 and 2005, the share of social security benefits increased from 4.9 to 23.9 percent of the national income (National Institute of Population and Social Security Research 2007). Moreover, the proportion of the social security expenditure allotted to the pension schemes increased from 22.7 percent in 1964 to 52.7 percent in 2005, while the corresponding value for the medical schemes declined from 54.4 to 32.0 percent. Owing to population aging, as well as the maturity of the old-age pension schemes, the relative share of pension benefits paid out in national income has been on an upward trend in recent years.

Japan undertook major reforms of its public pension schemes in 2004. One of the primary objectives was to fix the level of future contributions for younger workers and thereby increase transparency, without reducing the benefits considerably. The government introduced a mechanism to automatically balance benefit levels according to future changes in the population age structure. The goal was to avoid repeated reforms and to restore the younger generations' trust in government pension schemes. This may be regarded as a paradigm shift in Japan's social security provisions (Sakamoto 2005). As a consequence of the 2004 reform, the replacement rate for the Japanese public pension declined considerably, and is projected to fall to 50.2 percent by 2023, after which, it is assumed, will remain unchanged up to 2050.

Such downward adjustments of benefits have been clearly reflected in the expectations of the Japanese. According to a national survey on the economic life of the elderly undertaken by the Cabinet Office during January to February, 2007 (The Nikkei 2008b), 56.9 percent of respondents aged fifty-five and over (including baby boomers nearing the mandatory retirement age) stated that their pension benefits would fall short of their living expenses from age sixty. In the 2002 round of this survey, the proportion of those who held this pessimistic view was 46.6 percent.

The second major component of social security benefits is medical. Subject to Japan's economic growth performance, the coverage in medical insurance plans has been revised on a periodic basis. Despite the changes that have taken place in the past few decades, the absolute amount of financial resources allotted to medical care services has been rising. One of the problems that have set Japan apart from other industrialized nations is an extremely long period of hospitalization (Ogawa et al. 2007). In 2005 it was 35.7 days, which is the longest among the nineteen Organization for Economic Cooperation and Development (OECD) countries, followed by 13.4 days in France (OECD 2007).

In response to the upward spiral in medical care costs, the government of Japan implemented the Long-Term Care Insurance (LTCI) scheme in 2000 with a view to reducing the average duration of hospitalization for inpatient care by facilitating in-home care. The LTCI scheme was expected to alleviate the care-giving burden to be placed upon family members, many of whom are middle-aged women (Ogawa and Retherford 1997). Because the expenditure for the LTCI scheme had grown at an alarming rate since its inception, the scope of its services was critically reviewed and downgraded in 2006 with a view to curbing future costs.

In April 2008, the government implemented a new medical insurance scheme specifically for senior citizens aged seventy-five and older as another step toward curbing the nation's mushrooming medical costs. Under this new medical scheme, premiums are automatically deducted from pension payouts. However, because premiums have actually become higher under the new scheme for a certain segment of the targeted elderly age group, a possible revision of the new scheme has already become an urgent political issue.

4.4   Weakening Familial Support and Abrupt Normative Shifts

As distinct from developed countries in the West, multigenerational living arrangements are still fairly common in Japan (Ogawa and Ermisch 1996; Ogawa, Retherford, and Matsukura 2009). Although three-generational households persist in Japan, the proportion of elderly living with adult children is declining and with it the potential for family support for the elderly. As shown in figure 4.4, the proportion of those aged sixty-five and over coresiding with their adult children declined from 70 percent in 1980 to 43 percent in 2005. In addition, the index called the familial support ratio (expressed as the ratio of women aged forty to fifty-nine to elderly persons aged sixty-five to seventy-nine) is expected to decline substantially over the next twenty years. The value of this index was 1.30 in 1990, and is projected to be 0.65 in 2010, a 50 percent decline. The present value of this index is the lowest in the entire world and is expected to continue to be so for another twenty years.

Apart from these demographic transformations, value shifts among Japanese people have been dramatic. These value changes are well captured in the data gathered in the *National Survey on Family Planning* series, conducted

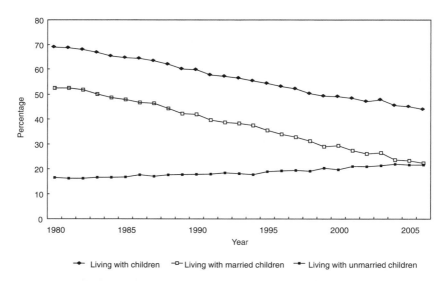

◆ Living with children   ▫ Living with married children   ■ Living with unmarried children

Fig. 4.4   Change in proportion of those aged sixty-five and over coresiding with their adult children: Japan, 1980–2006

Source: Ministry of Health, Labour, and Welfare, *Comprehensive Survey of Living Conditions of the People: Health and Welfare,* various years.

every other year from 1950 to 2004 by the Mainichi Newspapers (Population Problems Research Council 2004). Since the first round of the survey, except for a few rounds, a question regarding dependence on children for old-age security had been directed to currently married women of reproductive age who have at least one child. In addition to these time-series data obtained by the Mainichi Newspapers, we have extended the time span, as depicted in figure 4.5, by utilizing data collected in the *National Survey on Work and Family,* undertaken by the Nihon University Population Research Institute in 2007.

The precoded responses were as follows: (a) "expect to depend on children," (b) "do not expect to depend on children," and (c) "never thought about it." The proportion of respondents who expect to depend on their children declined almost continuously over the period from 1950 to 2004. Almost two-thirds of Japanese married women in 1950 expected to depend on their children for old-age security, but only 9 percent in 2007 expected to do so. These long-term downward trends in parents' expectations for familial support closely parallel the expansion of old-age public pensions since the early 1960s.

In the *National Survey* conducted by the Mainichi Newspapers since 1963, the question on the attitude of married women towards taking care of their aged parents was asked in successive rounds. The precoded response cat-

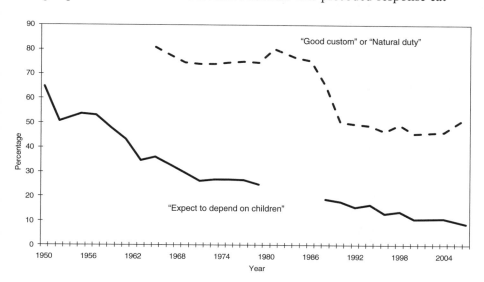

Fig. 4.5   Trends in values and expectations about care for the elderly: Japan, 1950–2007

Sources: Mainichi Newspapers of Japan, *Summary of Twenty-fifth National Survey on Family Planning,* 2005. Mainichi Newspapers of Japan, *Summary of the 2004 round of the National Survey on Population, Families and Generations,* 2004. Nihon University Population Research Institute, *National Survey on Work and Family,* 2007.

egories are as follows: (a) "good custom," (b) "natural duty as children," (c) "unavoidable due to inadequacy of public support resources," and (d) "not a good custom." We have also supplemented these time-series data compiled by the Mainichi Newspapers with the data gathered by Nihon University. As indicated in figure 4.5, the proportion of those who chose one of the first two response categories ("good custom" and "natural duty as children") was stable from 1963 to 1986. From 1986 to 1988, however, a sudden decline occurred. In the years leading up to 2007, the proportion of married women of reproductive age who chose one of these two response categories was, by and large, declining.

Obviously, these demographic and socioeconomic transformations in postwar Japan have been affecting the pattern and mode of intergenerational transfers over time. To analyze these changes in intergenerational transfers, we will draw heavily upon some of the principal findings recently generated from the National Transfer Account (NTA) project for Japan. A detailed explanation of NTA's basic concept, the crucial computational assumptions used, and the definitions of key variables are available on the NTA home page (http://www.ntaccounts.org).

4.5   Population Aging, Intergenerational Transfers, and Two Demographic Dividends

The economic life cycle is fundamental to understanding the macroeconomic effects of population aging. As has been recently discussed elsewhere (Bloom and Williamson 1998; Mason 2001, 2007; Mason and Lee 2006, 2007), the divergence between production and consumption interacts with changing population age structure to generate a demographic dividend, which has been substantial but transitory in Asia. Mason and Lee have shown that a second and sustainable dividend is possible due to increased accumulation of physical or human capital (Lee and Mason 2009; Mason 2007; Mason and Lee 2007). One of the key components of the NTA system is detailed information pertaining to the life cycle of production (labor income) and consumption. This information can be used to calculate the economic support ratio and quantify the extent to which per capita income has been influenced by changes in the working share of the population; that is, the first demographic dividend. The economic life cycle also provides key information for modeling the second demographic dividend, as explained below.

Fertility decline leads to the first demographic dividend because the population in the working ages increases relative to nonworking ages. This is incomplete, however, because gains depend both on what is produced at each age and what is consumed. The first demographic dividend arises because the population is concentrated in ages during which production exceeds consumption. Measuring the dividend in growth terms, the first demographic

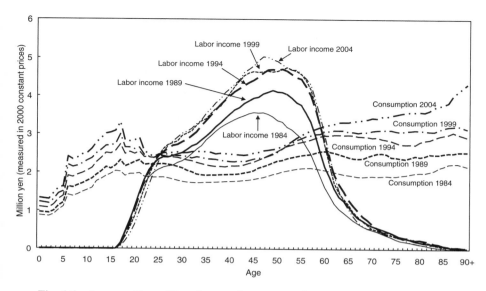

Fig. 4.6   **Age-specific profiles of per capita consumption and production: Japan, 1984–2004**

dividend is positive when the growth rate of the number of effective producers exceeds that of the number of effective consumers (Mason 2007).

Figure 4.6 shows estimates of age profiles of per capita consumption, both private and public sectors combined, and per capita production (labor income) in five selected years: 1984, 1989, 1994, 1999, and 2004. These profiles have been estimated by drawing upon private-sector data from five rounds of the *National Survey of Family Income and Expenditure* (NSFIE) from 1984 to 2004, carried out by the Statistics Bureau of Japan, and public-sector data for the corresponding five years, gleaned from various government publications. The estimates are expressed in terms of 2000 prices using the GDP deflator.

A few points of interest emerge from this graphical exposition. First, as expected, throughout the time periods under review, there are sizeable income-consumption deficits at both young and older life-cycle stages. These life-cycle deficits must be funded with reallocations coming largely from the surplus of income generated at the life cycle surplus stage.

Second, the age at which an average individual shifts from a net consumer to a net producer gradually increased from twenty-four in 1984 and 1989 to twenty-five in 1994, and to twenty-six in 1999 and 2004. A number of factors contributed to the upward trend in the crossing age: (a) earnings profiles, (b) hours worked, (c) women's labor force participation and the availability of child-care and old-age leave schemes, (d) sectoral shifts in the labor force, (e) higher enrolment rates in tertiary education, and (f) a marked increase in *freeters* (those aged fifteen to thirty-four who lack full-time employment or are unemployed) and NEETs (those not currently engaged in employment, education or training).

At the other end of the life cycle, the age transition from a net producer to a net consumer rose marginally from fifty-eight in 1984 and 1989 to fifty-nine in 1994, 1999, and 2004. The persistency of the crossing age at the later stage of the life cycle can be traced to Japan's mandatory retirement age of sixty. The length of time in the cross-section when individuals are producing more through their labor than they are consuming ranged from thirty-three to thirty-four years, only two-fifths of the average length of life in present day Japan.

Third, labor income increased substantially between 1984 and 1994 reflecting the substantial economic growth during the "bubble economy" phase. The age profiles of per capita production changed little between 1994 and 2004 reflecting the influence of Japan's "lost decade." The growth in labor income that occurred during the entire twenty-year period is concentrated in the prime working ages. Labor income below age twenty-five or above age sixty-five was essentially constant or declined.

Fourth and more importantly, the age profiles of per capita consumption rose almost continuously, particularly at the younger and older ages. Of particular note is the emergence of an upward sloping consumption curve among those aged sixty-five and over in 2004. This is accounted for by the implementation of the LTCI scheme starting from the year 2000. In-home care for the frail elderly, which had until then been informally provided by their family members, became formalized as a part of the market economy. As a result, Japan's per capita consumption profiles have been increasingly similar to those in Finland, the United States, Sweden, and Costa Rica among the NTA member countries.

How and why the economic life cycle is changing in Japan is an important issue, but the concern here is the effects of age structure given the age patterns of consumption and labor income observed in Japan. This analysis is based on an average of the five sets of profiles shown in figure 4.6. The age-specific values, shown in figure 4.7, are used as weights to calculate the effective number of producers and the effective number of consumers over the period from 1925 to 2025. The ratio of producers to consumers is the economic support ratio. The first demographic dividend is defined as the annual growth rate of the economic support ratio, which measures the change in output per effective consumer due solely to changes in age structure (figure 4.8). For thirty-four consecutive years from 1945 to 1979, the effective number of producers grew more rapidly than the effective number of consumers in Japan. The magnitude of the positive first demographic dividend was large, adding just over 1 percent per year to economic growth during the rapid economic growth of the 1960s and the early 1970s.

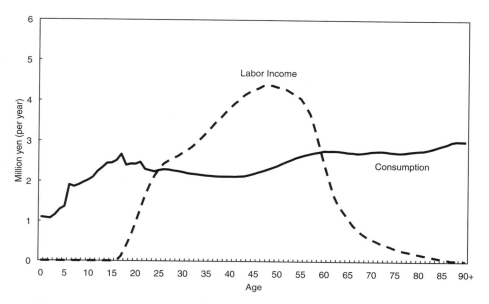

Fig. 4.7   Average age-specific profiles of annual per capita consumption and production: Japan, 1984–2004

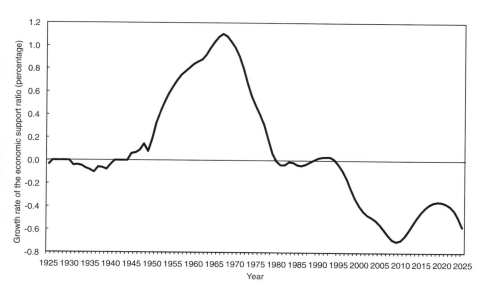

Fig. 4.8   Trend in first demographic dividend: Japan, 1925–2025

As has been the case with other developed countries, Japan's first demographic dividend lasted for a few decades, but proved inherently transitory in nature. Since the mid-1990s the effective number of producers has been growing more slowly than the effective number of consumers, the economic support ratio has been declining, and the first dividend has turned decidedly negative. This change is a direct consequence of population aging.

The same demographic forces that produce an end to the first dividend may lead to a second demographic dividend. Implicit in the large gap between consumption and production at old ages is the life cycle demand for wealth. To support consumption which in old-age greatly exceeds production, life cycle pension wealth must be accumulated in one of the two following forms. One form is transfer wealth or the net present value of public and private transfers. The second form is assets, which consists of capital, land, foreign assets, and the like. As a population ages, the demand for life-cycle pension wealth increases substantially. In part, this occurs because the duration of retirement is longer due to increased life expectancy and, in part, because of changes in the age composition of the population. If the demand for wealth is met by expanding transfer wealth, then population aging leads to large implicit debts imposed on future generations. If countries rely on capital accumulation to meet the retirement needs of the elderly, population aging provides a powerful incentive to accumulate capital and other assets. A key point is that in countries that rely on transfers, both public and familial, in meeting the retirement needs of the elderly, the second demographic dividend will not emerge. While the first dividend is purely accounting-oriented, the second dividend consists of both compositional and behavioral effects (Mason 2007; Ogawa and Matsukura 2007; Mason and Lee 2007). The second dividend is affected not only by the numbers of the elderly persons relative to younger persons, but also by the extent to which consumers and policy makers are forward-looking and respond effectively to the demographic changes that are anticipated in the years ahead. When life expectancy is increasing, for example, the impetus for accumulating wealth is stimulated, which, in turn, leads to a permanent increase in income. To summarize, if capital accumulation rather than familial or public transfer programs dominate the age reallocation systems for supporting the elderly, population aging may yield a second demographic dividend due to higher rates of saving and capital intensification of the economy.

Compared with the first dividend, measuring the second dividend is difficult, in part because the accumulation of wealth is intrinsically forward-looking. The demand for wealth depends on expectations about the future that can not be directly measured. In the present study, we have followed a relatively simple partial equilibrium method. As fully discussed elsewhere (Mason 2007), the second dividend is defined as the growth rate of productivity or output per labor income that arises because of an increase in the demand for assets as a consequence of population aging.

The estimates of the second demographic dividend over the period from 1960 to 2035 are shown in figure 4.9. Japan's second demographic dividend is very high in the 1980s, generating almost 1.5 percentage points of additional economic growth. Beginning from the 1990s, the second demographic dividend fluctuates to a considerable extent, with a trough in the 2010s, followed by a small upsurge in the 2020s. These oscillations occur primarily because the second generation of baby boomers enters the age group of fifty years old and over, in which they are expected to save at a high rate.

Undoubtedly, depending on how the Japanese elderly utilize or allocate their current and future accumulated wealth, the Japanese economy's future scenarios will be substantially different. Numerous banks and life insurance companies are aware of this phenomenon and have recently been paying great attention to the baby boomers born between 1947 and 1949, who are now approaching their mandatory age of retirement. They have already contributed greatly to creating both first and second demographic dividends over the course of Japan's demographic transition after World War II, and they are expected to enjoy the fruits of the second demographic dividend during their retirement life, as hinted in figure 4.9.

Figure 4.10 plots the age profile of asset holding in Japan in 1999 among those aged sixty and over. Using the 1999 round of NSFIE, we have estimated their age-specific stock of real and financial assets. In addition, we have computed the present value of the expected future stream of public pension benefits. The detailed computational procedure and assumptions employed are available elsewhere (Ogawa and Matsukura 2007). A quick glance at this graph reveals that the Japanese elderly are wealthy. At age

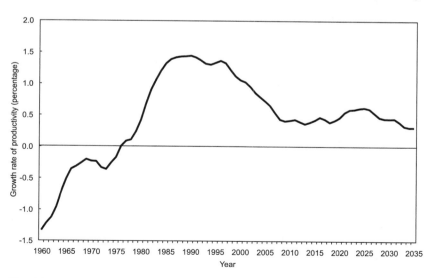

Fig. 4.9   Trend in second demographic dividend: Japan, 1960–2035

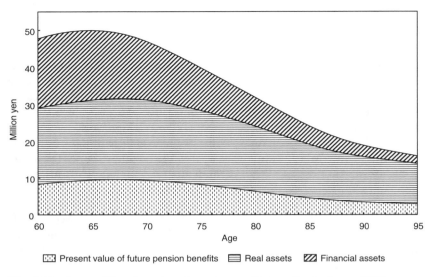

Fig. 4.10   Age profiles of assets and pension wealth transfers in Japan, 1999

sixty, the total amount of assets an average person owns is more than 50 million yen, or U.S. $0.5 million. In fact, they are wealthier than what this graph shows, because private pensions are not included in the computation. Also, familial transfers are not included in figure 4.10, but they are discussed below.

A striking feature of the graph is that the present value of public pension benefits to be paid to the elderly is greater than that of real assets at a relatively early stage of retirement life, but the latter exceeds the former by a great margin at a later stage of retirement life. A possible explanation is that the liquidation of real assets such as land and housing is crucial for very old persons, particularly those who are living alone. There seems to be a substantial potential for developing various financial schemes such as the reverse mortgage plan. These are cross-section estimates, however, so that other explanations may be important.

An additional feature of the demand for wealth in Japan is that the preference for land has declined considerably over the last fifteen years or so, during Japan's lost decade. According to various rounds of the *National Opinion Survey on Land Issues* conducted by the Ministry of the National Land, Infrastructure, Transport and Tourism, the proportion of those aged sixty and over who thought that land was a better asset than financial assets such as savings and securities declined from 63 percent in 1994 to 37 percent in 2007 (figure 4.11). This suggests that an increasing proportion of the Japanese elderly need more information regarding investment opportunities. Caution should be exercised, however, with regard to the lack of

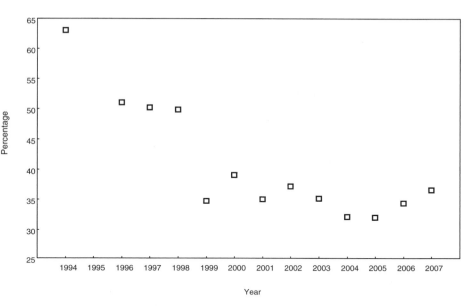

Fig. 4.11   Changing preference for land as an asset among the elderly aged sixty and over: Japan, 1994–2007

Source: Ministry of Land, Infrastructure, Transport, and Tourism, *National Opinion Survey on Land Issues,* 2007.

appropriate knowledge pertaining to various financial markets. According to a recent report released by the Organization for Economic Cooperation and Development (OECD [2005]), 71 percent of the population aged twenty and over have no knowledge about investment in equities and bonds, 57 percent have no knowledge of financial products in general, and 29 percent have no knowledge about insurance, pensions, and tax. The ongoing global financial crisis will surely influence preferences and knowledge over the coming years.

To cope with these problems, the Financial Services Agency of the Japanese Government implemented the Financial Instruments and Exchange Law, effective from September 30, 2007. This financial business law aims at enhancing investor protection by tightening the rules for financial institutions' sales of stocks, investment trusts, and other products that could cause holders to suffer a loss of principal. As a result, in order to avoid possible regulatory trouble, one of the major banks decided not to sell risk instruments to customers aged eighty and over unless they can demonstrate sufficient knowledge of investing or are accompanied by other family members at the time of purchase (The Nikkei 2007). The large bank requires that customers aged seventy and over receive explanation concerning the risks involved at least twice before they purchase an investment trust or variable annuities.

Another leading bank has recently begun the practice of visiting customers aged ninety and over once every three months, even if their products do not suffer any losses.

4.6   Changing Pattern of Life Cycle Deficits and Age Reallocations

The effect of population aging on the accumulation of assets will depend on the system for reallocating resources across age. The NTA system provides a comprehensive framework for estimating consumption, production, and resource reallocations by age. The NTA measures intergenerational flows for a certain period of time (usually a calendar or fiscal year), and its flow account is governed by the following expression:

$$\underbrace{Y^l(x) + Y^A(x) + \tau^+(x)}_{Inflows} = \underbrace{C(x) + S(x) + \tau^-(x)}_{Outflows},$$

where Y^l = labor income, Y^A = asset income, τ^+ = transfers received, C = consumption, S = saving, and τ^- = transfers given. It should be noted that this flow identity holds for each age x as well as the whole economy.

Rearranging the terms, the life cycle deficit, namely, the difference between consumption and labor income, $C(x) - Y^l(x)$, must be equal to the inter-age flows or reallocations that come in the following two forms: net transfers, $\tau(x) = \tau^+(x) - \tau^-(x)$, and asset-based reallocations, $Y^A(x) - S(x)$; thereby giving us the following equation:

$$\underbrace{C(x) - Y^l(x)}_{Life\ cycle\ deficit} = \underbrace{\underbrace{\tau^+(x) - \tau^-(x)}_{Net\ transfers} + \underbrace{Y^A(x) - S(x)}_{Asset\text{-}based\ reallocations}}_{Age\ reallocations}.$$

The age reallocations can be further disaggregated into public-sector and private-sector age reallocations. That is,

$$C(x) - Y^l(x) = \lfloor \tau_g^+(x) - \tau_g^-(x) \rfloor + \lfloor \tau_f^+(x) - \tau_f^-(x) \rfloor$$
$$+ \lfloor Y^{Ag}(x) - S_g(x) \rfloor + \lfloor Y^{Af}(x) - S_f(x) \rfloor,$$

where subscripts, g and f, refer to public and private age reallocations, respectively.

Before we proceed to the discussion of computational results, we would like to caution the reader about the following two points. First, both "familial transfers" and "private transfers" are used interchangeably in this chapter; both of the terms refer to transfers coming from other family members of the same or different households. Second, the private transfers presented here are limited to current transfers. Capital transfers, for example, bequests and inter vivos capital transfers, are not included.

It is also important to note that the estimated values for the totals are adjusted to match aggregates from National Income and Product Accounts

(NIPA), thus insuring consistency with NIPA. Labor income, however, does not exactly correspond to the NIPA counterpart, because the income of those self-employed (mixed income) includes returns to labor and capital. Based upon the result derived from one of the recent studies (Gollin 2002), we have opted to allocate two-thirds of this income to labor and one-third to capital.

Figure 4.12 presents the changing pattern of three components of the age reallocations for 1984 to 2004. The three components consist of reallocations through assets, net public transfers, and net private transfers. All values are measured in terms of 2000 constant prices and on an annual basis. Panel A presents age reallocations for 1984, panel B for 1994, and panel C for 2004.

There are many important changes in age reallocations over this twenty-year period. First, the impact of the rapid growth of the elderly population upon transfers is very clear. Net total transfers to those aged sixty-five and older increased by three times from 1984 to 2004. The increase is entirely a consequence of net public transfers to the elderly that grew 4.4 times in real terms. In contrast, the amount of net familial transfers to the elderly declines by 75 percent during the same period. Assets have become extremely important for the elderly population—asset-based reallocations increased by ten times in real terms from 1984 to 2004. Despite such phenomenal growth of asset-based reallocations, net public transfers dominated asset-based reallocations for the elderly population in 2004.

Second, despite a large decline in the young population, net transfers to those aged zero to nineteen grew by 9 percent during the two decades. The composition of the net transfers changed appreciably over time. Net public transfers to this age group rose by 35 percent in real terms, while net familial transfers declined by 7 percent.

Third, though relevant tables are omitted, on a per capita basis, net public transfers to both elderly and young persons doubled over the period in question. More importantly, while the amount of net familial transfers to the young population during the two decades rose by 34 percent, there was a 70 percent decline for the elderly population.

Fourth, net public transfers are negative for the productive age groups twenty to fifty-nine with the peak shifting rightward (to higher ages) over time, reflecting the influence of population aging (figure 4.12). In 2004, the peak occurred approximately at age fifty-seven, while in the earlier years the peak occurred between ages forty to fifty. On a per capita basis, however, the peak of the tax burden remained relatively stable in the vicinity of age fifty-five during the period under consideration.

Fifth, the role of asset-based reallocations became increasingly important over time particularly for the elderly, as can be clearly seen from the three panels of figure 4.12. Although asset-based reallocations occur in both private and public sectors, the amount of asset-based reallocations

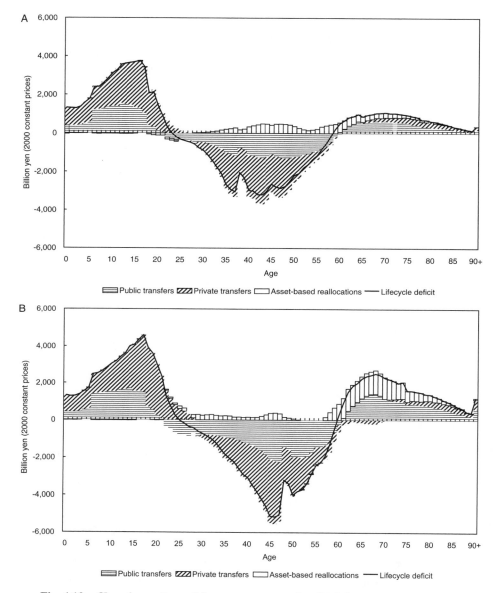

Fig. 4.12   Changing pattern of three components of reallocations: Japan, 1984–2004: *A*, 1984; *B*, 1994; *C*, 2004.

in the private sector has consistently dominated those in the public sector. Furthermore, a positive asset-based reallocation implies that people receive asset income in excess of their saving. In 2004, for instance, positive asset-based reallocations reach their peak when people are in their sixties, and are comprised largely of the return to private assets (e.g., property income). In

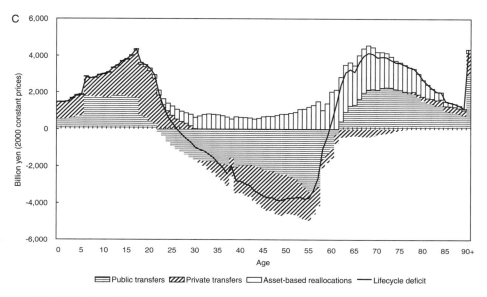

Fig. 4.12   (cont.)

contrast, the small negative asset-based reallocation at young ages in 1984 occurred mainly owing to public saving exceeding public asset income.

Sixth, a careful examination of the three panels reveals that net familial transfers are negative among relatively young elderly persons. This phenomenon is particularly pronounced in 2004 among the elderly in their sixties and seventies (panel C of figure 4.12). The financial assistance relatively young elderly persons provided to their adult children and/or grandchildren exceeded the monetary assistance the young elderly received. The magnitude of negative net familial transfers for relatively young elderly rose during the period of Japan's lost decade in which the unemployment rate remained at a very high level and labor income hardly grew at all in either nominal or real terms. The data displayed in figure 4.13 further substantiates the validity of this interpretation: all age groups received positive net intra-household transfers from the sixty- to seventy-four-year old age group.

Moreover, according to a nationwide survey undertaken by the Nihon University Population Research Institute in April 2007, the proportion of the survey respondents in their forties who had received financial assistance from their parents over the previous twelve months was approximately 50 percent higher than that of those who had provided financial assistance to their parents. These results suggest that despite the fact that multigenerational coresidence has been eroding over the past few decades, the Japanese elderly are still playing a vital role in providing financial support for their offspring when the latter encounter economic difficulties. Although older persons in Japan are often considered a liability for the country, they are

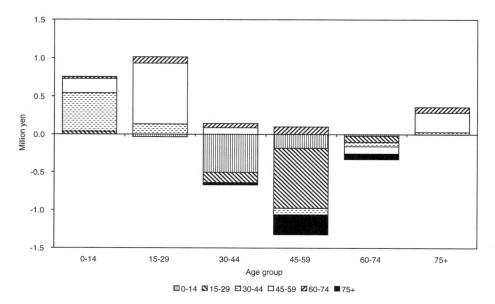

Fig. 4.13   Net per capita annual intra-household transfers between broad age groups: Japan, 2004

actually playing a key role as a safety net. For this reason, they should be considered latent assets in contemporary Japanese society. Ironically, filial norms among the middle-aged have been deteriorating since the late 1980s as displayed in figure 4.5, and this could be interpreted as partial evidence that elderly parents, despite such deterioration, still, to a considerable extent, remain altruistic toward their children and grandchildren.

Further to our discussion with regard to figure 4.13, we have also plotted net familial transfers to the elderly by age and year in figure 4.14. The data show an upward shift of the age at which net familial transfers to the elderly become positive. Over the period of two decades, that age rose from sixty-three years old in 1984 to sixty-four years old in 1989, seventy-one years old in 1994, seventy-four years old in 1999, and seventy-seven years old in 2004. These upward shifts over time seem to be closely related to the improved pension benefits due to the maturity of the pension schemes, but causality is difficult to infer here. It is also interesting to observe in figure 4.14 that for any given cohort, the importance of familial transfers does not increase much as the cohort members age. The ratio of net familial transfers to life cycle deficits for the elderly who turned sixty-five in 1984 remained virtually unchanged, around 0.15, over the subsequent fifteen years, until they reached age eighty in 1999. Similar observations are applicable to those who were seventy and seventy-five in 1984. These plotted results indicate that, from a cohort perspective, there is virtually no age gradient. This seems

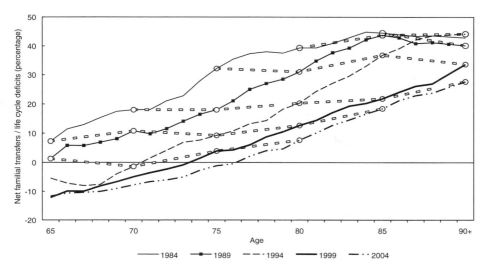

Fig. 4.14   Net familial transfers to the elderly aged sixty-five and older: Japan, 1984–2004

to be accounted for by the intercohort differentials in old-age pension maturity levels, which are heavily affected by the age of each cohort at which the universal coverage of public pension schemes was implemented.

In figure 4.15, we have plotted the change in the pattern of funding consumption among the two elderly groups (sixty-five and older, and eighty-five and older) from 1984 to 2004. Among those aged sixty-five and over, the role of public pensions was becoming increasingly important. In contrast, as has been already mentioned, familial transfers were becoming less important over time. Surprisingly, in 2004, the share of net familial transfers in funding consumption among the elderly aged sixty-five and over virtually disappeared, although a substantial proportion of the elderly in this age group were still coresiding with their adult children. It should be emphasized, however, that the inflow of familial transfers from the younger population is still significant among those aged eighty-five and over. This may be largely due to the fact that the elderly of this old age group receive a relatively limited amount of pension benefits as a result of (a) their shorter contribution period and (b) the dominance of women receiving a survivor's pension in this very old age group.

Moreover, the data plotted in figure 4.15 indicate the share of asset-based reallocations has been growing substantially over time, particularly among the relatively young elderly, which is consistent with our earlier discussion in connection with figure 4.10. In the case of those aged sixty-five and over, the proportion of consumption funded by asset-based reallocations grew from 14 percent in 1984 to 36 percent in 2004.

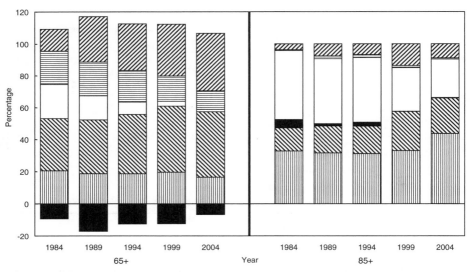

Fig. 4.15   Change in the pattern of financing consumption among the two elderly groups: Japan, 1984–2004

It is also worth remarking that the share of public transfers in the form of medical care services rose to a considerable extent, especially between 1999 and 2004, which is in agreement with our earlier discussion concerning the rise of per capita consumption among the elderly depicted in figure 4.6. It is also interesting to observe in figure 4.15 that, although declining over time, the share of labor income is considerable, which is consistent with the high labor force participation rate among the elderly population in contemporary Japan.

4.7   Concluding Remarks

In this chapter, we have analyzed some of the important impacts of Japan's unprecedented population aging on its postwar economy, by drawing heavily upon estimates from the NTA-Japan project, ranging from the first and second demographic dividends to life cycle reallocations. We have also shed light on the rapidly changing roles of public and familial support systems for the elderly in Japan, that have evolved together with the family organizational transformation and the rapid development of the social security system over the past several decades.

As extensively discussed in the literature, Japan's demographic landscape in the twenty-first century is extremely gloomy. In hope of raising marital fertility to alleviate the burden of rapid population aging on the economy, the Japanese government has formulated and implemented a series of pro-natalist programs and policies since the early 1990s (Ogawa and Retherford 1993; Retherford and Ogawa 2006). And yet, despite such strenuous efforts, the country's fertility remains very low. Judging from the extensive experience of many industrialized countries in the West, there is no apparent panacea for restoring fertility to the replacement level. Moreover, the use of immigration measures is inconceivable in contemporary Japanese society. In view of the results of various recent opinion surveys on the importation of unskilled foreign workers to Japan, it seems safe to say that the introduction of a large-scale immigration policy in Japan is a rather remote possibility. In contrast to this, although the awareness of the two demographic dividends is still fairly limited in Japan, their use, particularly that of the accumulated second demographic dividend which is likely to remain substantial for the next few decades, could be an option for Japan to resume steady economic growth.

One crucial question remains: how can Japanese elderly make use of their accumulated wealth? Depending upon where they invest their financial resources, Japan's future economic growth performance is prone to differ considerably. If Japanese elderly persons are provided with sufficient knowledge about the dynamics of the financial market, they may have a good potential for investing their accumulated assets possibly outside Japan. Moreover, the timing of the first demographic dividend for selected Asian countries varies considerably, as presented in figure 4.16. As examined earlier, Japan's first dividend ended in 1979. In contrast, in the case of China, for instance, the first dividend lasts for forty-one years—from 1973 to 2014.

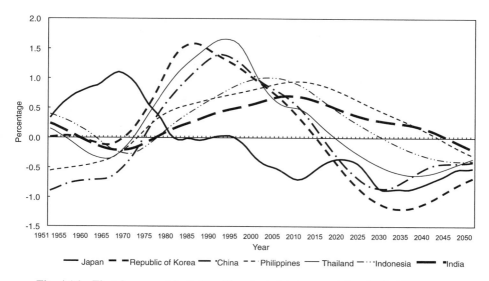

Fig. 4.16   First demographic dividend in selected Asian countries, 1950–2050

In an era of globalization, the healthier and wealthier among the Japanese elderly will have the opportunity to invest their assets in a dynamically growing Chinese economy, and bring financial gains back to Japan.

In contemporary Japan, the elderly are generally considered to be liabilities. However, the analyses developed in this chapter indicate that the Japanese elderly represent a powerful asset to keep the country on a sound and steady path of growth in the years to come. Furthermore, over the past decade or so, they have been informally playing the role of the society's safety net by providing financial assistance to their adult children and grandchildren suffering from financial difficulties.

In addition, as discussed elsewhere (Ogawa and Matsukura 2007), the number of healthy elderly persons in Japan is expected to increase significantly in the years ahead, and their educational attainment will be higher than that of the elderly in the past. In other words, Japan's future elderly will possess a substantial proportion of both the country's human and financial resources.

Before closing this chapter, it seems appropriate to offer a few words of caution concerning the interpretation of some of the numerical results computed from the NTA-Japan project. First, as pointed out earlier, bequests and other capital transfers are an important flow not included in the present paper. Estimating these flows is a difficult task but one that we hope to address in future work.

Second, although private-sector information derived from the five rounds of the National Survey of Family Income and Expenditure (NSFIE) from 1984 to 2004 is one of the most vital inputs in the NTA-Japan project, the data derived from the NSFIE have limitations. For instance, although there are significant seasonal variations in the consumption pattern, each round of the NSFIE covers only three months of the year (i.e., from September to November). Therefore, familial transfers in the form of wedding gifts, monetary contributions in case of death, financial assistance for university tuitions and housing, and so forth, may be rather poorly captured in the survey, which makes the estimates of familial transfers less reliable. Despite these data limitations, adult children are almost certainly contributing substantially less to their elderly parents through familial transfers than in 1984.

References

Bloom, D., and J. Williamson. 1998. Demographic transitions and economic miracles in emerging Asia. *World Bank Review* 12:419–56.

Clark, R., N. Ogawa, S.-H. Lee, and R. Matsukura. 2008. Older workers and national productivity in Japan. *Population Development Review* 34 (Supplement): S257–S274.

Ermisch, J. 2003. *An economic analysis of the family.* Princeton, NJ: Princeton University Press.

Gollin, D. 2002. Getting income shares right. *Journal of Political Economy* 110: 458–74.

Hodge, R., and N. Ogawa. 1991. *Fertility change in contemporary Japan.* Chicago: University of Chicago Press.

International Institute for Management Development. 2008. *IMD World Competitiveness Yearbook 2008.* Lausanne, Switzerland: IMD.

Japan Institute of Labour Policy and Training. 2004. *Law Concerning Stabilization of Employment of Older Persons.* Law no. 103 of June 11, 2004.

Lee, R., and A. Mason. 2009. Fertility, human capital, and economic growth over the demographic transition. *European Journal of Population* (published online on June 19).

Lutz, W., W. Sanderson, and S. Scherbov. 2004. *The end of world population growth in the 21st century: New challenges for human capital formation and sustainable development.* London and Sterling, VA: Earthscan.

Mason, A., ed. 2001. *Population change and economic development in East Asia: Challenges met, and opportunities seized.* Stanford: Stanford University Press.

———. 2007. Demographic transition and demographic dividends in developed and developing countries. United Nations Expert Group Meeting on Social and Economic Implications of Changing Population Age Structures. 31 August–2 September, 2005, Mexico City. New York: United Nations, pp. 81–102.

Mason, A., and R. Lee. 2006. Reform and support systems for the elderly in developing countries: Capturing the second demographic dividend. *Genus* 62 (2): 11–35.

———. 2007. Transfers, capital, and consumption over the demographic transition. In *Population Aging, Intergenerational Transfers and the Macroeconomy*, eds. R. Clark, N. Ogawa, and A. Mason, 128–62. Northampton, MA: Edward Elgar.

MacKellar, L. 2003. The predicament of population aging: A review essay. *Vienna Yearbook of Population Research* 2003:73–99.

McDonald, P. 2009. Explanations of low fertility in East Asia in comparative perspective. In *Ultra-low fertility in Pacific Asia: Trends, causes and policy issues,* ed. G. Jones, P. Straughan, and A. Chan, 23–39. Abington, Oxon: Routledge.

Matsukura, R., N. Ogawa, and R. L. Clark. 2007. Analysis of employment patterns and the changing demographic structure of Japan. *The Japanese Economy* 34:82–153.

National Institute of Population and Social Security Research. 2007. *Social security benefits for fiscal year 2007.* Published on the website of the National Institute of Population and Social Security Research Institute, http://www.ipss.go.jp/.

Organization for Economic Cooperation and Development (OECD). 2005. Recommendation on principles and good practices for financial education and awareness. Paris: OECD.

———. 2007. *OECD health DATA 2007.* Paris: OECD.

Ogawa, N., and J. Ermisch. 1996. Family structure, home time demands, and the employment patterns of Japanese married women. *Journal of Labor Economics* 14:677–702.

Ogawa, N., M. Kondo, M. Tamura, R. Matsukura, T. Saito, A. Mason, S. Tuljapurkar, and N. Li. 2003. Long-term perspectives for Japan: An analysis based on a macroeconomic-demographic-social security model with emphasis on human capital. Tokyo: Nihon University Population Research Institute.

Ogawa, N., S.-H. Lee, and R. Matsukura. 2005. Health and its impact on work and dependency among the elderly in Japan. *Asian Population Studies* 1:121–45.

Ogawa, N., A. Mason, Maliki, R. Matsukura, and K. Nemoto. 2007. Population aging and health care spending in Japan: public- and private-sector responses. In *Population aging, intergenerational transfers and the macroeconomy,* eds. R. Clark, N. Ogawa, and A. Mason, 192–223. Northampton, MA: Edward Elgar.

Ogawa, N., and R. Matsukura. 2007. Ageing in Japan: The health and wealth of older persons. United Nations Expert Group Meeting on Social and Economic Implications of Changing Population Age Structures. 31 August–2 September, 2005, Mexico City. New York: United Nations, 199–220.

Ogawa, N., and R. Retherford. 1993. The resumption of fertility decline in Japan: 1973–92. *Population and Development Review* 19 (4): 703–41.

———. 1997. Shifting costs of caring for the elderly back to families in Japan. *Population Development Reviews* 23 (1): 59–94.

Ogawa, N., R. D. Retherford, and R. Matsukura. 2009. Japan's declining fertility and policy responses. In *Ultra-low fertility in Pacific Asia: Trends, causes and policy issues,* ed. G. Jones, P. Straughan, and A. Chan, 40–72. Abington, Oxon: Routledge.

Population Problems Research Council. 2004. *National survey on population, families and generations.* Tokyo: Mainichi Newspapers.

Retherford, R. D., and N. Ogawa. 2006. Japan's baby bust: Causes, implications, and policy responses. In *The baby bust: Who will do the work? Who will pay the taxes?* ed. F. R. Harris, 5–47. Lanham: Rowman & Littlefield Publishers, Inc.

Sakamoto, J. 2005. Population challenges and social security—the case of Japan. Paper presented at the Forum on Population and Development in East Asia. 16–17 May, Beijing, China.

The Asahi Shimbun. 2007. Life insurance premiums to drop in April, March 10.

The Nikkei. 2007. Law prompts banks to heighten protection for elderly customers, October 1.

The Nikkei. 2008a. Annuity, medical insurance contracts top life policies, June 24.

The Nikkei. 2008b. 57% say pension payouts not enough for living expenses, May 13.

United Nations. 2007. *World population prospects: The 2006 revision.* New York: United Nations.

Washington Post. 2008. Japan steadily becoming a land of few children, May 6.

Yoshikawa, H. 2001. *Japan's lost decade.* Tokyo: International House of Japan.

Comment   Worawan Chandoevwit

The main objective of this chapter is to study the impact of population aging on both public and private intergenerational transfers in Japan in the last two decades. The highlights of the chapter are the last two sections relating to: (a) population aging, (b) intergeneration transfers, (c) two demographic dividends and changing pattern of lifecycle deficits, and (d) life cycle reallocations. The result from the last part is quite interesting.

This chapter systematically elaborates the facts about a rapid demographic transition, and changes of social security expenditure and family support. Generally, many of us know that Japan has already moved into aging population, but this chapter shows how it had evolved.

Worawan Chandoevwit is research director of the Thailand Development Research Institute.

The declining of total fertility rate (TFR) and mortality rate including a higher life expectancy are factors that resulted in a higher share of elderly and aging society. In the fifty-five-year period of 1950 to 2005, TFR declined from 3.6 to 1.3. Life expectancy at birth for both males and females increased approximately by twenty years. It would have been interesting if the chapter had estimated which factors between declining TFR and mortality rate had a stronger effect on a rapid increasing share of elderly.

It is quite well known that TFR in Japan is currently low—one of the lowest in the world. But, in fact, not many people know that the sharp reduction of TFR occurred between 1947 and 1957 (figure 4.2). In this decade TFR reduced from 4.5 to 2. This chapter should have mentioned what caused these substantial reductions. Was it because of the effectiveness of the abortion law in 1948 that made the number of births reduce by almost 500,000 in 1950? It was shown in a National Institute of Population and Social Security Research (IPSS) study (2006) that about 35 percent of married Japanese women experienced induced abortion in 1967. This chapter should have also mentioned why the TFR reduced from 2.2 to 1.6 in 1966 and then rebounded to 2.3 in 1967. What kind of shock decreased the number of births by 500,000 in only one year?

The first three parts of this chapter are the overview of Japanese demographic transition, public transfers, values of family support, and social security systems and the reforms. The authors generally emphasize the roles of universal pension and health insurance in 1961, Japan's structural reform in 1973, the bubble in mid-1980, and the lost decade in 1990s. These factors are raised to explain age structural shift of Japanese population and changes of family role on supporting elderly. The roles of pension and health insurance may be important, but sometimes are overemphasized. For example, the changes of expectation of Japanese married women to depend on their children for old-age security were remarkable from 1950 to 1960, before Japan had the universal pension (figure 4.5). In that ten-year period, the proportion of Japanese married women expecting to depend on their children for old-age security declined from 65 to 35 percent; or reduced by 30 percentage points. After 1961—or the first year of the universal pension—the proportion declined from 35 to 10 percent in 2005. It took forty-four years for the proportion to decline by 25 percentage points. It may be inaccurate to conclude that the change of expectation was from the public pension.

One of the upsides of this chapter is the use of survey data to explain Japanese behavior and attitude. Such surveys are not easy for nonJapanese to obtain, particularly for the long series of the survey results.

What is so serious for Japan is the population prospect. To prove this we can simply compare the share of elderly in the twenty-year period of 1985 to 2005, and 2005 to 2025. In 1985, the share of those aged above sixty-five was 10.3 and total dependency ratio was 46.7. In 2005, the share of those aged above sixty-five increased by 10 percentage points to 20.2, and total dependency ratio increased by 4 percentage points to 50.6. In 2025, the share will increase by 11 percentage points to 31.0, and total dependency ratio will increase by 20 percentage points to 70. It will be hard for the working-age group to live in such a burden.

Some countries make policy responses by helping families cope with child care burdens. For example, mothers in France are flexible to work from home so that they can take care of their children while working. No mothers in Japan have such an option. In Japan, about half of employed married women work part-time, and about 75 percent of part-time workers are women. The Child Care and Family Care Leave Law (2005) does not guarantee that these workers will not be terminated from their jobs if they ask for child care leave. There are loopholes in the law that allow employers to do so (Hassett 2008). In addition, in January 2007, Japan's Health, Labor, and Welfare Minister stated that "The number of women aged between fifteen to fifty is fixed. Because the number of birth-giving machines and devices is fixed, all we can do is ask them to do their best per head" (McCurry 2007).

This chapter illustrates the first and second demographic dividends quite well. When fertility and mortality are falling, the changes of population age structure lead to an increase in the working ages relative to nonworking age group(s), and the first demographic dividend. Japan experienced the first demographic dividend in 1945 to mid-1990. When the first demographic dividend was moving close to zero between 1975 and 1980, the second demographic dividend was moving into the positive zone. Figures 4.8 and 4.9 show that the period between 2005 and 2025 is not a good time for Japanese.

Elderly in Japan do accumulate wealth as the source of support for their consumption. Such action could have a positive effect on growth. However, one should also consider the distribution of wealth that has been ignored. This chapter emphasizes the role of second dividend as it states that "A key point is that in countries that rely on transfers, both public and familial, in meeting the retirement needs of the elderly, the second demographic dividend will not emerge. . . . The second dividend is affected not only by the numbers of the elderly persons relative to younger persons, but also by the extent to which consumers and policy makers are forward-looking and respond effectively to the demographic changes that are anticipated in the years ahead" (p. 146). In developing countries where the distribution of wealth and income are unequal, the policy promoting individual wealth accumulation for retirement only may end up with a large pool of poor elderly who were unable to save or accumulate wealth.

Wealth accumulation in the form of real and financial assets cannot be done without risks. Wealth accumulation in the form of land has become less popular among the elderly. It could be because their prices have gone too high. It might be because they know that population is declining, which should not make an upward trend for the demand for land as it has in the past when population was growing. Providing information about financial market risks and how to manage them may help people to make decisions about their wealth management. Life-time saving just to find that only half is remaining at the retirement age is painful. The chapter also mentions that 71 percent of population aged twenty and over have no knowledge about investment in equities and bonds and 57 percent have no knowledge about financial products.

Contemporary young Japanese are, in general, not happy with being in an aging society. However, the last part of the chapter shows a positive impact of elderly on younger generation. People in early retirement (sixty to seventy-five years old) actually make net intrafamily transfers to other age groups (figure 4.13). Their large portions of consumption are from labor income and income from assets (figure 4.15).

Why do older people decide to make a transfer to their offspring, knowing that pension benefits would fall short of their living expenses from age sixty? It could be altruism or intrafamily old age insurance. Once they retire, they live in a quiet and lonely environment. Any accident could happen easily to an elderly person at home. If they live with their children, those incidents will be mitigated. Should they live alone, they have to make some contribution in exchange of the visits from their children and grandchildren. The visits have some cost. Transfers from the elderly, therefore, could be a reward for their tender-loving care to their parents.

References

Hassett, M. 2008. Where did all the babies go? *The Japan Times* online, 10 June 2008.
National Institute for Population and Social Security Research (IPSS). 2006. Population Statistics of Japan 2006. Available at: www.ipss.go.jp/p-info/e/PSJ2006 .pdf.
McCurry, J. 2007. Japanese minister wants "birth-giving machines," aka women, to have more babies, *The Guardian,* 29 January 2007.

Comment   Alejandro N. Herrin

While providing an interesting account of Japan's experiences in population aging, the chapter also provides insights for analyzing policy issues related to economic-demographic and social changes in developing countries currently undergoing age structure change of varying timing and speed, and at varying stage of socioeconomic development. I focus my comments on these insights for developing countries.

Alejandro N. Herrin is a visiting research fellow at the Philippine Institute for Development Studies.

Effect of Economic, Social and Policy Changes
on the Age Pattern of Consumption and Production

The chapter describes Japan's changing age profiles of per capita consumption and per capita production (figure 4.7) as influenced by a number of interacting factors. These factors include patterns of economic growth, labor and social security policies, and social change. The last factor involves value shifts in family support for the elderly, and preferences for composition of assets; for example, land versus others forms. While one could speculate on what would have happened to the profiles of Japan's per capita consumption and production over the past twenty years had these factors been different in timing and speed, of practical interest is the effectiveness of recent policy reforms in the areas of, for example, mandatory retirement age, public pension schemes, long-term care insurance schemes, and medical insurance schemes.

Broadly, the analysis provides insights into possible factors to consider in macro-demographic simulations to test out various scenarios for other countries. For example, what would be the profile of consumption and production in countries characterized by slow and uneven economic growth, high poverty rates, slow demographic transition, and limited coverage of institutional mechanisms for public transfers? In these countries, high and low income groups are likely to have different demographic profiles, capacities for human and capital formation and patterns of transfers. What is the impact on overall poverty and income distribution over the longer term for such diverging economic and demographic profiles among major social groups within the country?

The analysis of Japan's experience provided by the chapter also points to some policy insights for developing countries trying to catch up economically, demographically, and institutionally with the developed world. For example, on economic policies, in the face of rapid growth of the absolute size of the labor force, would emphasis on achieving full employment first, rather than focusing on labor policies to protect the workers through social security and pension schemes (which tend to raise the cost of labor relative to capital, and reduce labor absorption), have more far reaching impacts on overall patterns of consumption and production and economic growth?

Effect of Age Structure on Economic Growth Given
Age Patterns of Consumption and Labor Income

The chapter estimates the first and second demographic dividend in Japan. The authors find that the magnitude of the positive first demographic dividend (annual growth rate of the economic support ratio, which measures the change in output per effective consumer due solely to changes in age structure) was large, adding just over 1 percentage point per year to economic growth during the 1960s and 1970s (figure 4.8). However, since the mid-1990s, the economic support ratio has been declining, and the first dividend has become negative.

The estimate of the second demographic dividend (i.e., the growth rate of productivity or output per labor income that arises because of an increase in the demand for assets as a consequence of population aging) is made over the period from 1960 to 2035. In the 1980s, the second demographic dividend generated almost 1.5 percentage points of additional economic growth (figure 4.9). Beginning from the 1990s, the second demographic dividend has declined to around 0.5 percentage point, with the prospect of maintaining this lower rate up to 2035.

Figure 4.16 shows estimates of the first demographic dividend for selected Asian countries. Following Japan's experience in rapid demographic transition, South Korea, Thailand, and China added another 1.0 to 1.5 percentage points to their economic growth solely due to age structure change. The pace of fertility decline was relatively much slower in Indonesia, Philippines, and India. As a result, the first demographic dividend added only less than 1 percentage point to economic growth. For the latter three countries, and similarly situated countries, an immediate goal is how to reap the full benefits of the first demographic dividend both in an accounting sense—through a more rapid decline in fertility—and, in a behavioral sense through better economic policies and stronger institutions. While age structure change through fertility decline can add to economic growth, other factors, such as continued rapid total population growth because of slower fertility decline, misguided economic policies, and weak institutions, could easily negate the contribution of age structure change to economic growth. The resulting overall slower economic growth and development would have implications for the pattern of consumption and production, asset accumulation, and the age reallocations, and, in turn, on the capacity to generate the second demographic dividend.

Changing Patterns of Age Reallocations

The third part of the chapter describes the effect of aging on the changing pattern of age reallocations for 1984 to 2004. The reallocations are made through assets, net public transfers, and net private transfers.

The chapter shows important changes in age reallocations resulting from the rapid growth of the elderly population (figure 4.12, panels A to C). In general, over this period, net total transfers increased by three times, with the increase coming mainly from public transfers, while net familial transfers have declined. Furthermore, asset-based reallocations have become important, increasing ten times during the period, although net public transfers still dominate in 2004.

How well an aging population can support the consumption of the elderly depends on how well the demand for life cycle pension wealth is accumulated. The authors note that for countries which rely on capital accumulation to meet the retirement needs of the elderly, population aging would provide an incentive to accumulate capital and other assets, and thus usher in the second demographic dividend.

Countries lagging behind the demographic transition would nonetheless undergo an aging process. But the slow demographic transition carries with it lost opportunities for faster economic growth and poverty reduction. Moreover, countries with slow demographic transition and limited coverage of the institutions for public saving (e.g., social security schemes and social health insurance)—such as the Philippines—are likely to also experience limited capacity in the future for age reallocations either in the form of transfer wealth (public and private) or in the form of asset accumulation to support the aging population and reap the second demographic dividend.

Putting Interrelationships Together: Policy Simulation Modeling

The chapter examined three different aspects of Japan's postwar economic-demographic experience: (a) the role of economic, social, and policy changes on the age pattern of consumption and production, (b) given an average age pattern of consumption and production, the effect of age structure on economic growth, and (c) depending on the nature of the age reallocations, the emergence of the second demographic dividend. For policy simulation, it might be instructive to put economic, social, and policy parameters to interact with age structure change that could simultaneously produce different levels and shapes of the age pattern of consumption and production, different patterns of the first demographic dividend, and different age reallocations. The empirical analysis for Japan described in the chapter provides building blocks for such policy discussions in developing countries.

Pension Issues in Japan
How Can We Cope with the Declining Population?

Noriyuki Takayama

5.1 Introduction

Japan already has the oldest population in the world. It has built generous social security programs. In 2002 the income statement of the principal program of social security pensions moved into deficit and its balance sheet has continued to suffer from huge excess liabilities. This has been accompanied by a growing distrust of the government's commitment on public pensions and increased concern with the incentive-compatibility problem. The 2004 pension reforms went some way toward addressing these issues.

This chapter uses a balance sheet approach to describe the current financial performance of social security pensions in Japan, and analyzes the impact of the recent reform measures.

The balance sheet approach was first used about 700 years ago in Italy and since then has become one of the two major accounting tools. However, it has been underutilized for public policy analyses.

Benefits of the balance sheet approach include: first, that it describes the current financial status in stock terms by presenting assets and liabilities with their compositions; second, it implies how smoothly future financing will be carried out; and third, it makes clear the impacts of alternative policy measures on future financing.

Before going into a discussion on the design flaws of Japanese pensions, some remarks have to be made on their implementation issues, since there

Noriyuki Takayama is a professor of economics at the Institute of Economic Research, Hitotsubashi University.

This is a revised and extended version of (Takayama 2008). The present author is grateful to Takatoshi Ito, Worawan Chandoevwit, Hyungpyo Moon, Ronald Lee, Naohiro Ogawa, and Francis Lui for their valuable comments and advices at the nineteenth EASE meeting, Seoul, June, 2008.

arose a serious pension record-keeping problem in Japan from May 2007. Namely, around 50 million pension records of social security are found to be floating, not being integrated to the unified specific pension numbers. The pending records are due to human errors made by enrollees, their employers, and agencies. There has been no integrated collection of taxes and social security contributions in Japan, and additionally no monitoring organizations have been effectively implemented in the field of pension administration. Government officials in Japan used to be regarded as the best and brightest, and thus too much reliance on bureaucracy was observed in the past. The general public were under the illusion that government officials were able to do and did everything correctly without committing any errors. However, human errors are inevitable anywhere. Regular and prompt examinations over possible errors are required for proper record-keeping of pensions. Upon any no-match identified, a two-way notification and confirmation with correction should follow in due course. The trustworthy government with its competent and neat implementation is, thus, the basis for any pension system.

This chapter begins with a brief sketch of the Japanese demography and its impact on financing social security. It then explains the Japanese social security pension program and summarizes Japan's major pension problems. It further examines the 2004 pension reform and uses the balance sheet approach to analyze its economic implications. The chapter discusses future policy options on pensions, as well.

5.2   Demography and Its Impact on Financing Social Security

In December 2006, the Japanese National Institute of Population and Social Security Research (NIPSSR) released its latest population projections. These indicated that the total population will peak at 128 million in 2004 and then will begin to fall steadily, decreasing to about 50 percent of the current number by 2080.

The total fertility rate (TFR) was 1.26 in 2005 and there is little sign that it will stabilize or return to a higher level. The 2006 *medium variant* projections assume that it will record the historical low of 1.21 in 2013 and will gradually rise to 1.26 around 2050, remaining unchanged at 1.26 thereafter. The number of births in 2005 was about 1.06 million and will continue to decrease to less than 1.0 million by 2008, falling further to 0.49 million in 2050.

Because it has the world's longest life expectancy,[1] Japan is now experiencing a very rapid aging of its population. The number of the elderly (sixty-five years and above) was 25.8 million in 2005. This will increase sharply to reach 36 million by 2020, remaining around 36 to 39 million thereafter until around 2060. Consequently the proportion of the elderly

---

1. Further declining mortality is almost ignored by the NIPSSR projections. Things will be much worse than imagined here.

(sixty-five years and above) will go up very rapidly from 20.2 percent in 2005 to 30 percent by 2023, rising further to more than 40 percent by 2052. Japan already has one of the oldest populations in the world.

In Japan, around 70 percent of social security benefits are currently distributed to the elderly. Along with the ailing domestic economy, the rapid population aging will certainly put increased stresses on the financing of social security.

In May 2006 the Ministry of Health, Labor, and Welfare published the latest estimates of the cost of social security just after the 2006 health care reform, using the 2002 population projections of the NIPSSR. According to these estimates, the aggregate cost of social security was 17.5 percent of gross domestic product (GDP) in 2006. This is expected to steadily increase to 19.0 percent by 2025.[2]

5.3   Japanese Pension Provisions before the 2004 Reform

Since 1980, Japan has undertaken piecemeal pension reforms every five years, mainly due to great stresses caused by anticipated demographic and economic factors. This has resulted in a step by step reduction in the generous pension benefits, an increase of the normal pensionable age from sixty to sixty-five, and an increase in the pension contribution rate. Yet, in 2004, the pension provisions still remained generous and the system seemed likely to face serious financial difficulties in the future.

Japan currently has a two-tier benefit system. All sectors of the population receive the first-tier, flat-rate basic benefit. The second-tier earnings-related benefit applies only to employees.[3] The system operates largely like a Pay-As-You-Go (PAYGO) defined benefit program.

The flat-rate basic pension covers all residents aged twenty to sixty. A minimum twenty-five-year contribution is required to receive an old-age benefit. The full old-age pension is payable after forty years of contributions, provided the contributions were made before sixty years of age. The maximum *monthly* pension of 66,000 yen (in 2008 prices) per person is payable from age sixty-five.[4] This benefit was indexed annually to reflect changes in the consumer price index (CPI). The pension may be claimed at any age between sixty and seventy years and is subject to actuarial reduction if claimed before age sixty-five, or actuarial increase if claimed after sixty-five years.

Earnings-related benefits are given to all employees. The accrual rate

2. Of the various social security costs, that of pensions is predominant, amounting to 9.2 percent of GDP in 2006, with an expected decrease to 8.7 percent by 2025 after the 2004 reform. The cost for health care is 5.4 percent in 2006, but is projected to steadily rise to 6.4 percent by 2025.

3. A detailed explanation of the Japanese social security pension system is given by Takayama (1998, 2003).

4. 1,000 yen = US$10.59 = Euro7.50 = UK £6.42, as of 19 August 2009.

for the earnings-related component of old-age benefits was 0.5481 percent per year; forty years' contributions would thus earn 28.5 percent of career average monthly real earnings.[5]

The career-average monthly earnings are calculated over the employee's entire period of coverage, adjusted by a net-wage index factor, and converted to the current earnings level. The full earnings-related pension is normally payable from age sixty-five to an employee who is fully retired.[6] An earnings test is applied to those who are not fully retired. The current replacement rate (including basic benefits) for take-home pay or net income is about 60 percent for a typical male retiree (with an average salary earned during forty years of coverage) and his dependent wife. This translates to a *monthly* benefit of about 233,000 yen in 2008.

Equal percentage contributions are required from employees and their employers. The contributions are based on annual standard earnings, including bonuses. Before the 2004 reforms, the total contribution rate for the principal program for private-sector employees (Kosei Nenkin Hoken, KNH), was 13.58 percent. Nonemployed persons between the ages of twenty to sixty years paid flat-rate individual contributions. The 2004 rate since April 1998 was 13,300 yen per month. And those who cannot pay for financial reasons are exempt. The flat-rate basic benefits for the period of exemption were one-third of the normal amount.

Moreover, if the husband has the pension contribution for social security deducted from his salary, his dependent wife is automatically entitled to the flat-rate basic benefits, and she is not required to make any individual payments to the public pension system.

The government subsidized one-third of the total cost of the flat-rate basic benefits plus administrative expenses. There is, however, no subsidy for the earnings-related part. All social security pension contributions are tax-deductible, while overwhelming parts of their benefits are virtually tax-exempt.

For 2004 the aggregate amount of social security pension benefits is estimated at around 46 trillion yen, or about 9 percent of GDP.[7]

5.4   Some Basic Facts on Pensions

Any pension reform proposal must take into account the current basic facts on social security pensions. Of these, the following five are especially crucial.

---

5. A semiannual bonus equivalent to 3.6 months salary is typically assumed.

6. The normal pensionable age of the KNH is sixty-five, though Japan has special arrangements for a transition period between 2000 and 2025. See Takayama (2003) for more details.

7. Almost all Japanese employees receive occupational pensions and/or lump-sum retirement benefits, as well. See Takayama (2003) for more information.

5.4.1   A Persistent Deficit in the Income Statement

Since 2002, the pension scheme for private sector employees (KNH) has been facing an income statement deficit. It recorded a deficit of 1.3 trillion yen in 2002, increasing to 9.8 trillion yen in 2005. It is estimated that this deficit will persist for a long time, unless radical remedies are made in the KNH financing.

5.4.2   Huge Excess Liabilities in the Balance Sheet

The KNH balance sheet is shown in table 5.1. In calculating the balance sheet, it was assumed that: the annual increases in wages and the CPI were 2.1 percent and 1.0 percent respectively, nominal, while the discount rate was 3.2 percent annually; and the 2003 contribution rate of the KNH of 13.58 percentage points would remain unchanged over the projection period (to the year 2100).

Table 5.1 indicates that, as at the end of March 2005, excess liabilities of the KNH are estimated at 550 trillion yen, which is a quarter of the total liabilities.[8]

The balance sheet set out in table 5.1 has two parts. Part One illustrates the assets and liabilities accrued from past contributions, while Part Two refers to assets and liabilities accrued from future contributions.[9] It can be seen that as far as Part Two is concerned, any excess liabilities are almost eliminated. That is, the funding sources of the current provisions will be sufficient to finance future benefits. Here the only task left is to slim down future benefits by 4.5 percent.

But if we look at Part One of the balance sheet, things appear quite different. The remaining pension liabilities are estimated to be 800 trillion yen, while pension assets are only 300 trillion yen (comprising a funded reserve of 170 trillion yen plus transfers from general revenue of 130 trillion yen). The difference is quite large, about 500 trillion yen,[10] which accounts for most of the excess liabilities in the KNH and is equivalent to about 100 percent of GDP of Japan in 2004.

In the past, too many pension promises were made, while sufficient funding sources had not been arranged. As a result, the Japanese have enjoyed a long history of generous social security pensions. However, contributions

8. Excess liabilities of all social security pension programs in Japan as at the end of March 2005 amounted to around 650 trillion yen, which is equivalent to 1.3 times the year 2004 GDP of Japan.

9. The balance sheet approach is slightly different from the generational accounting one, which is initiated by L. Kotlikoff.

10. The amount of excess liabilities (EL) will vary depending on alternative discount rates. For example, a 2.1 percent discount rate induces EL of 650 trillion yen, while another 4.0 percent discount rate produces EL of 420 trillion yen. Part One excess liabilities can be termed as "accrued-to-date net liabilities" or "net termination liabilities." See Franco (1995) and Holzmann, Palacios, and Zviniene (2004).

Table 5.1   **Balance sheet of the KNH before reform as of 31 March 2005**

	Trillion yen
1. Part one	
Assets	
Financial reserves	170
Transfers from general revenue	130
Liabilities	
Pensions due to past contributions	800
Excess liabilities	500
2. Part two	
Assets	
Contributions	920
Transfers from general revenue	130
Liabilities	
Pensions due to future contributions	1,100
Excess liabilities	50

Note: The author's own calculation.

made in the past were relatively small, resulting in a fairly small funded reserve. Consequently, the focus of the true crisis in Japanese social security pensions is how to handle the excess liabilities of 500 trillion yen representing entitlements from contributions made in the past.

5.4.3   The Heavy Burden of Pension Contributions

In Japanese public policy debates, one of the principal issues has been how to cut down personal and corporate income tax. But recently the situation has changed drastically. Social security contributions (for pensions, health care, unemployment, work injury, and long-term care) were 55.6 trillion yen (11.2 percent of GDP) for Fiscal Year (FY) 2003, more than all tax revenues (43.9 trillion yen) of the central government for the same year. Since 1998, the central government has received more revenue from social security contributions than from tax on incomes; FY 2003 revenue from personal income tax was 13.8 trillion yen and from corporate income tax 9.1 trillion yen, while revenue from social security pension contributions stood at 29.0 trillion yen. As a result, many Japanese now feel that the burden of social security pension contributions is far too heavy and employers have begun to express serious concerns about any further increases in social security contributions.

5.4.4   Overshooting the Income Transfer between Generations

Currently, in Japan the elderly are better off than those aged thirty to forty-four in terms of per capita income after redistribution (see Takayama [1998, 126] for more details). This amazing fact suggests that current pension

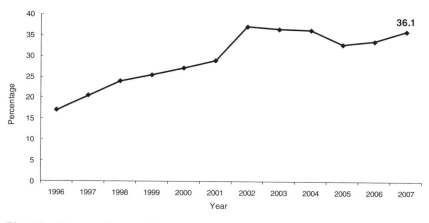

Fig. 5.1   Drop-out from social security pensions (category 1 nonemployees), delinquency in paying pension contributions
Source: Social Insurance Agency, Japan.

benefits may be too generous and there is still room for reduction in benefits provided to the current retired population (which would address the excess liabilities indicated by the balance sheet).

5.4.5   An Increasing Drop-Out Rate

In the past thirty years, the Japanese government has made repeated changes to the pension program, increasing social security pension contributions and reducing benefits through raising the normal pensionable age while reducing the accrual rate. Similar piecemeal reforms are likely to continue into the future.

Many Japanese feel that the government is breaking its promise. As distrust of the government's pension commitment builds up, nonparticipation is growing.

In 2007, 54 percent of nonsalaried workers and persons with no occupations dropped out from the basic level of old-age income protection, owing to exemption or failure to pay contributions (see figure 5.1). Any further escalation in the social security contribution rate will surely induce a higher drop-out rate.[11]

5.5   The 2004 Pension Reform: Main Features and Remaining Difficulties

The administration of Prime Minister Koizumi Jun'ichirō submitted a set of pension reform bills to the National Diet on February 10, 2004. These

---

11. Integrated collection of social security pension and health care contributions can reduce drop-out rates.

were enacted on June 5. This section will describe the gist of the approved reforms and explore issues that remain to be addressed.[12]

5.5.1   Increases in Contributions

Salaried workers are, as a rule, enrolled in the KNH, which is part of the public pension system. Contributions under this plan had since October 1996 been set at 13.58 percent of annual income, paid half by the worker and half by the employer. The newly enacted reforms raised this rate by 0.354 percentage points in October 2004. The rate will rise every September thereafter by the same amount until 2017, after which it will remain fixed at 18.30 percent of annual income. The portion paid by workers will accordingly rise to 9.15 percent of annual income.

For an "average" male company employee earning 360,000 yen a month plus an annual bonus equivalent to 3.6 months' pay, total contributions will increase by nearly 20,000 yen a year starting from October 2004, and by the time they stop rising in September 2017, they will have reached just under 1.03 million yen a year (of which the share paid by the worker will be just over 514,000 yen, or 35 percent more than the 2004 level of contributions).

Those who are not enrolled in the KNH or other public pension schemes for civil servants are required to participate in the National Pension plan (Kokumin Nenkin, KN), which provides the so-called basic pension *only* (the basic pension also forms the first tier of benefits under the KNH and other public pension systems for civil servants). Contributions under this plan will rise by 280 yen each April, from 13,300 yen per month in 2004 until they plateau at 16,900 yen (at 2004 prices) in April 2017. The actual rise in National Pension contributions will be adjusted according to increases in general wage levels.

In addition, the government will increase its subsidies for the basic pension. Currently one-third of the cost of basic pension benefits is paid from the national treasury; this share is to be raised in stages until it reaches one-half in 2009.

5.5.2   Reductions in Benefits

Benefits under the KNH consist of two tiers; the flat-rate basic pension, which is paid to all public pension plan participants, and a separate earnings-related component. The latter is calculated on the basis of the worker's average preretirement income, converted to current values. Until now, the index used to convert past income to current values was the rate of increase in take-home pay. Under the recently enacted reforms, however, this index is subject to a negative adjustment over a transition period based on changes in two demographic factors—the decline in the number of par-

---

12. This section draws heavily on Takayama (2004).

ticipants and the increase in life expectancy. This period of adjustment is expected to last through to 2023.

The application of the first demographic factor means that benefit levels will be cut to reflect the fact that fewer people are supporting the pension system. The actual number of people enrolled in all public pension schemes will be ascertained each year, and the rate of decline will be calculated based on this figure. The average annual decline is projected to be around 0.6 points.

The second demographic factor will adjust for the fact that people are living longer and thus collecting their pensions for more years; the aim is to slow the pace of increase in the total amount of benefits paid as a result of increased longevity. This factor will not be calculated by tracking future movements in life expectancy; instead, it has been set at an annual rate of about 0.3 percentage points on the basis of current demographic projections for the period through 2025. Together, the two demographic factors are thus expected to lead to a negative adjustment of about 0.9 points a year during the period in question.

How will these changes affect people's actual retirement benefits? Let us consider the case of a pair of "typical" KNH beneficiaries as defined by the Ministry of Health, Labor, and Welfare: a sixty-five-year-old man who earned the average wage throughout his forty-year career and his sixty-five-year-old wife who was a full-time homemaker for forty years from her twentieth birthday. In FY 2004, this typical couple would receive 233,000 yen a month.

How does this amount compare to what employees are currently taking home? The average monthly income of a salaried worker in 2004 was around 360,000 yen, before taxes and social insurance deductions. Assuming that this is supplemented by bonuses totaling an equivalent of 3.6 months' pay, the average annual income is roughly 5.6 million yen. Deducting 16 percent of this figure for taxes and social insurance payments leaves a figure for annual take-home pay of about 4.7 million yen, or 393,000 yen a month.

The 233,000 yen provided to the typical pensioners is 59.3 percent of 393,000 yen. However, under the 2004 reforms this percentage, or replacement rate, will gradually decline to an estimated figure of 50.2 percent by FY 2023 (assuming that consumer prices and nominal wages rise according to government projections by 1.0 percent and 2.1 percent a year, respectively). Over the next two decades, then, benefit levels are projected to decline by roughly 15 percent by comparison with wage levels.

The revised pension legislation stipulates that the income replacement rate is not to fall below 50 percent for the typical case previously described, so the transition period of negative adjustment will come to an end once the replacement rate declines to 50 percent. This provision was included to alleviate fears that retirement benefits would continue to shrink without limit.

How will the reforms affect those who are already receiving their pensions? Until now, benefits for those sixty-five years old and over were adjusted for fluctuations in the consumer price index. This ensured that pensioners' real purchasing power remained unchanged and helped ease postretirement worries. But this cost-of-living link will effectively be severed during the transition period, since the application of the demographic factors will pull down real benefits by around 0.9 points a year. In principle, however, nominal benefits are not to be cut unless there has also been a drop in consumer prices. Once the transition period is over, the link to the consumer price index is to be restored.

5.5.3   Changes to Provisions for Working Seniors and Divorcees

People aged sixty to sixty-four who were receiving pensions and also had wage income had their benefits reduced by a flat 20 percent, regardless of how much or little they earned. This rule was abolished in the 2004 reforms so as not to discourage older people from working. However, these older workers will still be subject to the previous rule that if the sum of wages and pension benefits exceeds 280,000 yen a month (after factoring in annual bonuses), the pension benefits are to be cut by 50 percent of the amount in excess of this level.

Workers aged seventy and over, meanwhile, have been exempt from paying into the KNH, even if they are still on a company's payroll. And they did not have their benefits reduced no matter how much they earned. Beginning in April 2007, however, their benefits are reduced if they are high-income earners. Those receiving more than an equivalent of 480,000 yen a month in wages and pension benefits will have their benefits cut by 50 percent of the amount in excess of this level. This is a rule that currently applies to those aged sixty-five to sixty-nine, as well. The over-seventy group will still be entitled to the full amount of the basic pension, and they will continue to be exempt from paying contributions.

Divorced wives were not legally entitled to any portion of their former husbands' earnings-related pension benefits, but this changed under the 2004 reforms. Couples who divorce after April 2007 are able to split the rights to the earnings-related portion of the husband's pension that accrued during their marriage. The wife is able to receive a share of up to 50 percent of these rights with the actual share to be determined by agreement between the two. For rights accruing after April 2008, moreover, a full-time homemaker is able to automatically receive half of her husband's benefits in case of divorce by filing a claim at a social insurance office. Underlying this rule is the assumption that even though the contributions are paid in the husband's name, the wife has provided half of the couple's livelihood through her work as a homemaker.[13]

---

13. The provisions for working husbands and dependent homemaker wives apply conversely in cases where a homemaker husband is dependent on the wife.

5.5.4   Improved Survivors' Benefits and Child-Raising Concessions

Until now, widowed spouses younger than thirty and without children under the age of eighteen have been entitled to lifelong benefits under the survivor's pension scheme (based on the earnings of the deceased spouse). After April 2007, however, they receive benefits for no longer than five years.

Workers taking child care leave are exempt from making pension contributions, and to prevent a decrease in their future benefits due to this period of nonpayment, they are treated as having continued their full payments, even when they have no income. This special exemption can now be claimed for up to one year after childbirth, but starting in April 2005 the period is extended until the child reaches age three.

Also, from April 2005, parents who change their working arrangements to put in shorter hours so as to care for children under age three and who take a corresponding cut in pay are treated as having worked full time and earned a full salary. Actual contributions during this three-year period, though, are based on the lower earnings.

5.5.5   Other Public and Private Pension Reforms

As a rule, a person cannot simultaneously receive more than one public pension. But the recent reforms have created an exception. People with disabilities who had gainful employment and paid pension contributions are, from April 2006, entitled to not only their basic disability pension but also the earnings-related component of the old-age pension or survivor's pension. This measure is designed to encourage greater employment among these people.

Participants in the National Pension plan who had low incomes paid either half of the regular contributions or none at all. There is a finer tuning of payment exemptions starting in July 2006, when low-income earners may also be exempt from paying one-quarter or three-quarters of the regular contributions.

Also, the administrative processes are improved and streamlined. In the past, pension plan participants found out how much they would receive in benefits only by going to a social insurance office with their pension passbooks after they had reached age fifty-five. From April 2008, however, such information is disclosed to all contributors each year, along with their payment records.

The reforms cover private pension plans as well. From October 2004, the upper limit of the amount that can be put aside each month under company-funded defined contribution pension plans was raised from 36,000 yen to 46,000 yen in cases where there is no other corporate pension plan, and from 18,000 yen to 23,000 yen where there is another plan in effect. The ceiling on monthly installments under individually-funded defined contribution plans for salaried workers was raised from 15,000 yen to 18,000 yen where there is no corporate pension coverage, while the cap for the self-employed remained unchanged at 68,000 yen. The higher ceilings for private plans are designed to make up for the anticipated smaller benefits of public old-age schemes.

5.5.6   Is the 2004 Reform Incentive-Compatible?

Social insurance contributions in Japan already exceed the amount collected in national taxes, and contributions to the pension system are by far the biggest social insurance item. If this already huge sum is increased by more than 1 trillion yen a year, as the government plans, both individuals and companies are very likely to change their behavior. Government projections of revenues and expenditures, though, completely ignore the prospect of such change.

It is possible that companies will reconsider their hiring plans and wage scales to avoid the higher social insurance burden. They may cut back on recruitment of new graduates and become more selective about midcareer hiring as well. Many young people will be stripped of employment opportunities and driven out of the labor market, instead of being enlisted to support the pension system with a percentage of their income. As well, the employment options for middle-aged women who wish to reenter the workforce will be reduced and, as only a few older workers will be able to continue commanding high wages, there is likely to be a dramatic rise in the number of aging workers who will be forced to choose between remaining on the payroll with a cut in pay or settling for retirement. It is possible that many more companies will either choose or be forced to leave the KNH, causing the number of subscribers to fall far below the government's projections and pushing the system closer to bankruptcy.

If these events come to fruition, the jobless rate on the whole could rise. The Japan Ministry of Economy, Trade, and Industry has estimated that higher pension contributions could lead to the loss of 1 million jobs and boost the unemployment rate by 1.3 percentage points.

The government plan to increase pension contributions annually for the next ten years will therefore exert ongoing deflationary pressure on the Japanese economy. For the worker, a rise in contribution levels means less take-home pay; as a result, consumer spending is likely to fall, and this will surely hinder prospects for an economic recovery and return to steady growth, which is one of the most important factors for Japan to make social security sustainable.

Another problem with increasing pension contributions is that they are regressive, since there is a ceiling for the earnings on which payment calculations are based and unearned income is not included in the calculations at all.

One major objective of the 2004 reforms is to eventually eliminate the

Table 5.2   **Balance sheet of the KNH after reform as of 31 March 2005**

	Trillion yen
1. Part one	
Assets	
Financial reserves	170
Transfers from general revenue	150
Liabilities	
Pensions due to past contributions	740
Excess liabilities	420
2. Part two	
Assets	
Contributions	1,200
Transfers from general revenue	190
Liabilities	
Pensions due to future contributions	970
Excess assets	420

Source: Ministry of Health, Labor and Welfare Japan, *The 2005 Financial Recalculation of the KNH,* 2004 (in Japanese).

huge excess liabilities in the balance sheet of the KNH. The plan is to generate a surplus by (a) increasing contributions; (b) increasing payments from the national treasury; and (c) reducing benefits. The policy measures adopted in the 2004 pension reform bill will induce huge *excess assets* of 420 trillion yen in Part Two of the balance sheet while offsetting excess liabilities of the same amount in Part One, as shown in table 5.2.[14] Huge excess assets of Part Two of the balance sheet imply that future generations will be forced to pay more in contributions than the anticipated benefits they will receive. That is, it is estimated that in aggregate the present value of future benefits will be around 80 percent of the present value of future contributions.

It is as if the Japanese government is cutting paper not with scissors but with a saw. Younger generations are most likely to intensify their distrust against government and the incentive-compatibility issue or drop-out problem will intensify. The management lobby (Nippon Keidanren) and trade unions (Rengo) both oppose any further increases of more than 15 percentage points in the KNH contribution rate.

5.5.7   A Declining Replacement Rate

As noted before, those who are already receiving their pensions will see their benefits decline in real terms by an average 0.9 percentage points per year. The government scenario sees consumer prices eventually rising 1.0 percent a year and take-home pay by 2.1 percent a year. This means that the

14. Assumptions in table 5.2 are the same as those described in section 5.4 in this chapter. Annual productivity growth of 0.7 percent is incorporated.

typical beneficiary who begins receiving 233,000 yen a month at age sixty-five in 2004 will get roughly 240,000 yen at age eighty-four in 2023; in other words, nominal benefits will remain virtually unchanged for two decades, despite the fact that average take-home pay of the working population is projected to have risen by over 40 percent. The income replacement rate, which stood at nearly 60 percent at age sixty-five, will dwindle to 43 percent by the time the typical recipient turns eighty-four. The promise of benefits in excess of 50 percent of take-home pay does not apply, therefore, to those who are already on old-age pensions.

5.5.8   Automatic Balance Mechanism: Still Incomplete

The so-called demographic factors are likely to continue changing for the foreseeable future. The government itself foresees the number of participants in public pension plans declining over the coming century. The estimated figure of 69.4 million participants in 2005 is expected to fall to 61.0 million in 2025, 45.3 million in 2050, and 29.2 million in 2100. This corresponds to an average annual decline of 0.6 percent through 2025, 1.2 percent of the quarter century from 2025, and 0.9 percent for the half century from 2050. In other words, the decline in the number of workers who are financially supporting the public pension system will continue for many decades.

The 2004 reforms, however, adjust benefit levels in line with the decline in the contribution-paying population for the next twenty years only; the government's "standard case" does not foresee any further downward revisions, even if the number of participants continues to fall. If the government really anticipates an ongoing decline in participation, there is no good reason to abruptly stop adjusting benefit levels after a certain period of time.[15]

The decision to keep the typical income replacement rate at 50 percent at the point when pension payments commence represents, in effect, the adoption of a defined benefit formula. Maintaining both fixed contributions on the one hand and defined benefit levels on the other is not an easy task, as there is little room to deal with unforeseen developments. The government will be confronted with a fiscal emergency should its projections for growth in contributions and a reversal in the falling birth rate veer widely from the underlying assumptions.

For example, the government has based its population figures on the January 2002 projections of the NIPSSR. Under these projections, the medium variant for the total fertility rate (the average number of childbirths per woman) falls to 1.31 in 2007, after which it begins climbing, reaching 1.39 in 2050 and 1.73 in 2100. Actual figures since the projections were released

---

15. The replacement rate at 50 percent can be regarded as still too high, since many people will also receive occupational pensions.

have been slightly lower than this variant, and there are no signs whatsoever that the fertility rate will stop declining in 2007.

5.5.9   The Normal Pensionable Age

If the government is to keep its promise on an upper limit for contributions and a lower limit for benefits, the only policy option it will have in the event of a financial shortfall will be to raise the age at which people begin receiving benefits. The reform package makes no mention of such a possibility; policymakers no doubt chose to simply put this task off to a future date.[16]

5.5.10   Increasing Transfers from General Revenue—Why?

By FY 2009 the share of the basic pension benefits funded by the national treasury will be raised from one-third to one-half. This means that more taxes will be used to cover the cost of benefits. Taxes are by nature different from contributions paid by participants in specific pension plans, and there is a need to reconsider the benefits that are to be funded by tax revenues.

The leaders of Japanese industry tend to be quite advanced in years. For the most part, they are over the age of sixty-five, which means that they are qualified to receive the flat-rate basic pension. Even though they are among the wealthiest people in the country, they are entitled to the same basic pension as other older people hovering around the poverty line. Using tax revenues to finance a bigger share of the basic pension essentially means asking taxpayers to foot a bigger bill for the benefits of wealthy households as well. For an elderly couple, the tax-financed portion of the basic pension will rise from 530,000 yen a year to 800,000 yen. If a need arises to raise taxes at a future date, who will then actually agree to pay more? Few people will be willing to tolerate such wasteful uses of tax revenue.

5.6   Future Policy Options in Social Security Pensions

There are five major policy options discussed in Japan, as follows.

5.6.1   Option 1: Privatizing the Second-Tier Earnings-Related Pension

The background for privatization is that too many promises have been made on social security pensions and their downsizing is required. Japan Association of Corporate Executives (Keizai Doyu Kai) proposes a privatization of the earnings-related portion, paying off the reduced earned entitlement by around 30 to 40 percent. The proportion of this reduction is to be decided by the remaining funded reserve of the KNH.

---

16. Raising the normal pensionable age will be implemented for financial reasons as in the United States, the United Kingdom, and Germany, even though it might not be socially acceptable.

The proposed payoff scheme is unpopular, however. It is still an open question how to make the privatization politically feasible.

5.6.2   Option 2: A Move to a Fully-Funded Plan

Many economists in Japan believe that any Pay-As-You-Go pension program is financially vulnerable to an aging population with declining fertility. They recommend a move to a mandated fully-funded pension plan to avoid the demographic risks (see Hatta and Oguchi [1992] for an example).

Others say, however, that it is *not* the Pay-As-You-Go program *but* the defined benefit (DB) plan that is financially fragile under demographic changes. The KNK (Kosei Nenkin Kikin), a typical occupational DB pension plan, which enables a contracted-out from social security pensions in Japan, faced a huge financial risk after the bubble burst in the 1990s. It turned quite unpopular and a majority of them have been abolished since then. Any move to a fully-funded DB plan can no longer promise sound financing.

5.6.3   Option 3: A Switch to Universal Pensions

The drop-out problem is getting more and more serious in recent Japan. The elderly receiving no social security pension benefits were 420,000 persons in January 2007, and the number will increase to 1.18 million in the near future. Those elderly with a smaller monthly amount of pension benefits of less than 30,000 Japanese yen amounted to 1.03 million in number, and 90 percent of them were female (see Takayama [2009] for more details).

In order to overcome these difficulties, the Democratic Party, Nippon Keidanren, Rengo, members from the private sector of the National Council on Economic and Fiscal Policy, Japan, and Nikkei newspaper group have proposed to shift from the current contribution-based basic pension to a universal pension, which is wholly financed by taxes.

Figure 5.2 illustrates changes in net burdens among different cohorts through this shift. In estimating these changes, it is assumed[17] that (a) a universal pension is to be introduced in 2007; (b) its benefit level is the same as that of the current flat-rate basic pension; (c) the flat-rate monthly contributions of 14,100 Japanese yen per person for nonemployees are abolished and the employees' portion of the KNH contributions (around 7.5 percent of their annual salaries) is reduced by 5.0 percentage points, while the employers' portion of the KNH contributions remains unchanged; (d) instead, an earmarked consumption-based tax of around 4.3 percent is newly introduced to finance the universal pension on a fully Pay-As-You-Go basis; and

---

17. See Takayama and Miyake (2008) for more details on the assumptions and estimating procedures here. The National Council on Social Security, Japan (2008) made a different estimate, assuming that both employees' and their employers' portions of the KNH contributions are reduced by the same percentage points. The effects of the switch on the balance sheet remain to be studied in the future.

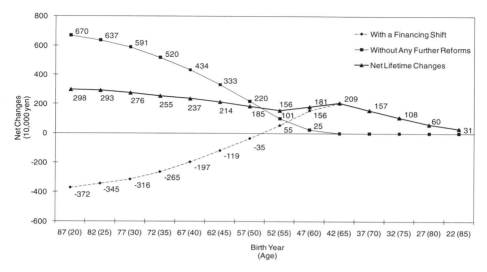

Fig. 5.2   Net changes in lifetime burdens of social security pensions
Source: The author's own calculation.
Note: Ages are in 2007.

(e) the tax base is 90 percent of the total consumption expenditure. A typical life course is assumed, as well. That is, a man starts working as an employee at age twenty, continuing working until age sixty-five when he begins to receive pension benefits, and dies at age eighty. At age thirty, he marries a woman, four years younger, who becomes a full-time housewife, without divorcing until his death. His wife lives longer, dying at age eighty-five.

Unless the shift of the aforementioned financing sources takes place, the contribution rate of the KNH will gradually rise from around 15 percent in 2007 to 18.3 percent by 2017. With these increases in pension contributions, the younger the cohort, the heavier his or her lifetime burdens after 2007. Needless to say, current elderly people age sixty-five and over will not incur any additional pension burdens in this setting.

The alternative financing shift to a universal pension brings a varying effect on pension burdens among different cohorts. Current pensioners will be forced to cover additional burdens of the newly introduced earmarked consumption-based tax, whereas the younger cohorts born after around 1955 can enjoy some net decreases in pension burdens through the switch of financing sources from contributions to consumption-based tax. The overall net lifetime impact will be increased burdens for everybody, as is shown in figure 5.2, although the financing shift to a consumption-based tax will induce smoother increases in pension burdens among different cohorts.

Any increases in social security burdens on the current elderly still look politically hard in Japan. Without these changes, however, their children and grandchildren will surely be forced to bear much heavier burdens for social security.

If we want to minimize increases in the consumption-based tax, it is worth considering a Canadian type of the clawback scheme, which is applied to pension beneficiaries with a higher income.

5.6.4   Option 4: A Move to Notional Defined Contribution

The Japan Ministry of Health, Labor, and Welfare has shown a great interest in switching the pension system to an NDC (notional defined contribution) arrangement. It has indicated, however, that it does not consider such a switch to be realistic until the KNH contribution rate reaches its peak level in 2017.

However, switching to an NDC arrangement can be introduced in Japan sooner, if we *separate* the "legacy pension" problem from the issue of rebuilding a sustainable pension system for the future.

The legacy pension problem is equivalent to *sunk costs* in the economic perspective. It can be solved not by increasing the KNH contribution rate but by introducing a new tax—for example, a 3.2 percent earmarked consumption-based tax and intensive interjection of the increased transfers from general revenue.[18] Needless to say, the current generous benefits can also be reduced more or less by the same percentage in the aggregate level, as implemented in the 2004 pension reform.

As far as Part Two of the balance sheet that relates to future contributions and promised pension benefits entitled by future contributions is concerned, a switch to the NDC is possible. The KNH contribution rate can be kept unchanged at around current 15 percentage points. As well, the notional rate of return may be endogenous, following a Swedish-type automatic balance mechanism.

Importantly, with the NDC plan, the incentive-compatibility problem can be avoided. Indeed, every dollar counts in the NDC, and this would be the most important element of a switch to an NDC plan. It will be demonstrated to the public that everybody gets a pension equivalent to his or her own contribution payments.[19]

Further, an NDC plan is expected to be rather neutral to the retirement decision. The labor force participation rate for Japanese elderly males still remains at a considerably high level (70.9 percent in 2006 for those age sixty to sixty-four) as compared with other developed countries. The shift to NDC arrangements can also induce later retirement in Japan, but its effect may not be so significant.

---

18. In the NDC plan stated previously, the balance sheet will turn healthy. Alternatively, a 2 percent earmarked consumption tax might be alright, since the remaining excess liabilities of 90 trillion yen may be acceptable as a "hidden" national debt.

19. See Könberg (2002), Palmer (2003) and Settergren (2001) for more details. The NDC is still a Pay-As-You-Go scheme, but it is no longer financially vulnerable.

A move to NDC may lead to lower replacement rates at age sixty-five. However, this can be compensated by working longer (to age sixty-seven or so), or by more voluntary saving.

While not explicitly considering NDC arrangements, the Japanese government has signaled increased support of financial defined contributions (FDC) arrangements by deciding to give more tax incentives to the existing defined contribution plan from October 2004 onward.[20]

5.6.5   Option 5: Introducing a Minimum Guaranteed Pension

The NDC does not suffice, however, when we also need to take account of *social adequacy.*

One way to resolve this problem is to introduce a minimum guaranteed pension, as the Yomiuri Group suggests. The National Council of Social Security, Japan (2008) estimated the cost of introducing such a pension with income testing. According to the estimate, the cost will be around 1.0 trillion yen, looking politically more feasible than other options. It remains a future task to specify the provision of income testing and tax sources, earmarking, or general revenue.[21]

An evidence-based policy decision is recommended. There remains a lot of empirical research before the Japanese adopt wise and appropriate policy measures for the future.

5.7   Concluding Remarks

The December 2006 release of future population projections by the NIPSSR made social security financing more serious. The majority of the population has recognized the gravity of the problem. The Japanese can forgive and forget.

Socioeconomic conditions will change very rapidly. The changes that take place will often be beyond our expectations. Neverending reforms of social security are inevitable in Japan, where only fine-tuning of programs even in the face of changing circumstances is acceptable in the political arena.

The Japanese are increasingly concerned with the "taste of pie" rather than the "size of pie" or the "distribution of pie." When it comes to social security pensions, the most important question is whether or not they are worth buying. It has become a secondary concern how big or how fair they are. Despite the comprehensive 2004 reforms, many issues remain. In particular, the basic design of the pension program has to be incentive-compatible. Contributions must be much more directly linked with old-age pension ben-

20. Mandating a partial FDC can be an option, when the KNH benefit level is further reduced.
21. The effects of introducing a minimum guaranteed pension on the balance sheet remain to be studied in the future. Another option is to raise the returns on the Government Pension Investment Fund (GPIF). Deregulations will bring higher returns.

efits, while an element of social adequacy should be incorporated in a separate tier of pension benefits financed by sources other than contributions.

Traditionally, the current (and projected future) income statement has been the major tool for describing the financial performance of social security pensions all over the world. It can only give half the story, however. Financial sustainability of social security pensions is often unattained even if its income statement enjoys a surplus. The balance sheet approach is now an indispensable tool for people to understand the long-run financial sustainability of social security pensions and to evaluate varying financial impacts of different reform alternatives. This chapter provides a typical example of applying the balance sheet approach to analyzing social security pensions.

Balance sheet of social security pensions in the United States, Sweden, Germany, Spain, Korea, Singapore, and China have also been available for some time. This approach could be useful for future policy developments around the world.

References

Franco, D. 1995. Pension liabilities: Their use and misuse in the assessment of fiscal policies. European Commission. Economic Papers no. 110.

Hatta, T., and N. Oguchi. 1992. Changing the Japanese Social Security system from pay as you go to actuarially fair. In *Topics in the economics of aging,* ed. D. Wise, 207–48. Chicago: University of Chicago Press.

Holzmann, R., R. Palacios, and A. Zviniene. 2004. Implicit pension debt: Issues, measurement and scope in international perspective. Social Protection Discussion Paper Series no. 0403. Washington, DC: World Bank.

Könberg, B. 2002. The Swedish pension reform: Some lessons. Center for Intergenerational Studies, Institute of Economic Research, Hitotsubashi University. Discussion Paper no. 46.

National Council on Social Security, Japan. 2008. *The interim report.* (In Japanese.)

Palmer, E. 2003. Pension reform in Sweden. In *Taste of pie: Searching for better pension provisions in developed countries,* ed. N. Takayama, Chapter 7. Tokyo: Maruzen, Ltd.

Settergren, O. 2001. The automatic balance mechanism of the Swedish pension system. Available at: www.rfv.se.

Takayama, N. 1998. *The morning after in Japan: Its declining population, too generous pensions and a weakened economy.* Tokyo: Maruzen, Ltd.

———. 2003. Pension arrangements in the oldest country: The Japanese case. In *Taste of pie: Searching for better pension provisions in developed countries,* ed. N. Takayama, Chapter 5. Tokyo: Maruzen, Ltd.

———. 2004. Changes in the pension system. *Japan Echo* 31 (5): 9–12.

———. 2008. Japanese responses to the aging society. In *Social policy at a crossroads,* ed. S. H. Lee, A. Mason, and K. E. Sul, 147–69. KDI Press.

———. 2009. Pension coverage in Japan. In *Closing the coverage gap,* ed. R. Holzmann, D. A. Robalino, and N. Takayama, 111–18. Washington, DC: World Bank.

Takayama, N., and H. Miyake. 2008. Shifting the basic pension to a tax-financed pension in Japan: A rough estimate. PIE/CIS Discussion Paper no. 386, July. (In Japanese.)

Comment   Worawan Chandoevwit

Takayama's chapter describes pension reforms and financial performance of pension systems in Japan. The chapter explains details of pension reform in 2004, assuming that readers have some background on the Japanese pension system and contemporary disputes on the reforms. It is worth clarifying the pension system in Japan as it is unique and helps readers understand this chapter easily. Therefore, in this comment, I will elaborate more on pension systems in Japan and discuss policy options.

For social security (pension and health care) administrative purposes, residents of Japan aged between twenty and sixty are grouped into three categories as follows.

Category I: Self-employed, students, and all registered residents aged twenty to sixty years excluding categories II and III. About 30 percent of the insured population are in this category.

Category II: Salaried employees in the private sector, central and local government employees, and private school teachers and employees in private schools. Over 50 percent of the insured population are in this category.

Category III: Dependent spouse of category II (aged twenty to sixty).

Japan also has a separate occupation based on social insurance system for seamen because they do not fall into these three categories.

The public pension system in Japan can be characterized as a universal and defined benefit system. Pension is composed of *basic pension* (or National Pension) and *income-related pension*.

National Pension (Kokumin Nenkin) is operated by municipalities and is called a regional-based pension. Everybody is entitled to basic pension, provided that they have paid premium for a certain period. The system is called a Pay-As-You-Go (PAYGO) flat rate benefit system. The pension includes five types of benefits: old-age, disability, survivor, widow, and death benefit. Those who receive disability basic pension or public assistance are exempted from paying contribution. Students and low income workers can postpone their contribution for some periods. An important issue of the National Pension is its coverage. Because of the aging population, the number of working age population who distrust the public pension system has increased. In 2002, the number of delinquent contributors rose by 8.3 mil-

Worawan Chandoevwit is the research director of the Thailand Development Research Institute.

lion. The system could include only 62.8 percent of eligible population in the program. In other words, the delinquency ratio was 37.2 percent (in figure 5.1 of this chapter). The ratio dropped by a few percentage points after that year. The situation was improved by a few more percentage points after the 2004 reform.

Income-related pension is mandatory for employees in companies with five or more employees, public employees, and teachers and employees in private schools. Basic pension and income-related pension for private employees are jointly operated (called Employees' Pension Insurance, Kosei Nenkin Hoken, or KNH) and a single contribution rate is paid by employee and employer. The Employees' Pension Insurance covers employees and spouse (insured persons in categories II and III). The joint basic pension and income-related pension for public employees and teachers and employees in private schools are operated by the National Government Employees' Mutual Aid Association, Local Government Employees' Mutual Aid Association, and Private School Teachers and Employees' Mutual Aid Association. Pension schemes for private employees, public employees, and private school teachers are unified. As described by the author, this public pension system currently faces many challenges: a persistent deficit in the income statement, huge excess liabilities in the balance sheet, and heavy burden of contribution.

Population forecast by Japan's National Institute for Population and Social Security Research (IPSS) implies that the Japanese pension systems will become more seriously unhealthy. Figure 5C.1 shows that each of young Japanese will have to bear the burden from at least one elderly in 2050. The government will no longer commit an expansion of the old-age pension benefit. There are serious questions about whether the system will be financially sustained.

The author mentions five policy options that have been discussed in Japan: privatization of earning-related pension, a move to a fully-funded plan, the use of tax revenue to finance basic pension, a move to notional defined contribution, and an introduction of a minimum guaranteed pension. It should be noted that extension of retirement age beyond sixty-five is not an option, although life expectancy among Japanese is longer than other nations. Moreover, the option of taxing pension income has been overlooked.

From the discussion, it is not quite clear which part of pension schemes should be changed to fully-funded, the basic pension or the earning-related pension or both. One alternative would be to change the earning-related pension to a fully-funded defined contribution system and the basic pension to the minimum guaranteed pension. This means that the options do not have to be mutually exclusive.

It is quite interesting to see that an earmarked consumption tax has been proposed to be an alternative source for financing basic pension. If financed by general tax revenue, the basic pension holds the principle of income redis-

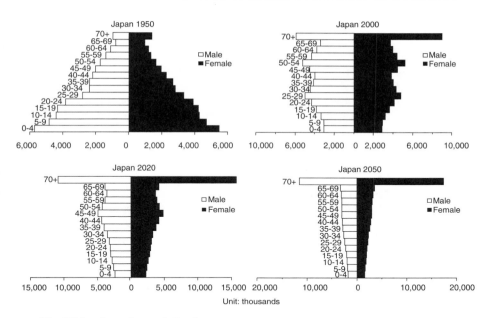

Fig. 5C.1   Japan's population by age group
Source: IPSS (www.ipss.go.jp/site-ad/TopPageData/p_age2.xls, accessed January 30, 2007).

tribution. Consumption tax is regressive in nature. It hurts the poor more than the rich. Additional consumption tax increase may increase the number of poor elderly in Japan. Then, new social issues will arise.

The Japanese pension reform is all about the intergeneration share of "pie." Looking at the balance sheet, we learn that the piece of pie the old will have is getting smaller and smaller. But, the number of old will be larger. The young will have to share their pie with the old. This is not easy since the author shows that the 2004 reform made the present value of future benefits account for only 80 percent of the present value of future contribution. The question is how to make the young willing to share their pie with the old when they are not sure that the number of their offspring will not be large enough to make a big pie that is shareable?

Comment   Hyungpyo Moon

In his excellent chapter, Professor Takayama provides very comprehensive reviews and appraisals of the current pension issues in Japan from the per-

Hyungpyo Moon is director of the Economic Information and Education Center of the Korea Development Institute.

spectives of financial sustainability and distributional equity. In particular, he analyzes lucidly the contributions and limitations of the 2004 Pension Reform in Japan using the ingenuous balance sheet approach, which enables separate accounting of past pension liabilities from future ones. He goes further to outline a possible new pension reform option that could be more sustainable and incentive-compatible.

As described in the chapter, the 2004 pension reform's major target is to make the pension plans—both earnings-related pension (KNH) and basic pension—more sustainable in a super-aged society. The KNH achieved this goal through a substantial increase in contribution rate as well as reduction in benefit levels. The contribution rate will increase gradually from 13.59 percent in 2004 to 18.30 percent in 2017. Benefits will be lowered automatically by introducing the built-in stabilizer to neutralize demographic factors, which is equivalent to the negative benefit adjustment of approximately 0.9 percentage point per year. By this measure, the average income replacement rate of the KNH is projected to decline by 9.1 percentage points during the next twenty years. Reduction schedule will be halted in 2023, so that the average replacement rate does not fall below the 50 percent level.

The KNH reform in 2004 will undoubtedly enhance its financial stability. However, it is still questionable whether the reform fully recovers the plan's longer-term financial sustainability. If the contribution rate will be fixed after 2017 and benefit levels will be fixed after 2023, what will happen after 2023? There is no doubt that population aging in Japan will continue even after 2023. According the projections, old-age dependency rate is expected to go up as high as 40 percent in 2052, due to both increased longevity and low fertility. This trend will inevitably create financial shortage problems even after 2023, despite the recent reform.

Even if both contribution rate and benefit level are fixed, we can still maintain the plan's financial balance by adjusting the minimum pensionable age. But my question is whether the minimum replacement rate target of 50 percent is really the "Masino line" to guarantee social adequacy. The 2004 reform promised that the KNH replacement rate will not fall below the 50 percent level for the full participants. However, many developed countries provide less generous public pension benefits and complement the inadequacy through fostering corporate/individual annuity markets. As almost all the KNH participants in Japan receive corporate level retirement benefits, the total replacement rate can still be high despite the KNH benefit cut. In addition, increasing the role of private pensions will strengthen the prefunding of the entire old-age income security system, thereby making the entire system less vulnerable (more sustainable) to demographic changes. Considering this, it seems to me that setting the "adequacy" target for the old-age income security system as a whole, rather than for the public pension provision only, may be more effective.

Professor Takayama proposes that the NHK be converted to the notional defined contribution (NDC) plan to make the plan more sustainable and more incentive-compatible. This can be done by separating the past liabilities—or legacy debt—and financing them through the increase in consumption tax. My second question is whether the NDC is really incentive-compatible or actuarially fair. A shift to the NDC will increase the marginal linkage between contributions and benefits conceptually: "Every dollar counts in the NDC," as Takayama puts it. However, the NDC is still a PAYGO system, and vulnerable to demographic changes. While the unfunded defined benefit plans often neutralize the negative impacts of demographic changes by adjusting the benefit levels, the NDC does this by adjusting the internal rate of return: that is, the rate of return applied to the NDC—notional rate of return—is a function of aging factors as well as wage growth rate. Hence, increasing longevity and low fertility will inevitably lower the notional rate of return. In this case, people still can compare the rate of return on the NDC with those of other financial portfolios to find out the NDC is not attractive (actuarially fair) anyhow.

Another question is whether tax financing of the past KNH liabilities is socially equitable. As mentioned in the chapter, the past liabilities are "sunk costs" and can be financed by tax revenues. An introduction of the earmarked consumption tax will not only reduce the deadweight loss, as it is more broadly-based than income taxes, but it will also increase intergenerational equity as the old generations will share the burden. However, the KNH plan is for the employees only, excluding nonemployees. In this case, tax financing of the KNH legacy debt will inevitably result in transfers from nonemployees to employees, and thereby creating intragenerational inequity.

My final question is whether a shift to the funded defined contribution (FDC) plan cannot be an option in Japan. From the perspectives of financial sustainability and intergenerational equity, the effective countermeasure to depopulation would be a transition from the conventional PAYGO system to a funded system. Sweden, for example, recently introduced the mandated FDC with 2.5 percent of contribution rate to supplement the NDC. Is it impossible for Japan to introduce the FDC partially together with a shift to the NDC? If the "double taxation burden" problem matters, is it impossible to spread the burden intertemporally through a proper mixture of tax financing and debt financing?

Professor Takayama also proposes that the current basic pension be shifted to a noncontributory universal pension, instead of increasing government's matching subsidy to the basic pension as in the 2004 reform. I agree that this shift could solve the noncompliance problem, and improve both efficiency (by utilizing more broadly-based consumption tax) and equity (by making the system more progressive). In spite of that, one thing we should take into consideration from the perspective of financial burden is the rapid population aging in Japanese society. The significant demographic changes in the future signal that there will be a tremendous increase in financial burden when a universal noncontributory basic pension is introduced and the consumption tax rate will have to increase to a substantial degree, thereby reducing economic efficiency.

6

The Effects of Demographic Change on Public Education in Japan

Fumio Ohtake and Shinpei Sano

6.1   Introduction

Many developed countries are experiencing the population aging. Japan is one of the countries experiencing such aging at the most rapid pace. According to the Japanese census, the percentage of elderly over the age of sixty-five increased to 17.3 percent in 2000 from 7.1 percent in 1970. Furthermore, the Institute for Social Security and Population Research estimated that the ratio would reach 31.8 percent in 2030.

How does population aging affect the structure of government expenditure? Median voter theory indicates that the preference of the median voter determines the size of government expenditure. If the elderly become median voters, government expenditure such as social security and medical services, which is directly related to the elderly, will be increased. On the other hand, government expenditure such as education, which is not directly related to the elderly, will be decreased by the aging of median voters. In particular, the local governments in Japan will be affected by this problem since the share of their expenditure on education as well as medical and social welfare is high. Thus, it is expected that the government expenditure on education will be decreased by the increase in the share of the elderly in the population.

However, the elderly may support the government's decision to increase

Fumio Ohtake is a professor at the Institute of Social and Economic Research, Osaka University. Shinpei Sano is an assistant professor at the Graduate School of Economics, Kobe University.

The authors thank Takatoshi Ito, Daeil Kim, Ronald Lee, Chang-Gyun Park, Andrew Rose, and an anonymous referee for invaluable comments and suggestions. We also thank Atsushi Morimoto for excellent research assistance.

expenditure on education. Poterba (1997, 1998) pointed out several possibilities. First, the elderly may have a long time horizon with regard to decision making and voting. Expenditure on education is beneficial to the old as well as the young generations in the long run, because monetary transfer from the young to the old generations may be increased by the growth in productivity caused by the increase in educational investment.

Second, the elderly may have an altruistic preference. The utility of the elderly will be increased by the increase in investment on education to their grandchildren or by the increase in consumption of their grandchildren by productivity growth caused by investment on education if they have an altruistic preference toward their children.

Third, an increase in government expenditure on education may indirectly benefit the elderly. The increase in expenditure on education by a local government may raise the land prices in that area because the quality of education would be higher in that area. If most of the elderly own real estate, they would benefit from the increase in land prices. Moreover, the elderly may benefit by the reduction in the crime rate caused by the socialization effects of better education.

Fourth, Tiebout sorting (voting by foot) also affects the relationship between population aging and education expenditure by the government. If a local government imposes higher taxes for better education, the elderly who oppose the increase in taxes would shift to other areas. In this sense, the share of the elderly and education expenditure in the local area are simultaneously determined. Thus, the effects of aging on the change in government expenditure on compulsory education can be regarded as an empirical problem.

Although issues on education have recently attracted public attention in Japan, most of the discussions are not based on empirical research. It is important to analyze the effects of population aging on public expenditure on compulsory education in order to discuss the role of the government in providing education. In particular, this analysis is important in Japan because Japan is the most rapidly aging society. Figure 6.1 shows the time series change in the ratio of people over the age of sixty-five in selected countries. Among the developed countries, although the ratio of the elderly in Japan was relatively low in the 1980s, it rapidly increased from the late 1980s to the 1990s. In 2000, the ratio of the elderly in Japan was the highest among four countries. It is expected that Japanese society will face a higher rate of population aging in the future.

Citing the results of Hoxby (1998), Poterba (1998) pointed that the correlation between the ratio of the elderly and government education expenditure, which was positive in the early 1900s, has recently become negative. However, Poterba (1998) did not empirically test the hypothesis and merely speculated that this change in the sign of the relationship had been caused by the increase in nuclear families.

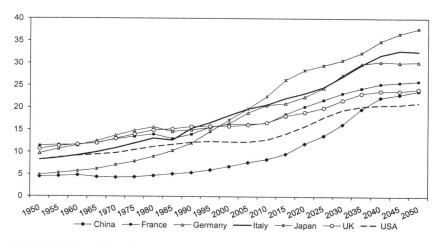

Fig. 6.1   Share of people at the age of sixty-five and over in selected countries
Source: "Population Statistics 2007," National Institute of Population and Social Security Research.

Japan is an ideal testing field for conducting empirical research on the relationship between population aging and public education expenditure. This is because the country recently experienced rapid population aging and a drastic change in household structures—namely, from extended families to nuclear families.

In this chapter, we analyze the effects of population aging on the public expenditure on compulsory education using prefectural panel data from 1975 to 2005 in Japan. The results of the chapter are summarized as follows. The higher ratio of the elderly increased the per-student public expenditure on compulsory education before the 1980s; however, it decreased the per-student public expenditure on compulsory education after the 1990s. Since the elderly began to live independently from their children who are old enough to receive compulsory education, they may have become less concerned about public expenditure on compulsory education. However, the reversal cannot be explained by the change in the living arrangements of the elderly in our analysis. We speculate that the change was caused by the change in the subsidy system on compulsory education from the national government to the local governments.

This chapter is structured as follows. In section 6.2 we review previous research. In section 6.3 we describe the estimation models and the data for empirical analysis. The estimation results and the explanation that the aging population had different effects on the expenditure on compulsory education between the 1980s and the 1990s are presented in section 6.4. In section 6.5 we examine the effects of the changes in the living arrangements of the elderly on the level of public expenditure on compulsory education both in the 1980s and 1990s. In section 6.6 we summarize the results and note the problems for future research.

6.2   Previous Research

First, we review the theoretical background on the relationship between population aging and the size of government expenditure on compulsory education. According to the median voter theory, the size of government expenditure is determined by the preference of median voters. Person and Tabellini (2000) and Gradstein, Justman, and Meier (2005) show that the preference for public expenditure on the education of voters should be single-peaked with income for the existence of a voting equilibrium. Intuitively, this condition implies that the demand for public expenditure on education monotonically increases with an increase in income (Oberndorfer and Steiner 2006). The aging of median voters increases the public expenditure on goods and services that are demanded by the elderly. If the elderly do not wish to support an increase in public expenditure on compulsory education, population aging decreases the government expenditure on education.[1]

Poterba (1997, 1998) pointed out the possibility of a positive correlation between the size of public expenditure on compulsory education and population aging. The elderly support the increase in government expenditure on compulsory education if they are altruistic toward the younger generation or if they are indirectly benefited by the appreciation of land prices, reduction in the crime rate, and increase in future productivity owing to an increase in the expenditure on compulsory education. Thus, because of theoretical ambiguity, the relationship between population aging and expenditure on compulsory education is an empirical problem.

In Europe and the United States, empirical research on the relationship between population aging and government expenditure on compulsory education has been accumulated. Poterba (1997, 1998) analyzed the impact of population aging on government expenditure on compulsory education (K through 12) using state-level panel data from 1961 to 1991 in the United States. According to his estimation results, a 1 percent increase in the ratio of the elderly—aged at least sixty-five years—reduces the per-student public expenditure on education by about 0.26 percent.

Harris, Evans, and Schwab (2001) estimated the relation using school

---

1. Even parents of school-age kids would be against public expenditure if the private sector can do it better. This might be true for high income parents who send their kids to private school. However, the percentage of pupils in private school in compulsory education is very low in Japan. Of elementary school pupils, 99.0 percent went to public school and of junior high school students, 93.5 percent went to public school in 2004. Sugimoto and Nakagawa (2007) argued the role of public education on fertility during the industrialized process. They demonstrated the vicious cycle between population aging and the undersupply of public education in advanced economies.

district-level data for 1972, 1982, and 1992 because the population structure and education expenditure changed in school districts even if they
were located in the same state. The estimated negative effects of the ratio
of the elderly on education expenditure are smaller than those obtained
by Poterba—there is a negative correlation between population aging and
education expenditure.

Ladd and Murray (2001) conducted research using the county-level data
for 1970, 1980, and 1990 in the United States. Their results reveal that the
impact of the ratio of the elderly on education expenditure by the government is not statistically significant.

Using individual cross-section data, Rubinfeld (1977) indicated that the
elderly do not tend to vote for policies that increase the expenditure on
education. Based on household data, Brunner and Balsdon (2004) examined whether respondents agree with hypothetical educational policies at the
national and regional levels. They reveal that the elderly tend to support
an increase in government expenditure on education at the regional rather
than the national level. However, they do not identify the reason for the preference of the elderly for local government education expenditure—whether
the elderly wish to raise the local land price or if they have an altruistic
preference toward the young generation.

Using the state-level data from 1990 to 2002 in Switzerland, Grob and
Wolter (2005) found that an increase in the ratio of the elderly (retired) decreases the per-student expenditure on compulsory education (elementary
and junior high school). They also showed that the effects of the decrease
in public expenditure on education caused by the increase in the ratio of
the elderly are greater than those caused by the decrease in the number of
students.[2]

By contrast, no study has been conducted on the relationship between
population aging and government expenditure on education in Japan. Although Doi (1998a, 1998b) empirically examined the median voting theory
using Japanese data, he analyzed the determinants of the size of overall
public expenditure rather than categorizing public expenditure such as education.

This chapter is the first attempt to examine the effects of aging on government expenditure on education in Japan. Japan is an ideal testing field for
analyzing this problem because it has experienced a rapid change in both
population and household structures in the last three decades.

Hoxby (1998) indicated a positive correlation between the ratio of the
elderly and government expenditure in the early 1900s in the United States.
She also revealed that the correlation gradually changed from positive to

---

2. Oberndorfer and Steiner (2006) examined the effects of political variables on higher education in Germany. They found that leftist governments increase education expenditure.

negative in the nineteenth century. Goldin and Katz (1998) showed the same change of correlation between population aging and public expenditure on higher education.

Poterba (1998) conjectured that the change of correlation between the elderly and public expenditure on education was caused by the trend toward nuclear families, although he did not empirically examine the hypothesis.

Because there is a growing trend toward nuclear families in the last three decades in Japan as well as a rapid increase in the ratio of the elderly, we are able to test the effects of population aging as well as the change in the household structure on public expenditure on education.

6.3   Empirical Analysis

6.3.1   The Fiscal System of Public Education in Japan

In Japan, there is a substantial variation in the per-student government expenditure on compulsory education among local governments because the cost of compulsory education is borne both by the central and local governments. The subsidy system from the national government to local governments for the costs of compulsory education is as follows.

The number of classes and teachers are determined by the Compulsory Education Standards Law. The law stipulates the maximum number of students per class as forty from 1998 (forty-five from 1968 to 1997). The national treasury burdens of compulsory education costs subsidizes local governments for the half the cost of the compensations for teachers including lump sum retirement allowance, mutual aid benefit (social security benefit for teachers), travel expenses, and education materials if the number of teachers is determined by the Compulsory Education Standards Law. After the introduction of this subsidy system in 1952, the Japanese government increased the amount of subsidy to local governments for compulsory education costs in order to equalize the national level of the quality of education. The Japanese government's equalization policy for the quality of education changed the relationship between per pupil education costs and the financial capability of the local government. According to Kariya (2006), a positive correlation existed between the per pupil costs of public elementary school and the financial capability index of the local governments in 1965; however, this correlation changed to negative in 2003.

From 1985, the subsidy for compensation for teachers has been gradually reduced. In 1985, the Japanese government discontinued subsidies to the local governments for the costs of education material and travel expenses. From 1986, the subsidies for the costs of social security benefits and the lump sum retirement allowance for teachers have been gradually reduced. The subsidy for the costs of lump sum retirement allowance was abolished in 1993, and the subsidy for the costs of social security benefits for teachers was abolished in 2003. From 2006, the subsidy for the salary of teachers from the national government to local governments was reduced from one-half to one-third of the total salary of the teachers.

At the same time, the discretionary power of local governments on compulsory education has been increased. Until 2003, the local governments were not able to reduce the class size below forty students per class. Although this restriction was lifted in 2003, the national government did not subsidize the salaries of teachers that exceeded the standard number of teachers determined by the standard class size of forty pupils.

Prefectural governments have discretionary power on hiring of teachers. Municipal governments were not able to hire full-time teachers for municipal elementary and junior high schools by their own financial resources because the prefectural boards of education appointed teachers for municipal schools and prefectures bore the salary for the teachers of municipal schools.[3] Except for the hiring of the teachers, municipal governments can determine the size of expenditure on educational costs such as costs for educational materials, libraries, and travel in municipal schools from 1985.[4]

There are large differentials between standard financial needs for compulsory education—which determine the size of the local allocation tax grant for prefectures—and actual expenditure on the compulsory education by the prefectures. For example, the maximum value of the ratio of actual expenditure on educational materials for compulsory schools to the standard financial needs in the local allocation tax grant for prefectures was 163.7 percent in Tokyo and the minimum value of the ratio was 35.6 percent in Tokushima in 2003 (the average value was 75.7 percent).

As shown in figure 6.2, the subsidies for local governments on compulsory education had decreased in the 1980s and had been stable in the 1990s. On the contrary, by 1995, the expenditure of local governments on compulsory education continued to increase. Figure 6.3 shows the change in the educational costs per pupil by the national and local governments. From 1985, the per-student educational costs by local governments has been increasing. However, the subsidy from the national government gradually increased in the same period.

These changes in the fiscal system of compulsory education in Japan might have affected the expenditure of local governments on public education. As local governments increased the discretional power for determining the expenditure on compulsory education, the level of education costs was determined by political pressure.

---

3. This regulation was relaxed in the special zone for structural reform from 2002.

4. Although municipal level analysis would be desirable if municipal level data were available, we were not able to get municipal level data in this analysis. Thus, we use prefectural level data in this chapter. Prefectural level analysis can be justified because the share of labor cost is very high (about 75 percent from 1997 to 2005) in educational expenditure.

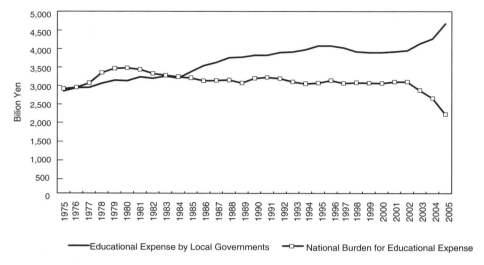

Fig. 6.2   Total expenditure on compulsory education by national and local governments
Note: Deflated by CPI in 2000.

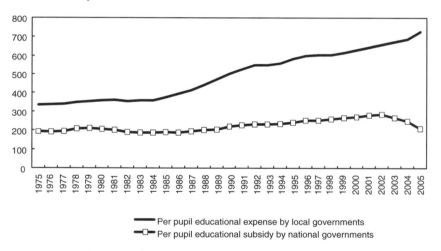

Fig. 6.3   Per pupil educational expense by national and local governments
Note: Deflated by CPI in 2000.

6.3.2   Estimation Model

Similar to Poterba (1997, 1998), we estimate the following model to test the effects of population aging.

$$Educ_{it} = \beta_1 OLD_{it} + \beta_2 KID_{it} + \beta_3 Income_{it} + \beta_4 Aid_{it}$$
$$+ \beta_5 Unemp_{it} + \beta_6 House_{it} + \beta_7 Urban_{it} + u_{it}$$

$$u_{it} = \tau_t + \alpha_i + \varepsilon_{it}.$$

The subscripts i and t stand for prefecture and time, respectively. Variable $Educ_{it}$ represents the per student compulsory education costs of prefecture i at time t. Similarly, OLD is the percentage of the elderly who are sixty-five years of age or above, and KID is the percentage of people old enough to receive compulsory school education in prefecture i at time t. These variables capture the demographic effects on public education costs.

In order to control for the effects of the subsidy from the central government, we added the per-student subsidy from the central government to the local government (Aid) to the estimation model. Variable House is the house ownership rate and it controls for the difference in the preference with regard to public expenditure on education between households with and without ownership of their houses. Variable Income is the per capita prefectural income; Unemp, the unemployment rate; and Urban, the percentage of people who live in urban areas. These variables capture the information on the income distribution of the prefectures. Variable u_{it} is the error term and it is assumed that the error term is decomposed to time effect (τ_t), prefecture fixed effect (α_i), and the idiosyncratic error (ε_{it}), with mean 0 and constant variance.

We are most interested in the coefficient of OLD in the estimation. If this coefficient is negative, we can interpret the situation as follows: the elderly support policies that directly benefit them because of their self-interest. On the other hand, if the coefficient of OLD is positive, we interpret the situation as follows: the elderly support the increase in public education either because they recognize the benefit of public education—since they are altruistic or long-term decision makers—or because their welfare will be raised by the decrease in crime rate and increase of land prices. However, we cannot identify the reasons that the elderly support the increase of public expenditure on compulsory education when the coefficient of OLD is positive in the estimation.

Let us discuss the other explanatory variables. The coefficient of KID is expected to be negative because the per-student public education costs would be reduced by an increase in the per capita number of children if the total government expenditure on education does not increase along with the number of children. The coefficient of House is expected to be positive because homeowners will benefit from the increase in land prices due to an increase in the quality of education. The coefficient of Income is expected to be positive since a higher income household would demand a higher level of education. The coefficient of Unemp is expected to be negative because people may prefer the strengthening of measures for unemployment to increasing the education quality when the unemployment rate is high. Variable Urban is expected to have a negative coefficient since people living in urban areas, where private schools are located, may prefer private schools to public ones.

We use the panel estimation method with prefectural fixed effects. This estimation method provides a consistent estimator when the unobserved prefectural factors are correlated with both education costs and demographic change.

Harris, Evans, and Schwab (2001) and Ladd and Murray (2001) pointed out that the ratio of the elderly might be endogenously determined. Under Tiebout sorting, if the elderly are self-interested, they may shift from the high-quality education area because of higher taxes. In this case, the estimated coefficients by ordinary least squares (OLS) are biased because the expenditure on compulsory education and the ratio of the elderly are simultaneously determined. To avoid this bias, we use the ratio of the elderly five years ago as an instrumental variable (IV). This variable is adequate as an IV because we can consider that the ratio of the elderly five years ago is independent from the current level of government expenditure on education.[5]

6.3.3   Data

We use prefectural panel data from 1975 to 2005 to estimate the model. Since we use the census survey that is conducted every five years, we use the prefectural panel data with a five-year interval. The definitions and sources of the data are as follows.

The amount of government expenditure on compulsory education is obtained from the "Survey of the Educational Costs by the Local Governments" (Ministry of Education, Culture, Sports, Science, and Technology [MEXT]). The costs include the expenditures on elementary and junior high schools paid by prefectures and municipalities. The numbers of students are obtained from the "Basic Survey on Schools" (MEXT). The per-student education costs are obtained by dividing the total expenditure on compulsory education by the number of students.

The ratio of the elderly aged sixty-five years or above (OLD) and the ratio of young people aged between five and fourteen years (KID) are calculated from "the Population Census" (Ministry of Internal Affairs and Communications [MIC]).

The per-student subsidy from the central government (Aid) is the amount of subsidy for compulsory education from the central government divided by the number of students ("Survey of the Educational Costs by the Local Governments").

The per capita prefectural income (Income) is the prefectural income ("Annual Report on Prefectural Accounts" [Cabinet Office]) divided by the prefectural population. The Prefectural Unemployment rates (Unemp) are calculated from the Population Census.

The house ownership rate (House) is taken from "The Housing and Land Survey" (MIC). This survey was conducted two years before the Population Census, which we use for the other variables. We use the ratio of population

---

5. Harris, Evans, and Schwab (2001) and Ladd and Murray (2001) reported that the estimation results by OLS and IV are similar.

in a densely inhabited district from the Population Census for the proxy of the degree of urbanization. We realized monetary variables by the consumer price index (CPI) in 2000. Since all the variables are logarithmically transformed, as in the previous research, the estimated coefficient implies elasticity. Table 6.1 shows the descriptive statistics of the variables.

Figure 6.4 shows the scatter plot between the per-student education costs (Educ) and the ratio of the elderly aged sixty-five years or above (OLD). Although there is positive correlation between Educ and OLD, this correlation might be caused by the other variables. For example, the prefectures that have a higher ratio of young people aged between five and fourteen years (KID) show the higher Educ because there is scale economy due to fixed costs in educational expenditure, as shown in figure 6.5.

Table 6.1   **Descriptive statistics**

Variable	Observations	Mean	Standard deviation	Min	Max
	1975–2005				
Per-pupil local educational expenditure	329	499.43	152.91	267.74	930.95
Population share of old (%)	329	14.53	5.00	5.27	27.09
Population share of kid (%)	329	13.11	2.60	7.54	20.55
Per-pupil subsidy	329	2,525.79	555.96	1,484.60	4,884.71
Per capita income	329	235.27	42.77	147.62	377.58
Unemployment rate (%)	329	3.64	1.64	1.23	11.85
House occupation rate (%)	329	67.83	8.89	39.44	85.73
Population density index	329	47.75	18.61	21.85	98.03
	1975–1985				
Per-pupil local educational expenditure	141	358.29	40.14	267.74	547.24
Population share of old (%)	141	10.29	2.10	5.27	15.32
Population share of kid (%)	141	15.60	1.10	12.72	20.55
Per-pupil subsidy	141	2,078.50	351.43	1,484.60	3,743.86
Per capita income	141	215.40	34.50	147.62	298.64
Unemployment rate (%)	141	2.70	1.17	1.23	8.09
House occupation rate (%)	141	68.66	9.76	39.44	85.73
Population density index	141	44.74	18.31	21.85	97.21
	1990–2005				
Per-pupil local educational expenditure	188	605.27	116.29	411.65	930.95
Population share of old (%)	188	17.71	4.10	8.28	27.09
Population share of kid (%)	188	11.24	1.66	7.54	16.93
Per-pupil subsidy	188	2,861.26	430.92	2,066.31	4,884.71
Per capita income	188	250.17	42.38	171.84	377.58
Unemployment rate (%)	188	4.36	1.59	1.73	11.85
House occupation rate (%)	188	67.21	8.16	39.59	84.88
Population density index	188	50.01	18.56	24.16	98.03

Source: "The Population Census" (Ministry of Internal Affairs and Communications).

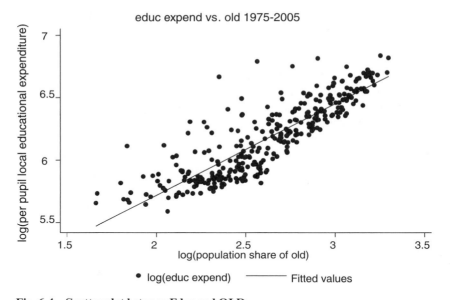

Fig. 6.4   Scatter plot between Educ and OLD

Note: This figure plots the relationship between the per-student education costs (Educ) and the ratio of the elderly aged sixty-five years or above (OLD) from 1975 to 2005.

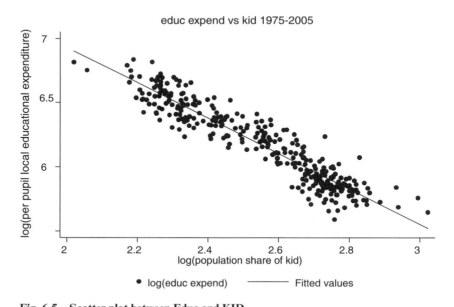

Fig. 6.5   Scatter plot between Educ and KID

Note: This figure plots the relationship between the per-student education costs (Educ) and the ratio of young people aged between five and fourteen years (KID) from 1975 to 2005.

6.4   Estimation Results

6.4.1   Base Model

Let us examine the estimation results of the effects of population aging on the per-student compulsory education costs. Table 6.2 reports the benchmark estimation results. Columns (1) to (3) in table 6.2 show the estimation results by OLS in specifications with and without the variables of unemployment rate and the ratio of population in a densely inhabited district.

The estimated coefficients of the ratio of the elderly by OLS are not statistically significant, although they are positive. However, the estimation results by OLS might be biased if the unobserved fixed effects are correlated with the explanatory variables. In order to check this possibility, we conducted the Breusch-Pagan and Hausman tests. First, the random effect model is supported between OLS and the random effect model by the Breusch-Pagan test. Second, the fixed effect model is supported between the fixed effect model and the random effect model by the Hausman test. Thus, we use the fixed effect model for estimation.

Figures in columns (4) to (6) in table 6.2 report the estimation results by the fixed effect model and show that the percentage of people aged sixty-five years or above significantly reduces the per-student public education costs.

Let us focus on other variables. The coefficient of the ratio of people below fifteen years of age is significantly negative. This implies that the increase in the ratio of people old enough to receive compulsory school education decreases the per-student compulsory education costs. The coefficient of per capita prefectural income, which denotes the income level of a household, is significantly positive. The amount of per-student subsidy for compulsory schools from the central government has a significant positive effect on the per-student compulsory school costs paid by the local governments. The estimated coefficient of the house ownership rate is significantly negative in the OLS; however, it is not significantly positive in the fixed effect estimation. The unemployment rate is not significant in the fixed effect estimation when we control the ratio of population in a densely inhabited district. The estimated coefficient of the ratio of population in a densely inhabited district is not significantly negative.

As shown in figure 6.1, Japan experienced rapid population aging in the 1990s, leading to the possibility of structural change in the relationship between population aging and the per-student education costs. Thus, we conducted the Chow test to test the stability of coefficients in the estimation period. Concretely speaking, we conducted the test for the structural change that occurred in the following years—1980, 1985, 1990, 1995, and 2000. The results are shown in table 6.3. According to this table, the null hypothesis of no structural change is rejected at the 5 percent significance level. We also

Table 6.2   Estimation results of the effects of the aging on per student public education costs

	1975–2005 (OLS) (1)	1975–2005 (OLS) (2)	1975–2005 (OLS) (3)	1975–2005 FE (4)	1975–2005 FE (5)	1975–2005 FE (6)
log(per-pupil educational cost)						
log(Population share of old)	0.0526	0.0394	0.00481	-0.118**	-0.119**	-0.129**
	(0.0336)	(0.0338)	(0.0376)	(0.0597)	(0.0599)	(0.0601)
log(Population share of kid)	-0.566***	-0.563***	-0.597***	-0.544***	-0.549***	-0.542***
	(0.0621)	(0.0628)	(0.0653)	(0.0700)	(0.0714)	(0.0714)
log(per capita income)	0.274***	0.213***	0.211***	0.132**	0.134**	0.140**
	(0.0531)	(0.0587)	(0.0575)	(0.0587)	(0.0592)	(0.0591)
log(per-pupil subsidy)	0.574***	0.585***	0.574***	0.194***	0.194***	0.186***
	(0.0399)	(0.0394)	(0.0381)	(0.0464)	(0.0466)	(0.0468)
log(Unemployment rate)	-0.197***	-0.266***	-0.313***	0.0292	0.0278	0.00374
	(0.0379)	(0.0427)	(0.0517)	(0.0807)	(0.0809)	(0.0822)
log(House occupation rate)		-0.0478***	-0.0436***		-0.00795	-0.00429
		(0.0160)	(0.0164)		(0.0246)	(0.0246)
log(Population density index)			-0.0419**			-0.0856
			(0.0192)			(0.0547)
Constant	2.958***	3.707***	4.299***	5.417***	5.424***	5.842***
	(0.634)	(0.690)	(0.715)	(0.699)	(0.701)	(0.748)
Observations	329	329	329	329	329	329
R²	0.964	0.964	0.965	0.984	0.984	0.984
Number of pref	47	47	47	47	47	47
Year effect	Yes	Yes	Yes	Yes	Yes	Yes

Note: Figures in parentheses are standard errors. FE = fixed effects.

***Significant at the 1 percent level.

**Significant at the 5 percent level.

*Significant at the 10 percent level.

Table 6.3   **Tests for structural change**

Structural break point	F-statistics	P-value
1980	1.06	0.39
1985	1.73	0.08
1990	2.09	0.03
1995	3.35	> 0.001
2000	4.82	> 0.001

Note: The Chow test was used to test the structural change that occurred between the first and second years' statistics.

conducted a sequential test for structural change using the yearly panel data from 1975 to 2005, eliminating those variables that are only available at five-year intervals—for instance, the housing ownership and unemployment rates. In the sequential test for structural change, we test the possibility of structural change for every year. First, we conduct the Chow test to test the structural change that occurred between the first and second years. Second, we examine the change that occurred between the second and third years, and so on. We infer that the structural change occurred in the year that takes the maximum value of F (test statistic). According to appendix figures 6A.1 and 6A.2, which present the results of the sequential tests for structural change (Chow tests and cumulative sum [CUSUM] test, respectively), we can infer that the structural change occurred around 1993. We estimated the model using a separated sample period because the effect of population aging on public education costs may have changed between the 1980s and 1990s, according to the results of the structural change.

Table 6.4 reports the results of the fixed effect estimation using the separated sample periods—the sample before 1985 and after 1990. Table 6.4 shows that the estimated coefficients of the ratio of the elderly are significantly positive when we use the sample before 1985. The coefficient changes to significantly negative when we use the sample of the 1990s. The estimated coefficients of other variables do not change between the 1980s and 1990s.

Figure 6.6 plots the relationship between the log of the per-student education costs (Educ) and the ratio of the elderly aged sixty-five years or above (OLD), after adjusting for KID, Aid, Income, Unemp, House, and prefectural fixed effects from 1975 to 2005. There is negative relationship between Educ and OLD if we adjust other explanatory variables as shown in column (1) of table 6.4. Figures 6.7 and 6.8 are scatter plots for divided samples for 1975 to 1985 and 1990 to 2005, corresponding to columns (2) and (3) of table 6.4. These figures show that the relationship between Educ and OLD changed from negative to positive after 1990. In sum, similar to the case observed by Poterba (1997) in the United States, population aging decreased the per-student compulsory education costs in the 1990s in Japan.

Table 6.4   **Estimation results of the effects of aging on per-student public education costs based on the divided sample periods**

log(per-pupil educational cost)	1975–2005 FE (1)	1975–1985 FE (2)	1990–2005 FE (3)
log(Population share of old)	−0.129**	0.315*	−0.495***
	(0.0601)	(0.174)	(0.116)
log(Population share of kid)	−0.542***	−0.593***	−0.775***
	(0.0714)	(0.126)	(0.167)
log(per capita income)	0.140**	0.255**	0.151*
	(0.0591)	(0.112)	(0.0895)
log(per-pupil subsidy)	0.186***	0.332***	0.124**
	(0.0468)	(0.0972)	(0.0565)
log(Unemployment rate)	0.00374	0.212	−0.0717
	(0.0822)	(0.133)	(0.197)
log(House occupation rate)	−0.00429	−0.0789	0.0255
	(0.0246)	(0.0581)	(0.0440)
log(Population density index)	−0.0856	−0.0523	−0.0681
	(0.0547)	(0.118)	(0.114)
Constant	5.842***	2.423*	8.527***
	(0.748)	(1.387)	(1.407)
Observations	329	141	188
Number of pref	47	47	47
R^2	0.984	0.770	0.963
Year effect	Yes	Yes	Yes

Notes: Figures in parentheses are standard errors. FE = fixed effects.
***Significant at the 1 percent level.
**Significant at the 5 percent level.
*Significant at the 10 percent level.

6.4.2   Estimation Results by IV

If voting by foot works, the elderly would shift from the regions where they have to pay higher taxes to finance higher costs for public education. In this case, the ratio of the elderly and the public education costs are simultaneously determined and the ratio of the elderly should be considered as an endogenous variable in the estimation. Harris, Evans, and Schwab (2001) and Ladd and Murray (2001) used the ratio of the elderly in previous census as an IV for the current ratio of the elderly. Since the current level of government expenditure on compulsory education does not affect the percentage of the elderly five years earlier, the ratio satisfies the conditions of an IV. Therefore, we use the ratio of the elderly five years earlier as an IV. Moreover, we estimate the model using the divided samples of the 1980s and 1990s.

Estimation results by IV are shown in table 6.5. The ratio of the elderly does not have a significant effect on the per-student government expenditure on compulsory education, either in the entire sample period nor in the

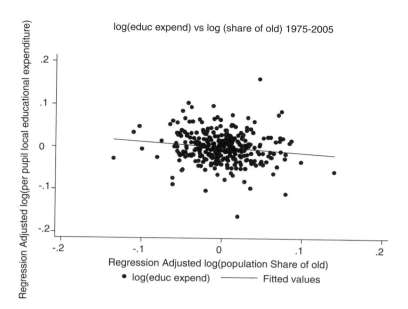

Fig. 6.6   Scatter plot between Educ and OLD after regression adjusted from 1975 to 2005

Note: This figure plots the relationship between the per-student education costs (Educ) and the ratio of the elderly aged sixty-five years or above (OLD), after adjusting for KID, Aid Income, Unemp, House, and prefectural fixed effects from 1975 to 2005.

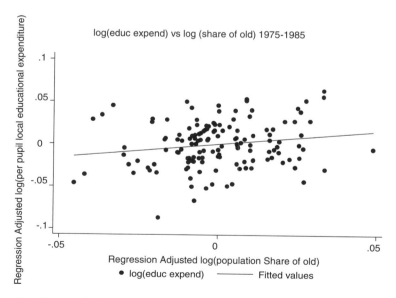

Fig. 6.7   Scatter plot between Educ and OLD after regression adjusted from 1975 to 1985

Note: This figure plots the relationship between the per-student education costs (Educ) and the ratio of the elderly aged sixty-five years or above (OLD), after adjusting for KID, Aid, Income, Unemp, House, and prefectural fixed effects from 1975 to 1985.

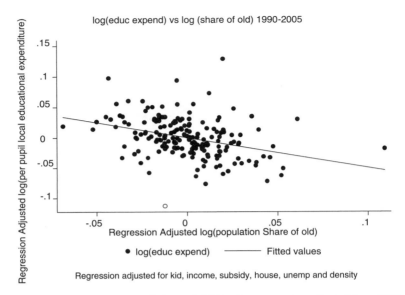

Fig. 6.8   Scatter plot between Educ and OLD after regression adjusted from 1990 to 2005

Note: This figure plots the relationship between the per-student education costs (Educ) and the ratio of the elderly aged sixty-five years or above (OLD), after adjusting for KID, Aid, Income, Unemp, House, and prefectural fixed effects from 1990 to 2005.

1980s. However, similar to the OLS results in table 6.4, the ratio of the elderly significantly decreases the per-student compulsory education costs in the sample of the 1990s when we use the IV method that provides the consistent estimator shown in table 6.5.

These results imply that the elderly in Japan have become self-interested since the 1990s and that population aging decreases the per-student compulsory school costs. The results obtained in Japan in the 1990s are similar to those obtained by Poterba (1997) and Harris, Evans, and Schwab (2001) in the United States and by Grob and Wolter (2005) in Switzerland.

Demographic change has both negative and positive effects on public education costs. The increase in the ratio of the elderly population decreases the per-student public education costs because of political pressure from the elderly. On the other hand, the decrease in the ratio of children old enough to receive compulsory education increases the per-student public education costs because of the adjustment costs for changing the number of teachers and consolidating schools. What are the net effects of the demographic change on public education costs?

According to table 6.5, the 1 percent increase in the ratio of the elderly decreases the per-student education costs by around 0.6 percent. The 1 per-

Table 6.5   **Estimation results using IV**

log(per pupil educational cost)	1975–2005 FEIV (1)	1975–1985 FEIV (2)	1990–2005 FEIV (3)
log(Population share of old)	–0.0421	0.321	–0.599***
	(0.0700)	(0.246)	(0.150)
log(Population share of kid)	–0.514***	–0.592***	–0.795***
	(0.0725)	(0.128)	(0.169)
log(per capita income)	0.148**	0.255**	0.125
	(0.0595)	(0.112)	(0.0929)
log(per pupil subsidy)	0.192***	0.331***	0.117**
	(0.0470)	(0.101)	(0.0570)
log(Unemployment rate)	–0.0373	0.210	0.0133
	(0.0841)	(0.142)	(0.212)
log(House occupation rate)	–0.00313	–0.0794	0.0209
	(0.0247)	(0.0596)	(0.0444)
log(Population density index)	–0.0767	–0.0513	–0.0746
	(0.0550)	(0.121)	(0.114)
Constant	5.619***	2.419*	8.504***
	(0.756)	(1.393)	(1.428)
First stage			
log(Population share of old 5 yrs ago)	0.832***	0.623***	0.981***
	(0.030)	(0.068)	(0.070)
F-statistics	776.76	84.84	196.83
Partial R^2	0.743	0.500	0.600
Observations	329	141	188
Number of pref	47	47	47
Year effect	Yes	Yes	Yes

Note: Figures in parentheses are standard errors.
***Significant at the 1 percent level.
**Significant at the 5 percent level.
*Significant at the 10 percent level.

cent decrease in the ratio of children old enough to receive compulsory education increases the per-student education costs by around 0.8 percent. According to the population projections by the National Institute of Population and Social Security Research of the Japanese government, the ratio of the population of children old enough to receive compulsory school attendance will decrease by 29.7 percent from 2005 to 2030, and the ratio of the population of the elderly who are sixty-five years or above will increase by 57.4 in the same period. Consequently, the net effect of the demographic change will be a 10.2 percent decrease in the per-student public education costs: per-student education costs will be increased by 23.8 percent through the decrease in the number of children and will be decreased by 34.4 percent through the increase in the population of the elderly.

6.5   Why Did the Effects of Demographics on Public Education Change in the 1990s?

What caused the change from no correlation in the 1980s to a negative relation in the 1990s in the effects of the ratio of the elderly on the per-student compulsory education costs? Let us examine several possibilities.

First, the disposition of the elderly in Japan might have changed from altruistic to self-interested or from being short-term to long-term decision makers around the 1990s. However, the following question then arises: why did the preferences of the elderly change in the 1990s?

Second, the change in the voting rates might have affected the relationship between the ratio of the elderly and public education costs. Recently, voting rates have been decreasing in Japan. Moreover, the percentage of young voters has dropped, although that of the elderly is stable. Thus, the political power of the elderly has been strengthened more than expected as a result of the demographic change. This change in voting behavior by age group might have enabled the elderly to acquire political power and implement policies that are beneficial to them.

Third, the change in the household structure might cause the change in the effects of population aging on public education costs. It is expected that elderly people became self-interested and no longer focused on children and grandchildren because the percentage of the elderly living independently from their children increased, while the percentage of the elderly living with their children and grandchildren as extended family members decreased. The estimation results of Hoxby (1998) also indicate that the effects of aging on public education changed from positive in the early 1900s to negative in the 1990s. Poterba (1998) speculated that this reversal of the effects of population aging on public education costs was caused by the increase in the ratio of the elderly who lived independently. If the elderly have children or grandchildren old enough to receive compulsory education within the same household, they are interested in public education and understand its importance. However, they would prefer policies that are more directly beneficial to them than to public education if they live independently from their children.

Fourth, the change in the effects of the coefficient of the ratio of the elderly on public education costs might not be caused by the change in the preference of the elderly with regard to education. Rather, it might be caused by the change in the public finance system of local governments, as explained in section 6.3.1.

In Japan, the ratio of three-generation families has decreased, while the ratio of single-member families of the elderly has increased. These changes in the family structure might affect the attitudes of the elderly toward public education.

In this section, we analyze the effects of the change in the family structure

Table 6.6   **Change of household structure (national average: %)**

	Population share of old	Household share of three-generation family	Household share of nuclear family	Household share of elderly family
1975	9.05	21.99	67.48	5.92
1980	10.25	18.68	58.21	5.84
1985	11.56	17.82	57.95	7.46
1990	13.58	15.95	57.72	9.68
1995	16.31	13.80	57.08	12.33
2000	19.15	11.41	57.26	15.27
2005	21.79	9.45	57.11	18.41

Source: "The Population Census" (Ministry of Internal Affairs and Communications).

on compulsory education. We used the ratios of three-generation families, nuclear families, and single-member families from the census as the explanatory variables of household structure. Table 6.6 presents the change in the ratios of the family structure variables. During the last three decades, the percentage of single-member families of the elderly has increased, while that of three-generation families has decreased, as shown in table 6.6. Thus, the Japanese elderly began to live independently from their children when they were old enough to receive compulsory education.

Table 6.7 provides the estimation results for the models, including the share of single-member households of the elderly as an explanatory variable to test the effect of the change in the living arrangements of the elderly on public education. Columns (1) to (3) show the results of the fixed effect models for the entire sample, the sample of the 1980s, and the sample of the 1990s, respectively. Columns (4) to (6) show the results of IV estimation for the same sample periods. The inclusion of the share of single-member households as explanatory variables does not change the estimated coefficients of the population share of the elderly. To examine the effect of the living arrangement on the public educational spending, we use the other types of variables different from the previous estimation. The other types of variables, such as the share of elderly households or the share of households with their children living nearby, are obtained from the "National Livelihood Survey" conducted by the Health, Labor, and Welfare Ministry.[6] The sample periods are from 1986 to 2004 because of data availability. The estimation results of regressions for several specifications are reported in table 6.8. Column (1) shows the benchmark result. Columns (2) to (4) show the results of adding the living arrangement variables. The negative coefficient

6. National Livelihood Survey is conducted at intervals of three years. It is available from 1986. Total number of observation is 329 (= 47×7 waves), but the figure of Hyogo in 1994 is not available because of the Hansin-Awaji earthquake.

Table 6.7   The effects of elderly single-member households on public education

	1975–2005 FE (1)	1975–1985 FE (2)	1990–2005 FE (3)	1975–2005 FEIV (4)	1975–1985 FEIV (5)	1990–2005 FEIV (6)
log(per pupil educational cost)						
log(Population share of old)	-0.0104	0.680**	-0.379*	0.156	0.943**	-0.707**
	(0.105)	(0.261)	(0.198)	(0.130)	(0.441)	(0.276)
log(Proportion of old family)	-0.0606	-0.200*	-0.0681	-0.0953*	-0.291*	0.0601
	(0.0440)	(0.107)	(0.0937)	(0.0497)	(0.150)	(0.113)
log(Population share of kid)	-0.540***	-0.573***	-0.774***	-0.507***	-0.553***	-0.797***
	(0.0713)	(0.125)	(0.167)	(0.0710)	(0.123)	(0.164)
log(per capita income)	0.160***	0.310***	0.162*	0.181***	0.332***	0.114
	(0.0607)	(0.114)	(0.0909)	(0.0606)	(0.112)	(0.0943)
log(per-pupil subsidy)	0.180***	0.319***	0.128**	0.184***	0.298***	0.113**
	(0.0469)	(0.0961)	(0.0569)	(0.0460)	(0.0977)	(0.0561)
log(Unemployment rate)	0.00128	0.248*	-0.0791	-0.0463	0.237*	0.0246
	(0.0820)	(0.133)	(0.198)	(0.0824)	(0.132)	(0.210)
log(House occupation rate)	0.0213	-0.0310	0.0448	0.0374	-0.0162	0.00359
	(0.0308)	(0.0628)	(0.0515)	(0.0321)	(0.0624)	(0.0549)
log(Population density index)	-0.0941*	-0.0369	-0.0687	-0.0888**	-0.0153	-0.0745
	(0.0549)	(0.117)	(0.114)	(0.0539)	(0.117)	(0.111)
Constant	5.239***	0.201	7.883***	4.654***	5.675***	3.346***
	(0.866)	(1.817)	(1.665)	(0.472)	(1.303)	(0.775)

First stage

	(1)	(2)	(3)
log(Population share of old)			
log(Population share of old 5 yrs ago)	0.694***	0.418***	0.700***
	(0.051)	(0.104)	(0.109)
log(Proportion of old family 5 yrs ago)	0.068***	0.107**	0.129***
	(0.020)	(0.419)	(0.039)
F-statistics	409.03	48.41	111.12
Partial R^2	0.626	0.316	0.484
Observations	329	141	188
Number of pref	47	47	47
R^2	0.984	0.776	0.963
Year effect	Yes	Yes	Yes
log(Proportion of old family)			
log(Population share of old 5 yrs ago)	−0.197*	−0.322*	−0.372**
	(0.075)	(0.172)	(0.152)
log(Proportion of old family 5 yrs ago)	0.933***	0.862***	0.982***
	(0.030)	(0.070)	(0.055)
F-statistics	1314.11	151.88	336.80
Partial R^2	0.755	0.462	0.643
Observations	329	141	188
Number of pref	47	47	47
R^2	0.984	0.779	0.964
Year effect	Yes	Yes	Yes

Note: Figures in parentheses are standard errors.

***Significant at the 1 percent level.

**Significant at the 5 percent level.

*Significant at the 10 percent level.

Table 6.8   **The effects of living arrangements of elderly on public education costs (1986 to 2004)**

log(per pupil educational cost)	FE (1)	FE (2)	FE (3)	FE (4)
log(Population share of old)	−0.487***	−0.480***	−0.470***	−0.486***
	(0.0633)	(0.0683)	(0.0694)	(0.0699)
log(Share of elderly households)		0.0332	0.0608	−0.115
		(0.0298)	(0.0447)	(0.222)
log(Share of elderly households without children)		−0.0340**	−0.0410**	
		(0.0149)	(0.0172)	
log(Share of households with children living nearby)			−0.0190	0.0412
			(0.0230)	(0.0723)
log(Share of households without children)				0.0706
				(0.149)
log(Population share of kid)	−0.708***	−0.733***	−0.733***	−0.715***
	(0.0743)	(0.0748)	(0.0749)	(0.0755)
log(per capita income)	0.0711**	0.0680*	0.0698*	0.0699*
	(0.0361)	(0.0361)	(0.0361)	(0.0365)
log(per-pupil subsidy)	0.167***	0.155**	0.150**	0.164**
	(0.0636)	(0.0635)	(0.0637)	(0.0645)
Constant	7.745***	7.845***	7.807***	7.867***
	(0.684)	(0.683)	(0.685)	(0.724)
Observations	328	328	328	328
Number of pref	47	47	47	47
R^2	0.979	0.979	0.979	0.979
Year effect	Yes	Yes	Yes	Yes

Notes: Living arrangement variables such as share of elderly households are obtained from the National Livelihood Survey (Health, Labor, and Welfare Ministry). The National Livelihood Survey is conducted at intervals of three years. It is available from 1986. Total number of observation is 329 (= 47×7 waves), but the figure of Hyogo in 1994 is not available because of the Hansin-Awaji earthquake. Figures in parentheses are standard errors.

***Significant at the 1 percent level.

**Significant at the 5 percent level.

*Significant at the 10 percent level.

of the share of the elderly does not change when the living arrangement variables are included in the explanatory variables.

The hypothesis that the change in the living arrangements of the elderly in Japan caused the change in the preference for public education among the elderly was not accepted.

We speculate that the change in the subsidy system for compulsory education from the national to the local governments affected the change in the estimation results between the 1980s and 1990s. From 1985, the subsidy from the national government for the salary of teachers has been gradually reduced. Thus, the burden of the local governments with regard to public education has been increased in the last two decades. This change is shown in table 6.5. Although the elasticity of the subsidy for per-student education costs was about 0.3 in the 1980s, it became about 0.1 in the 1990s.

As the discretionary power and the fiscal burden of the local governments with regard to compulsory education increased, the local governments began to be affected by political pressure from the elderly voters who were less supportive in terms of increasing the public education costs.

6.6   Conclusion

This chapter examined the effects of demographic change on compulsory education costs using prefectural panel data from 1975 to 2005 in Japan. If the elderly are self-interested and short-term decision makers, they would try to reduce government expenditure on compulsory education. On the other hand, the elderly would try to increase public education costs if they are altruistic or long-term decision makers.

Our estimation results indicate that the higher share of the elderly increased the expenditure on compulsory education per student by local governments in the 1980s; however, this relationship was reversed in the 1990s.

We did not find evidence that this change was caused by the change in the living arrangements of the elderly in Japan. Thus, we suspect that the change in the relationship between public education costs and population aging was caused by the changes in the fiscal system, which increased the discretionary power of the local governments in determining public education costs.

Three issues are pointed out for future research. First, we need a detailed analysis of the effects of the changes in the subsidy system on compulsory education and on the relationship between population aging and public education costs. Second, a municipal level analysis would be more useful since there are many more variations in both demographic and education costs. Third, the quality of education and demographic change should be analyzed directly.

Appendix

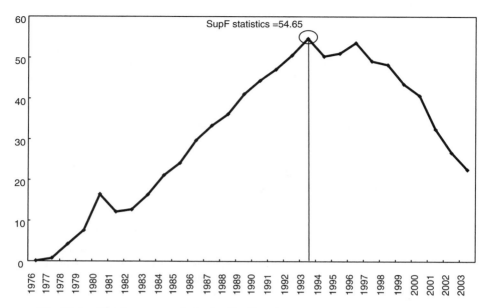

Fig. 6A.1   Test for structural change (SupF test)

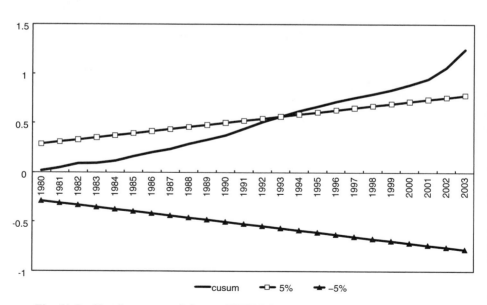

Fig. 6A.2   Test for structural change (CUSUM test)

References

Brunner, E., and E. Balsodon. 2004. Intergenerational conflict and the political economy of school spending. *Journal of Urban Economics* 56 (2): 369–88.

Doi, T. 1998a. Empirics of the median voter hypothesis in Japan. Discussion Paper Series No. F-69, Institute of Social Science, University of Tokyo.

———.1998b. New evidence on the median voter hypothesis in Japan. Discussion Paper Series No. F-72, Institute of Social Science, University of Tokyo.

Goldin, C., and L. F. Katz. 1998. The origins of state-level differences in the public provision of higher education: 1890–1940. *American Economic Review* 88 (2): 303–08.

Gradstein, M., M. Justman, and V. Meier. 2005. *The political economy of education: Implication for growth and inequality.* Cambridge, MA: MIT Press.

Grob, U., and S. C. Wolter. 2005. Demographic change and public education spending: A conflict between young and old? CESifo Working Paper no. 1555, October. Munich: Ifo Institute for Economic Research.

Harris, A. R., W. N. Evans, and R. M. Schwab. 2001. Education spending in an aging America. *Journal of Public Economics* 81 (3): 449–72.

Hoxby, C. M. 1998. How much does school spending depend on family income? The historical origins of current school finance dilemma. *American Economic Review* 88 (2): 309–14.

Kariya, T. 2006. Change of equal opportunity in education. *ASTEION* no. 65. (In Japanese.)

Ladd, H. F., and S. E. Murry. 2001. Intergenerational conflict reconsidered: Country demographic structure and the demand for public education. *Economics of Education Review* 20:343–57.

Oberndorfer, U., and V. Steiner. 2006. Intergenerational conflict, partisan politics, and public higher education spending: Evidence from the German states. IZA Discussion Paper no. 2417 November. Institute for the Study of Labor.

Person, T., and G. Tabellini. 2000. *Political economics: Explaining economic policy.* Cambridge, MA: MIT Press.

Poterba, J. 1997. Demographic structure and the political economy of public education. *Journal of Policy Analysis and Management* 16 (1): 48–66.

———. 1998. Demographic change, intergenerational linkage, and public education. *American Economic Review* 88 (2): 315–20.

Rubinfeld, D. L. 1977. Voting in a local school election: A micro analysis. *Review of Economics and Statistics* 59 (1): 30–42.

Sugimoto, Y., and M. Nakagawa. 2007. From duty to right: The role of public education in the transition to aging societies. ISER Discussion Paper no. 700. Institute of Social and Economic Research, Osaka University.

Comment   Dae Il Kim

The authors of this chapter present quite important and interesting empirical findings. The share of the elderly population negatively affects the level of public educational expenditure in recent years in Japan, as was found

Dae Il Kim is a professor of economics at Seoul National University.

in the United States. This result deserves careful attention because many other countries are similarly experiencing population aging and also because high-quality education has been increasingly emphasized in the face of rapid technological progress and increased world market competition. To the extent that the causality is robust, we will have to work hard to find a way to deal with population aging without sacrificing the quality of our education systems.

Given that the result has such a strong implication, the authors need to substantiate their interpretation with additional empirical evidence. The authors suggest several theories, but they are not quite successful in singling out the one behind the empirical findings. They test the possibility that the elderly may have become more selfish and short-sighted, and conclude otherwise as the changes in living arrangement do not explain the results. The power of the test, however, does not appear sufficiently strong for a couple of reasons. First, living arrangement itself may not be a valid indicator for how uninterested the elderly are in their children's and grandchildren's welfare in an Asian country such as Japan, where family values are strongly emphasized. At the same time, to the extent that intrafamily transfer is an important income source for the elderly, the elderly may not really benefit from being so selfish as to place political pressure against educational expenditure. Greater subsidy for the elderly financed by lower educational expenditure, for example, may induce a smaller intrafamily transfer, leading to no changes in their actual income. Indeed, public transfer crowds out private transfer (from their children) among the Korean elderly households almost one to one, and Japan may not be much different from Korea in that aspect. Second, the regression with the changes in living arrangement as an additional explanatory variable serves only as an indirect test, and a more direct test would be investigating whether elderly population induces an increase in the public expenditure directly linked to the welfare of the elderly, such as income transfer and health care.

The authors speculate, in conclusion, that the changes in the subsidy from central government may have caused the negative effects of the elderly population on the educational expenditure. The possibility cannot be excluded, but two interrelated questions still remain. First, why would the effect of the changes in subsidy from central government show up in the relationship between the *elderly population* and the *educational expenditure*? I think it is possible that such changes affect the educational expenditure at local governments, but how are they related to the size of the elderly population? Second, what is the mechanism through which the changes in subsidy system affect the results? Little information is given regarding these two questions, and readers will love to see more information to better understand the chapter. Further regarding the issue, the authors may wish to pay more attention for the 2000 to 2005 period during which the central government's subsidy fell considerably from the previously stable trend. If the period stands out in terms of the correlation between the elderly population and the educational expenditure, the authors' speculation can be more persuasive.

Now I turn to the choice of variables in the regression. In particular, the authors need to pay more attention to the OLD and KID variables in the regression. As suggested by the authors, a greater share of schoolkids in population tends to reduce the per-student educational expenditure. But at the same time, a greater share of schoolkids implies a greater share of households with kids, whose parents may vote for a greater expenditure for education. These two effects offset each other, but the relative magnitudes of these effects may also depend on population aging, to the extent the aging arises from a lower fertility rate. In other words, a decline in fertility rate may reduce the share of schoolkids in population, but not so much the fraction of the households with schoolkids. As only the share of schoolkids (KID) is controlled for in the regression, the effects through the fraction of the households with schoolkids may show up in the coefficients on the elderly population. If so, the educational expenditure is not adversely affected by the increasing size of the elderly population. Instead, the educational expenditure is adversely affected by the declining size of the fraction of the households with kids, which is represented as an increase of the elderly population in the data.

Another complication arises in the regression as the increase in the share of the elderly, given that the share of kids partly reflects a smaller working-age population. To the extent that the smaller workforce means smaller tax revenue, the negative coefficients on the elderly population may simply represent the local government's ability to spend. The positive coefficient on the per capita income is consistent with this alternative interpretation.

An alternative way to interpret the authors' results is the nonlinearity in the relationship between political power and the population size. The median voter theory used by the authors actually suggests such nonlinearity. An increase in the elderly population will have a stronger effect on public policy when their population is sufficiently large that the elderly are near the median. Instead, when their population is too small or too large, an increase in their population will have no marginal effect on the public policy. Thus the empirical results are consistent with the following interpretation. First, the elderly have always been selfish. Second, their selfishness has finally started to affect the public policies in the 1990s because the elderly population has sufficiently grown. One way to consider this hypothesis is to compare the sizes of elderly population between Japan and the United States at the time when the relationship between the elderly population and the educational expenditure started to turn negative in each country.

Again, I wish to emphasize that the empirical relationship documented in this chapter is very important and deserves careful attention. I would like to thank the authors for providing the interesting results and also encourage further works on the issue. Identifying the causality and the underlying hypothesis will make a substantial contribution to the literature.

Comment   Chang-Gyun Park

The chapter examines the relationship between demographic structure and government expenditure on compulsory public education with Japanese data. A standard theoretical model would predict that if the median voter is old enough to be without kids under compulsory public education and does not take the external effect on general productivity level into account, we would observe the positive correlation between the two variables. Several researchers had already tackled the issue and provided evidence conforming to the implication of generational competition theory. However, Japan seems to be an ideal test site to reexamine the issue because it has experienced one of the fastest demographic changes in human history.

The authors report an interesting finding. While the share of elderly population had a positive relation with per capita expenditure on public education in the 1970s and 1980s, the relation was reversed in 1990s when demographic change measured by the proportion of the elderly of sixty-five years or older was significantly accelerated. They conjecture that the result may reflect the institutional shift in the mid-1980s, which helped political pressure from demographic structure project more clearly into collective decision making on public expenditure. From 1985, Japanese central government had gradually reduced the subsidies to local governments to cover part of teachers' salary and local governments were forced to bear more fiscal burden with regard to compulsory education. One can infer that as the fiscal burden increased the decision making on compulsory education of local governments, it began to be affected by political pressure from the elderly, who are thought to be less supportive for increasing expenditure on public education. Plausible as it sounds, the authors do not offer much empirical evidence to support the conjecture. Further in-depth investigation on the issue should be done before it is accepted as a reliable explanation on the sign reversal repeatedly reported in the chapter.

We should be very careful in interpreting the true implication of estimates of the key explanatory variable, the proportion of the elderly among the entire population. Though it is not entirely clear from the chapter, it seems that the authors include both current and capital expenditure in measuring the dependent variable, per pupil expenditure on compulsory public

Chang-Gyun Park is an assistant professor in the College of Business Administration at Chung-Ang University.

education. As aging progresses, some portion of capital expenditure, such as construction of new school buildings, may decrease even in the absence of generational competition in political decision making. Considering the lumpy nature of capital expenditure, we may observe, at least in the short run, a significant decrease in per-pupil expenditure on compulsory education without lowering the quality or intensity of education and may simply reflect projected decrease in demand for compulsory education. Data permitting, it would be a useful exercise to conduct the empirical investigation for the current expenditure as well as the total expenditure.

Next, I would like to suggest a minor robust check for the key explanatory variable. The authors take the proportion of the elderly to approximate the political pressure from the older generations, who are presumed to be less supportive for public education. Considering considerably different voter turnout ratios across generations and time, one can construct a better proxy for political pressure from the elderly by combining the proportion of the elderly and turnout ratio of the corresponding group.

Finally, the main reason we pay attention to the issue is that generational competition may do harm to accumulation of human capital that is widely believed to be the crucial factor in maintaining economic growth. We can easily accept the possibility that generational competition in allocation of public resources may result in divergence from socially optimal level of human capital investment to suboptimal resource allocation. Therefore, the findings in the chapter have significant policy implications as well as theoretical substance. However, public education is just a part of human capital investment and the decreased public expenditure could be compensated by increased expenditure on private education by worrying parents. Consequently, competition among voting generations in the arena of public expenditure may not have major effects in terms of efficiency of resource allocation. We may need to examine the expenditure on education both public and private to address the issue, especially in the context of Japan, where expenditures on private education such as extracurricular activities and private tutoring constitute a significant part of the total human capital investment.

III

Korea

Intergenerational Transfers and Old-Age Security in Korea

Hisam Kim

7.1 Introduction

Korea entered an aging society as of 2000, when people over age sixty-five made up 7.2 percent of the population. The ratio of the elderly population in Korea is projected to reach 14.3 percent by 2018 before it becomes a super-aged society in 2026, with the share reaching 20.8 percent. Consequently, the elderly dependency ratio, which is defined as people aged sixty-five and over per people aged fifteen to sixty-four years, is projected to increase three times from 12.6 percent in 2005 to 37.7 percent in 2030, according to the Korea National Statistical Office.

In spite of its population aging at an unprecedented pace in the world, Korea has been unsuccessful in building up a social safety net for the elderly. Instead, adult children (mostly eldest sons) have undertaken the responsibilities of supporting their elderly parents in Korea's extended family. For this reason, empirical analysis of the financial support given to elderly parents by adult children is important in preparing an income guarantee policy that suits the current trend of the population aging and its subsequent social and economic changes.

Even though a substantial portion of Korean elderly have been living on financial assistance received from their children, studies on intergenerational transfers in Korea are rare and microeconomic empirical studies are even rarer. Part of the reason for this is there had been few microdata on intergenerational transfers until the twenty-first century. Now we have such data from at least three data sets: the Korean Labor and Income Panel Study (KLIPS), the Korean Longitudinal Study of Aging (KLoSA), and the

Hisam Kim is an associate fellow of the Korea Development Institute.

Korean Retirement and Income Study (KReIS). This study examines micro-economic behavior on intergenerational transfers using these data sets.

First of all, this study directly looks into variables regarding intergenerational transfers in the three Korean data sets and compares them with those in the Health and Retirement Study (HRS), one of the elderly panel data sets that the KLoSA and the KReIS have tried to benchmark. Compared with the author's previous paper (Kim 2006) that uses data from the KLIPS, this study has both similarity and complementarity. The previous study analyzes a broad range of issues on private transfers—such as the magnitude and frequency of transfers, the determinants of transfer receipts and gifts, the crowding out of private transfers by public transfers, and the dead zones and loopholes of public assistance—and, therefore, some issues certainly overlap with this study. If we find similar results regarding the patterns and motivations of intergenerational transfers from these different data sets, we may get closer to stylized facts with the findings. Therefore, I cite or mention selected results from the previous study in some places of this chapter.

At the same time, however, this study deals with some unexplored issues using new features of the KLoSA and the KReIS data. First, the KLoSA respondents report their transfer receipts and gifts with all adult children who do not live with them. This resultant sibling sample motivates family fixed-effect models to examine which child gives more transfers to elderly parents or lives with them.

Second, the KReIS data report intergenerational transfers between parents and coresident children as well as between parents and noncoresident children. Considering that intergenerational transfers are reported only for noncoresident adult children in other data sets, we can have an unusual opportunity to examine intergenerational transfers by children's coresidence status and conjecture the motivations of those transfers.

Third, the KReIS survey has explicit questions on the existence of grandchildren who respondents and/or spouses are taking care of, the hours of caregiving, and the magnitude of pecuniary compensation, if any. These data items enable us to directly test whether there exists an exchange motive in adult children's cash transfers to their parents who look after grandchildren.

Fourth, the KLoSA survey asks about the respondents' subjective expectation feelings to several issues: for instance, the financial situation in their future, the relative financial situation of their children's generation compared to their own generation, and potential support for their old age by government. I use these variables to examine how individuals' expectations on tomorrow's situations affect their transfer behavior today.

Finally, the KLoSA and the KReIS data contain information on inheritances and detailed items of assets and debts. Using these variables that have rarely been observed in other data sets, this study first documents some basic statistics on inheritance and wealth in Korea.

This chapter proceeds as follows. Section 7.2 quantifies intergenerational transfers focusing on adult children's transfers given to their elderly parents. Section 7.3 examines the characteristics of the donor and the recipient of such transfers to uncover which parents benefit more from their children and which child in the family gives more to the parents. Section 7.4 documents ongoing changes in familial support mechanism and suggests policy implications for old-age income security, based on observed profiles of income and wealth by age and by income quintile. The last section concludes.

7.2   Patterns of Intergenerational Transfers

In this section, I tabulate descriptive statistics on intergenerational transfers in Korea, and then those in the United States as well, for a cross-country comparison. First, I examine "inter-vivos" transfers; that is, transfers made while both the donor and the recipient are alive. Then, I look at reported and expected inheritance as another way that intergenerational transfers are made.

7.2.1   Inter-Vivos Transfers

First, I describe inter-vivos transfers in Korea, observed in the KLoSA, the KLIPS, and KReIS data sets focusing on adult children's financial help given to their elderly parents. The HRS data show striking differences in intergenerational transfer patterns between the United States and Korea.

KLoSA Data

The Korean Longitudinal Study of Aging (KLoSA) started in 2006 for the purpose of creating a basic data set needed to devise and implement effective policies to population aging.[1] The KLoSA survey interviews middle/old-aged population (aged forty-five or older) nationwide, excluding Jeju Island. The total number of samples is 10,254 in 2006. Topics under KLoSA are grouped into the following seven main categories: (a) Demographics; (b) Family; (c) Health; (d) Employment; (e) Income; (f) Assets; (g) Subjective Expectations and Satisfaction.[2]

Specifically, rich information on intergenerational transfers in the Family section is extremely useful for this study. In the 2006 KLoSA data, financial transfers between the respondent and each child during the last calendar year (2005) are asked if the child does not live with the respondent. According to the KLoSA questionnaire, financial help (or transfer) means giving

1. Basic survey for KLoSA will be conducted every even-numbered year starting from 2006, mostly using the same survey categories. The first KLoSA baseline survey was conducted over a six-month period from July 2006. The surveys thereafter will also be held in the second half of the year.
2. The data and questionnaires of the 2006 KLoSA are available online at the website of Korea Labor Institute (www.kli.re.kr).

money, helping pay bills, or covering specific types of costs (such as those for medical care or insurance, schooling, down payment for a home, rent, etc.), but it does not count any shared housing or shared food. Respondents are told that financial help can be considered as either a gift or a loan. The survey separately reports transfers made on a regular basis and those made irregularly. Regular monetary transfer refers to the case in which respondents received monetary transfers regularly in a certain time interval (e.g., each month, every two months), such as monthly allowances. Occasional (or irregular) monetary transfer refers to the case in which respondents received monetary transfers without any regularity, such as paying for medical bills or schooling and occasional allowances. I calculate annual regular transfer amount by multiplying the average amount of regular transfer by the number of months such transfer is made.

Intergenerational transfers in the KLoSA survey are reported not only for survey respondents and their children but also for the respondents and their own parents. The later generation data on the respondents and their children will be used in the main analyses of this study. The average age of parents (i.e., respondents) is 69.5, and that of their children is 41.5. In the earlier generation data on the respondents and their parents, the average age of respondents who have at least one living parent is 52.3, and their fathers and mothers are, on average, 79.1 and 78.8 years old, respectively.[3] I add up financial assistance given to and received from the father and the mother if they are both alive. We have observations on intergenerational transfers made in 6,496 families for the later generation and those made in 3,159 families for the earlier generation.

Table 7.1 reports descriptive statistics on annual intergenerational transfers for each generation. Forty percent of respondents received financial transfers from their children and 11.4 percent gave financial help to their children. Average receipt amount is 1,040,000 won and average gift amount is 850,000 won, which yields average net transfer receipt of 190,000 won (surplus) for parents.

Looking at the earlier generation, 41.5 percent of respondents gave financial help to their elderly parents and 6 percent received financial support from them. Mean amount (both conditional and unconditional one) of net transfer is larger—more than double—for the earlier generation than for the later generation. Note that the former measures average net transfer received only from respondents, excluding those from their siblings, but the latter measures average net transfer received from all children of the respondents. Taking this different survey structure into account, the smaller amount of average net transfer receipt for the parents in the later generation may reflect a weakening role of children's financial support for their old parents. Other-

---

3. Given that at least one parent is alive, the fraction of the father's being alive is 0.323 and that of the mother's is 0.932.

Table 7.1   Annual intergenerational transfers in Korea: KLoSA data
(%, 10,000 won)

		Fraction (%)	Unconditional mean	Conditional on making each transfer	
				Mean	Median
Later generation (6,496 families)					
From children (A)	Regular	10.6	65	615	360
	Irregular	35.3	39	111	60
	Total[a]	40.1	104	260	100
To children (B)	Regular	5.0	54	1,079	720
	Irregular	7.4	31	419	50
	Total[a]	11.4	85	749	315
Net transfer receipt	Regular[b]	15.1	11	71	240
from children (A – B)	Irregular[b]	38.9	8	21	50
	Total[b]	46.3	19	41	70
Earlier generation (3,159 families)					
To parents (C)	Regular	10.2	42	413	240
	Irregular	31.7	19	59	40
	Total[a]	41.5	61	147	50
From parents (D)	Regular	0.7	1	82	12
	Irregular	5.4	14	267	30
	Total[a]	6.1	15	247	30
Net transfer gift to	Regular[c]	10.8	41	383	234
parents (C – D)	Irregular[c]	35.6	4	12	30
	Total[c]	45.8	46	100	50

Source: Calculated by the author, using the 2006 KLoSA data.

Note: All numbers are calculated using weights assigned to family respondents.

[a]Either regular or irregular, or both transfers are made.

[b]Either from or to children, or both, some transfers are made.

[c]Either to or from parents, or both, some transfers are made.

wise, it may reflect that the relative financial situation of parents to their children in the later generation is better than that in the earlier generation. Or, instead, it may simply reflect age difference between the parents in the two generations. At least the last conjecture seems to be supported by table 7.2. Net transfer receipt from children increases with the respondents' age from their fifties to early seventies. As parents get older, they are more likely to receive a large net transfer.[4]

4. Another possibility is a measurement error. In particular, we might need to account for potential underreporting bias when the respondents are asked to report their transfer receipts as opposed to their transfer gifts (see Gale and Scholz [1994] and Brown and Weisbenner [2002] for this bias). If KLoSA respondents indeed underreported transfers from their children (A) and/or from their parents (D), net transfer receipt from their children (A–B) should be underestimated and/or net transfer gift to their parents (C–D) should be overestimated in table 7.1.

Table 7.2   **Mean amount of annual intergenerational transfer in Korea by age: KLoSA data (10,000 won)**

		Respondent age (no. of families)						
		45–49 (1,128)	50–54 (840)	55–59 (789)	60–64 (809)	65–69 (953)	70–74 (785)	75– (1,192)
From children (A)	Regular	5	18	49	67	134	162	115
	Irregular	7	13	30	57	70	71	65
	Total[a]	12	31	79	124	204	233	180
To children (B)	Regular	98	129	49	28	13	4	1
	Irregular	34	23	51	49	22	21	3
	Total[a]	132	152	100	77	35	25	5
Net transfer receipt from	Regular[b]	–93	–111	1	39	121	159	113
children (A–B)	Irregular[b]	–28	–10	–21	8	49	49	61
	Total[b]	–120	–121	–20	47	170	208	175

Source: Calculated by the author, using the 2006 KLoSA data.

Note: All numbers are calculated using weights assigned to family respondents.

[a]Either regular or irregular, or both transfers are made.

[b]Either from or to children, or both, some transfers are made.

In addition, table 7.2 shows that the direction of the net flow of inter-generational transfers is reversed from downward to upward around the parent's age sixty, a common retirement age. Transfer receipt from children increases as respondents get older, peaking at their mid-seventies, while transfer gift to children decreases after their fifties. Although these profiles are constructed from cross-section data, they probably depict a life cycle reallocation through intergenerational transfers within Korean families.

KLIPS Data

The Korean Labor and Income Panel Study (KLIPS) is an annual survey of 5,000 households and their members (aged fifteen and over) from the seven metropolitan cities and urban areas in eight provinces (excluding Jeju Island).[5] Since its fourth-year survey in 2001, the KLIPS has been collecting data on intergenerational transfers given to and received from parents. Related questions are separately asked for the household head's parents and for the spouse's parents. Using these questions, we know financial transfers in the last year given to and received from parents and parents-in-law who do not live with respondents and spouses. The average age of the KLIPS household heads is 45.4 in 2005.

Table 7.3 shows that at least 50 percent of KLIPS households make transfers to their parents or parents-in-law; however, the fraction of households who report transfer receipts from their parents or parents-in-law is at most 24 percent. Compared with the KLoSA data in table 7.1, the KLIPS data

5. The data and documentations of the KLIPS can be downloaded at the website of Korea Labor Institute (www.kli.re.kr).

Table 7.3   Annual intergenerational transfers in Korea: KLIPS data (%, 10,000 won)

Data (number of households)	To parents or parents-in-law				From parents or parents-in-law			
	Fraction (%)	Unconditional mean	Conditional mean	Conditional median	Fraction (%)	Unconditional mean	Conditional mean	Conditional median
KLIPS 2001 ($N = 2,771$)	50.7	73.7	145.4	80	18.1	42.0	232.2	70
KLIPS 2002 ($N = 2,723$)	56.1	97.1	173.1	100	18.8	47.3	251.4	80
KLIPS 2003 ($N = 2,979$)	58.5	106.9	182.7	120	20.4	108.5	532.0	100
KLIPS 2004 ($N = 3,056$)	65.5	140.6	214.7	120	23.7	54.9	231.5	80
KLIPS 2005 ($N = 3,112$)	62.4	122.6	196.4	120	22.6	58.6	259.3	100

Source: Calculated by the author, using the 2001–2005 KLIPS data.

Note: All numbers are weighted using household weights of each wave.

report more prevalent, sizable transfers between parents and children. But it should be accounted for that the intergenerational transfers from the KLIPS data in table 7.3 include financial help from/to the spouses' parents as well as the household heads' parents, whereas those from the KLoSA data in table 7.1 do not include transfers from/to parents-in-law. In addition, unlike the KLoSA survey, the intergenerational transfers in the KLIPS survey include monetary value of in-kind transfers such as food or electronic appliances (evaluated at the purchase price).[6]

By its survey structure, the KLIPS provides an opportunity to investigate potential differences between transfers from/to the husband's parents and those from/to the wife's parents by separating them using information on the household head's gender.[7] Table 7.4 reveals that Korean households tend to give a larger amount of transfers (in terms of both average and median) to the husband's parents than to the wife's parents. As for the median amount of transfer gifts from parents, however, we do not observe such differences between the head's parents and the wife's parents. This gender difference might reflect asymmetric standings of the husband and the wife in their earnings and decision-making powers in the family. But it surely reflects traditional norms under which elderly parents have been supported mainly by their sons (especially their eldest sons) rather than their daughters.

KReIS Data

The Korean Retirement and Income Study (KReIS) started in 2005 to be conducted every odd-numbered year. The KReIS survey has the purpose of creating a basic data set needed to devise policies for effective old-age income security. The sample consists of nationally representative 5,110 households that have at least one person aged fifty or older (an "age-eligible respondent"). In addition, the KReIS included the age-eligible respondent's spouse irrespective of his/her age, resulting in a total sample of 8,689 respondents.

In the 2005 KReIS data, private transfers received by and given by the respondent or the spouse during the last calendar year (2004) are asked. Unlike the KLoSA and the KLIPS data, the KReIS reports transfers between the respondent (or the spouse) and coresident family members as well as noncoresident family members. According to the KReIS questionnaire, transfers include financial help in the form of money or in-kind transfers for living, schooling, and so forth, but do not include occasional gifts such as for birthdays or holidays.

6. By contrast, the KLoSA survey asked about in-kind transfers using separate questions on "nonmonetary" transfer. Suggested types of nonmonetary support in the questionnaire is leisure (e.g., travel), health-related products (e.g., vitamins, equipments, etc.), household items, electronics, dining out and foods, and other. But their monetary values are not reported.

7. The proportion of females among the KLIPS household heads has increased gradually: 15.3 percent in 2001, 16.0 percent in 2002, 18.0 percent in 2003, 18.3 percent in 2004, and 19.6 percent in 2005.

Table 7.4   Differential intergenerational transfers between husband and wife in Korea: KLIPS data (10,000 won)

Data	To husband's parents		To wife's parents		From husband's parents		From wife's parents	
	Fraction (Number of households)	Conditional mean (median)	Fraction (Number of households)	Conditional mean (median)	Fraction (Number of households)	Conditional mean (median)	Fraction (Number of households)	Conditional mean (median)
KLIPS 2001	53.1%	115.0	40.0%	72.2	16.6%	161.5	13.5%	103.5
	(N = 1,924)	(50)	(N = 2,273)	(30)	(N = 1,924)	(50)	(N = 2,273)	(40)
KLIPS 2002	57.5%	137.1	47.1%	69.0	15.9%	178.1	14.5%	150.2
	(N = 1,898)	(70)	(N = 2,224)	(40)	(N = 1,898)	(50)	(N = 2,224)	(50)
KLIPS 2003	59.8%	139.5	49.8%	86.6	18.3%	513.0	15.5%	93.2
	(N = 2,089)	(100)	(N = 2,398)	(50)	(N = 2,089)	(50)	(N = 2,398)	(50)
KLIPS 2004	65.8%	178.2	57.4%	77.3	21.3%	222.2	19.8%	139.7
	(N = 2,168)	(100)	(N = 2,439)	(50)	(N = 2,168)	(50)	(N = 2,439)	(50)
KLIPS 2005	64.4%	149.7	55.9%	84.5	19.5%	208.3	18.3%	144.2
	(N = 2,181)	(100)	(N = 2,437)	(50)	(N = 2,181)	(50)	(N = 2,437)	(50)

Source: Calculated by the author, using the 2001–2005 KLIPS data.

Note: Mean (median) transfer amounts are conditional on making transfers. All numbers are weighted using household weights of each wave.

Since private transfers are reported for every age-eligible respondent or spouse in the household, some households have multiple observations of different amounts of transfers when there are multiple respondents or couples in the same household. Thus, I specify a "financial respondent" for each household by naming the household head first, and then the spouse if the head is not a respondent, and then the head's parent if both are not respondents, and so on following the frequency of the respondent's relationship with the head in the data. The resulting age-eligible financial respondents, who were aged 64.9 on average in 2005, provide 4,800 household observations on private transfers.

Table 7.5 tabulates annual transfer receipts and gifts by the relationship of donors and recipients. The proportion of those who received transfers from noncoresident children is 45.8 percent, while that from coresident children is 16.5 percent. Because coresidence is another important way of supporting elderly parents and also because some coresident children may be still dependent on their parents, fewer coresident children tend to give transfers to their parents than their noncoresident siblings. The mean amount of transfer receipt from noncoresident children is 1,380,000 won and the conditional mean (median) amount is 3,010,000 (1,500,000) won.

The proportion of respondents who gave transfers to coresident children is 23.8 percent and the conditional mean (median) amount of transfer gift is 7,300,000 (6,000,000) won. This sizable amount may reflect parents' help for dependent children (e.g., college tuition help) who are relatively young compared to noncoresident children. In terms of mean amounts of transfer receipt and gift, coresident children tend to be "net receivers" whereas noncoresident children tend to be "net givers" from whom parents receive 950,000 (= 1,380,000 − 430,000) won, on average, a year.

Time is also transferable between family members through informal caregivings. Given that family caregivings are substitutes for formal caregivings that can be purchased from the market in many cases, intergenerational caregivings often have similar effects on the recipient with intergenerational financial help. Specifically, the KReIS data report respondents' childcare for their grandchildren and caregivings for their sick parents. As Table 7.6 shows, about 15 percent of age-eligible financial respondents or their spouses are currently looking after their grandchildren almost entirely, and their average (median) child care hours are fifty-four (forty-nine) hours a week—the equivalent of having a full-time job with no weekend and holiday. At the same time, 15 percent of grandparents said that they had an experience of quitting paid work or reducing the amount of time they worked in order to look after their grandchildren. Of those who provide child care services, two-thirds offer their services for free. The rest receive money with mean (median) amounts 360,000 (300,000) won a month, which suggests that some intergenerational transfers from adult children to elderly parents are motivated by an exchange motive—child care service for money.

Table 7.5   Private transfers in Korea: KReIS data (N = 4,800 households) (%, 10,000 won)

Relationship	Annual transfer receipt from				Annual transfer gift to			
	Fraction (%)	Unconditional Mean	Conditional Mean	Conditional Median	%	Mean	Mean > 0	Median > 0
Coresident								
Parents	0.5	1	180	54	3.4	6	166	60
Children or grandchildren	16.5	68	410	200	23.8	174	730	600
Other family members	0.1	0	171	120	0.1	0	93	30
Noncoresident								
Parents	0.8	4	478	100	9.6	16	168	100
Spouse	0.3	4	1,188	1,200	0.2	0	145	40
Children or grandchildren	45.8	138	301	150	23.3	43	184	50
Siblings	2.3	4	195	80	1.9	2	90	50
Other relatives	1.7	2	125	36	1.6	1	81	30
Ex-spouse	0.0	0	515	100	0	0	32	24
Social/religious organizations	2.4	3	126	20	12.4	11	89	35
All others	1.9	1	53	20	0.3	1	195	100
Total	61.5	225	366	200	54.4	252	463	130

Source: Calculated by the author, using the 2005 KReIS data.

Note: All numbers are weighted using household weights.

Table 7.6   **Family caregivings in Korea: KReIS data**

Caregivings for	Grandchildren (N = 3,290 households that have grandchildren)	Sick parents (N = 1,431 households whose parents are alive)
Proportion of caregiving households	14.7%	7.0%
Mean (median) caregiving hours per week	54 (49) hours	37 (21) hours
Proportion of caregivers who had to quit or reduce work for caregiving	15.2%	26.3%
Proportion of caregivers who receive money for caregiving	33.2%	n.a.
Mean (median) amount of money received for caregiving per month	360,000 (300,000) won	n.a.

Source: Calculated by the author, using the 2005 KReIS data.

Note: All numbers are weighted using household weights.

On the other hand, 7 percent of age-eligible financial respondents or their spouses are currently taking care of their sick parents and their average (median) caregiving hours are thirty-seven (twenty-one) hours a week. About 26 percent had an experience of quitting paid work or reducing the amount of time they worked in order to care for their sick parents.

Intergenerational Transfers in the United States: HRS Data

Now let us look at comparative data for the United States on intergenerational transfers. Among others, the Health and Retirement Study (HRS) provides useful information on financial transfers between parents and children. The HRS is a national panel study with an initial sample of 7,607 households (12,652 persons who were fifty-one to sixty-one years old in 1992).[8] To compare annual familial transfers between the United States and Korea, I use the first two waves of the HRS (1992, 1994) that report intergenerational transfers made in the past twelve months.[9] The 1992 wave of the HRS asked about financial assistance given to the parents and children of the respondent or spouse totaling 500 dollars or more in the past twelve months.[10] In the 1994 wave, the censoring amount was changed to 100 dollars, and financial assistance received from their parents and children was also reported.

Panel A and panel B in table 7.7 report the 1992/1994 HRS respondents' transfer gifts to their parents or parents-in-law and those to their children, respectively. Both waves of the HRS data show that the respondents make

8. The baseline 1992 survey consisted of in-home, face-to-face interviews with the 1931 to 1941 birth cohort and their spouses, if married. Follow-up interviews were given by telephone in 1994, 1996, 1998, 2000, 2002, 2004, and 2006.

9. In waves 3 through 8 the questions on financial transfers asked about transfers exceeding $500 in the past two years.

10. The financial help in the HRS data includes help with education but it does not include any shared housing or shared food, which is the same as the KLoSA data.

Table 7.7   **Annual intergenerational transfers in the United States: HRS 1992/1994 data (U.S. dollar in each year)**

Data (censoring amount)	Fraction % (N)	Unconditional mean	Conditional mean	Conditional median
A. To parents or parents-in-law				
HRS 1992 ($500 or more)	10.8 (2,180)	208	1,929	1,000
HRS 1994 ($100 or more)	16.5 (1,985)	89	903	500
B. to children				
HRS 1992 ($500 or more)	34.8 (3,920)	1,604	4,609	2,000
HRS 1994 ($100 or more)	45.1 (3,462)	1,750	3,934	1,400
C. From parents or parents-in-law				
HRS 1994 ($100 or more)	5.7 (1,984)	81	2,459	1,000
D. From children				
HRS 1994 ($100 or more)	8.0 (3,465)	90	1,505	600

Source: Calculated by the author, using the 1992/1994 HRS data.
Note: All numbers are weighted using household weights of each wave.

substantial transfers to their children, whereas transfers to their elderly parents are much fewer. Panel C and panel D report the 1994 HRS respondents' transfer receipts from their parents or parents-in-law and those from their children. The fraction of positive transfer receipts is very low from both directions.

To compare Koreans' transfers to their elderly parents with Americans,' we should pay attention to the 1994 HRS statistics in panel A, which are fairly comparable to the KLIPS statistics in table 7.3. Remember that KLIPS respondents are on average younger than HRS respondents, and therefore take the 2005 KLIPS statistics from table 7.3. About 62 percent of Korean households give some transfers to their parents or parents-in-law, and the average amount of transfers conditional on gift is 1,964,000 won (roughly $2,000 in 2005 dollars) a year. By contrast, only 16.5 percent of American households make transfers to their parents or parents-in-law, and the average transfer amount conditional on gift is just $117 (converted to 2005 dollars) a year.

Using later waves of the HRS, we can also see similar patterns of U.S. familial transfers, which are mostly headed for children and play only a limited role as a supplemental income for the elderly. Table 7.8 shows the fraction of U.S. households making intergenerational transfers exceeding 500 dollars in the last two years over six waves of the HRS survey fielded in 1996, 1998, 2000, 2002, 2004, and 2006.[11] The proportion of families who

11. The HRS sample was expanded in 1998, and every two years thereafter, by adding the Study of Assets and Health Dynamics Among the Oldest Old (AHEAD) sample and the new subsamples—War Babies (WB) and Children of the Depression (CODA)—to the original HRS sample interviewed previously in 1992, 1994, and 1996. Therefore, the number of households that responded to transfer questions increased substantially in 1998.

Table 7.8   **Fraction of U.S. households making intergenerational transfers exceeding 500 dollars in the last two years (% positive fraction [no. of households])**

Data	To children or grandchildren	From children or grandchildren	To parents or parents-in-law	From parents or parents-in-law
HRS 1996	39.9 (6,208)	4.0 (6,224)	Husband's parents: 15.0 (1,930) Wife's parents: 13.9 (2,960)	Husband's parents: 4.4 (1,940) Wife's parents: 6.0 (2,961)
HRS 1998	35.6 (12,764)	5.2 (12,802)	13.5 (3,900)	7.2 (3,902)
HRS 2000	35.7 (11,859)	5.9 (11,878)	15.3 (3,374)	7.1 (3,372)
HRS 2002	31.3 (12,038)	6.2 (12,049)	14.3 (4,299)	5.6 (4,307)
HRS 2004	37.9 (12,281)	6.5 (12,315)	16.7 (5,859)	6.9 (5,856)
HRS 2006	36.3 (11,494)	6.4 (11,521)	17.0 (4,742)	6.6 (4,741)

gave positive transfers to children is always over 30 percent, which is more than double the proportion of families who gave positive transfers to elderly parents.

Compared to Korean families in tables 7.1, 7.3, and 7.5, among which at least 40 percent give transfers to elderly parents in the last twelve months, fewer American families make such transfers, at most 17 percent, even in the last twenty-four months. This may reflect a cultural difference between two countries in that Korea has a tradition of extended families and Confucian ethics that requires children's responsibility of supporting their elders. But it may also reflect that even without help from children, American elderly can have relatively sufficient income from their savings or Social Security benefits.[12]

Also, unlike Korean families who exhibit noticeable gender differences in transfer behavior toward the husband's parents and the wife's parents (table 7.4), American families in the HRS data do not clearly show such differences. The 1996 wave of the HRS reports financial assistance from/to parents and parents-in-law separately. I identify the husband's parents and the wife's parents based on the family respondent's gender. The fraction of households who made transfers to the wife's parents is 14 percent, similar to the fraction of 15 percent for the husband's parents.[13]

12. For instance, the sources of American elderly household income as of 1984 for the highest and lowest income quintiles are as follows (Hurd 1990, table 12). The highest quintile households' average income of $34,061 consists of $9,450 earnings (27.2 percent), $13,289 property income (39.0 percent), $5,901 Social Security benefits (17.3 percent), and $5,421 other income (15.9 percent). The lowest quintile households' average income of $3,986 consists of $73 earnings (1.8 percent), $168 property income (4.2 percent), $3,102 Social Security benefits (77.8 percent), and $643 other income (16.1 percent). These amounts are in 1982 dollars and adjusted for family size.

13. The conditional mean (median) amount of positive transfer given to the husband's parents is $3,406 ($1,500) and that from the wife's parents is $2,639 ($1,000). The conditional mean (median) amount of positive transfer received from the husband's parents is $5,370 ($2,000)

Table 7.9   **Inheritances ever received: KLoSA and HRS data**

Data sample (no. of households)	Percentage of the households that have ever inherited	Mean amount conditional on receipt	Median amount conditional on receipt
KLoSA 2006	2.4	₩150,658,000	₩50,000,000
All households ($N = 6{,}171$)		($157,665 in 2006)	($52,325 in 2006)
KLoSA 2006	3.3	₩201,659,000	₩80,000,000
Age 51–61 cohort ($N = 1{,}781$)		($211,038 in 2006)	($83,721 in 2006)
HRS 1992	28.1	$50,818	$20,000
Age 51–61 cohort ($N = 7{,}538$)		($73,021 in 2006)	($28,738 in 2006)

Notes: In converting won (₩) to dollar ($) amount, I use the year-average exchange rate in 2006 (1 dollar = 955.56 won) from the Bank of Korea. The 1992 dollar amounts are converted to the 2006 dollars using the Consumer Price Index.

7.2.2   Inheritances

Inheritances Ever Received

The 2006 KLoSA survey asks about money or property that the respondent has ever received in the form of an inheritance, a trust fund, or an insurance settlement. As shown in table 7.9, the fraction of KLoSA households who have ever received any of these is only 2.4 percent.[14] However, the magnitude of inheritance is quite sizable. The mean and median amounts of inheritances conditional on receipt are about 151 million won ($158,000) and 50 million won ($52,000), respectively.

The 1992 HRS survey contains a similar question on inheritance receipt, which reads: "Have you [or your (husband/wife/partner)] ever received an inheritance, or been given substantial assets in the form of a trust?"[15] The fraction of HRS households who have ever received an inheritance is 28 percent. The mean and median amounts of inheritances conditional on receipt are about $51,000 and $20,000, respectively.

Considering different age distributions of the 2006 KLoSA (age forty-five or over) and the 1992 HRS (age fifty-one to sixty-one) respondents, in the middle row of table 7.9, I restrict the KLoSA sample to those who were

---

and that from the wife's parents is $6,334 ($3,000). So if I were to point out anything at all, the wife's parents appear to receive slightly less and give slightly more than the husband's parents in the United States.

14. To compare with the HRS data that report inheritances that the respondent or spouse has ever received, I add up a couple's inheritance receipts if both are KLoSA respondents and therefore both report their inheritances. But if the spouse is not an eligible KLoSA respondent (probably because younger than forty-five years old), her or his inheritance receipt cannot be counted in.

15. The 1992 HRS data report the following three receipts separately: (a) an inheritance or a trust; (b) money or assets totaling $10,000 or more; and (c) a life insurance settlement of $10,000 or more. I add up these three forms of receipts and find that among 7,538 respondents the number of people with zero, one, two, and three forms of receipts is 5,420, 1,908, 203, and 7, respectively.

aged between fifty-one and sixty-one at the time of survey. Compared to the whole KLoSA sample, this subsample reports a higher fraction of positive receipts and a larger conditional mean and median. Nevertheless, there still exists a sharp contrast between the HRS and the KLoSA in inheritance patterns.

According to the table, Korean parents tend to concentrate their bequests on a child (arguably the eldest son who has taken care of them in their old age), which limits the number of inheritors to a small fraction but increases the amount of inheritance. On the contrary, American parents are known to distribute their estates almost equally among their children.[16]

In light of this, we may infer that, together with traditional norms of filial piety, potential bequests could have been used as leverage for Korean parents to get old-age support from their children, or their eldest sons to be more specific. A cross-cultural study by Shin, Cho, and Walker (1997) also finds that Korean children and their parents (specifically, mothers and mothers-in-law in their study) are more likely to endorse distributing larger shares of inheritance to the child who cares for her/his parents than American counterparts.

The KLoSA data also report the form of the largest inheritance receipt and the relationship of its donor to the recipient. Table 7.10 shows that about 70 percent of donors are recipients' fathers, which may reflect that the household head has the ownership of major household properties like a house. The form of the largest amount of inheritance is real estates in most cases. This implies that the most common case of inheritance in Korea is the eldest son's inheriting his parents' house or land when they died, finishing their coresidence with him. The eldest son is more likely to stay with his elderly parents after marriage than any other child in the family (see table 7.18 in section 7.4). Therefore, Korean parents have been able to provide a material incentive for the child who takes care of them in old age (mostly the eldest son) using their house as a promising inheritance.

The KReIS data report inheritances that respondents and spouses have ever received and bequests that they have ever left. Table 7.11 shows that 28.6 percent of the age-eligible financial respondents' households received inheritances, which is a much larger proportion compared to the KLoSA households in table 7.9, but quite similar to the HRS households. This discrepancy between the KReIS data and the KLoSA data in terms of the fraction of households receiving inheritances may arise at least in part from the fact that these two data sets use different wordings in their questions on inheritance. The KReIS asks about inheritances received by the spouse as well as the respondent, and explicitly refers to land or a house—the most

16. For example, Wilhelm (1996) finds that 68.6 percent of decedents divide their estates exactly equally between their children, and 76.6 percent divide their estates so that each child receives within 2 percent of the average inheritance across all children. McGarry (1999) also finds that bequests are mostly shared equally, whereas inter-vivo transfers tend to be more compensatory.

Table 7.10   **Who leaves what as an inheritance in Korea? KLoSA data**

Relationship of donor	No. of cases (%)	Form of inheritance	No. of cases (%)
Father	99 (67.8)	Real estate	137 (93.8)
Spouse	28 (19.2)	Cash or financial assets	5 (3.4)
Mother	12 (8.2)	Insurance settlement	2 (1.4)
Father-in-law or mother-in-law	4 (2.7)	Pension settlement	1 (0.7)
Other relative	3 (2.1)	Other	1 (0.7)
Total	146 (100.0)	Total	146 (100.0)

Table 7.11   **Inheritances and bequests in Korea: KReIS data (N = 4,800 households)**

Inheritances ever received		Bequests ever left	
Proportion of recipients (%)	28.6	Proportion of donors (%)	31.7
Donor	% donor[a]	Main recipient	% main recipient
Parents		Eldest son	52.6
Parents-in-law	79.3	Evenly to every child	17.6
Grandparents		Eldest daughter	15.5
Grandparents-in-law		Noneldest son	9.3
Spouse (deceased)	21.1	Noneldest daughter	3.5
		Social organization	0.6
		Sibling	0.1

Source: Calculated by the author, using the 2005 KReIS data.

Note: All numbers are weighted using household weights.

[a]The sum of "% donor" is 100.4 because a few households received inheritances from both their parents and their spouses.

common form of inheritances in Korea. Looking at bequests that the KReIS respondents and spouses have ever left, we can find that the tradition of primogeniture still prevails but different patterns also make an appearance. The proportion of the eldest son as the main recipient of bequests is 52.6, still more than half, but the proportion of equal distribution across children is now the second most frequent case.

Expectation about Inheritances

While having not yet received any inheritance, people may expect to receive inheritances in the future. They may also expect to leave bequests. The KLoSA and the HRS surveys have questions on subjective expectations about inheritances.[17] Table 7.12 reports such expectations. The sample mean of the subjective chances that the KLoSA respondents will receive inheri-

17. The related KLoSA questions read: "Including property and other valuables that you might own, what are the chances that you will leave an inheritance totaling 100,000,000 Korean won or more? And how about the chances that you will receive an inheritance totaling 100,000,000 Korean won or more?" The corresponding HRS questions read: "What are the

Table 7.12   Subjective expectations about inheritances: KLoSA and HRS data

Data	Chances of receiving an inheritance	Chances of leaving a bequest
KLoSA 2006	₩100,000,000 or more: 0.17 (N = 3,163)	₩100,000,000 or more: 0.38 (N = 10,254)
HRS 1994	0.21 (N = 5,905)	$10,000 or more: 0.60 ($N$ = 5,901)
	Mean (median) amount: $51,127 ($20,000)	$100,000 or more: 0.42 ($N$ = 5,139)
HRS 1996	0.20 (N = 6,316)	$10,000 or more: 0.65 ($N$ = 6,309)
	Mean (median) amount: $62,996 ($25,000)	$100,000 or more: 0.44 ($N$ = 4,885)
HRS 1998	0.18 (N = 6,027)	$10,000 or more: 0.65 ($N$ = 6,000)
	Mean (median) amount: $75,220 ($25,000)	$100,000 or more: 0.45 ($N$ = 4,778)
HRS 2000	0.17 (N = 5,697)	$10,000 or more: 0.66 ($N$ = 5,660)
	Mean (median) amount: $172,661 ($20,000)	$100,000 or more: 0.48 ($N$ = 4,563)

tances exceeding 100,000,000 won is 0.17, which is much higher than the fraction of the KLoSA households that have ever inherited in table 7.9. This subjective probability is quite comparable to the HRS respondents' expectations in table 7.12, although the HRS questions did not give any censoring amount (herein a lower limit) to the respondents. Therefore, the KLoSA respondents appear to have more optimistic expectations about substantial amounts of inheritance receipts than the HRS respondents. As for the subjective probability of leaving an inheritance exceeding 100,000,000 won (roughly $100,000 in 2006), the KLoSA respondents report 0.38 on average and the corresponding HRS figures range from 0.42 to 0.48.

Considering substantial differences between the KLoSA and the HRS in terms of inheritance receipts, their expectations about inheritances seem fairly similar to each other. This probably suggests that Koreans' behaviors toward inheritances are getting closer to Americans'. That is, Koreans' bequests are being more equally distributed among children, as the eldest son's burden of supporting elderly parents is being distributed to a broader range of supporters, including other sons, daughters, and parents themselves (see table 7.19 in section 7.4). Incidentally, high chances that Koreans expect to leave sizable inheritances exceeding 100,000,000 won might reflect the recent housing market boom in Korea, considering that the most common form of their inheritance is real estate.

7.3   Characteristics of Donor and Recipient

Intergenerational transfers given by adult children to their elderly parents have played a crucial role in the old-age income security in Korea. As shown in the previous section, Korean elderly parents are more likely to be net ben-

---

chances that you [or your (husband/wife/partner)] will leave an inheritance totaling $10,000 [$100,000] or more? And how about the chances that you will receive an inheritance within the next 10 years? About how large do you expect that inheritance to be?"

eficiaries in financial exchanges with their children. This section investigates the characteristics of the donor and the recipient to better understand the motivation and other realities of familial transfers in Korea.

First, I introduce a simple model of intergenerational transfers for setting up a basic specification of empirical models and review existing empirical results. Based on these backgrounds, I examine parents' characteristics as the explanatory variables in the regressions of the parents' net transfer receipt from their children. Then I examine children's characteristics using family fixed-effect models to figure out which child will provide the largest financial help, which is what many parents are probably curious about.

7.3.1   Background

The theoretical framework in this section is adopted from Cox, Hansen, and Jimenez (2004). Consider a family in which financial transfers are made between two family members. For simplicity, I assume that the "net giver" whose transfer gift is bigger than transfer receipt has an altruistic preference, while the "net receiver" does not. So the two family members are assumed to consist of an altruistic donor and a nonaltruistic recipient.

Suppose the utility of the donor, U_d, is given by:

$$(1) \qquad U_d = U(C_d, s, V(C_r, s)),$$

where V is the well-being of the recipient; C_d and C_r are consumption levels for the donor and the recipient, respectively; and s denotes "services" that the recipient might provide to the donor.[18] The donor's altruistic motive is indicated by $\partial U/\partial V > 0$. Exchange motives may be present as well if the donor values services from the recipient, $\partial U/\partial s > 0$, and the recipient's utility falls with provision of services, $\partial V/\partial s < 0$.

The budget constraints for donor and recipient can be written:

$$(2) \qquad C_d = I_d - T \text{ and } C_r = I_r + T,$$

where T denotes financial transfers given by the donor to the recipient; and I_d and I_r are pretransfer incomes of the donor and the recipient, respectively. Since C_r is a normal good for the donor, transfers are increasing in the donor's pretransfer income, $\partial T/\partial I_d > 0$.

If transfers are altruistically motivated, we expect $\partial T/\partial I_r < 0$ because the donor believes that the recipient with higher (lower) pretransfer income requires smaller (larger) transfers to attain the optimal level of consumption. Instead, if transfers are exchange-motivated, the relationship between T and I_r will be ambiguous. Suppose transfers are payments for services that the

---

18. Cox, Hansen, and Jimenez (2004) consider "services" as a catchall term standing for anything provided by the recipient in return for the money received from the donor. It can be, for example, help with home production, babysitting, visiting, caregiving, behaving in a way the donor prefers, or future financial transfers as the discounted value of repayments if the money received from the donor is a loan.

donor purchases from the recipient at an implicit price, p, so that $T = ps$. Cox (1987) shows $\partial s/\partial I_r < 0$ and $\partial p/\partial I_r > 0$; that is, a richer recipient will provide smaller services to the donor, and the donor has to pay a higher price for the services provided by a richer recipient. Therefore, transfers can rise or fall with I_r, depending on whether the price effect dominates the quantity effect. In this case, the functional form of transfers in the recipient's pretransfer income will be nonlinear.

As seen in the previous section, the dominant direction of private transfers in the United States is downward; therefore, most empirical studies using U.S. data focus on the motivation of parental transfers to their children rather than adult children's transfers to their elderly parents. The extensive empirical literature comes to mixed conclusions on whether inter-vivos transfers are compensatory or not. McGarry and Schoeni (1995, 1997), Dunn and Phillips (1997), McGarry (1999, 2000), and Hochguertel and Ohlsson (2000), for example, report that parental transfers compensate worse-off children. But Laferrère and Wolff (2004) discuss some empirical studies providing evidence against compensatory transfers and rejecting altruism. Cox (1987), Cox and Rank (1992), and Cox, Eser, and Jimenez (1998) also suggest that transfers may represent payment to the recipient for the provision of services rather than altruism. Cox and Jakubson (1995) even argue that the anti-poverty effectiveness of public transfers can be magnified by private-transfer responses that are basically exchange-motivated.

By contrast, the direction of familial transfers observed in Korean data sets is more likely to be upward; as a result, this study has a different angle. In the remaining parts of this section, I estimate the familial transfer model in which adult children are net givers and their elderly parents are net receivers. If children's transfers are made in a compensatory fashion from their altruistic motive, an increase in their parents' pretransfer income, for example, by public assistance leads to a decrease in their transfers to the parents. This altruism story and resultant crowding-out of private transfers by public transfers are supported in Korean empirical studies by Kang and Jeon (2005) and Kim (2006). But Jin (1999) and Sung (2006) do not find such evidence.

7.3.2   Which Parents Benefit More from Children?

Here I examine parental characteristics as explanatory variables for net transfer receipt from children. The regression results using data from the KLoSA and the KReIS are provided in turn.

KLoSA Regression Results

In the 2006 KLoSA data, financial transfers received from and given to each child in 2005 are reported by the respondent of the Children section in the survey. Regular transfers and irregular (or occasional) transfers are added up to construct total transfers. I calculate net total annual transfer receipt from each child by subtracting total annual transfer gift to the child from total annual transfer receipt from the child. Then I sum up net total annual transfer receipt from every child of the respondent to generate the sum of net total annual transfer receipt of the respondent as the dependent variable.

The simple model discussed previously provides some guidance to the empirical specifications of transfer functions. First, as long as we do not know the motivation of transfers ex ante, the functional form of transfers needs to be nonlinear in the recipient's pretransfer income. After trying polynomials of the third and the fourth order that turned out inappropriate in criteria of statistical significance, I choose a quadratic function. Second, considering heterogeneous budget constraints depending on household characteristics given pretransfer incomes, I control for the recipient's age, gender, family size, education level, wealth, health status, work status, and region of residence. Third, in order to account for differential numbers of donors in a family, we need to control for the number of children of the respondent; I further control for the number of daughters and sons separately to address potential gender differences in supporting elderly parents. Finally, I attempt to address other observed characteristics that might affect transfer behavior, such as religious preference, the number of grandchildren, expectations about financial situation of recipients and their children, and expectations about public support for their old age.

Baseline regression results are reported in columns (a) and (b) of table 7.13. First, transfer surplus (i.e., the sum of net total annual transfer receipt from every adult child in the family) increases with the recipient's age until the late seventies, and then decreases. Remember that a similar pattern is also found in the transfer in/out profiles by parent age in table 7.2. Female respondents report more transfer surplus from their children, conditional on their marital status.

Second, transfer surplus is negatively correlated with the recipient's income for almost the entire range of their income distribution. The recipient's net worth also reduces transfer surplus. These results clearly show the main motivation of familial transfers in Korea—an altruistic motive to alleviate the recipient's financial difficulties.[19]

Third, the son provides bigger financial help to the parents than the daughter. The parameter estimates for the number of sons and the number of daughters in column (a) suggest that one more son gives his parents additional transfer surplus of 346,000 won while one more daughter gives her

19. As mentioned earlier, using the KLIPS data, Kim (2006) also concludes that private transfers are altruistically motivated in Korea, from findings that private transfer receipts are negatively correlated with the recipient income and they are crowded out by public assistance. Moreover, Kim (2006) finds qualitatively similar results when both the donor's and the recipient's characteristics, including their incomes, are controlled for using a split-off children sample.

Table 7.13   Which parents benefit more from children? KLoSA data (10,000 won)

Dependent variable: Net transfer from noncoresident children

	(A)		(B)		(C)		(D)	
	Parameter	t-value	Parameter	t-value	Parameter	t-value	Parameter	t-value
Intercept	−1,353.6	−5.05***	−1,342.4	−5.00***	−1,420.5	−5.29***	−1,408.3	−5.23***
Age	31.7	3.91***	32.6	3.99***	32.1	3.95***	32.9	4.03***
Age squared	−0.2	−2.84***	−0.2	−3.04***	−0.2	−2.88***	−0.2	−3.06***
Female	40.5	1.93*	38.2	1.81*	40.1	1.91*	37.8	1.80*
Annual income/10^3	−15.6	−2.83***	−15.3	−2.79***	−15.1	−2.75***	−14.9	−2.72***
Annual income squared/10^6	0.1	2.22**	0.1	2.18**	0.1	2.18**	0.1	2.15**
Net worth/10^6	−644.2	−3.10***	−637.2	−3.06***	−653.2	−3.14***	−646.8	−3.11***
Number of daughters	14.3	1.82*	2.9	0.28	14.5	1.84*	3.8	0.37
Number of sons	34.6	3.47***	23.4	1.96**	34.2	3.43***	23.7	1.99**
Number of household members	0.4	0.07	1.1	0.17	0.0	0.00	0.6	0.09
Marital status (omitted: Currently married)								
Separated	33.7	0.49	36.5	0.53	30.2	0.44	32.8	0.47
Divorced	73.8	1.47	75.6	1.49	80.3	1.60	82.1	1.62*
Widowed	−28.6	−1.13	−30.7	−1.20	−24.5	−0.97	−26.4	−1.03
Health status (omitted: Fair)								
Very good	−54.6	−1.29	−53.7	−1.27	−55.6	−1.32	−54.8	−1.30
Good	13.9	0.67	13.8	0.67	14.8	0.71	14.7	0.71
Poor	42.1	1.79*	43.5	1.85*	44.2	1.88*	45.6	1.93*
Very poor	−0.6	−0.01	2.0	0.05	1.9	0.05	4.3	0.11
Years of education	20.1	2.92***	20.6	2.99***	20.3	2.95***	20.8	3.02***
Years of education squared	−1.1	−3.02***	−1.1	−3.06***	−1.1	−3.09***	−1.1	−3.12***
Not working	2.2	0.11	2.3	0.11	4.7	0.23	4.8	0.23

	Model 1		Model 2		Model 3		Model 4	
Province (omitted: Metropolitan area)								
Gangwon	−142.6	−3.08***	−143.6	−3.10***	−148.3	−3.18***	−149.3	−3.20***
Gyeongsang	−58.2	−2.84***	−59.1	−2.87***	−56.0	−2.71***	−57.0	−2.75***
Jeolla	−81.1	−2.92***	−82.1	−2.95***	−85.7	−3.06***	−86.4	−3.08***
Chungcheong	−7.1	−0.24	−8.5	−0.29	−5.1	−0.17	−6.5	−0.22
Religious preference (omitted: No preference)								
Protestant	31.5	1.38	32.0	1.40	32.4	1.42	32.9	1.44
Catholic	10.6	0.35	11.7	0.38	11.4	0.38	12.5	0.41
Buddhist	15.2	0.71	15.8	0.74	16.2	0.76	16.8	0.79
Won Buddhist	110.4	0.59	112.1	0.59	111.6	0.59	113.1	0.60
Other	42.0	0.48	43.5	0.49	35.0	0.40	36.4	0.41
Number of grandchildren			7.6	1.78*			7.2	1.68*
Subjective expectation feeling (chances: 0–1)								
Financial situation will be worse					25.0	0.76	26.0	0.79
Children's generation will be better off					94.6	2.55**	91.8	2.47**
Government will provide old-age support					−67.0	−1.89*	−67.0	−1.89*
Number of families	6,488		6,474		6,488		6,474	
F	10.94		10.69		10.24		10.02	
Adjusted R²	.0412		.0416		.0423		.0427	

***Significant at the 1 percent level.

**Significant at the 5 percent level.

*Significant at the 10 percent level.

parents additional transfer surplus of 143,000 won. When the number of the recipient's grandchildren is included in the set of explanatory variables as in column (b), the magnitudes of the coefficients for the number of sons and the number of daughters are reduced significantly so that one more daughter, in particular, does not increase transfer surplus anymore. Therefore, one may imagine that the motivation of daughters' financial transfers to their elderly parents is closely related to their children (e.g., in return for grandparents' babysitting service).

Fourth, parental education level increases transfer surplus until nine years of completed schooling (high school entrance level), but further parental education decreases transfer surplus. This nonlinear relationship between parental education and net transfers from children probably reflects the fact that parental education delivers indirect information on their children's economic standings. If undereducated parents tend to have low-income children, parents' additional education implies their children's higher income that can increase net transfers from the children to some levels of parental education. But highly educated parents may not need financial help from their children or are even able to give net transfers to their children, so parental education eventually decreases transfer surplus from a certain level of their education.[20]

Fifth, those who live in the Metropolitan area (Seoul, Incheon, and Gyeonggi province) report a larger transfer surplus than those in other provinces, which probably reflects the recipient's higher living cost and/or the donor's higher income in that area. More transfer surplus seems to go to divorced parents and those who reported their health status as poor. Other parental characteristics such as work status and religious preference do not affect transfer surplus to a degree that has statistical significance.

Furthermore, the KLoSA data contain survey results on respondents' subjective expectation feelings to several issues. Among others, I select their expectations about the financial situation in their future, the relative financial situation of their children's generation compared to theirs, and potential support of their old age by government. These expectations are rescaled between 0 and 1 with an interval of 0.1 and additionally included in the set of explanatory variables in columns (c) and (d) to see how they are correlated with familial transfer behavior.

The results show that expectations on tomorrow's situations affect today's transfer behavior. Those who expect their children's generation will be better off than their generation tend to have more transfer surplus than those

20. The KLoSA data contain detailed information on the respondents' formal education—the highest level of school they attended and whether they got the diploma, just completed course of study, dropped out, or passed an equivalency test. Using these variables, I construct a variable of imputed years of education that is used in the regressions. According to this variable, the KLoSA respondents have 8.2 years of schooling on average, and 62.5 percent have education levels of nine years or below.

who do not expect it. They probably make fewer transfers to their children or receive more transfers from their children, who may have similar expectations. A pessimistic expectation about their future financial situation might also yield transfer surplus, but the relationship is not statistically significant. So an expectation about the relative financial situation of the respondents to their children seems more important than an expectation about the absolute level of their own financial situation in determining transfer balance between them.

The most interesting part would be the effect of an expectation about public support on private transfer behavior. The result suggests that those who expect that government will provide old-age support have smaller transfer surplus within their families. They probably make more transfers to their children or receive fewer transfers from their children, who may have similar expectations. As long as familial transfers are not observed by government in general and public transfers are made in a compensatory fashion, this can be regarded as a "moral hazard" behavior.

The crowding-out effect of realized public transfers on private transfers has been documented in the literature (see Kang and Jeon [2005] and Kim [2006], for example), but this potential crowding-out effect of a positive expectation about public transfers on private transfers is first suggested in this study.

KReIS Regression Results

Since the KReIS survey asked about transfers that respondents or spouses received from and gave to coresident children as well as noncoresident children, table 7.13 reports regression results on net annual transfer receipts by children's coresidence status.[21] Column (a) uses net transfer receipts from all children irrespective of coresidence status as the dependent variable, and columns (b) and (c) use net transfer receipts from coresident children and from noncoresident children, respectively. Therefore, column (c) results are most comparable to the KLoSA regression results in table 7.12.

In every specification, net transfers are negatively correlated with the recipient's income for almost the entire range of their income distribution, which confirms that Korean familial transfers operate in a compensatory fashion. The crowding-out of noncoresident children's transfers by transfers from coresident children and others listed in table 7.5 also supports the altruism theory. Net worth is also negatively correlated with net transfers, although the relationship is not significant for net transfers from noncoresident children. Parental education level exhibits a nonlinear relationship

---

21. The unit of analysis here is an individual (or a respondent), not a family. Therefore, I estimate the model with clustered error terms to control for correlation within families and calculate the White-Huber robust standard errors. A household-level analysis using the age-eligible financial respondents' observations yields qualitatively similar results.

with net transfer receipts from their children, which is also found in table 7.13 of the KLoSA results.

On the other hand, net transfers from coresident children show different relationships with some parental characteristics compared to those from noncoresident children. First, female respondents, household heads, or those who live with their spouses tend to have larger transfer deficits from their coresident children, whereas they tend to have larger transfer surpluses from their noncoresident children.

Second, the age structure of household members has different effects on parents' net transfer receipts by children's coresidence status. The number of household members aged zero to four is positively correlated with net transfers from coresident children but it is negatively correlated with those from noncoresident children. This may reflect coresident children's transfers in return for their parents' babysitting service because coresident infants are probably coresident children's children, not noncoresident children's. The number of household members aged ten to nineteen (and aged twenty to thirty-nine) in the household is negatively correlated with net transfers from coresident children, reflecting parents' substantial expenditure on teenagers (and probably single children in their twenties or thirties) for schooling, private tutoring, clothing, and so on. The number of household members aged forty to sixty-four is negatively correlated with net transfers from noncoresident children, which may suggest that the existence of potential supporters for elderly parents in the household reduces transfers from non-coresident children.[22]

Third, noncoresident sons give more transfers than noncoresident daughters. One more son gives his parents additional transfer surplus of 250,000 won, while one more daughter gives her parents additional transfer surplus of 150,000 won. But coresident children ("net receivers" on average) show no significant difference by gender (see table 7.14).

Finally, more net transfer receipts are reported by those who are caring for their grandchildren (regardless of whether they live together or not) almost entirely. Grandparents who provide extensive caregiving to their grandchildren get more transfer surplus of 1,981,000 won from noncoresident children (probably the grandchildren's parents) than grandparents who do not. This result provides evidence to the existence of exchange motive in familial transfers.

7.3.3   Which Child Gives More to Parents?

Now I turn to the child's side to examine the donor's characteristics. We can also control for the donor's and the recipient's observed characteristics

---

22. Those aged forty to sixty-four may include parents themselves, but the KReIS data do not provide more detailed information on the age structure other than these age categories.

Table 7.14   Which parents benefit more from children?: KReIS Data (1,000 won)

		Dependent variable: Net transfer from				
	(A) All children		(B) Coresident children		(C) Noncoresident children	
	Parameter	t-value	Parameter	t-value	Parameter	t-value
Annual income	-.06375	-7.14***	-.03338	-4.71***	-.03341	-6.42***
Annual income squared/10^3	.00011	5.32***	.00007	5.00***	.00004	3.59***
Net transfer from coresident children			-.05471	-5.20***	-.04079	-4.95***
Net transfer from noncoresident children						
Net transfer from others	.01395	0.18	.07711	1.05	-.06352	-1.95**
Annual saving	-.02392	-1.19	-.03064	-1.92*	.00585	0.66
Net worth	-.00142	-2.85***	-.00146	-3.49***	-.00002	-0.06
Age	1,234.4	13.82***	1,130.1	15.04***	156.3	2.83***
Age squared	-8.2	-12.87***	-7.8	-14.87***	-0.8	-1.91*
Female	-245.3	-1.71*	-757.9	-6.33***	510.1	5.93***
Household head	-942.7	-5.87***	-1,620.7	-11.51***	649.5	7.83***
Education level (omitted: No schooling)						
Primary school	1,059.0	6.88***	428.9	3.94***	682.6	6.05***
Middle school	1,701.6	7.87***	867.3	5.14***	916.0	6.40***
High school	1,046.8	3.91***	22.0	0.11	1,082.6	5.67***
College	303.5	0.68	-416.6	-1.21	743.0	2.48**
Graduate school	-2,206.6	-1.73*	-2,168.1	-2.07**	-129.1	-0.16*
Married	146.5	0.26	405.2	0.86	-256.5	-0.75
Living with spouse	-453.6	-0.79	-1,370.7	-2.80***	912.1	2.62***

(continued)

Table 7.14 (continued)

	(A) All children		(B) Coresident children		(C) Noncoresident children	
	Parameter	t-value	Parameter	t-value	Parameter	t-value
Number of household members						
Age 0–4	365.2	1.12	1,089.9	3.74***	−720.4	−4.13***
Age 5–9	−24.0	−0.09	320.6	1.48	−350.7	−1.97**
Age 10–19	−1,489.6	−7.65***	−1,466.2	−7.95***	−84.5	−1.02
Age 20–39	−495.1	−3.59***	−416.4	−3.45***	−100.0	−1.33
Age 40–64	−680.5	−4.23***	26.5	0.20	−745.1	−7.76***
Age 65 or older	−597.6	−2.75***	−345.5	−1.76*	−280.1	−2.60***
Number of sons	220.1	2.98***	−17.7	−0.35	250.3	4.46***
Number of daughters	114.2	1.85*	−31.2	−0.65	152.2	3.71***
Caring for grandchild	2,762.6	9.56***	920.8	4.75***	1,981.6	8.95***
Province (omitted: Metropolitan area)						
Gangwon	−1,134.9	−3.41***	−390.0	−1.72*	−802.2	−3.30***
Gyeongsang	−481.4	−2.30**	−277.5	−1.68*	−226.6	−1.63
Jeolla	−545.8	−1.93*	−657.9	−3.28***	91.5	0.45
Chungcheong	−757.0	−2.93***	−466.3	−2.22**	−325.9	−2.01**
Jeju	−1,246.8	−2.54**	−706.2	−1.72*	−599.4	−2.32**
Intercept	−42,086.3	−13.18***	−37,142.7	−13.63***	−6,733.2	−3.51***
Number of observations	8,629		8,629		8,629	
F	35.10		23.61		20.16	
R²	0.233		0.204		0.107	

***Significant at the 1 percent level.
**Significant at the 5 percent level.
*Significant at the 10 percent level.

simultaneously in a cross-section model with a parent-child pair being the unit of analysis. But familial transfer behavior can be affected by unobserved family-specific characteristics, which are arguably common across children within a family. Thus, to investigate which child gives more to her or his parents in a family, the best empirical strategy would be a family fixed-effect specification using a sibling sample that consists of multiple parent-child pairs in the family. I confine children to adults (aged nineteen or over) and those who do not live with their parents and are not students at the time of survey. Considering potential differences in the effects of donor's characteristics depending on whether the transfer is regular financial support or occasional irregular transfer, I use three different dependent variables: the amounts of net total/regular/irregular transfer receipts from each adult child in the family.

The main interest is how net transfer receipt is affected by the child's demographic characteristics such as age, birth order, gender, marital status, number of children, and financial status. Since the KLoSA data do not have information on children's income or wealth, I use years of education, home ownership, and work status as proxies for their financial status. In addition, I use variables related to intimacy in the relationship between the respondent and each child. These variables are the child's residential distance from the respondent; frequency of contact in person and by phone, mail, or e-mail; and receipts and gifts of various in-kind transfers. One may have interest in how in-kind transfer variables are related to financial transfers.

Table 7.15 reports regression results from these within-family estimations. To account for the potential relationship of in-kind transfers with net financial transfers, I include dummies for in-kind transfer gift and receipt in specification (a), and then dummies for detailed items of in-kind transfer gift and receipt in specification (b).

Children's demographic variables exhibit some interesting relationships, with net transfers given to their parents. First, the eldest child in the family gives more net regular financial support to the parents by 230,000 won per year. Similarly, the son gives more by 230,000 won per year than the daughter. Thus, both estimates imply that the eldest son makes more transfers than his siblings on a regular base by 460,000 won per year. This reflects an old tradition that the eldest son usually undertakes the responsibility to support his elderly parents and inherits their property (and also the duty of celebrating annual Confucian memorial services for his ancestors) afterwards.

Second, a more educated child gives more total transfer surplus to the parent by 90,000 won per additional one year of education. Looking at regular transfer only, additional transfer surplus from the child's one more year of education is 65,000 won per year. Irregular transfer surplus from child education does not have any statistical significance in every

Table 7.15 Which child gives more to parents? Family fixed-effect models, KLoSA data

	(A)			(B)		
	Total	Regular	Irregular	Total	Regular	Irregular
Intercept	−167.9	−133.0	−34.9	−184.0	−142.1	−41.9
Age	−0.8	−1.0	0.2	−0.9	−0.9	0.1
Eldest child	20.6	22.9***	−2.2	22.2	22.5***	−0.3
Son	31.3**	22.7***	8.5	30.1*	23.0***	7.0
Years of education	9.1***	6.5***	2.6	9.0***	6.7***	2.3
Home ownership	33.3**	34.0***	−0.7	34.5**	33.4***	1.1
Working	−2.8	31.2***	−34.0**	−1.2	30.9***	−32.1**
Marital status (omitted: Single)						
Currently married	15.1	30.3**	−15.2	19.3	29.8*	−10.5
Separated	−49.9	−48.6	−1.2	−45.4	−48.4	3.0
Divorced	24.1	35.0	−10.9	22.2	28.4	−6.3
Widowed	116.4	66.8	49.6	120.7	64.6	56.0
Number of children	0.5	−3.5	4.0	0.9	−3.3	4.2
Distance from parents (omitted: More than a 2-hour distance by public transportation)						
Within a 30-minute distance	6.6	−12.5	19.1	4.4	−12.4	16.8
Within a 1-hour distance	−39.8*	−0.5	−39.3**	−39.8*	−0.2	−39.7**
Within a 2-hour distance	−8.6	−2.3	−6.2	−10.6	−2.5	−8.1
Frequency of face-to-face contact (omitted: Never)						
More than 4 times a week	226.5	119.7	106.9	217.7	116.4	101.3
2–3 times a week	158.1	139.8	18.4	150.5	136.5	14.0
Once a week	153.1	152.2	0.9	144.8	150.4	−5.6
Twice a month	160.6	128.0	32.6	151.9	125.5	26.4
Once a month	142.5	115.4	27.1	134.1	112.3	21.7
5–6 times a year	149.1	110.7	38.4	142.2	107.9	34.3

Dependent variable: Net annual transfer from each child to parents (unit: 10,000 won)

	(1)	(2)	(3)	(4)	(5)	(6)
3–4 times a year	143.4	110.7	32.6	133.7	106.3	27.4
1–2 times a year	149.1	116.2	32.9	138.0	113.1	24.9
Almost never (in a year)	130.6	88.2	42.4	123.1	87.9	35.2
Frequency of phone/(e-)mail contact (omitted: Never)						
More than 4 times a week	33.8	15.5	18.4	60.1	19.8	40.3
2–3 times a week	−19.2	−28.1	8.9	9.6	−22.0	31.6
Once a week	−44.4	−38.7	−5.7	−14.6	−33.1	18.4
Twice a month	−54.3	−51.1	−3.1	−29.5	−45.7	16.2
Once a month	−52.1	−50.6	−1.5	−22.8	−45.2	22.5
5–6 times a year	−68.3	−63.3	−5.1	−49.0	−59.1	10.1
3–4 times a year	−90.7	−89.6	−1.1	−61.5	−83.5	22.0
1–2 times a year	−138.1	−138.2	0.1	−107.3	−133.2	25.9
Almost never (in a year)	−72.2	−40.3	−32.0	−51.0	−37.5	−13.5
Giving in-kind transfer to parents	−11.5	−10.2	−1.3			
Leisure (e.g., travel)				145.2*	149.2***	−4.0
Health-related products (e.g., vitamins, equipments, etc.)				−5.3	−2.2	−3.1
Household items				11.3	5.9	5.4
Electronics				−25.3	−55.4*	30.1
Dining out and foods				−12.5	−13.3	0.8
Other				0.4	15.3	−14.9
Receiving in-kind transfer from parents	82.2***	−2.4	84.6***			
Leisure (e.g., travel)				−106.9	−22.4	−84.5
Health-related products (e.g., vitamins, equipments, etc.)				367.8***	−7.8	375.6***
Household items				−122.1*	−57.4	−64.7
Electronics				−2.9	39.0	−41.9
Dining out and foods				48.9	12.1	36.8
Other				43.0	−10.7	53.7
Observations: 6,299 (2,052 families)						
R^2 (within families)	.020	.044	.012	.024	.048	.016

***Significant at the 1 percent level.
**Significant at the 5 percent level.
*Significant at the 10 percent level.

specification.[23] In addition, when a college graduate dummy is included instead of years of education, total (regular) transfer surplus from the child's college graduation is 430,000 won (260,000 won) per year. Therefore, a college-graduate child gives more net regular transfers than her/his siblings who have not graduated from college by only 20,000 won (roughly 20 dollars) per month. If children's education has been funded mainly by their parents, this "repayment" looks too small.[24] In light of this, child education can hardly be a retirement plan for the parents.

Third, a child who has her or his own home makes a larger amount of regular transfer (by 340,000 won per year) than siblings who do not have home ownership. Since the 2006 KLoSA data have no information on children's income or assets other than home, home ownership can be used as a reliable proxy for the economic standing of the child. This result seems trivial, but consistent with the theory that transfers are increasing in the donor's pretransfer income.

Fourth, when we look at total transfers, the child's work status does not seem to be related with transfer behavior. However, looking at regular transfers and irregular transfers separately, we can find an interesting pattern of transfer behavior by the child's work status. A child who has a job makes more regular transfers by 310,000 won per year than her or his sibling who has no job. But the latter makes more irregular transfers than the former by the similar amount, which leads to roughly the same amount of resultant total transfers regardless of the child's work status.

Fifth, a child who is currently married makes more regular transfers than a child who is still single. A child with other marital status does not show any significant difference compared with an unmarried child.

Sixth, parents seem to have the least financial gain from a child who lives within a one-hour distance (by public transportation) than other children living closer or farther. The frequency of a child's face-to-face contact or phone/mail/e-mail contact with the respondent does not show any significant relationship with transfer behavior.[25]

23. Although not provided in this chapter, the specification that includes the square term of years of education is estimated with statistical significance only for the model of net regular transfer. The estimated quadratic function of net regular transfer is increasing in the years of education higher than 11.5 years. But 83.5 percent of the children in the regression sample have at least twelve years of education, so in most cases net transfers from children are positively correlated with their education levels.

24. According to the Organization for Economic Cooperation and Development's (OECD's) *Education at a Glance 2007,* annual expenditure per student on public education in Korea as of 2004 was estimated as 4,490 dollars for primary education, 6,761 dollars for secondary education, and 7,068 dollars for tertiary education. Furthermore, it is well-known that Korean parents spend large sums of money on the private tutoring for their children. As of 2007, average monthly spending per student on private tutoring is estimated by 276 dollars for primary school, 338 dollars for middle school, and 386 dollars for high school (Korea National Statistical Office, February 2008).

25. At the beginning of my estimation, a regression using the entire KLoSA children sample showed that a child who had never contacted the respondent in person made a significantly

Table 7.16   **Major financial supporter among children: KReIS data (%)**

Eldest son	42.4 (53.6)	Other children	46.4
Firstborn and only son	9.8	Other son	10.8
Non-firstborn but only son	5.5	Daughter with no brother	6.7
Non-only son but eldest son	27.2	Daughter with 1 brother	15.6
Non-only son but can be eldest son	(11.2)	Daughter with 2 or more brothers	13.3

Source: Calculated by the author using the 2005 KReIS data.
Note: All numbers are weighted using household weights.

Finally, parents receive a larger amount of net irregular transfer from children whom they gave some in-kind transfers than from other children whom they did not. If this is because parents gave a smaller amount of irregular financial help to the child who received some in-kind transfers, the relationship implies that in-kind transfer and irregular financial transfer are substitutes. Instead, if this is because the child gave a greater amount of irregular financial help to the parents, the relationship implies that children's occasional financial transfers are made in return for the in-kind transfers received from their parents. Specification (b) examines what type of in-kind transfers are related to financial transfers. The results show that a child who provides parents with a leisure gift such as travel gift certificates is probably a regular financial helper to the parents. In addition, a child's occasional financial transfer is made probably in return for a parental gift of health-related products.

The KReIS data do not have any information on the respondents' children except the number of sons and daughters. But the KReIS survey contains a useful question for this study, which reads: "Which child is providing the biggest financial help to you with nothing in return?" To this question, the respondent reports the birth order and gender of the child so that we can identify the major financial supporter's birth order and gender. Table 7.16 summarizes the best information that can be drawn from the data. We find again a dominant role of the eldest son in supporting elderly parents. At least 42 percent of KReIS households pinpoint their eldest sons as major financial supporters.

7.4   Deteriorating Familial Support and Policies for Old-Age Security

The tradition of familial support for the elderly in Korea is on a decreasing turn due to broadly documented socioeconomic factors such as nuclear fam-

---

larger transfer than other children who had been in some contact. But this result was driven by an extreme outlier who made a huge amount of net transfer (43,200,000 won a year), which I have dropped from the sample.

ily, individualism, population aging, and changing preferences for multigenerational coresidence. In this regard, the demand and expectation that the government should expand programs to guarantee the income of the elderly are growing. This section describes changes in familial support mechanism and discusses potential income sources of the elderly.

7.4.1   Changes in Familial Support Mechanism

Decreasing Portion of Familial Transfer as Main Source of Elderly Income

Familial transfer has been losing importance as a private safety net for Korean elderly. As shown in table 7.17, the proportion of Korean elderly aged sixty or older who report that their main source of income is financial assistance from their children has decreased from 72 percent in 1980 to 56 percent in 1995, and 31 percent in 2003. Instead, the proportion of public transfers as the main source of income has increased, owing to welfare expansion after the late 1990s financial crisis in Korea. As a result, a quarter of the elderly aged sixty or older was living mainly on public transfers as of 2003. Considering that public transfers tend to crowd out private transfers, private demand for welfare programs for the elderly is likely to increase further.

Changing Patterns of Children's Coresidence with
and Support for Elderly Parents

This study focuses on intergenerational transfer as a pillar of familial support mechanism. But another pillar should be intergenerational coresidence. Coresidence implies sharing of food and utilities as well as housing, so it may be altruistic from the standpoint of the richer member in the family. However, intergenerational coresidence is sometimes demanded by children

Table 7.17   **Changing patterns of main source of the elderly (aged sixty or older) income in Korea (%)**

Income source	Items	1980	1995	2003
Labor	Wage, own business, etc.	16.2	26.6	30.4
Property	Rent, interest, dividend, deposit withdrawal, private pension, etc.	5.5	9.9	9.9
Private transfers	Subtotal	75.6	56.6	31.4
	From children	72.4	56.3	31.1
	From other persons	3.2	0.3	0.3
Public transfers	Subtotal	2.0	6.6	25.6
	Public pension, social insurance	0.8	2.9	10.6
	Public assistance	1.2	3.7	15.0

Sources: Kim (2006, Table 2-13, 58). The 1980 and 1995 figures are from Seok and Kim (2000) who cited Japanese government's cross-country survey, and the 2003 figures are calculated by Kim (2006), using the additional survey for the aged cohort in the 2003 KLIPS data.

who need parents' help for living. Anyway, relatively high prevalence of coresidence between elderly parents and adult children in Korea is generally interpreted as a structural manifestation of traditional family norms.

Although fewer parents are expecting to live with their adult children these days, some parents are probably curious about which child will live with them in their old age.[26] Table 7.18 provides an answer to this question. Using KLoSA data, I investigate adult children's characteristics as the determinants of their status of coresidence with their parents. Again, I confine the children sample to those who were aged nineteen or older and were not students at the time of survey. To control for unobserved familial heterogeneity and also to see the results from a parent's point of view, I compare the likelihoods of coresidence with elderly parents between siblings within a family using fixed-effect logit estimation (Chamberlain logit model).

Column (a) reports the likelihood of coresidence is high when the child is the eldest and a son, which reflects a traditional norm of the eldest son's coresidence with his parents. The positive effect of the years of education of a child on the coresidence likelihood implies that more investment in a child's education and resultant higher earning potential of the child would place more responsibility of supporting elderly parents on the child. The positive effect of a child's home ownership and having a job also indicates that elderly parents tend to live with children with better economic standings. The positive correlation of coresidence with the number of children of the child suggests that there is another motivation of coresidence with parents—taking care of grandchildren. The formation of three-generation households has been motivated partly by this instrumental concern of exchanging the adult child's old-age support with the elderly parents' child care service. Looking at marital status, married children are less likely to live with their parents than unmarried children. However, if they get separated, divorced, or widowed, the probability of their coresidence with their parents increases again.

In columns (b) and (c), I examine the effects of home ownership and work status interacted by marital status. Home ownership and employment raise the likelihood of married children's coresidence with their parents, which shows again that abler children are more likely to support their elderly parents. Unmarried children, however, are more likely to leave their parents if they have a necessary condition for independence—jobs.

In traditional extended families, the eldest sons undertake the most responsibility to support their elderly parents. The regression results in table 7.18 show that there still remains a tendency of the eldest son's supporting elderly parents by intergenerational coresidence as well. However, recent

26. According to a survey of Korean Baby Boomers (born between 1955 and 1963), conducted in 2007, 69.7 percent believe that children should leave parental home after marriage (*The Korea Economic Daily* [*Han-Gook-Gyeong-Je-Sin-Moon*], June 18, 2007).

Table 7.18   **Which child lives with elderly parents? Fixed-effect logit models, KLoSA data**

	Dependent variable: Whether living with parents					
	(A)		(B)		(C)	
	Parameter	z-value	Parameter	z-value	Parameter	z-value
Age	0.016	1.69*	0.019	1.98**	0.019	2.05**
Eldest child	0.190	2.33**	0.186	2.26**	0.177	2.16**
Son	1.020	12.39***	0.872	10.19***	1.200	15.82***
Years of education	0.066	3.55***	0.063	3.39***	0.088	4.80***
Number of children	0.190	3.83***	0.199	3.98***	0.195	3.97***
Home ownership	0.264	2.81***				
Working	0.323	3.72***				
Married	−3.009	−23.02***	−3.609	−22.24***		
Married and own home			0.276	2.74***		
Married and working			0.762	6.35***		
Separated	−0.712	−1.65*	−1.843	−3.00***	1.149	1.84*
Separated and own home			−0.138	−0.10	0.204	0.14
Separated and working			2.368	2.58***	2.365	2.51**
Divorced	−0.519	−2.55**	−0.863	−2.75***	2.164	6.93***
Divorced and own home			−0.229	−0.50	−0.264	−0.57
Divorced and working			0.600	1.61	0.567	1.48
Widowed	−1.328	−4.77***	−1.556	−3.89***	1.580	4.10***
Widowed and own home			−0.369	−0.73	−0.448	−0.87
Widowed and working			0.544	1.12	0.482	0.97
Single					3.366	19.20***
Single and own home					−0.244	−0.86
Single and working					−0.529	−3.44***
Number of observations	7,164		7,164		7,164	
Log likelihood	−1,631.7		−1,609.0		−1,632.1	
Pseudo R^2	0.343		0.352		0.342	

***Significant at the 1 percent level.
**Significant at the 5 percent level.
*Significant at the 10 percent level.

socioeconomic changes in Korea are raising doubts about the sustainability of the tradition of familial support.

The 2003 KLIPS contains an additional survey for the aged (the KLIPS respondents who are aged fifty or older at the time of survey), in which the respondents were asked who undertook the responsibility of supporting their elderly parents. As shown in table 7.19, 71 percent of aged respondents report that the eldest sons lived with or supported their deceased parents while they were alive (question [a]), whereas only 45 percent report that the eldest sons are currently undertaking the responsibility of supporting their elderly parents (question [b]). Meanwhile, the proportion of the elderly taking care of themselves without children's support has increased from 19 percent to 35 percent. Considering that the average age of the respondents

Table 7.19   **Changing patterns of undertaking responsibility to support the elderly: KLIPS data**

Coresident or supporter for the elderly parents	(A) Who lived with or supported your deceased parents while they were alive? (%, n = 2,597)	(B) Who lives with or supports your elderly parents now? (%, n = 799)	Changes (% point)
Alone by themselves	18.6	34.5	15.9
The eldest son/daughter-in-law	70.6	45.2	−25.4
Other sons/daughters-in-law	6.5	13.8	7.2
Daughters/sons-in-law	2.8	4.1	1.4
All children together	1.5	2.5	1.0

Source: The additional survey for the old cohort (aged fifty or older) in the 2003 KLIPS.

whose parents are still alive must be lower than that of the respondents whose parents have died, we can infer that traditional norms of the eldest son's responsibility to support his elderly parents have been deteriorating and that the responsibility has been shifting to the elderly themselves.[27]

7.4.2   Policies for Old-Age Income Security

As seen before, Korean elderly have been undertaking more responsibilities for their income security. Do they have adequate means to do that? I briefly describe their incomes and wealth by age and by income quintile to find potential ways to old-age security.

The 2005 KReIS and the 2006 KLoSA have a fairly comprehensive set of data items on the respondent's assets and debts as well as detailed components of annual income. In particular, the availability of household wealth data is good news for researchers given the rarity of official wealth data.[28] Tables 7.20 and 7.21, respectively, report mean amounts of annual income, assets, and debts by the KReIS and the KLoSA respondents' ages. Table 7.22 reports the same items for the KLoSA respondents aged sixty or older by their income quintiles. When constructing income quintiles, I exclude those

27. Although this study deals with financial aspects of elderly life, emotional difficulties suffered by the lonely elderly also cause serious social problems such as elderly suicide. As of 2004, 4,118 elderly people aged sixty or older committed suicide in Korea; that is, eleven persons a day. The elderly suicide rate has increased four times for a decade in Korea, ranked top among OECD countries. The suicide rate of the elderly living alone is three times higher than that of the average elderly. According to the 2006 elderly statistics reported by Korea National Statistical Office, 18 percent of people aged sixty-five or older live alone without any family members.

28. The 2006 Household Wealth Survey (Korea National Statistical Office, 2007) conducted by Korea National Statistical Office can be regarded as a starting point of collecting wealth data although the raw data of the survey are not available to the public. I reorganize the items of asset and debts in the 2006 KLoSA wealth data following the classification of the 2006 Household Wealth Survey.

Table 7.20   Average income and wealth of Koreans by age: KReIS data (10,000 won)

	All (8,664)	50–54 (1,296)	55–59 (1,468)	60–64 (1,569)	65–69 (1,567)	70–74 (1,103)	75– (1,227)
				Respondent age (Number of respondents)			
Total annual income (in 2004)	1,384	2,169	1,733	1,564	1,023	799	498
1 Wage	381	849	575	286	147	52	7
2 Own business	211	420	316	164	112	25	5
3 Agricultural and fisheries	97	117	105	143	105	110	28
4 Side job	14	20	15	22	9	7	3
(1–4) Earnings (%)	50.8	64.8	58.3	39.4	36.4	24.3	8.8
5 Rent	145	241	155	175	121	97	49
6 Interest	76	156	46	162	32	27	15
(5–6) Property incomes (%)	16.0	18.3	11.6	21.6	15.0	15.6	13.0
7 National pension benefit	23	2	11	65	50	24	4
8 Occupational pension benefit	45	10	37	77	62	80	48
9 Private pension benefit	3	1	8	7	2	1	1
(7–9) Pensions (%)	5.1	0.6	3.3	9.6	11.1	13.1	10.6
10 Unemployment compensation	1	5	0	0	0	0	0
11 Workers' compensation	3	9	4	0	0	0	0
12 National Basic Livelihood Security	9	5	4	4	8	22	23
13 Veteran benefit	7	0	8	1	2	25	16
14 Other welfare benefit	4	0	1	0	8	13	14
(10–14) Public transfers (%)	1.7	0.9	1.0	0.3	1.7	7.6	10.6

15 Private transfers from children	209	145	201	230	275	281	254
16 Private transfers from others	17	30	25	10	7	12	8
(15–16) Private transfers (%)	16.3	8.1	13.0	15.3	27.6	36.6	52.6
17 Other income	141	159	221	216	83	23	22
Annual savings	199	360	269	145	87	69	29
Saving rate (%)	14.3	16.6	15.5	9.3	8.5	8.6	5.9
Total assets (A)	17,317	23,487	20,855	18,647	12,457	10,610	7,160
1 Deposits	1,078	1,338	1,271	1,142	933	923	499
2 Savings-type insurance ever paid	286	570	400	193	85	31	9
3 Private pension ever paid	94	200	124	48	19	2	0
4 Installment-type fund ever paid	17	35	25	4	0	0	0
5 Stocks	121	175	84	185	248	12	0
6 Bonds	3	4	5	2	2	0	0
7 Personal loans made to others	66	128	82	48	25	43	3
8 Other financial assets	0	0	0	0	0	0	0
9 Home	9,390	12,396	10,800	9,916	7,188	5,753	4,836
10 Business	1,136	2,178	1,898	759	410	126	107
11 Real estate other than home	4,782	5,957	5,716	5,999	3,341	3,630	1,660
12 Other assets	344	506	451	351	205	87	45
Total debts (B)	2,454	3,603	2,813	3,144	1,648	890	654
Net worth (A − B)	14,863	19,884	18,042	15,503	10,809	9,720	6,506

Table 7.21   Average income and wealth of Koreans by age: KLoSA data (10,000 won)

	Respondent age (Number of respondents)						
	45–49 (1,796)	50–54 (1,513)	55–59 (1,400)	60–64 (1,390)	65–69 (1,505)	70–74 (1,171)	75– (1,479)
Total annual income (in 2005)	1,578	1,460	1,139	966	783	510	452
1 Wage	863	733	503	312	106	27	15
2 Own business	402	316	246	139	53	24	26
3 Agricultural and fisheries	43	82	89	198	257	98	109
4 Side job	8	16	8	10	5	3	1
(1–4) Earnings (%)	83.4	78.6	74.3	68.2	53.8	29.8	33.4
5 Rent	15	20	28	11	6	12	6
6 Interest	109	85	68	42	57	31	32
(5–6) Property incomes (%)	7.8	7.2	8.4	5.5	8.1	8.4	8.5
7 National pension benefit	1	2	14	46	44	22	9
8 Occupational pension benefit	1	4	31	60	54	44	28
9 Private pension benefit	0	0	1	11	4	2	3
(7–9) Pensions (%)	0.1	0.4	4.0	12.1	13.0	13.3	8.8
10 Unemployment compensation	1	1	2	0	0	0	0
11 Workers' compensation	1	3	0	1	1	4	0
12 National Basic Livelihood Security	7	5	4	5	9	13	20
13 Veteran benefit	0	1	7	5	1	7	13
14 Other welfare benefit	1	1	1	1	6	10	8
(10–14) Public transfers (%)	0.6	0.8	1.2	1.2	2.2	6.7	9.1
15 Financial help received from children	8	17	45	73	128	155	144
16 Financial help received from parents	17	2	1	0	0	0	0
(15–16) Private transfers (%)	1.6	1.3	4.0	7.5	16.4	30.4	31.8
17 Other income	102	172	91	52	51	58	38

Total assets (A)	16,461	16,484	16,495	16,911	12,195	12,037	10,943
1 Cash and checking account balance	396	460	421	312	301	217	159
2 Saving account balance	352	256	739	1,040	59	896	44
(1–2) Deposits (%)	4.5	4.3	7.0	8.0	3.0	9.2	1.9
3 Term life insurance ever paid	172	150	82	36	28	2	1
4 Whole life insurance ever paid	133	69	37	11	2	0	0
5 Annuity insurance ever paid	236	54	23	9	1	1	1
(3–4) Insurances (%)	3.3	1.7	0.9	0.3	0.3	0.0	0.0
6 Stocks and mutual funds	115	145	79	7	11	81	4
7 Bonds	6	0	1	1	0	0	0
8 GYE money owed by others	14	8	4	1	3	0	0
9 Personal loans made to others	71	59	45	20	11	31	1
10 Other financial assets	4	3	1	7	0	0	0
11 JEON-SE security deposit paid	875	553	537	423	409	487	1,098
12 WOL-SE security deposit paid	78	90	86	77	67	51	31
13 Home	10,705	11,151	11,307	11,792	9,588	8,966	8,651
14 Real estate other than home	2,924	3,139	2,878	2,870	1,595	1,257	909
15 Farm	40	31	12	112	27	12	31
(13–15) Real estates	83.0	86.9	86.1	87.4	91.9	85.0	87.6
16 Vehicles	299	288	238	179	87	37	11
17 Other assets	41	27	5	15	6	0	1
Total debts (B)	1,489	1,394	1,609	2,135	884	663	392
1 Loans from financial institutions	803	675	674	488	337	245	78
2 Loans from relatives and friends	134	130	58	33	40	71	12
3 Other debts	9	2	13	1	3	4	1
4 GYE money owing others	6	7	3	3	0	0	0
5 JEON-SE security deposit received	200	341	521	1,268	336	202	230
6 WOL-SE security deposit received	54	98	131	105	73	60	24
7 Other security deposit received	281	143	208	238	96	82	46
Net worth (A − B)	14,972	15,090	14,886	14,776	11,311	11,373	10,551

Table 7.22   Average income and wealth of Korean elderly aged sixty or older and having some income by income quintile: KLoSA data (10,000 won)

			Income quintile [Income range]			
	All (N = 4,159)	Lowest [1, 60]	Second fifth [60, 196]	Middle fifth [196, 456]	Fourth fifth [456, 1,062]	Highest 1,062 and over
Total annual income (in 2005)	924	24	116	309	704	3,161
1 Wage	199	0	2	15	152	751
2 Own business	99	0	1	4	35	417
3 Agricultural and fisheries	234	0	4	32	141	906
4 Side job	7	0	1	7	9	18
(1–4) Earnings (%)	58.3	2.6	6.4	18.7	47.9	66.2
5 Rent	12	0	1	2	13	41
6 Interest	56	1	12	13	43	190
(5–6) Property incomes (%)	7.3	3.6	10.7	4.8	7.9	7.3
7 National pension benefit	44	0	17	52	51	91
8 Occupational pension benefit	65	0	1	3	10	286
9 Private pension benefit	8	0	2	6	5	23
(7–9) Pensions (%)	12.7	1.4	17.2	19.5	9.3	12.7
10 Unemployment compensation	0	0	0	0	0	0
11 Workers' compensation	1	0	0	0	1	5
12 National Basic Livelihood Security	14	0	2	39	27	3
13 Veteran benefit	8	0	1	4	11	24
14 Other welfare benefit	7	7	7	9	9	3
(10–14) Public transfers (%)	3.4	30.8	8.9	16.8	6.9	1.1
15 Financial help received from children	156	14	66	123	192	348
(15) Private transfers (%)	16.9	61.4	56.8	40.0	27.2	11.0
16 Other income	13	0	0	0	5	54

Total assets (A)	13,886	8,593	11,193	12,035	12,301	23,689
1 Cash and checking account balance	290	97	178	226	287	608
2 Saving account balance	566	9	71	86	118	2,329
(1–2) Deposits (%)	6.2	1.2	2.2	2.6	3.3	12.4
3 Term life insurance ever paid	22	3	7	19	19	56
4 Whole life insurance ever paid	4	0	1	0	3	16
5 Annuity insurance ever paid	4	0	0	9	0	9
(3–4) Insurances (%)	0.2	0.0	0.1	0.2	0.2	0.3
6 Stocks and mutual funds	27	0	1	1	100	29
7 Bonds	0	0	0	0	0	2
8 GYE money owed by others	1	0	1	0	1	3
9 Personal loans made to others	19	1	5	30	9	47
10 Other financial assets	3	0	0	11	6	0
11 JEON-SE security deposit paid	622	445	1,431	511	423	248
12 WOL-SE security deposit paid	53	62	60	43	52	51
(11–12) Housing security deposit paid	4.9	5.9	13.3	4.6	3.9	1.3
13 Home	9,930	7,310	8,157	9,327	9,686	14,427
14 Real estate other than home	2,157	627	1,133	1,668	1,410	5,461
15 Farm	73	13	93	36	131	79
(13–15) Real estates	87.6	92.5	83.8	91.7	91.3	84.3
16 Vehicles	104	24	56	60	55	298
17 Other assets	8	1	0	8	1	27
Total debts (B)	1,007	862	851	762	1,046	1,455
1 Loans from financial institutions	348	373	209	295	362	503
2 Loans from relatives and friends	41	48	87	31	21	19
3 Other debts	3	0	0	3	9	0
4 GYE money owing others	1	0	0	3	0	3
5 JEON-SE security deposit received	367	295	299	254	412	547
6 WOL-SE security deposit received	76	53	68	71	81	103
7 Other security deposit received	171	94	188	105	161	279
Net worth (A – B)	12,879	7,730	10,343	11,272	11,254	22,235

who do not have any income from the sample. Of 4,159 KLoSA respondents aged sixty or older, 25.6 percent are reported to have no income.[29] Table 7.23 repeats table 7.22 for those aged sixty-five or older. In reading tables 7.21, 7.22, and 7.23, it should be noted that real estate and related security deposits could have been counted redundantly for multiple respondents in the same family, probably a couple, because KLoSA data report assets and debts at the respondent's individual level, not at the household level. In table 7.20, however, assets and debts are reported in the unit of a couple (the KReIS respondent and his or her spouse, if exists).

The 2005 KReIS survey classifies annual income items and private transfer income into the same section, so I add up these variables to construct a variable of total annual income in 2004. Missing and/or refused answers in some income items are imputed with zeros. Using the 2006 KLoSA data, I construct a variable of total annual income in 2005 by summing up income items in the Income section, rent and interest in the Asset section, and private transfers in the Family section.[30] Table 7.20 and table 7.21 show that total annual income decreases monotonously with the respondent's age. A sharp decline of earnings is not sufficiently compensated by supplementary incomes such as pension benefits and public or private transfers. As a result, the average total annual income of those in their seventies is below half of that of those in their fifties. In the following, I briefly discuss how to make up for the elderly income deficiency by examining each source of income.

Earnings

Tables 7.17 and 7.19 imply that an increasing number of elderly people now have to make ends meet by themselves. In this regard, one of the most promising income sources would be their jobs. Table 7.22 shows that the main income source of the highest quintile among those aged sixty or older is their employment, own businesses, or farms (66 percent of total annual income). For the highest income quintile among those aged sixty-five or older in table 7.23, the proportion of wage gets lower because of retirement between age sixty and sixty-five, but still 53 percent of their total annual income comes from their jobs, specifically farms. Therefore, job opportunity seems crucial to the income security of the elderly as of yet.

Retirement age has been virtually shortened since the late 1990s financial crisis that has made layoffs easier and pushed early retirement. As a result, the employment of those aged between fifty-five and sixty-four has been declining in Korea while that in major advanced countries was on the uphill.

29. This proportion of the elderly living without income does not necessarily seem to be overestimated. According to the whole population statistics based on the 2007 National Health Insurance data, 30 percent of 4,178,946 elderly households in which at least one person are aged sixty-five or older are reported not to have any income.

30. Of course, private transfer receipts reported in the Family section are not included in the annual income that is used as an explanatory variable in the regression models of table 7.13.

Table 7.23   Average income and wealth of Korean elderly aged sixty-five or older and having some income by income quintile: KLoSA data (10,000 won)

			Income quintile [Income range]			
	All (N = 3,212)	Lowest [1, 52]	Second fifth [52, 160]	Middle fifth [160, 372]	Fourth fifth [372, 870]	Highest 870 and over
Total annual income (in 2005)	712	21	99	259	573	2,661
1 Wage	67	0	1	7	58	274
2 Own business	46	0	0	2	21	211
3 Agricultural and fisheries	207	0	4	25	99	926
4 Side job	4	0	1	5	5	7
(1–4) Earnings (%)	45.4	2.1	5.9	15.2	32.0	53.3
5 Rent	10	0	1	2	8	40
6 Interest	53	1	9	13	29	217
(5–6) Property incomes (%)	8.9	2.8	10.4	5.9	6.6	9.7
7 National pension benefit	33	0	7	32	44	82
8 Occupational pension benefit	54	0	1	2	7	267
9 Private pension benefit	4	0	1	3	2	13
(7–9) Pensions (%)	12.7	0.8	9.2	14.1	9.3	13.6
10 Unemployment compensation	0	0	0	0	1	0
11 Workers' compensation	2	0	0	0	0	8
12 National Basic Livelihood Security	18	0	1	30	52	4
13 Veteran benefit	9	0	1	4	5	35
14 Other welfare benefit	10	8	10	12	11	7
(10–14) Public transfers (%)	5.3	39.7	11.8	17.8	12.1	2.0
15 Financial help received from children	183	11	62	120	225	502
(15) Private transfers (%)	25.7	53.9	62.6	46.6	39.3	18.8
16 Other income	14	0	0	1	4	69
Total assets (A)	11,584	8,297	9,729	9,982	10,505	19,618
1 Cash and checking account balance	258	88	119	178	239	678
2 Saving account balance	82	6	61	69	76	198
(1–2) Deposits (%)	2.9	1.1	1.8	2.5	3.0	4.5

(continued)

Table 7.23   (continued)

Income quintile [Income range]	All (N = 3,212)	Lowest [1, 52]	Second fifth [52, 160]	Middle fifth [160, 372]	Fourth fifth [372, 870]	Highest 870 and over
3 Term life insurance ever paid	14	1	0	4	18	46
4 Whole life insurance ever paid	1	0	0	0	0	4
5 Annuity insurance ever paid	1	0	0	3	0	0
(3–4) Insurances (%)	0.1	0.0	0.0	0.1	0.2	0.3
6 Stocks and mutual funds	36	0	0	0	143	37
7 Bonds	0	0	0	0	0	0
8 GYE money owed by others	1	0	0	0	1	6
9 Personal loans made to others	17	2	7	25	25	23
10 Other financial assets	0	0	0	0	0	0
11 JEON-SE security deposit paid	738	466	2,038	410	437	331
12 WOL-SE security deposit paid	48	54	38	43	48	55
(11–12) Housing security deposit paid	6.8	6.3	21.3	4.5	4.6	2.0
13 Home	8,764	7,129	6,866	7,993	7,811	14,170
14 Real estate other than home	1,540	518	550	1,170	1,641	3,877
15 Farm	31	17	26	53	21	41
(13–15) Real estates	89.2	92.4	76.5	92.3	90.2	92.2
16 Vehicles	51	16	24	22	43	151
17 Other assets	3	1	0	11	0	1
Total debts (B)	668	679	487	431	837	914
1 Loans from financial institutions	247	223	111	169	372	361
2 Loans from relatives and friends	44	40	107	38	12	22
3 Other debts	3	0	0	0	16	0
4 GYE money owing others	0	0	0	0	0	0
5 JEON-SE security deposit received	235	265	213	145	279	278
6 WOL-SE security deposit received	50	65	20	45	44	76
7 Other security deposit received	89	86	36	34	113	177
Net worth (A − B)	10,916	7,618	9,241	9,551	9,668	18,704

In Korea, people generally exit from their main career at an average age of fifty-four and work for another thirteen to fourteen years at new workplaces with substantially worsened working conditions until they permanently stop working at the age of sixty-eight.

Now to postpone retirement in a rapidly aging society like Korea, systematic efforts would be needed. For example, we may consider a wider adoption of the Wage Peak System to address employers' concern about an increase in labor cost by retaining the aged under seniority-based payment scheme. And we may also consider a deferred pension and annuity system to give employees an incentive to delay their retirement.

Given that Korea's economically active population aged between twenty-five and fifty-four declines from 2009, employment of the aged plays a role not just in elderly income but also for addressing a possible labor shortage. Stereotypical perceptions of employing the elderly, and the extent to which workers invest in their own human capital, are also factors. One option might be to facilitate employers' investment in developing the aged-friendly training programs and strengthen self-motivated capability development by the aged workers. Elderly employment projects could also target more competitive programs by tailoring job opportunities to each elderly individual's need, ability, and willingness to work.

Property Incomes

As shown in tables 7.20 through 7.23, most properties of Korean elderly are real estates (more than 80 percent of total assets), and the majority of elderly has virtually nothing other than their residential home. In this regard, the Reverse Mortgage Loan was introduced in 2007 to let those who are "house-rich but cash-poor" have regular income by liquidation of their residential home with staying in their home until they die. In addition, even though few elderly have stocks, mutual funds, or bonds right now, the proportion of financial assets in elderly nest eggs will rise as capital markets are rapidly growing.[31]

Pensions

Public and private pension systems have a relatively short history in Korea compared to advanced western economies. Hence, the coverage and sufficiency of benefits are not yet up to the level of a major source of retirement income as seen in tables 7.20 and 7.21. Compared to the National Pension that started in 1988 and has not yet matured, occupational pensions have longer histories and higher replacement rates. Tables 7.22 and 7.23 show that the beneficiaries of occupational pensions are likely to occupy the highest income quintile among Korean elderly. Occupational pensions,

---

31. An and Jun (2006) suggest that household savings for retirement are positively associated with household head's education, job security, income stability, and housing security.

however, cover very limited occupations such as public employees, teachers, or soldiers, in spite of requiring substantial inflow of government budget. Moreover, the National Pension system is likely to face fiscal drain in several decades if the current scheme will not be drastically reformed soon. A corporate pension scheme that has been recently introduced is one alternative step toward a multipillar old-age security system based on public-private pension linkage.[32] However, institutional rearrangements might be needed if private pensions or annuities were to be used as a means of securing retirement income. Tables 7.20 and 7.21 suggest that private pension/annuity (insurance) application of the elderly has been negligible, although those in their forties and fifties now seem to have more interest in that.

Public Transfers

Elderly households are far more prone to poverty. Using KLIPS data, Cho (2007) finds that as of 2005, 45.6 percent of households in absolute poverty are elderly households. Table 7.15 also suggests that the dependency on public assistance increases with age. Tables 7.22 and 7.23 show that those who do not take up the National Basic Livelihood Security benefits find themselves in the lowest income quintile among the elderly. It is not clear whether they are indeed not eligible for the benefits or they are unfairly excluded from them; however, according to Kim (2006), who uses the 2003 KLIPS data on aged respondents, at least 11.3 percent of elderly households whose heads are aged sixty or older are estimated to have been unfairly excluded from the National Basic Livelihood Security benefits despite living in absolute poverty.

The Basic Old-Age Pension benefits supposedly cover a broader range of Korean elderly aged sixty-five or older—60 percent in 2008, with the maximum benefit at 84,000 won per month. The growing role of governmental efforts in assisting elderly income may indicate the overall improvement of Korea's social welfare.

Private Transfers

Financial assistance from adult children still occupies a substantial portion of elderly incomes. Table 7.21 reports that the proportion of familial transfer receipts in the KLoSA respondents' total annual income increases after retirement to reach as much as 30 percent in their seventies. Tables 7.22 and 7.23, however, show that the average amount of children's financial transfers received by the highest income quintile elderly is far larger than that of the lowest income quintile elderly.[33] For the elderly below the middle

---

32. To establish a multipillar model of old-age income security in Korea, Moon et al. (2005, 2007) provides policy suggestions focusing on pension reforms and the development of pension systems.

33. Since affluent elderly parents tend to make substantial transfers to their children, their net transfer receipts from their children are probably much smaller than their gross transfer receipts.

income quintile, the average amount of familial transfer receipts is at most 660,000 won (roughly 600 dollars) a year, despite the fact that familial transfers occupy more than half the total annual income. This surely reflects a positive income correlation between parents and children. But it also shows that the anti-poverty effectiveness of private transfers is limited because they are essentially income redistribution within families.

At least for a while, familial support will play a transient role as a private safety net for the elderly until a comprehensive system for old-age income security will have been full-fledged and stabilized. As shown earlier, however, familial support for the elderly is deteriorating in terms of both financial transfers and coresidence with elderly parents.[34] Moreover, the expansion of elderly welfare will further decrease the role of families in old-age security. But, as Ogawa and Retherford (1997) point out, government seems unable to reverse the trend of a weakening role of familial support.[35] Encouraging retirement savings through enhancement of long-term saving incentives and promoting elderly employment might be options if the government does not wish to support a growing elderly population.

7.5 Conclusion

This study investigates intergenerational transfers in Korea, focusing on children's financial assistance to their elderly parents. According to KLoSA and KLIPS data, two or three out of five households provided some type of financial support for their aged parents. The average amount of net annual transfers from children is approaching 2 million won after retirement age. Even though it is not always sufficient, financial help from adult children has alleviated income deficiency of Korean elderly.

Among many findings from this study, I select four as key stylized facts. First, the negative effect of the recipient's income (and net worth) on net transfer receipt suggests that altruism is the main motive of familial transfers in Korea. This is consistent with the existing literature that concludes altruism prevails as the motivation of private transfers until public transfer programs are well established (see Cox, Hansen, and Jimenez [2004], for example). The exchange motive, however, also appears to operate in the form of more transfers to the parents who look after their grandchildren.

Second, as the theory predicts, as long as private transfers are made in

---

34. A survey (conducted by Chosun Ilbo Co. and Mirae Asset Securities Co. in August 2005) of 1,001 Korean adults suggests that the current generation has an asymmetric view about the responsibility of supporting their elders and the expectation of being supported by their children. According to the survey, 47.4 percent feel they should support their elderly parents. But only 26.9 percent expect their children will support them after retirement.

35. On the factors that make Japanese government's efforts to shift some burden of supporting the elderly back to families unsuccessful, Ogawa and Retherford list rapid population ageing, decreases in intergenerational coresidence, increases in women's labor market participation and resultant decreases in available caregivers for impaired elderly, and depreciating values of filial piety.

a compensatory fashion, they are crowded out by public transfers made in the same fashion. The KLIPS data show that there exists almost a dollar-for-dollar crowding-out of private transfers by public assistance benefits (Kim 2006), and the KLoSA data even suggest that positive expectations about public support also decrease elderly parents' net transfer receipt in the family.

Third, intergenerational transfers in Korean families have been under the influence of traditional norms, specifically Confucian ethics that have institutionalized the eldest son's responsibility of taking care of elderly parents. Therefore, even as of 2005, among other children the eldest son undertakes the heaviest burden of supporting his elderly parents through financial help or coresidence with them.

Fourth, I find that child education can hardly be a retirement plan. A child's additional one year of education compared to his siblings only leads to an additional net transfer of 90,000 won per year for the elderly parents. Therefore, parental spending on children's education can be an investment but cannot be the one for the old-age income security of the parents.

Moreover, familial support mechanism has been deteriorating in Korea. Seven out of ten Korean elderly people lived mainly on transfers from their children in 1980, but the proportion is only three out of ten in 2003. This gap has been filled with expansions of public assistance programs and an increased role of self-support. So the burden of supporting the increasing number of the elderly has shifted from families to government; and within a family, it has shifted from the eldest son to the elderly parents themselves.

In light of these findings and ongoing changes, this study leaves some messages for households and government. For households, it suggests preparation for retirement. In the face of rapid population aging and prevailing individualism, the social norm for supporting the elderly is changing from transfers to self-responsibilities. As such, individuals might have to consider longevity risk as well as keeping a balance between savings for their old age and spending on their children, and investing in their own human capital.

Finding an optimal role in the old-age security is a big challenge to the government coping with rapid population aging due to unprecedented low fertility rates, increasing life expectancy, and cohort effect of the Baby Boomers' imminent retirement. Possible alternatives include making more job opportunities for the elderly, enhancing long-term saving incentives, and pension reforms. In front of an increasing elderly population, political settlements tend to introduce universal welfare that covers most elderly people and generous benefits. However, considering that roughly half of households living in poverty are elderly households, poverty reduction for the elderly may come to the forefront. In addition, before introducing new welfare programs, the existence and magnitude of latent demands for the service and potential crowding-out effect of the program on private sectors should be accounted for and measured in a reasonable way.

References

An, C.-B., and S.-H. Jun. 2006. Retirement plans and household saving behaviors. The 7th Conference of Korean Labor and Income Panel Study, February 2, 2006 (in Korean).

Brown, J. R., and S. J. Weisbenner. 2002. Is a bird in hand worth more than a bird in the bush? Intergenerational transfers and savings behavior. NBER Working Paper no. 8753. Cambridge, MA: National Bureau of Economic Research, January.

Cho, Y.-S. 2007. The realities of recent elderly poverty and policy implications. The 8th Conference of Korean Labor and Income Panel Study, February 1, 2007 (in Korean).

Cox, D. 1987. Motives for private income transfers. *Journal of Political Economy* 95 (3): 508–46.

Cox, D., Z. Eser, and E. Jimenez. 1998. Motives for private transfers over the life cycle. *Journal of Development Economics* 55 (1): 57–80.

Cox, D., B. E. Hansen, and E. Jimenez. 2004. How responsive are private transfers to income? Evidence from a laissez-faire economy. *Journal of Public Economics* 88 (9–10): 2193–219.

Cox, D., and G. Jakubson. 1995. The connection between public transfers and private interfamily transfers. *Journal of Public Economics* 57 (1): 129–67.

Cox, D., and M. Rank. 1992. Inter vivos transfers and intergenerational exchange. *Review of Economics and Statistics* 74 (2): 305–14.

Dunn, T. A., and J. W. Phillips. 1997. The timing and division of parental transfers to children. *Economic Letters* 54 (2): 135–37.

Gale, W. G., and J. K. Scholz. 1994. Intergenerational transfers and the accumulation of wealth. *Journal of Economic Perspectives* 8 (4): 145–60.

Hochguertel, S., and H. Ohlsson. 2000. Compensatory inter vivos gifts. Working Papers in Economics 31, Göteborg University, Sweden.

Hurd, M. D. 1990. Research on the elderly: Economic status, retirement, and consumption and saving. *Journal of Economic Literature* 28 (2): 565–637.

Jin, J.-M. 1999. An analysis on the relationship between Social Security transfers and private transfers. *Social Welfare Studies (Sa-Hoe-Bok-Ji- Yeon-Goo)* 13:167–99 (in Korean).

Kang, S.-J., and H.-J. Jeon. 2005. A study on the motivation of private transfer income and the crowding-out effect of public transfer income. *Public Economics (Gong-Gong-Gyeong-Je)* 10 (1): 23–46 (in Korean).

Kim, H. 2006. Population ageing and income transfers: Microeconomic approach. In *Population ageing and income transfers,* National Research Council for Economics, Humanities and Social Sciences, Joint Research Project Report 06-05-03. Korea Development Institute: 7–70 (in Korean).

Korea National Statistical Office. 2007. *The 2006 household wealth survey report.* KNSO, March (in Korean).

Korea National Statistical Office. 2008. *The 2007 Survey on Private Tutoring Expenditure.* KNSO, February (in Korean).

Laferrère, A., and F.-C. Wolff. 2004. Microeconomic models of family transfers. In *Handbook of giving, reciprocity and altruism,* ed. L.-A. Gerard-Varet, S.-C. Kolm, and J. Mercier Ythier, chapter 12. North Holland: Elsevier.

McGarry, K. 1999. Inter vivos transfers and intended bequests. *Journal of Public Economics* 73 (3): 321–51.

———. 2000. Testing parental altruism: Implications of a dynamic model. NBER Working Paper no. 7593. Cambridge, MA: National Bureau of Economic Research, March.

McGarry, K., and R. F. Schoeni. 1995. Transfer behavior in the health and retirement study: Measurement and the redistribution of resources within the family. *Journal of Human Resources* 30:S184–S226.

———. 1997. Transfer behavior within the family: Results from the asset and health dynamics study. *Journals of Gerontology* 52B (Special Issue): 82–92.

Moon, Hyungpyo et al. 2005. *Population ageing and old-age income security.* National Research Council for Economics, Humanities and Social Sciences, Joint Research Project Report 05-10-02, Korea Development Institute (in Korean).

Moon, Hyungpyo et al. 2007. *A comprehensive study on constructing an old-age income security system in Korea.* National Research Council for Economics, Humanities and Social Sciences, Joint Research Project Report 07-01-01, Korea Development Institute (in Korean).

Ogawa, N., and R. D. Retherford. 1997. Shifting costs of caring for the elderly back to families in Japan: Will it work? *Population and Development Review* 23 (1): 59–94.

Organization for Economic Cooperation and Development (OECD) 2007. *Education at a glance, 2007:* Paris: OECD.

Seok, J.-E., and T.-W. Kim. 2000. *The reality of elderly income and policies for the improvement of income security system.* Korea Institute for Health and Social Affairs (in Korean).

Shin, H. Y., B. E. Cho, and A. J. Walker. 1997. A comparative study on caregiving and inheritance patterns: Korea vs. U.S.A. *Korean Journal of Home Management (Han-Gook-Ga-Jeong-Gwan-Ri-Hak-Hoe-Jee)* 15:125–36 (in Korean).

Sung, J.-M. 2006. Private transfers in the Korean labor and income panel study data. Korea Labor Institute, *Monthly Labor Review* 15:75–83 (in Korean).

Wilhelm, M. O. 1996. Bequest behavior and the effect of heirs' earnings: Testing the altruistic model of bequests. *American Economic Review* 86 (4): 874–92.

Comment   Jiyeun Chang

Investigating intergenerational transfers is essential in order to understand the economic status and security of the Korean elderly. Previous researches and journalistic articles reported that they highly depend upon transfers from their adult children to live, although it is also known that the proportion of private transfers among old-age income has been rapidly decreasing for the last few decades. However, empirical studies have been insufficient, mostly because we lacked in data. Based on the new panel data, such as the Korean Longitudinal Study of Aging (KLoSA), many empirical studies are to be expected. "Intergenerational Transfers and Old-Age Security in Korea" by Hisam Kim, although it could use only the data of a single year, makes a great contribution in our understanding, with detailed analysis and plenteous implications.

The most important finding of this chapter is about the motivation of

Jiyeun Chang is a research fellow at the Korea Labor Institute and a visiting scholar at the Center for Advanced Social Science Research, New York University.

intergenerational transfers. Examining which parents benefit more from children, he found that the net transfer was negatively correlated with the recipient's income. This was suggested as a result of altruistic motivation of familial transfers. One step further, the author implies the crowding-out effect of public transfer programs on private transfers. However, these findings could not provide any rationale to restrict the expansion of the public transfer system. Rather, private transfers have filled up the deficiency of public transfers. If the economic condition of the Korean elderly is frail because it relies upon familiar transfers motivated by the donors' altruism, a government focus on poverty reduction for the elderly might be an option.

Besides the altruistic motivation of private transfer, the chapter presents the following findings. First, exchange motivation is also inferred by observing that there are more transfers to the old people who take care of their grandchildren. Second, the eldest son tends to provide coresidency or cash transfers to their parents, reflecting traditional Confucian ethics. Third, parents' investments for the child's education can hardly be rewarded as cash transfers in their later lives.

In spite of the great contribution of the chapter, two more considerations would be worthy to make. First, coresidency must be counted in the intergenerational net transfers. In the regression model of which parents benefit more from children, using KLoSA data, he analyzed net transfers only from noncoresident children. "Selection problem" is inherent in this model. Simply gathering information on cash transfers between coresident parents and children cannot solve this problem. Cash transfers among families who share their consumptions have completely different characteristics from transfers among noncoresident families. If we consider the selection of which child lives with his parents in the analytical model, the implication on the altruism or the exchange motivation might be changed. It is a quite reasonable idea that coresident children would give more to parents if they had not lived with them. Please be reminded that this chapter reported that the highly educated working homeowner child tends to live with their elderly parents with a higher rate than their counterparts, although it did not analyze the relationship in terms of the recipient parents. If you can say that the higher economic status you have, the more it is possible you live with your adult children, the analytical models with considering the selection process will present to us the weaker effect of economic status on the net transfers from children, which might limit us to interpret the implication of altruistic motivation. On the other hand, this chapter reported that people who have many children tend to reside with their parents, which makes us expect stronger exchange motivation in models reflecting the selection.

Regarding the second consideration, long-term exchange is worthy to consider in this research area, although the current data situation limits empirical analyses. This chapter revealed the exchange between elderly parents' caregiving for their grandchildren and cash transfers from their adult children. The revealed exchange could be only a part of the entire exchange process. The extra contributions of the eldest son may be understood as part of a long-term exchange. Although you admit the strong relationship between the contributions of the eldest son in Korea and the traditional Confucian ethics, you can still understand the Confucian values inducing the long-term exchange. If you recall that older parents gave special care and extra investment for their eldest son under the sense of Confucian values, it is acceptable to comprehend the greater contribution of the eldest son as one of the long-term exchange processes.

Labor Force Participation of Older Males in Korea: 1955 to 2005

Chulhee Lee

8.1 Introduction

This chapter estimates the labor force participation rate (LFPR) of older men in Korea for the last fifty years, and provides explanations for the patterns of long-term change in retirement behaviors. This study found that the LFPR of older men increased substantially from the mid-1960s to the late 1990s, in sharp contrast to the historical experiences of most Organization for Economic Cooperation and Development (OECD) countries, where the LFPR of older males declined rapidly over the last century. The rise in the LFPR of older males in Korea between 1965 and 1995 is largely explained by the dramatic increase in the labor market activity of the rural elderly population. The study suggests that the acceleration of population aging in rural areas due to the selective out-migration of younger persons was the major cause of the sharp increase in the LFPR of older males. Likewise, evidence provides the suggestion that the LFPR of older males that fell dramatically after 1997 was due to the adverse labor-market effect of the financial crisis.

Population aging is one of the most critical economic and social issues in many nations today. Due to the rapidly rising life expectancy and low fertility rates, the proportion of the elderly population has increased with an alarming speed in most of the developed countries and in many of the

Chulhee Lee is a professor of economics at Seoul National University.

This article extends and improves on the previous paper of the author (Lee 2007) by utilizing the newly released 2005 population census, offering a new literature survey, and conducting some additional analyses. I thank J. Kwon for the research assistance and the participants of the Nineteenth NBER East Asian Seminar on Economics, especially Kyungsoo Choi, Takatoshi Ito, Fumio Ohtake, and Andrew Rose, for their helpful comments and suggestions. The errors in this report are solely the responsibility of the author.

emerging nations as well. Korea is no exception to this global process of population aging. In fact, its current pace of aging is much faster than that most of the OECD countries.[1] The proportion of the population aged sixty-five and older is currently 10 percent, and projected to increase to 23 percent by 2030. It is anticipated that the increase in the relative size of the elderly population will radically change the fundamental features of the economy and society. Labor shortages, lowered productivity, and intensified financial pressure on the social insurance programs are among the most frequently mentioned economic consequences of ongoing population aging. Thus, it is no surprise that there was a recent surge in research on fertility decline and the health of the elderly populations, the major determinants of the pace of population aging.

For economists, especially those who specialize in labor economics and public finance, a central research topic related to population aging is the trend and determinant of the labor force participation of older individuals, especially males. One of the most marked labor market changes in developed countries over the last several decades has been the sharp decline in the LFPR of older males. In the countries that industrialized ahead of the others, the long-term decrease in the labor market activity of elderly males began even earlier. In the United States, for example, nearly four out of five men aged sixty-five and older were gainfully employed in 1880. Today, less than 20 percent of males at these ages participate in the labor market. Similar trends in the LFPR of older men are observed in Great Britain and Germany for the same period (Costa 1998).

Early retirement, defined as leaving the labor force permanently before reaching the age of sixty-five, also became common in most OECD countries over the last four decades. In Germany, Belgium, the Netherlands, and France, the LFPR of men aged sixty to sixty-four fell from over 70 percent in the 1960s to around 20 to 30 percent in 1995. Other countries such as the United States, Sweden, Spain, and Italy experienced a relatively modest but nevertheless substantial rise in early retirement during the same period. Japan is an exception among the OECD countries, showing a relatively stable LFPR for men aged sixty to sixty-four over time (Gruber and Wise 1999; Abe 2001; OECD 2004).

As the increase in the relative size of the aged population has accelerated, this changing retirement behavior has become a major social issue in developed countries. It is feared that the fall in the labor market activity of this growing age group will aggravate the problems anticipated to arise from

1. The United Nations classifies a nation in which the share of the population aged sixty-five and older is 7 percent or higher as "aging society," and a nation in which the population aged sixty-five and older is 14 percent as "aged society." It is expected that Korea will transform from an aging society (2000) to an aged society (2019) in just nineteen years, whereas it took 115 years for France, seventy-two years for the United States, and twenty-four years for Japan to complete the same kind of transition (Korea National Statistical Office 2001).

population aging, such as labor shortages and financial pressure on pension funds (Lee 2001; Nyce and Sylvester 2005). A key policy measure proposed in response to the potential labor market problems associated with the aging of society is to boost the employment of older workers. A better understanding of the labor market behavior of older individuals will provide a useful basis for making effective policies.

The purpose of this study is to estimate the LFPR of older men in Korea for the last fifty years, and to provide an explanation for the patterns of long-term change in retirement behaviors. Reflecting the growing interest in the economic impacts of population aging, a number of studies have recently examined the labor market status of aged workers in Korea. However, as will be discussed later in detail, these studies cover a relatively short period in recent years and have some limitations arising from relatively small samples of the elderly population. The present study can overcome some of these limitations by analyzing micro samples of the censuses covering longer periods of time.

Recent progress in the comparative study of the economics of aging has been remarkable, as can be seen in the research of Gruber and Wise (1999, 2004), OECD (2000), and Ogura, Tachibanaki, and Wise (2001). However, existing studies have focused mainly on Europe, North America, and Japan. Korea certainly shares with the other OECD countries a lot of common features in retirement patterns. As such, there is no reason to believe that standard economic models of retirement that have been utilized in studying the cases of developed countries cannot be applied to Korea. On the other hand, some of its labor market and institutional characteristics are distinct from those of the other advanced countries. For example, the self-employed account for a much higher proportion of the labor force, especially those aged forty-five and older in Korea, than in the other nations with a comparable phase of economic development. In addition, the Korean social insurance programs for old-age security are less developed than most of the other OECD countries. These are major explanations for the relatively high labor market activity of older males in Korea, although the high labor force participation rate does not mean employment stability. It is largely acknowledged that retirement from formal wage and salary jobs in Korea is more forced than voluntary, especially after the Financial Crisis (Chang 2003; Cho and Kim 2005). Due to these particularities, the retirement behaviors of Korean older males could differ from the other populations. In this light, this study may add some additional insights to the comparative study of retirement.

8.2 Background

Due to the growing interest in the economic impacts of population aging, the determining factors of retirement decisions and the causes of the secular decline in the LFPR of older men have attracted the attention of many economists in recent years. They have attributed the decline in the involvement of older males in the labor market to the factors that influence labor supply decisions of older persons. In particular, a great deal of attention has been paid to the retirement effect of the implementation and expansion of social insurance programs such as social security. A particularly large number of studies have focused on the impact of the implementation and expansion of the social insurance programs, especially social security, on the labor force participation of older men (Boskin 1977; Parsons 1980 1991; Hurd and Boskin 1984; Krueger and Pischke 1992; Lee 1998a; Gruber and Wise 1999, 2004).

As for the United States, it has been suggested that the Old Age Assistance (OAA) was the main underlying force behind the sharp decline in the LFPR of older men during the 1930s (Parsons 1991). Many have attributed the fall in the LFPR of older males starting in the 1960s to the increase in the real Social Security benefits (Boskin 1977; Parsons 1980; Hurd and Boskin 1984). Recent comparative studies have concluded that measures of work disincentives arising from old-age pension programs were strongly related to the size of labor market activity of older males around the world (Gruber and Wise 1999, 2004). Aside from Social Security, the major supply-side factors of retirement that the existing literature suggests include health status (McGarry 2004), health insurance (Gruber and Madrian 1995), and wealth (Gustman and Steinmeier 2002).

Although studied less extensively than supply-side factors, demand-side factors such as the features of the workplace, production technology, managerial practices, work organization, employment relations, and labor market conditions are also potentially important determinants of retirement decisions. For example, Hurd (1996) and Hurd and McGarry (1993) found that the flexibility of the job and financial aspects were important determinants of retirement decisions. It has also been reported that shifts in the industrial structure increased the pressure toward retirement by diminishing the relative size of the sectors that were more favorable of the employment of older workers (Lee 2002, 2005). A recent study by Lee (2009) suggested that technological changes strongly affected the labor market status of older male manufacturing workers in early twentieth-century America.

In Korea, research on the labor market status of older persons has been growing over the last decade, reflecting the rising concern over the coming of the aging society. In recent years, a large number of in-depth studies on retirement have been produced, utilizing newly released micro-panel data, such as the Korea Labor and Income Panel Survey (KLIPS) and the Korea Longitudinal Study of Aging (KLoSA). An example of these studies is the undertaking by Chang (2002), which was based on the data from the 2000 to 2001 KLIPS. Chang reported that the odds of retirement were associated negatively with health and educational attainment, and positively with real estate wealth. She also suggested that the average retirement age of Korean males increased by two years from 1987 to 1997, before it began to decrease after the financial crisis in 1998.

Cho and Kim (2005) investigate the nature of mandatory retirement in Korea using the data from the Workplace Panel Survey (WPS). They find that Korean corporations, especially after the financial crisis in 1998, use mandatory retirement as a means to deal with exorbitant wage increases that outpace productivity and were in part generated by the traditional seniority-based wage system. According to this study, mandatory retirement for many firms also plays an alleviating role to the problem of backlogs in promotion by circumventing the rigidity of the personnel dismissal system under the Korean labor law. Finally, this study suggests that the labor unions may tacitly approve this practice.

Sung and Ahn (2006) examine the determinants of the decision of older persons to work, based on the data from the KLIPS. They also investigate the factors that determine the classification of workers as fit for wage and salary jobs or self-employment. They find that age and years of schooling are negatively related to the probability of employment of individuals aged forty-five and older. Healthier persons are more likely to be employed than those who reported poor health. Local unemployment rate has a strong negative effect on the probability of employment. Individuals who were employed as nonwage workers at the age of forty-five are more likely to be employed today than those employed in wage and salary jobs, suggesting that job characteristics are important determinants of employment decisions.

By analyzing a sample of two-earner households drawn from the KLIPS, Choi (2006) finds that the retirement decisions of husbands are significantly affected by the health and wages of the spouses, as well as their own pension wealth and other retirement incentives. In contrast, the results show that the retirement behaviors of the wives are not strongly influenced by the characteristics of their spouses. By estimating the cross wage elasticity of retirement of the couples, this study suggests that the leisure times of a couple complement each other, and that the complementarities are much stronger for men than for women. For men, the substitution effect of the wages of their spouses dominates the income effect, whereas substitution and income effects cancel out for women.

Lee (2008) explores how retirement expectations differ between the self-employed (SE) and wage and salary earners (WS) and why they differ. The results generally confirm the widely held belief that the SE expect to remain in the labor market longer than the WS. Differences in the retirement incomes, health, productivity, job characteristics, and the presence of compulsory retirement in the workplaces of the WS do not explain the observed disparity in the retirement expectations by employment status. This study suggests that the difference between the SE and WS in the quality of matching between the job and the worker is an important factor in explaining the late retirement of the SE compared to WS.

These studies provide useful implications for the reasons why older Korean workers leave the labor market. However, the data used in these studies only cover recent years. The KLIPS started with the year 1998, and the first wave of the KLoSA was collected in 2006. Furthermore, recent studies based on the micro-panel data, such as KLIPS, are subject to limitations arising from the relatively small sample of the elderly population. The present study can overcome some of these limitations by analyzing the micro samples of the censuses that cover a longer period.

8.3   Data and Definition of Labor Force Participation

This study is largely based on the Population and Housing Census (Census, hereafter), provided by the National Statistical Office of Korea (Korea National Statistical Office 1955, 1960, 1966, 1970, 1975, 1980, 1985, 1990, 1995a, 1995b, 2000a, 2000b, and 2005). In particular, the micro samples of the Censuses for 1980, 1985, 1990, 1995, 2000, and 2005 are the principal basis for the empirical analysis of the labor force participation patterns of older males. Additionally, the Economically Active Population Survey (EAP, hereafter) is used in estimating the LFPR of older males.

The EAP is the most widely used micro-level labor survey that provides basic information on employment and unemployment in Korea. One advantage of this source over the census data is that the continuous yearly estimate of the LFPR from 1963 through today can be obtained from the data. In addition, by using this survey we can consistently apply to each year the most widely used definition of employed and unemployed persons as labor force participants.

The employed are defined as all persons who work at least one hour or more for pay or profits, including those who work eighteen hours or more as unpaid family workers during the reference week. Persons who have a job but are temporarily absent from work due to bad weather, temporary illness, and other reasons are also classified as employed. The unemployed include all persons who are not working at all, but are available for work and are actively seeking work during the reference week. Those who are not working or seeking work, but are expected to start a new job within a month of the reference week, are also considered unemployed (Korea National Statistical Office 2001).

A disadvantage of using the EAP is its relatively small sample size. Prior to 1988, only 17,500 households were sampled in the survey. Since the percentage of the elderly population then was much smaller than it is today, the sample size of older males may not be large enough to generate a reliable estimate of their LFPR. This potential problem can be mitigated with the current data because after 1988, the number of sample households increased to 32,500.

The Census Report has been published every five years since 1949. With a large sample size, it is a better source of data for in-depth analysis focusing on the elderly population. It also provides data on a broad range of socioeconomic variables that are not available from the EAP, such as the characteristics of housing and place of residence, and a much finer classification of family structure.

When using the Census, the researcher makes the definition of labor force participation as close as possible to that of the EAP. For the Censuses from 1955 through 1980, the published reports provide the number of the employed and the unemployed for each five-year age interval. The Census Reports for 1960, 1965, 1970, and 1980 further divide the unemployed according to whether they were seeking a job. Accordingly, for these years, labor force participants are defined as the employed and those unemployed who were seeking a job. For 1955 and 1975, all employed and unemployed persons are classified as participants. Since the number of the unemployed among men aged sixty and older is very small for these two years, the inclusion of the unemployed not seeking a job does not make a significant difference.[2]

The 2 percent random samples of the Censuses for 1980 through 2005 provide a finer classification of labor force status.[3] The following categories are classified as labor force participation: (a) working; (b) working occasionally while taking care of household affairs; (c) working occasionally while going to school; (d) working occasionally while doing other things; (e) temporarily absent from work; and (f) seeking a job. The following categories are regarded as nonparticipation: (g) housekeeping; (h) schooling; and (i) not working for other reasons, such as old age or sickness. The overwhelming majority of men aged fifty and older fall into categories (a) and (i). The results of the estimation of the LFPR and the analyses regarding the determinants of labor force participation are therefore not sensitive to whether these categories (b to h) are classified as participation or not.

2. The percentage of the unemployed among the male population aged sixty and older was 0.001 percent in 1955 and 0.5 percent in 1975.
3. The published Census Reports after 1980 classify the population into two categories of labor force status, the gainfully employed and the nonemployed. The former includes full-time and part-time workers and persons who have a job but are temporarily absent from work. The latter comprises the unemployed, unpaid family workers, students, and other nonparticipants. Since the published reports provide the number of age-specific population only for these two large categories, it is impossible to obtain an estimate of the LFPR that is comparable to the estimate based on the EAP or earlier Census Reports.

8.4   Long-Term Trend in the LFPR of Older Males

Table 8.1 reports the long-term trend in the age-specific LFPR of males aged fifty and older from 1955, estimated from the Census. Figure 8.1 graphically presents the estimates of the LFPR of males aged sixty and older from both the Census and the EAP. The most remarkable feature of the observed long-term trend is that the LFPR of males aged sixty and older in Korea *increased,* not decreased, between the mid-1960s and the late 1990s. According to the results based on the EAP, it rose from 40 percent in 1965 to 55 percent in 1997. The estimate from the Census shows a similar trend, with the LFPR rising from 44 to 53 percent between 1965 and 1995. This pattern is sharply distinct from the historical experience of most of the other OECD countries, as noted in the introduction. The long-term rise in labor market activity is less visible for males in their fifties. The LFPR of men aged fifty to fifty-nine based on the Census rose from 70 percent in 1965 to 72 percent in 1995.

The three decades of long-term increases in the labor market activity of older men were followed by a dramatic exodus of aged workers from the labor force from 1997 to 2000. The LFPR of males aged sixty and older estimated from the Census fell by 7 percentage points between 1995 and 2000. Males aged fifty to fifty-nine experienced an even greater decline in economic activity. The LFPR of men aged fifty-five to fifty-nine, for instance, dropped from 85 percent in 1995 to 72 percent in 2000.

The LFPR of men aged sixty and older for the period from 1955 to 1965 estimated from census reports suggests that the labor market activity of aged men was initially high and then declined dramatically with the beginning of industrialization, similar to what happened in other developed countries. If this pattern is confirmed, the truly special feature of the Korean experience is the turnaround of the trend in the middle of the 1960s. However, since the quality of the Censuses prior to 1965 was relatively poor, it is difficult to tell whether the drop in the LFPR of older men in the earlier period was real.

Another prominent feature of this analysis is the uneven change over time in the LFPR of older males in Korea. In particular, the series based on the EAP prior to the mid-1980s exhibits highly volatile year-to-year fluctuations. This is presumably due to the small sample size of the EAP prior to 1988, as previously noted. Consistent with this conjecture, the trend of the LFPR based on the EAP shows a much more continuous change after 1988, when the sample size nearly doubled. According to the estimates from the EAP, the LFPR of older men rose between the mid-1960s and the mid-1970s, fell during the following ten years, and then rapidly rose from the mid-1980s to 1997. The estimates of the LFPR from the Census generally matched those obtained from the EAP. The only exception is 1985, for which the Census shows a much higher rate of labor market activity of older males than does the EAP. Due to the discrepancy in the 1985 period, the trend

Table 8.1 Population share and labor force participation rate of males aged fifty and older by age group

Year	Population share					Labor force participation rate							
	50–54	55–59	60–64	65–69	70+	50–54	55–59	60–64	65–69	70+	50–59	50+	60+
1955	0.293	0.257	0.189	0.136	0.126	0.933	0.897	0.803	0.683	0.464	0.916	0.785	0.672
1960	0.324	0.224	0.181	0.129	0.142	0.899	0.873	0.711	0.507	0.291	0.889	0.718	0.521
1965	0.320	0.254	0.172	0.124	0.131	0.916	0.851	0.636	0.432	0.178	0.887	0.701	0.436
1970	0.314	0.253	0.187	0.112	0.134	0.919	0.854	0.676	0.494	0.230	0.890	0.717	0.491
1975	0.320	0.245	0.182	0.126	0.127	0.937	0.856	0.638	0.487	0.203	0.902	0.726	0.486
1980	0.298	0.255	0.179	0.128	0.140	0.851	0.764	0.654	0.510	0.253	0.811	0.667	0.487
1985	0.327	0.228	0.181	0.123	0.140	0.917	0.815	0.679	0.531	0.285	0.875	0.715	0.514
1990	0.326	0.247	0.162	0.122	0.143	0.911	0.817	0.642	0.494	0.263	0.871	0.701	0.473
1995	0.282	0.253	0.191	0.116	0.156	0.930	0.853	0.698	0.525	0.315	0.894	0.723	0.525
2000	0.273	0.225	0.197	0.142	0.163	0.830	0.719	0.581	0.467	0.293	0.779	0.617	0.455
2005	0.257	0.210	0.173	0.155	0.206	0.839	0.743	0.590	0.500	0.337	0.796	0.620	0.466

Sources: Published Population and Housing Census Reports for 1955–1975; Micro samples of Population and Housing Census for 1980–2005.

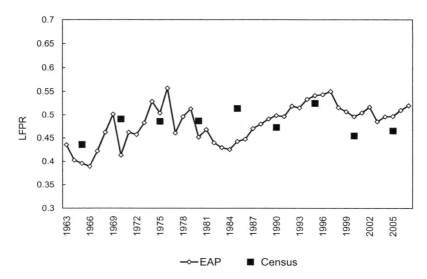

Fig. 8.1   LFPR of men aged sixty and older

estimated from the Census is somewhat different, with the economic activity of older men rising greatly between 1965 and 1970, remaining relatively stable over the next twenty years, and then increasing sharply between 1990 and 1995.

It is too early to determine whether the sharp decrease in the LFPR of older men between 1997 and 2000 heralds the beginning of the same long-term decline in the labor market activity of the elderly that has already been taking place in developed nations. It may simply reflect a temporary discouraged-worker effect resulting from the poor labor market prospect during the period of the financial crisis. Given that the decreasing trend of the LFPR of older men has been reversed since 2000, the latter story seems more likely. In addition, it appears that the labor market activity of older workers was at least strongly influenced by the recession during the financial crisis and subsequent restructuring of the economy. The fall in the LFPR was particularly pronounced for men aged fifty to sixty-four, whose unemployment rate was higher than that of men aged sixty-five and older. Likewise, as will be seen later, the fall in labor market activity was much greater in urban areas than in the countryside. However, since the main focus of this study is the long-term trend, the causes of the sharp decline and the rise in the LFPR of older males from 1997 will not be scrutinized here.

The rise in the LFPR since the mid-1960s of men aged sixty and older is not an artifact of a change in the age distribution. As indicated in table 8.1, an increase in the LFPR is observed for three different age groups, sixty to sixty-four, sixty-five to sixty-nine, and seventy and older. As a matter of

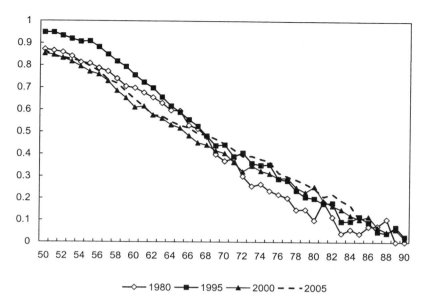

Legend: ◇ 1980   ■ 1995   ▲ 2000   - - - 2005

Fig. 8.2   Age-LFPR profile

fact, had the age distribution remained unchanged since 1965, the LFPR of men aged sixty and older in 1995 would have been practically the same as the actual rate, 51.9 percent instead of 52.5 percent.[4] A comparison of the age-LFPR profiles for 1980, 1995, 2000, and 2005, presented in figure 8.2, provides a more detailed structure of age-specific change in the LFPR for men aged fifty and older since 1980. Between 1980 and 1995, the rise of the LFPR was greater for men in their fifties and seventies than for men in their sixties. For the period 1995 to 2000, as noted previously, the exit from the labor force was concentrated among men aged fifty to sixty-four.

The size and time trends of the LFPR of older males were sharply different between urban and rural areas and between farm and nonfarm households. The Census reports classify lands into three administrative categories according to the degree of urbanization: *Dong, Eup,* and *Myon,* roughly corresponding to city, town, and countryside, respectively. Table 8.2 and figure 8.3 present the age-specific LFPR of men aged sixty and older for rural areas (Myon and Eup areas combined) and cities (Dong areas). It is evident from the results that the rise in the LFPR of older males in Korea between 1965 and 1995 is largely explained by the dramatic increase in the labor market activity of the elderly population in rural areas. The LFPR in rural areas increased by 30 percentage points, from 46 percent in 1965 to 70 percent in

---

4. Calculated based on the relative size of each age group in 1965 and the age-specific LFPR as of 1995, reported in table 8.1.

Table 8.2   Urban population share and labor force participation rate of males aged sixty and older by place of residence

Year	Share of urban dwellers				Labor force participation rate							
					60+		60–64		65–69		70+	
	60+	60–64	65–69	70+	Urban	Rural	Urban	Rural	Urban	Rural	Urban	Rural
1960	0.172	0.200	0.164	0.143	0.373	0.551	0.485	0.767	0.350	0.543	0.197	0.306
1965	0.206	0.235	0.199	0.174	0.351	0.458	0.491	0.680	0.317	0.461	0.142	0.185
1970	0.247	0.281	0.245	0.200	0.353	0.536	0.483	0.751	0.310	0.554	0.140	0.252
1975	0.304	0.336	0.312	0.252	0.337	0.551	0.487	0.782	0.288	0.578	0.110	0.235
1980	0.360	0.385	0.368	0.322	0.281	0.603	0.400	0.812	0.253	0.660	0.127	0.313
1985	0.436	0.470	0.439	0.389	0.333	0.654	0.481	0.853	0.305	0.708	0.128	0.386
1990	0.467	0.500	0.470	0.427	0.325	0.603	0.493	0.790	0.303	0.663	0.122	0.369
1995	0.571	0.606	0.574	0.525	0.391	0.703	0.588	0.868	0.348	0.762	0.149	0.498
2000	0.605	0.659	0.596	0.547	0.312	0.675	0.463	0.809	0.278	0.746	0.124	0.498
2005	0.566	0.659	0.562	0.493	0.311	0.668	0.483	0.795	0.302	0.754	0.136	0.541

Sources: Published Population and Housing Census Reports for 1955–1975; Micro samples of Population and Housing Census for 1980–2005.

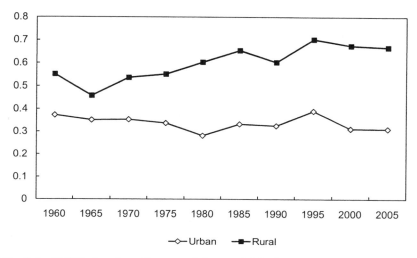

Fig. 8.3   LFPR of male residents aged sixty and older in urban and rural areas

1995, in sharp contrast to a rise of only 4 percentage points among urban dwellers. Within the rural areas, the aged men in the countryside (Myon areas) experienced a much greater increase in participation than those living in towns (Eup areas). These, however are not reported here. Similar patterns are observed for each of the three age groups: sixty to sixty-four, sixty-five to sixty-nine, and seventy and older.[5]

The LFPR of older males has been higher among the rural population than among city-dwellers throughout the period under study. The greater labor market activity of the aged in rural areas probably results from the greater flexibility of self-employment in such work as farming. Since health, desire to work, and other factors that affect labor force participation change gradually as a person gets older, an aging person might prefer to reduce the amount of work step by step rather than to work full time and then retire completely. Gradual retirement is an option for the self-employed who are able to reduce the hours and intensity of work to some extent.[6] Moreover, the self-employed are less likely to be covered by employer-sponsored or public

5. If the elderly population is classified into persons residing in farm households and those living in nonfarm households, a similar result emerges. The LFPR of men aged sixty and older residing in farm households increased from 47 percent in 1965 to 78 percent in 1995. By contrast, the male LFPR of the same age group dwelling in nonfarm households rose only modestly, from 33 to 42 percent during the three decades. These results suggest that the rise in the LFPR of older males in Korea between 1965 and 1995 was largely a rural and agricultural phenomenon.

6. For instance, aged farmers can reduce the amount of work efforts by adjusting acreage and crop-mix or by adopting mechanization (Pedersen 1950). In the United States, the LFPR of older males was likewise higher in the farm than in nonfarm households throughout the late nineteenth and the first half of the twentieth century (Lee 2002).

pension plans than wage earners. Therefore, it would be more difficult for the rural elderly population to finance retirement. In addition, the economic status of the rural population has been unfavorable compared with that of the urban population, particularly in recent years.

Since the 1960s, the proportion of the elderly male population living in urban areas has rapidly increased. The percentage of the population among males aged sixty and older who resided in urban areas increased from 17 percent in 1960 to 60 percent in 2000 (table 8.2). Similarly, the share of men aged sixty and older residing in farm households decreased from 72 percent in 1965 to 34 percent in 1995. This implies that, other things being equal, the LFPR of older men would have declined as a result of the shift toward the urban and nonfarm sectors. In the case of the United States, the decline of agriculture explains a substantial fraction of the fall in the LFPR of older men between 1880 and 1940 (Lee 2002, 2005). In Korea, the dramatic increase in the LFPR of aged men in rural areas more than offsets this countervailing force resulting from urbanization and agricultural decline.

It is unclear why aged workers in rural areas remain in the labor force much longer today than they did forty years ago. A possible explanation is the impact of the mass migration of the rural population into the urban and nonagricultural sectors (Yoon 1984; Moon et al. 1991; Lee 1993a; Kim et al. 1997). The relative importance of farm households, which accounted for 54 percent of all households in 1960, has since rapidly declined. In 1995, 40 percent of the economically active population (those aged fourteen and older) lived in the rural areas, compared with 65 percent in 1966. The selective out-migration of younger people has accelerated the aging of the population in rural areas. The proportion of individuals sixty and older to the population aged fourteen and over increased from 11 to 25 percent between 1966 and 1995, and rose from 6 to 9 percent in urban areas. In 1995, 30 percent of the economically active population living in the countryside (Myon) was composed of persons sixty and older.

This aging of the rural population may have produced a rise in the LFPR of older men for the following reasons: first, if young and older workers are substitutes in the labor market, the out-migration of the young may have increased the value of aged workers' marginal labor productivity, thereby raising the opportunity cost of retirement. Second, the self-employed, farmers in particular, may have been forced to work longer because of the loss of family labor. The potential effect of population aging on the labor force participation decisions of older workers will be examined following.

8.5   A Regression Model of the Labor Force
Participation Decisions at Older Ages

In this section, the determinants of labor force participation decisions of older males are examined. More specifically, it is estimated how the probability of labor force participation was affected by a number of potential factors in labor force participation decisions, such as age, education, marital status, family size, home ownership, residence in urban areas, and the extent of population aging and the industrial structure in the place of residence. Furthermore, the time and cohort effects on the economic activity of older men are considered. The results of this analysis not only reveal the patterns of retirement at a particular point in time, but also provide useful insights into the cause of the changes in the LFPR of older males over time. The logit regression analyses provided following are based on a pooled sample of the Censuses of 1980, 1985, 1990, 1995, 2000, and 2005.

The analyses start with a simple standard model of labor force participation decisions based on a choice between work and leisure.[7] At any given date, a person will choose either retirement or labor force participation based on his or her utility associated with each option. Well-being when working can be written as:

(1) $$U_W(Y + N, \overline{H}; \mathbf{Z}),$$

and utility when not working as

(2) $$U_R(N, 0; \mathbf{Z}),$$

where Y is labor income, N is nonlabor income, $\mathbf{Z}$ is a vector of demographic and socioeconomic variables to affect utility, and $\overline{H}$ is hours of work in the labor market. A decision function can be given as

(3) $$I^* = U_R(N, 0; \mathbf{Z}) - U_W(Y + N, \overline{H}; \mathbf{Z}).$$

Although the value of I^* is not observed, a discrete retirement indicator is observed, given by $I = 0$ if $I^* < 0$, $= 1$ otherwise, where 1 represents retirement and 0, labor force participation.

The decision function evaluated by the individual can be presented as

(4) $$I^* = U_R(N, 0; \mathbf{Z}) - U_W(Y + N, \overline{H}; \mathbf{Z}) = -\mathbf{X}'\beta - A\alpha - C\gamma - Y\varphi + \varepsilon,$$

where $\mathbf{X}$ is a vector containing proxy variables for Y, N, $\overline{H}$, $\mathbf{A}$ is a matrix of age dummies, $\mathbf{C}$ is a matrix of cohort dummies, $\mathbf{Y}$ is a matrix of year dummies, β, α, γ, and φ are parameter vectors, and ε is an error term. Using the indicator function I, the effects of the variables will be estimated by means of a logit,

(5) $$\text{Prob}(I = 1) = \text{Prob}(\varepsilon < \mathbf{X}'\beta + A\alpha + C\gamma + Y\varphi)$$
$$= \frac{\exp(\mathbf{X}'\beta + A\alpha + C\gamma + Y\varphi)}{1 + \exp(\mathbf{X}'\beta + A\alpha + C\gamma + Y\varphi)}$$
$$= \Phi(\mathbf{X}'\beta + A\alpha + C\gamma + Y\varphi).$$

7. The model given following is a modified version of the model used in Costa (1998, chapter 3).

Since there is a linear relationship across the three matrices A, C, and Y, the matrices of the dummies satisfy

$$(6) \qquad As_a = Cs_c + Ys_y,$$

where the s vectors are arithmetic sequences $\{0,1,2,3, \ldots \}$ of the length given by the number of columns of the matrix that premultiplies them. Since equation (6) is a single identity, it is impossible to estimate the equation (5).

To circumvent this problem, the following methods are employed. First, cohort dummies are dropped from the regression equation, ignoring the cohort effect. Second, adopting the method used by Deaton (1997, chapter 2), the age, cohort, and year effects are normalized assuming that any secular time trend in the LFPR of older men is attributable to the age and cohort effects and that the year effect captures the cyclical fluctuations or business cycle effect. A normalization that accomplishes this makes the year effect orthogonal to a time-trend, so that

$$(7) \qquad s_y' \varphi = 0.$$

To estimate the equation (5) subject to the normalization given by equation (7), three-year dummies defined as follows, from $t = 3, 4, 5$, are included in the regressions:

$$(8) \qquad d_t^* = d_t - [(t-1)d_2 - (t-2)d_i],$$

where d_t is the usual year dummy. This procedure satisfies the restriction (7), as well as the restriction that the year dummies should add to zero. The coefficients of the d_i^* give the third to the final year (1990 through 2005 in the present case) coefficients. The first and second can be computed from the two restrictions that all year effects add to zero, thus satisfying equation (7).

For many developed countries, especially the United States, a large number of studies have investigated the determinants of the timing of retirement. Some independent variables widely used in those studies include age, education, health status, characteristics of prior occupation, the size of the pension income, and family structure (Parson 1980; Hurd and Boskin 1984; Krueger and Pischke 1992; Costa 1998; Lee 1998b, 1999). Age, educational attainment, and health status are proxy variables for the individual's productivity in the labor market, which determines the opportunity cost of retirement. Health, family structure, and job attributes such as flexibility and physical demands are believed to be associated with the preference for work. Though it would be desirable to consider all the potential determining factors of labor force participation of older men, the selection of explanatory variables used in this study was limited by the information available from the data.

In the regression analyses, the following variables are included. Age is included as a dummy variable for each of the five-year age intervals.[8] Educational attainment is represented by the dummy variables denoted as "No schooling," "Elementary school," "Middle school," "High school," and "College."[9] It is well-documented that the degree of education is positively related with the size of the labor supply (Pencavel 1986). Accumulation of human capital in the form of education will increase wages, raising the opportunity cost of retirement (substitution effect). It should be noted, however, that the variables of education in this study could also capture the effect of income, because no income measure is included in the present analysis. Therefore, the direction of the effect of education will depend on the relative magnitudes of the substitution and income effects.

Variables of the marital status and the family size are included to capture the potential effects of having dependents and receiving family support. A larger family will require a greater household income, but will also have a greater potential for earnings from more family members. Therefore, the sign of the effect of the number of potential earners will depend on the relative sizes of these two different influences. A dummy variable of urban dwelling is included to measure the difference between urban and rural areas. The percentage of the male population aged sixty and older in each city or county is added to capture the effect of the extent of population aging in the locality. Finally, the percentage of the male population aged fifty and older employed in nonagricultural industries is included to show the influence of the local industrial structure.[10]

It should be emphasized that the regression model employed in this study is subject to limitations arising from the cross-sectional nature of the data, as well as the lack of information on a number of key determinants of the labor force participation decisions. First, some of the independent variables may have endogeneity problems. For instance, the family size could reflect outcomes rather than determine the factors of retirement decisions. Second, the retirement effect of job attributes cannot be considered fully in this study because information on the previous occupation and industry is unknown for the retired. Furthermore, the proxy variables employed in the analysis, such as age and education, are highly incomplete measures of labor and nonlabor incomes. Some of these shortcomings can be overcome by using the panel data. Unfortunately, such data sources are not available for the years prior to 1997. In spite of these limitations, the results of the regressions given following, if interpreted carefully, should be useful in understanding

8. If age is included as a continuous variable, the results do not show much change. Age has a strong negative effect on the odds of labor force participation, and the parameter estimates of other explanatory variables remain practically unchanged.

9. Each educational category includes both graduates and dropouts. "College" includes persons who had at least some college education.

10. Agricultural industries include agriculture, forestry, hunting, and fishing.

the reasons for the long-term change in the LFPR of older males since the 1980s.

8.6   Regression Results

Table 8.3 presents the results of pooled-sample logistic regressions, excluding the cohort dummies. The year dummy variables would capture Korea's various social, economic, and institutional changes, as well as the changing patterns of public policies and social programs such as medical care and pension plans that influenced the labor force participation decisions of older men. By allowing these variables, we can also consider the potential business cycle effect on employment and retirement of older males. Men aged fifty-five to seventy-four are included in the analyses. Three regressions are performed separately for men aged fifty-five to seventy-four who resided in urban and rural areas, as well as the entire sample of men at the same ages.

Age is negatively related to the odds of labor force participation, as antici-

Table 8.3   **Results of pooled-sample logistic regressions: Correlates of the probability of labor force participation for males aged fifty-five to seventy-four**

	All		Rural		Urban	
	Mean	$\partial P/\partial X$	Mean	$\partial P/\partial X$	Mean	$\partial P/\partial X$
Ages 60 to 64	0.285	−0.586***	0.284	−0.533***	0.286	−0.597***
65 to 69	0.211	−0.787***	0.226	−0.754***	0.202	−0.799***
70 to 74	0.137	−0.886***	0.155	−0.879***	0.126	−0.887***
Year 1985	0.145	0.147***	0.222	−0.013	0.098	0.377***
1990	0.135	0.096***	0.203	−0.071**	0.094	0.408***
1995	0.169	0.480***	0.130	−0.086**	0.193	0.990***
2000	0.198	0.013	0.137	−0.061**	0.235	0.226***
2005	0.254	0.227***	0.153	0.154***	0.317	0.447***
Elementary school	0.339	−0.022	0.421	−0.051***	0.288	0.155***
Middle school	0.163	−0.100***	0.121	−0.361***	0.190	0.213***
High school	0.190	−0.096***	0.100	−0.466***	0.246	0.237***
College	0.131	0.120***	0.051	−0.437***	0.181	0.537***
Married	0.916	1.446***	0.921	2.352***	0.913	0.991***
Family size	3.497	−0.043***	3.626	−0.076***	3.417	−0.017***
Urban dwelling	0.617	−0.276***	0.000	NI	1.000	NI
% Agriculture	45.294	0.013***	80.494	0.013***	23.476	0.013***
% Male 60+	7.674	0.045***	10.933	0.054***	5.655	0.044***
Number of observations	276,238		105,848		170,390	

Notes: NI stands for "Not Included." Omitted categories are: (1) ages 55 to 59, (2) year 1980, and (3) no schooling.

***Significant at the 1 percent level.

**Significant at the 5 percent level.

pated. The size of the estimated coefficient is similar for all three samples and remained stable over time. The results for the year dummies suggest that, if other variables included in the regressions are held constant, the increasing trend of the LFPR largely disappears for older men residing in rural areas. In contrast, the regression results for city dwellers are remarkably similar to the actual changes in the LFPR presented in figure 8.1. This indicates that the independent variables included in the regressions better explain the changes in the LFPR of the rural elderly population than those of older males living in urban areas.

The association between education and labor market activity of older men was markedly different between rural and urban areas. In urban areas, a strong positive relationship between education and the labor force participation of older males was found. In rural areas, by sharp contrast, males with no schooling were more likely to be in the labor force than the educated. A possible explanation is that formal education was less important in rural areas due to a larger fraction of the self-employed, such as farmers. Alternatively, it could reflect a stronger income effect associated with education in rural areas.

Married men were much more likely to be in the labor force than single men for both the urban and rural populations. The higher labor force participation of the married could have resulted from a greater need to support dependents. Alternatively, it could reflect a better environment for the labor market activity of married men owing to the spouses' assistance. On the other hand, the family size was negatively related to the probability of the labor force participation for both rural and urban areas. It appears that the presence of potential earners in the household enabled aged householders to leave the labor force. Additional family members diminished the probability of labor force participation of older men more strongly in rural areas than in cities. This rural-urban difference could be explained by the fact that the relative contribution of other family members to the family economy is much higher in the rural areas than in cities because the proportion of self-employed jobs is higher in the countryside. The observed negative effect of the family size on the probability of labor force participation supports the earlier conjecture that migrations of the rural population to cities should have increased the LFPR of older males in rural areas.

Older men who were residing in rural areas were much more likely to be active in the labor force than city-dwellers. In addition, the percentage of the economically active male population aged fifty and older employed outside agriculture in each city or county had a significant negative effect on the probability of the labor force participation of older males living in the locality. These results suggest that urbanization and the decline of agriculture in Korea, other things being equal, would have greatly lowered the LFPR of older males, as in the case in nineteenth- and early twentieth-century

America (Lee 2002).[11] Finally, the percentage of the male population aged sixty and older in each city or county, an indicator of the degree of population aging in the locality, stands out as a very powerful predictor of the labor force participation of older males. Its effect on the odds of labor force participation is strongly positive for both the rural and urban populations. The magnitude of the effect, however, was greater in the rural than in urban areas, consistent with the hypothesis that the population aging in rural areas caused by rural-urban migration increased the LFPR of older men in the countryside.[12]

The aforementioned results suggest that losing family labor in rural households owing to rural-urban migrations was a major cause of the rise of the LFPR of older males between 1980 and 1997. The changing age structure, urbanization, and the relative decline of agriculture were all countervailing forces that decreased the labor market activity of older men over the two decades under study. Improved educational attainments should have increased the labor force participation of older men in cities, and should have decreased the economic activity of aged men in rural areas. On the other hand, the decrease in the family size and population aging in each county or city should have increased the LFPR of older men, especially of those living in rural areas.

The effect of population aging in rural areas was particularly large in magnitude. A 1 percent increase in the proportion of the male population aged sixty and older was associated with a 5.4 percent rise in the probability of the labor force participation in rural areas. Since the average share of the population aged sixty and older in rural areas increased by 8.8 percentage points between 1980 and 1995, this change would have produced a 48 percent

11. The changing composition of business may have been an additional force that decreased the LFPR of older men. Among the men aged fifty-five to seventy-four in the labor force, the percentage of self-employed farmers declined from 66.6 percent in 1980 to 43.4 percent in 1995, while the fraction of wage and salary workers increased from 12.3 percent in 1980 to 35.1 percent in 1995. The percentage of nonfarm self-employed fell slightly, from 21.1 percent to 20.7 percent over the fifteen years. Between 1995 and 2000, the percentage of nonfarm self-employees increased to 25.1 percent while the share of wage and salary workers remained stable. Since the hazard rate of retirement had been much lower for self-employed farmers than the other types of jobs during the period 1980 to 2000 (Lee 2004), such changes in the composition of employment should have decreased the LFPR of older men.

12. Migration from urban to rural areas might itself be related to retirement if many older urban dwellers chose to relocate in the countryside after leaving the labor market. In contrast, in the case of the early twentieth-century United States (Moen 1994), older farmers could move to towns or cities after retirement. These possibilities were tested by including the dummy variables of migration across rural and urban areas during the five-year period prior to the census year instead of the urban dwelling dummy variable. Both urban-to-rural and rural-to-urban migrants were less likely to participate in the labor market than nonmigrants, indicating that the migration of older men was related to retirement decisions. However, since the percentage of migrants across rural and urban areas was very small (2.5 percent) and migrations in both directions are positively related to the probability of retirement, the observed migration-retirement link among older men does not explain the effects of urban dwelling and population aging on the probability of labor force participation as reported in the regression results.

increase in the LFPR of older males during the fifteen years, more than seven times the actual rise in the LFPR of males aged fifty-five to seventy-four in rural areas.[13] For the entire sample, the rise in the elderly population in each locality between 1980 and 1995 (3.5 percentage points) would have resulted in a 16 percent increase in the LFPR of older men, more than twice the actual rise in the LFPR of all males aged fifty-five to seventy-four.

Table 8.4 presents the results for the regressions, including those of the cohort dummies and normalized year dummies. "Dummy 1990," for instance, denotes d_3^* in equation (8). Since the geographic mobility of older men across urban and rural areas was very low during the period under study, it is reasonable to construct synthetic birth cohorts and perform the regression analysis separately for the urban and rural populations.[14] The estimated coefficients of the cohort dummies suggest that, starting from the cohorts born between 1931 and 1935; later cohorts were generally less likely to participate in the labor market than earlier cohorts. The year effects shown in the coefficients of the normalized year dummies are generally similar to those of the previous regressions excluding cohort dummies (see table 8.3). For the entire sample, the year effects for 1980 and 1985 recovered from the two restrictions are 0.073 and 0.059, respectively. The coefficients for the modified year dummies suggest that there was a strong transitory shock that increased the LFPR of older men in 1995.

The regression results for the variables of age, education, marital status, family size, urban dwelling, the percentage of the population engaged in nonagricultural work, and the percentage of males aged sixty and older are generally similar to those of the previous regressions reported in table 8.3. Even if the age and cohort effects, as well as the transitory time effect are considered, the aging of the population in each city or county emerges as the single most powerful factor explaining the increase in the LFPR of older men between 1980 and 1995.

Similar regressions were performed separately for each year and for the rural and urban areas, excluding the cohort and year dummies to see how

13. The strong effect of the extent of population aging on the labor force participation of older males is also observed for the period from 1970 through 1980. The published Census Reports for 1970, 1975, and 1980 provide statistics on the age-specific population and labor force participation rate separately for Dong, Eup, and Myon for the nine provinces (*Do*) and for the entire areas of the cities of Seoul and Pusan. Regressions were conducted using the eighty-seven observations (twenty-nine places for three years) obtained from these sources. The results, not presented here, indicate that a 1 percent increase in the share of the male population aged sixty and older was associated with a 2 to 3.5 percent rise in the LFPR of males aged sixty and older, depending on the inclusion of other control variables such as the dummy variables of Dong, Eup, and Myon (for province and city), as well as the year dummy variable. The share of the elderly population variable alone explains 75 percent of the variation in the LFPR of older males across places and times, and accounts for more than 100 percent of the change in the participation rate between 1970 and 1980.

14. Each Census provides information on the previous place of residence. Only 2.5 percent of men aged fifty-five to seventy-four in the pooled sample of the five Censuses had migrated across urban and rural areas during the five years prior to each census year.

Table 8.4 Results of logistic regressions for synthetic cohort analyses: Correlates of the probability of labor force participation for males aged fifty-five to seventy-four

	All		Rural		Urban	
	Mean	∂P/∂X	Mean	∂P/∂X	Mean	∂P/∂X
Ages 60 to 64	0.285	−0.596***	0.284	−0.555***	0.286	−0.598***
65 to 69	0.211	−0.796***	0.226	−0.768***	0.202	−0.799***
70 to 74	0.137	−0.886***	0.155	−0.877***	0.126	−0.889***
Cohort 1911–15	0.038	0.152***	0.063	0.359***	0.022	−0.121
1916–20	0.074	0.220***	0.119	0.564***	0.046	−0.071
1921–25	0.131	0.175***	0.186	0.716***	0.097	−0.110
1926–30	0.146	0.323***	0.179	0.900***	0.126	0.039
1931–35	0.191	0.516***	0.185	1.099***	0.195	0.226**
1936–40	0.187	0.463***	0.132	0.743***	0.222	0.251***
1941–45	0.137	0.214***	0.077	0.189**	0.174	0.099
1946–50	0.083	0.200***	0.037	−0.099	0.111	0.093
Dummy 1990	−0.057	−0.070***	−0.085	−0.144***	−0.039	0.013
1995	−0.070	0.193***	−0.225	−0.173***	0.026	0.339***
2000	−0.088	−0.165***	−0.285	−0.092***	0.034	−0.192***
2005	−0.079	0.056***	−0.336	0.272***	0.081	−0.030***
Elementary school	0.339	−0.049***	0.421	−0.095***	0.288	0.136***
Middle school	0.163	−0.122***	0.121	−0.371***	0.190	0.195***
High school	0.190	−0.119***	0.100	−0.475***	0.246	0.213***
College	0.131	0.087***	0.051	−0.456***	0.181	0.504***
Married	0.916	1.424***	0.921	2.290***	0.913	0.978***
Family size	3.497	−0.042***	3.626	−0.076***	3.417	−0.016***
Urban dwelling	0.617	0.281***	0.000	NI	1.000	NI
% Agriculture	45.294	0.013***	80.494	0.013***	23.476	0.013***
% Male 60+	7.674	0.045***	10.933	0.053***	5.655	0.044***
Number of observations	276,238		105,848		170,390	

Notes: NI stands for "Not Included." Omitted categories are: (1) ages 55 to 59, (2) cohort 1906–10, (3) year 1980, and (4) no schooling.

***Significant at the 1 percent level.

**Significant at the 5 percent level.

the effect of each independent variable changed over time. The results are reported in tables 8.5 (rural areas) and 8.6 (urban areas). A notable difference found across years is that the effect of education, especially that of college education on the labor force participation of the urban elderly population diminished over time (table 8.6). The estimated coefficient for college education was particularly small in 2000. This perhaps resulted from the fact that many aged white-collar workers were forced to retire on the basis of their age in the course of the restructuring of firms after the financial crisis and that a large fraction of these workers were college graduates.

Another notable result is that the effect of population aging in the locality on the probability of labor force participation has diminished in magnitude over time in both rural and urban areas. Moreover, the negative effect of the family size on the probability of remaining active in the labor market became

Table 8.5   **Results of logistic regressions for each year: Males in rural areas aged fifty-five to seventy-four ($\partial P/\partial X$)**

	1980	1985	1990	1995	2000	2005
Ages 60 to 64	−0.565***	−0.593***	−0.606***	−0.562***	−0.373***	−0369***
65 to 69	−0.813***	−0.823***	−0.810***	−0.795***	−0.558***	−0.532***
70 to 74	−0.931***	−0.921***	−0.909***	−0.893***	−0.77***	−0.712***
Elementary	−0.145***	−0.173***	−0.065*	−0.015*	0.006*	0.192***
Middle school	−0.488***	−0.523***	−0.319***	−0.340***	−0.362***	0.038***
High school	−0.361***	−0.575***	−0.359***	−0.463***	−0.475***	−0.291***
College	−0.230*	−0.502***	−0.111*	−0.416***	−0.549***	−0.389***
Married	2.004***	2.803***	1.855***	2.258***	1.996***	2.593***
Family size	−0.144***	−0.130***	0.014*	−0.009*	−0.001*	−0.067***
% Agriculture	0.037***	0.023***	0.006***	0.022***	0.019***	0.022***
% Male 60+	0.027*	0.053***	0.123***	0.031***	0.006*	0.032***
Number of observations	16,389	23,463	21,492	13,760	14,511	16,233

Note: NI stands for "Not Included." Omitted categories are: (1) ages 55 to 59, and (2) no schooling.
***Significant at the 1 percent level.
**Significant at the 5 percent level.
*Significant at the 10 percent level.

Table 8.6   **Results of logistic regressions for each year: Males in urban areas aged fifty-five to seventy-four ($\partial P/\partial X$)**

	1980	1985	1990	1995	2000	2005
Ages 60 to 64	−0.503***	−0.590***	−0.665***	−0.66***	−0.552***	−0.595***
65 to 69	−0.742***	−0.791***	−0.843***	−0.857***	−0.768***	−0.787***
70 to 74	−0.847***	−0.907***	−0.922***	−0.924***	−0.862***	−0.876***
Elementary school	0.261***	0.141**	0.132*	−0.078*	0.032*	0.261***
Middle school	0.480***	0.360***	0.303***	−0.091*	0.058*	0.210***
High school	0.824***	0.569***	0.681***	−0.010*	−0.052*	0.188***
College	2.134***	1.343***	1.708***	0.304***	0.092*	0.325***
Married	1.002***	1.090***	0.735***	0.891***	1.056***	1.063***
Family size	−0.045***	−0.037***	0.008*	0.010*	0.008*	−0.020***
% Agriculture	0.012***	0.010***	0.004***	0.013***	0.013***	0.014***
% Male 60+	0.443***	0.176***	0.107***	0.021***	0.016***	0.057***
Number of observations	10,813	16,700	15,934	32,862	40,116	53,965

Notes: NI stands for "Not Included." Omitted categories are: (1) ages 55 to 59, and (2) no schooling.
***Significant at the 1 percent level.
**Significant at the 5 percent level.
*Significant at the 10 percent level.

weaker over time. Its sign even turned positive for the urban sample from 1990 to 2000. As noted before, these two variables are perhaps the major forces that produced the increase in the LFPR of older men from 1980 to 1995, which dominated the countervailing influences of urbanization and agricultural decline. Thus, if the effects of these two variables diminish in the long run, as the regression results suggest, the LFPR of older men is likely to fall over time, other things being equal.

8.7   Discussions

The results of the previous sections suggest that the rise in the LFPR of aged Korean males over the last four decades was largely produced by the dramatic increase in the labor market activity of older men residing in rural areas. This study also indicates that the population aging produced by the mass migration of younger persons to urban areas was a major explanation for the increase in the LFPR of the rural elderly population. Although it is not entirely clear why the increase in the share of the elderly population in a county was related to a higher LFPR of older men in the locality, circumstantial evidence suggests that older householders are forced to continue to work because they are losing family labor.

The average size of farm households decreased from 6.4 persons in 1963 to 2.8 persons in 2006 (table 8.7). According to Kim et al. (1997), the households in Myon areas today have less than three persons on the average. It is particularly notable that the numbers of one-generation households and single-person households rapidly increased. In 1960, the majority of rural households were composed of two or three generations. The proportion of one-generation households in Myon areas increased from 4.4 percent in 1960 to 27.5 percent by 1995. The majority of the heads of these one-generation households are older persons. In 1995, for instance, 78 percent of the heads of the one-generation households were aged fifty-five or older. Similarly, the share of single-person households sharply increased from 2 percent in 1960 to 17 percent in 1995. Again, the majority of the single-person householders were aged fifty-five and older.

An intriguing question related to the rising LFPR of the rural elderly population is why the Korean case is so different from the historical experiences of other developed nations that also went through a large-scale population movement from rural to urban areas that would have accelerated the pace of the population aging in countryside. In early twentieth-century America, as in the case of Korea, farmers remained in the labor force longer than nonfarmers owing to the greater flexibility of farming. However, the pace of the decline in the LFPR of older males in the United States was not greatly different between farmers and nonfarmers from 1880 to 1940 (Lee 2002). It was quite common for an older farmer to sell his farm, move to a nearby town, and lead a relatively independent retirement (Moen 1994; Lee 1999).

Further investigation is needed to understand why so many older farmers in Korea do not follow the retirement pattern seen in the past among American farmers. A possible explanation is that the relative decline of the rural economy in the course of industrialization made it increasingly

Table 8.7   **Average size and income of farm and urban households in Korea, 1963–2006**

Year	Household size			Household income (won)		
	Farm	Urban	Ratio	Farm	Urban	Ratio
1963	6.39	5.56	1.15	7,765	5,990	1.30
1964	6.44	5.56	1.16	10,474	7,320	1.43
1965	6.29	5.56	1.13	9,350	8,450	1.11
1966	6.22	5.56	1.12	10,848	11,750	0.92
1967	6.12	5.85	1.05	12,456	18,180	0.69
1968	6.02	5.70	1.06	14,913	21,270	0.70
1969	5.99	5.53	1.08	18,156	24,650	0.74
1970	5.92	5.48	1.08	21,317	28,180	0.76
1971	5.83	5.40	1.08	29,699	33,340	0.89
1972	5.71	5.37	1.06	35,783	38,080	0.94
1973	5.72	5.26	1.09	40,059	40,380	0.99
1974	5.66	5.22	1.08	56,204	47,780	1.18
1975	5.63	5.18	1.09	72,744	65,540	1.11
1976	5.54	5.12	1.08	96,355	88,270	1.09
1977	5.52	4.83	1.14	119,401	105,910	1.13
1978	5.38	4.73	1.14	157,016	144,510	1.09
1979	5.20	4.66	1.12	185,624	194,749	0.95
1980	5.11	4.58	1.12	224,426	234,086	0.96
1981	5.05	4.56	1.11	307,321	280,953	1.09
1982	4.97	4.45	1.12	372,098	313,608	1.19
1983	4.99	4.37	1.14	427,354	359,041	1.19
1984	4.80	4.28	1.12	462,428	395,613	1.17
1985	4.70	4.21	1.12	478,021	423,788	1.13
1986	4.52	4.16	1.09	499,584	473,553	1.05
1987	4.33	4.08	1.06	544,610	553,099	0.98
1988	4.28	4.04	1.06	677,468	646,672	1.05
1989	4.12	4.02	1.02	786,389	804,938	0.98
1990	3.97	3.99	0.99	918,815	943,272	0.97
1991	3.82	3.97	0.96	1,092,087	1,158,608	0.94
1992	3.70	3.92	0.94	1,208,788	1,356,110	0.89
1993	3.78	3.84	0.98	1,410,664	1,477,828	0.95
1994	3.68	3.76	0.98	1,692,980	1,701,304	1.00
1995	3.56	3.73	0.95	1,816,880	1,911,064	0.95
1996	3.46	3.67	0.94	1,941,472	2,152,687	0.90
1997	3.39	3.63	0.93	1,957,363	2,287,335	0.86
1998	3.29	3.62	0.91	1,707,811	2,133,115	0.80
1999	3.23	3.59	0.90	1,860,246	2,224,743	0.84
2000	3.12	3.54	0.88	1,922,677	2,386,947	0.81
2001	3.05	3.49	0.87	1,992,231	2,625,118	0.76
2002	2.97	3.44	0.86	2,039,552	2,792,400	0.73
2003	2.96	3.45	0.86	2,239,799	2,940,026	0.76
2004	2.85	3.39	0.84	2,416,711	3,113,362	0.78
2005	2.83	3.35	0.84	2,541,918	3,250,837	0.78
2006	2.77	3.31	0.84	2,691,957	3,443,399	0.78

Source: Urban Household Income Survey, Farm Household Economic Statistics.

difficult for the rural elderly population to save for retirement. The ratio of the income of farm households to the income of urban households shows a long-term decreasing trend (table 8.7). Except for the late 1960s, when the average income of urban households rose rapidly, farm households fared relatively well until the mid-1980s. Beginning in the late 1980s, farm households began to lose ground, and they currently receive 78 percent of the income earned by urban households. According to the 1996 National Survey of Family Income and Expenditure, the average amount of net savings of rural households was only 76 percent of the net wealth held by urban households (Korea National Statistical Office 2000, 3-13). The result of the 1994 Social Statistics Survey indicates that the people living in rural areas are much less prepared financially for old-age security than city-dwellers. While 57 percent of urban respondents had made preparations for old age, only 41 percent of rural respondents had done so (Korea National Statistical Office 2000, 3-13).

Statistics on wealth holdings suggest that it is probably difficult for the majority of older farmers to finance retirement by selling their farm properties. In 1995, for instance, the average value of wealth held by farm households was 150 million won, about ten times the average farm household expenditure (Korea National Statistical Office 1995b). Since the wealth distribution in rural areas is highly skewed, the median value of wealth possessed by farm households should be much lower than the average.

If older males in rural areas tend to stay in the labor force longer involuntarily because of insufficient savings, a rise in the value of farm properties would stimulate retirement of the rural elderly population. Thus, the effect of the rate of appreciation of land value between 1985 and 1990 in each city or county on the probability of labor force participation of older men who resided in the locality was examined. For this particular analysis, the five-year period was selected because it was the only time interval between two census years prior to 1997 during which the LFPR of older men in rural areas declined and the average land price rapidly rose. The results of the logit regressions (not reported here), which employed a model similar to one used in the previous regressions (tables 8.3 and 8.4), show that the rate of change of the average land value between 1986 and 1990 had a strong negative effect on the probability of labor force participation of older males, especially those living in rural areas.[15]

It is noted earlier that the sharp decline in the LFPR of older males between 1995 and 2000 may have resulted from the deterioration of the labor market conditions after the financial crisis. To see if retirement decisions of older men in Korea were actually influenced by business cycles, additional pooled-sample logistic regressions similar to those reported in table 8.3 were

---

15. A 1 percent increase in the average land value was associated with a 0.4 percent decrease in the probability of labor force participation of older men in rural areas. The magnitude of the effect for the urban population was only a quarter of the magnitude for the rural population.

conducted. In this case, a variable pertaining to labor market nonparticipation of prime-age males (ages twenty-five to forty-nine) in each city or county of residence was added. For the purpose of the present analysis, men who did not work involuntarily were defined as nonparticipants. The 2005 Census was not included in the pooled sample, because it does not provide reasons for not working. The results are reported in table 8.8.

The results confirm the conjecture that poor labor market conditions may have pushed older male workers out of the labor force. As a whole, the 1 percent increase in the nonparticipation rate among prime-age males was associated with a 3 percent decline in the LFPR of males aged fifty-five to seventy-four. Between 1995 and 2000, the average nonparticipation rate of males aged twenty-five to forty-nine in the pooled sample of the Censuses rose from 8.4 percent to 13.1 percent. If the regression result is applied, the sliding job market conditions would have decreased the LFPR of older men by 14 percent. This suggests that the surge in unemployment following the financial crisis should be a major culprit of the exodus of older workers from the labor market after 1998.

Another possible explanation for the increase in the LFPR of older males

Table 8.8   **Results of 1980–2000 pooled-sample logistic regressions: Local labor market condition and the probability of labor force participation for males aged fifty-five to seventy-four**

	All		Rural		Urban	
	Mean	$\partial P/\partial X$	Mean	$\partial P/\partial X$	Mean	$\partial P/\partial X$
Ages 60 to 64	0.291	−0.601***	0.291	−0.550***	0.291	−0.610***
65 to 69	0.202	−0.808***	0.218	−0.788***	0.191	−0.815***
70 to 74	0.127	−0.905***	0.146	−0.905***	0.114	−0.902***
Year 1985	0.195	0.299***	0.266	0.215	0.149	0.407***
1990	0.182	0.179***	0.230	0.113**	0.150	0.367***
1995	0.226	0.548***	0.146	1.049	0.278	0.931***
2000	0.265	0.179***	0.155	1.300***	0.336	0.255***
Elementary school	0.356	0.007	0.428	−0.012***	0.310	0.131***
Middle school	0.153	0.027	0.096	−0.297***	0.189	0.291***
High school	0.161	0.076***	0.073	−0.388***	0.218	0.369***
College	0.118	0.439***	0.034	−0.342***	0.171	0.838***
Married	0.920	1.530***	0.922	2.563***	0.918	0.966***
Family size	3.876	−0.073***	3.809	−0.135***	3.920	−0.032***
Urban dwelling	0.608	−0.203***	0.000	NI	1.000	NI
% Agriculture	43.527	0.014***	81.082	0.015***	19.414	0.014***
% Male 60+	7.361	0.051***	10.234	0.056***	5.516	0.047***
% Nonparticipation	9.793	−0.030***	7.272	0.039***	11.415	−0.016***
Number of observations	206,040		80,676		125,364	

Notes: NI stands for "Not Included." Omitted categories are: (1) ages 55 to 59, (2) year 1980, and (3) no schooling.

***Significant at the 1 percent level.

**Significant at the 5 percent level.

in rural areas is the technological progress in agricultural production that may have allowed aging farmers to continue working. It appears that farmers increasingly adopted more technology- and capital-intensive production methods to overcome the growing labor shortage in rural areas (Koo 1991). Table 8.9 reports the number of the five major agricultural machines; namely, scuffler, tractor, rice transplanter, binder, and combine. The numbers are presented as fractions of the total number of farm households from 1980 through 2005. It is apparent from the table that Korean agriculture became increasingly mechanized since 1980.

To see if such technological changes in the agricultural sector increased the LFPR of older men in rural areas by diminishing their required work efforts, logistic regressions similar to those presented in table 8.5 were performed. The number of agricultural machines per farm household in each county of residence in the set of independent variables was included in the computation. Since the county-level statistics on farm machines are available only for the recent period, the regression analysis is confined to a sample from the 2005 census. The sample is further limited to 16,236 males aged fifty-five to seventy-four living in rural areas. The variables regarding the five major farm machines were included in the regressions one by one. Table 8.10 presents the estimated partial effects of the variables pertaining to farm machines, omitting the results for other independent variables that were included in the regressions.

The results suggest that technological progress may have encouraged the economic activity of older farmers in Korea. The probability of labor force participation of older males was higher in counties where scufflers, rice transplanters, and combines were more widely used. However, these relationships obtained from cross-sectional regressions do not tell the direction of the causality. It may have been a case where the growing aging population and labor shortage in rural areas produced both the increasing adoptions of farm machines and the rise of the LFPR of older farmers.

The rise of the economic activity of older males in rural areas may not be fully explained by the economic factors considered before. Older farmers could continue to work while living on the farm because they were emotion-

Table 8.9   Number of agricultural machines per farm household from 1980 to 2005

Agricultural machines	1980	1985	1990	1995	2000	2005
Scuffler	0.134	0.306	0.425	0.579	0.679	0.844
Tractor	0.001	0.006	0.023	0.067	0.136	0.179
Rice transplanter	0.005	0.022	0.078	0.165	0.247	0.261
Binder	0.006	0.013	0.031	0.045	0.052	0.047
Combine	0.001	0.006	0.025	0.048	0.063	0.068

Source: Korea National Statistical Office, Korea Statistical Information Service (http://www.kosis.kr).

Table 8.10   **Summary of results of five logistic regressions based on the 2005 Census: Diffusion of agricultural machines and the probability of labor force participation of older men**

	Mean	$\partial P/\partial X$	P-value
1. Scufflers per farm household	0.746	0.417	0.0712
2. Tractors per farm household	0.196	0.008	0.9813
3. Rise transplanters per farm household	0.295	0.472	0.0866
4. Binders per farm household	0.055	0.029	0.9138
5. Combines per farm household	0.076	8.984	0.0028

Notes: Similar independent variables as those used in the regressions reported in table 8.5 are used in these regressions but they are omitted from this table. The sample used for regressions is limited to the 16,236 males aged fifty-five to seventy-four living in rural areas in 2005. Dependent variable has a value of one if a man works, and zero otherwise.

ally attached to their lifelong job, place of residence, and neighbors (Lee 1993a; Koo 1991). Yoon (1984) reported that aged farmers stayed on the farm because the economic difficulties of their children or relatives living in urban areas made coresidency difficult. Moreover, they hoped to serve as a safety net for their migrant children. According to a survey conducted in 1983, migrant children received remittances from their parents twice as much as the amount they sent home, on average (Lee 1993b). It is also possible that some practically retired farmers are regarded as participants by maintaining some minor works while living in farm households. The economic and demographic changes explained previously, such as the large-scale city-bound migrations and relative decline of the rural economy, may have increased the number of such marginal participants among the elderly in rural areas. Other noneconomic factors not considered here, such as the changing attitudes toward work and improving health conditions, could have produced the same outcome.

8.8   Conclusions

This chapter has estimated the labor force participation rate of older males in Korea from 1955 to 2005 and analyzed the effects of several determining factors of the labor force participation decisions at older ages. The most remarkable result is the increase from 40 to 44 percent in 1965 to 53 to 55 percent in 1995 of the LFPR of older males aged sixty and older. This pattern is sharply distinct from the historical experiences of most OECD countries that witnessed a rapid decline in the labor force participation of older males over the last century. Although not highly reliable, the estimate from the early Census data indicates that the LFPR of older men fell from 1955 to the mid-1960s before it began to increase. The LFPR of older males fell dramatically after 1997, presumably due to the adverse labor market effect of the financial crisis.

The rise in the LFPR of older males in Korea between 1965 and 1995 is largely explained by the dramatic increase in the labor market activity among the rural elderly population. The LFPR of men aged sixty and older living in the rural areas increased from 46 to 70 percent during the same period, in sharp contrast to the 4 percentage point rise among urban dwellers. The results of the regression analyses suggest that the acceleration of population aging in rural areas due to the selective out-migration of younger persons was the major cause of the sharp increase in the LFPR of older males. It is likely that the relative decline of the rural economy in the course of industrialization made it increasingly difficult for the rural elderly population to save for retirement.

The results of this analysis suggest that the evolution of the labor market activity of older males in emerging economies may not be the same as the historical experiences of developed countries. In Korea, for instance, the pattern of the labor market activity of older men is distinct from that of the more developed countries in several respects. First, the overall LFPR of older males is much higher than those in other OECD countries. The relatively high participation rate may be attributable to the greater proportion of the self-employed among the elderly, as well as the late development of a public old-age pension program in Korea. Second, the trend of the LFPR of older males in Korea exhibits substantial fluctuations over time. This instability in the economic activity of older men is presumably due to the highly fragile labor market status of older workers in Korea that makes them vulnerable to recessions or structural changes in the economy.[16] Finally, as this chapter found out, the LFPR of aged males in Korea shows a long-term upward trend until 1997. As suggested before, this is likely to be an outcome of the relative decline of the rural economy in Korea. In sum, the features of the long-term trend of the *labor* market activity of older men in Korea reflect the characteristics of the social welfare system, labor market structure, and the legacy of past development strategy.

References

Abe, Y. 2001. Employees' pension benefits and the labor supply of older Japanese workers, 1980s–1990s. In *Aging issues in the United States and Japan,* ed., S. Ogura, T. Tachibabaki, and D. Wise, 273–305. Chicago: University of Chicago Press.

16. The length of job tenure, measured by the percentage of workers who hold the same job for five years at each age, was much shorter for Korean men after age fifty than for the other OECD countries such as the United States, United Kingdom, Germany, Japan, and France. More than a quarter of male workers fifty-five and older in Korea are employed in temporary positions that provide little job protection (OECD 2002).

Boskin, M. J. 1977. Social Security and retirement decisions. *Economic Inquiry* 15 (1): 1–25.

Chang, J. 2002. Transition paths from work to retirement. Paper presented at the Organization for Economic Cooperation and Development (OECD)/Korean Labor Institute (KLI) International Conference on Labor Market Policies in an Aging Era. Seoul, June 21, 2002.

———. 2003. Labor market policies in the era of population aging: the Korean case. KLI working paper, Korea Labor Institute.

Cho, J., and S. Kim. 2005. On using mandatory retirement to reduce workforce in Korea. *International Economic Journal* 19 (2): 283–303.

Choi, S.-H. 2006. Retirement behaviors of two wage earners households. *Korean Journal of Labor Economics* 29 (1): 129–52.

Costa, D. L. 1998. *The evolution of retirement.* Chicago: University of Chicago Press.

Deaton, A. 1997. *The analysis of household surveys.* Baltimore: Johns Hopkins University Press for World Bank.

Gruber, J., and B. C. Madrian. 1995. Health insurance availability and the retirement decision. *American Economic Review* 85 (4): 938–48.

Gruber, J., and D. Wise. 1999. *Social Security and retirement around the world.* Chicago: University of Chicago Press.

———. 2004. *Social Security Programs and retirement around the world: Microestimation.* Chicago: University of Chicago Press.

Gustman, A. L., and T. L. Steinmeier. 2002. Retirement and the stock market bubble. NBER Working Paper no. 9404. Cambridge, MA: National Bureau of Economic Research, December.

Hurd, M. D. 1996. The effect of labor market rigidities on the labor force behaviors of older workers. In *Advances in the economics of aging,* ed. D. A. Wise, 11–60. Chicago: University of Chicago Press.

Hurd, M. D., and M. J. Boskin. 1984. The effect of Social Security on retirement in the early 1970s. *Quarterly Journal of Economics* 99 (4): 767–90.

Hurd, M. D., and K. McGarry. 1993. The relationship between job characteristics and retirement. NBER Working paper no. 4558. Cambridge, MA: National Bureau of Economic Research, December.

Kim, N., S. Choi, W. Park, and K. Yang. 1997. *Population movement and changes in the characteristics of the rural population in Korea.* Korea National Statistical Office (in Korean).

Koo, J. 1991. Outmigration and the rural elderly in Korea. *Korean Gerontology* 11:235–50.

Korea National Statistical Office. 1955. *Population census report.* KNSO.

———. 1960. *Population and housing census report.* KNSO.

———. 1966. *Population census report.* KNSO.

———. 1970. *Population and housing census report.* KNSO.

———. 1975. *Population and housing census report.* KNSO.

———. 1980. *Population and housing census report.* KNSO.

———. 1985. *Population and housing census report.* KNSO.

———. 1990. *Population and housing census report.* KNSO.

———. 1995a. *Population and housing census report.* KNSO.

———. 1995b. *Farm household economy survey report.* KNSO.

———. 2000a. *Population and housing census report.* KNSO.

———. 2000b. *Social indicators in Korea.* KNSO.

———. 2001. *Population projections.* KNSO.

———. 2005. *Population and housing census report.* KNSO.

Kreuger, A. B., and J. Pischke. 1992. The effect of Social Security on labor supply: A cohort analysis of the notch generation. *Journal of Labor Economics* 10 (4): 412–37.

Lee, C. 1998a. Long-term unemployment and retirement in early-twentieth-century America. *Journal of Economic History* 58 (3): 844–56.

———. 1998b. Rise of the welfare state and labor force participation of older males. *American Economic Review* 88 (2): 222–26.

———. 1999. Farm value and retirement of farm owners in early-twentieth-century America. *Explorations in Economic History* 36 (4): 387–408.

———. 2001. The expected length of male retirement in the United States, 1850–1990. *Journal of Population Economics* 14 (4): 641–50.

———. 2002. Sectoral shift and labor-force participation of older males in America, 1880–1940. *Journal of Economic History* 62:512–23.

———. 2004. Changing industrial structure and economic activity of older males in Korea, 1980–2000. *Seoul Journal of Economics* 17 (2): 181–234.

———. 2005. Labor market status of older males in the United States, 1880–1940. *Social Science History* 29 (1): 77–106.

———. 2007. Long-term changes in the economic activity of older males in Korea. *Economic Development and Cultural Change* 56:99–124.

———. 2008. Retirement expectations of older self-employed workers in Korea: Comparison with wage and salary workers. *Korean Economic Review* 24:33–71.

———. 2009. Technological changes and employment of older manufacturing workers in early twentieth century America. NBER Working Paper no. 14746. Cambridge, MA: National Bureau of Economic Research, February.

Lee, E. W. 1993a. A study on rural-urban migration in Korea. PhD dissertation. Department of Economics, Seoul National University (in Korean).

———. 1993b. Rural-urban migration and its effects. *Korean Journal of Labor Economics* 16 (1): 107–29.

McGarry, K. 2004. Health and retirement: Do changes in health affect retirement expectation? *Journal of Human Resources* 39 (3): 624–48.

Moen, J. 1994. Rural non-farm households: Leaving the farm and the retirement of older men, 1860–1980. *Social Science History* 18 (1): 55–75.

Moon, H., Y. Hahn, H. Jun, and Y. Byun. 1991. *A study of migration.* Korea Institute for Health Social Affairs (in Korean).

Nyce, S. A., and S. J. Schieber. 2005. *The economic implications of aging society.* Cambridge: Cambridge University Press.

Ogura, S., T. Tachibanaki, and D. Wise. 2001. *Aging issues in the United States and Japan.* Chicago: University of Chicago Press.

Organization for Economic Cooperation and Development (OECD). 2000. *Reforms for an aging society: Social issues.* Paris: OECD.

———. 2002. *Older but wiser: Achieving better labour market prospects for older workers in Korea.* Paris: OECD.

———. 2004. *Ageing and employment policies: Japan.* Paris: OECD.

Parson, D. O. 1980. The decline in male labor force participation. *Journal of Political Economy* 88 (1): 117–34.

———. 1991. Male retirement behavior in the United States, 1930–1950. *Journal of Economic History* 51 (3): 657–74.

Pedersen, H. 1950. A cultural evaluation of the family farm concept. *Land Economics* 26 (1): 52–64.

Pencavel, J. 1986. Labor supply of men: A survey. In *Handbook of labor economics,* vol. 1, ed., O. Ashenfelter and R. Layard, 3–102. North Holland: Elsevier.

Sung, J.-M. and J.-Y. Ahn. 2006. Determining factors of older workers' employment. *Labor Policy Research* 6 (1): 39–74.

Yoon, S. 1984. Changes in the rural society caused by the migration of labor. PhD dissertation. Department of Sociology, Seoul National University (in Korean).

Comment   Kyungsoo Choi

Korea's elderly labor force participation rate (LFPR) is exceptionally high in comparison with other countries. As of 2002, Korea's male LFPR of sixty to sixty-four years old is 66.5 percent, while in most European countries the rate stands at below 40 percent, and in other Asian countries and in the United States the rates are around 50 to 60 percent.[1] The high participation rate did not decline despite the worldwide early retirement trend observed in most advanced economies since the 1960s. In European countries Gruber and Wise (1999) analyzed that the social security system, specifically the public pension system, is the main reason for the LFPR drop and for the United States, Burtless and Quinn (2000) claimed that the wealth accumulation, which made early retirement affordable for the elderly, was the dominant source. However, as shown by tables 8.1 and 8.2 in the text, the elderly LFPR (among males aged sixty to sixty-four) in Korea did not drop since the 1960s, despite the wealth accumulation created by the rapid economic growth. In rural areas it actually increased, and in urban areas, it remained roughly constant (see figure 8.3).

The reason for such uniqueness of the Korean elderly LFPR has not been well-known nor thoroughly investigated. Roughly it has been claimed that not enough wealth accumulation and insufficient provisions for old-age income security may be the causes for the lengthened labor participation among the Korean elderly. This chapter looks into this unique phenomenon of Korea, using rich sets of data both from the Census and monthly labor market survey data sets. The author finds that up to the 1990s, the LFPR of the elderly remained roughly constant in urban areas, whereas it rose in the rural area due to reduced share of rural population among the elderly, offsetting the LFPR drop. The large share of rural population among the elderly in Korea is obviously an important factor of the high elderly LFPR. Among sixty-five to sixty-nine-year-olds, rural LFPR rose from around

Kyungsoo Choi is a senior fellow at the Korea Development Institute.

1. The LFPR among men aged sixty to sixty-four in various countries are as follows (in percent): Japan 71.2, Korea 66.5, New Zealand 66.1, Sweden 60.1, United States 57.6, Canada 50.9, United Kingdom 50.8, Singapore 49.6, Australia 47.0, Thailand 46.8, Hong Kong 46.1, Russia 39.1, European Union 35.3, Germany 34.0, Italy 30.9, France 17.3 (http://www.jil.go.jp/kokunai/statistics/databook).

0.5 to 0.7 and among those aged seventy and more, it rose from 0.3 to 0.5 (table 8.2). The chapter points to the shortage of labor in the rural area due to emigration during the industrialization, deficient wealth accumulation caused by stagnant real estate price of farmland, and—although not fully supported by data—health improvement in the rural area as causes of the rise of LFPR among the rural elderly. This chapter considers a variety of candidate causes for LFPR rise and evaluates their importance from empirical data, comparing the Korean situation with that of the United States in the past. Further, the author provides a very kind and detailed description of changes that occurred in the rural area, which will be greatly helpful for foreigners in understanding the Korean situation. I agree with the author's view on the causes of LFPR in the rural area. Later studies may find the relative importance of the causes somewhat different; for example, they could find health improvement or technology change more important than evaluated in this chapter, but I expect that the empirical results given in this chapter would be maintained.

But then another obvious question is, "Why did the urban elderly men's LFPR not drop?" Among elderly men, the urban population is now more than 50 percent, and the fact that urban elderly male LFPR did not drop is as interesting a question as the rise of rural elderly male LFPR.[2] Needless to say, high urban LFPR need also be analyzed to explain the overall high LFPR. Rising rural LFPR prevented the elderly male LFPR from dropping by offsetting the fall caused by shrinking rural population share. But the high and persistent urban LFPR contributed as much to the persistent high level of elderly male LFPR of Korea.

In advanced economies the elderly LFPR continued to drop until the 1980s. Even in Japan, where the elderly LFPR is at roughly the same level as Korea, the rate dropped with the decline of self-employment in urban areas up to the 1980s. Unlike advanced countries, Korea did not have a mature pension system, public or private, and the social security system did not provide incentives for early retirement. But the wealth has increased a lot, education level has upgraded, and self-employment share dropped among the elderly in urban Korea. Education could have acted toward increasing the old-age labor participation, but urban income has greatly increased (table 8.7), and urban real estate prices soared at least several times in real terms during the last fifty years. The effects of land price rise on the elderly LPFR have been small in urban areas. The author estimates (in footnote 16) that the 1 percent rise of land prices has lowered urban elderly male LFPR by 0.1 percent, which is a quarter of the effect in rural areas. But the effect of income still remains to be explained.

2. Specifically, the urban population share is 65.9 percent among age sixty to sixty-four, 56.2 percent among age sixty-five to sixty-nine, and 49.3 percent among seventy and over (see table 8.2).

A very feasible cause for high participation is the large share of self-employment in the urban area, especially among the elderly, which is very high in Korea. Its employment share is 29.8 percent among men and 43.6 percent among men aged sixty to sixty-four. And the elderly self-employment does not show a long-term downward trend. Self-employment in the urban area acts like a bridge between employment and retirement in the Korean labor market. I think the self-employment structure in the urban sector of Korea needs to be analyzed to answer the question, "Why is the LFPR of older males so high in Korea?"

References

Burtless, G., and J. F. Quinn. 2000. Retirement trends and policies to encourage work among older Americans. Boston College Working Papers in Economics. Available at: http://scholarhip.bc.edu/econ_papers/175.
Gruber J., and D. A. Wise. 1999. *Social security and retirement around the World.* Chicago: University of Chicago Press.

Comment   Fumio Ohtake

The purposes of Lee's study were twofold: (a) to analyze the long-term trend in the labor force participation rate (LFPR) of older males in Korea, and (b) to examine the determinants of the labor force participation of the elderly through regression analysis of Census data. In his research conducted toward the first objective, the author used the following two data sources: the Population and Housing Census (Census) and the Economically Active Population Survey (EAP). He especially concentrated on the differences of the LFPR between rural and urban older males. The key variables in his analysis toward the second objective were family size and the percentage of males over the age of sixty in the area.

The major findings of the study were as follows. The LFPR of older men increased substantially from the mid-1960s to the late 1990s in Korea. The rise in the LFPR of older males in Korea between 1965 and 1995 is largely explained by the dramatic increase in the labor market activity of the rural elderly population. The estimation results showed that the labor force participation rate of the elderly increased in direct proportion to the decrease in family size and the increase in the percentage of males over the age of sixty in the local area. The acceleration of population aging in rural areas due to the selective out-migration of the younger workforce was the major cause of the sharp increase in the LFPR of older males. When younger workers

Fumio Ohtake is a Professor at the Institute of Social and Economic Research, Osaka University.

of a rural area out-migrate to an urban area, the elderly males in the rural area are left bereft of economic support, and thus forced to work.

I agree with the author's interpretation of the causality between the out-migration of younger workers from the rural area and the increase of the labor participation rate of the rural older males. However, there might be a reverse causality or omitted variable bias in the estimation. One possible explanation is the technological progress in the farm sector. If the technological progress in the farm sector increased the productivity of the elderly, it would lead to hitherto redundant labor being resurrected in rural areas. The out-migration of the younger workers from rural areas might be the result of this resurrection of redundant labor in rural areas that was caused by the technological progress in the farm sector. In this case, the reduction of the family size would not be the cause of the increased participation rate. A similar argument can be applied to the effects on the LFPR of the percentage of people over the age of sixty and the percentage of agricultural sector workers in the area. This is because these variables would also be affected by the technological progress in the farm sector. A possible way to avoid this bias would be to use instrumental variables for the percentage of people over the age of sixty and the percentage of agricultural sector workers. In section 8.7 of the final version of this chapter, the author added a discussion on this possibility. He found that there was technological progress in the rural areas and that the introduction of the new technology had increased the LFPR of elderly males.

The author has attributed the population aging resulting from the mass migration of the younger workforce to urban areas as a major explanation for the increase in the LFPR of the rural elderly population. However, apart from the abovementioned factor of technological progress, there are several other possible explanations to this phenomenon.

First, changes in the social security systems have been known to affect the LFPR of the elderly population in many advanced countries. For example, a reduction in social security benefits or an increase in the minimum age for pension payment eligibility increases the LFPR of the elderly. Thus, it might have proved informative if the author had added a discussion on the changes in the social security system in Korea and its effect on the LFPR of elderly males.

Second, the improvement in the general health conditions of the elderly increases their LFPR. And third, the unexpected increase in the life expectancy of the elderly causes an increase in their LFPR because the amount of money that they may have saved toward their retirement period proves inadequate.

Additionally, the author points out that Korea experienced a relative decline in its rural economy from the late 1980s onward. Using table 8.7, he shows that the ratio of the income of rural households to the income of urban households showed a long-term decreasing trend. However, if we examine the change in the ratio of per capita income of rural households to that of urban households, the decline becomes smaller since the difference in the relative family size between rural and urban areas also declined around the same period.

The findings of the study related to the increase of LFPR in Korea are very unique as compared to similar studies in other developed countries. The LFPR of the elderly Japanese decreased in the 1970s and the 1980s. The decline of the LFPR of Japanese males is caused due to the following two reasons: (a) the decrease in the number of younger workers in self-employed and agricultural sectors in which the elderly are capable of working, and (b) the increase in social security benefits during this period. However, the LFPR of the Japanese males in their sixties increased twice; once in the 1990s, and subsequently in the 2000s. First, in the early 1990s, the LFPR of males above the age of sixty increased. This increase was caused by the rise in labor demand during the bubble economy. Even after the collapse of bubble economy, the LFPR continued to stay at a high level almost throughout the 1990s. The LFPR of elderly males started to decline toward the end of the 1990s, and the trend continued till 2005. This LFPR rose again in the years 2006 and 2007. This increase was caused by the introduction of the "Law for the stabilization of the employment of the aged," which required companies to gradually raise the retirement age from sixty to sixty-five in 2007. Japanese experience shows that the LFPR of the elderly is affected by the share in the labor force of the self-employed and the agricultural sector, and by changes in the social security system, labor demand, and the labor law. The comparative economic analysis between the LFPR of the elderly in Korea and Japan would be an interesting research topic.

IV

China and Hong Kong

Long-Term Effects of Early-Life Development
Evidence from the 1959 to 1961 China Famine

Douglas Almond, Lena Edlund, Hongbin Li, and Junsen Zhang

9.1 Introduction

The dramatic success of China's One Child Policy in reducing fertility catapults the question of population aging to center stage. As China's dependency ratio increases, the health and productivity of those of working age will play key roles. So far, attention has generally focused on investments in these "working age" cohorts that occur after birth (e.g., educational investments). This chapter focuses instead on the prenatal environment and its impact on health and economic outcomes in adulthood, exploiting the 1959 to 1961 Chinese famine (henceforth, "the Famine") as a natural experiment in maternal stress and nutrition.

While starvation on the scale of the Famine may seem remote, maternal malnutrition is not. In the twenty years following the Famine, average nutrition was little improved from the 1930s (White 1991). Smil (1981) noted that "Chinese food availability has remained virtually static for at least half a century." Meat remained scarce and diets were heavily reliant on grains, which accounted for 90 percent of energy and 80 percent of protein (Smil 1981). Disruptions in grain production brought "permanent malnutrition

Douglas Almond is associate professor of economics at Columbia University and a faculty research fellow of the National Bureau of Economic Research. Lena Edlund is an associate professor of economics at Columbia University. Hongbin Li is a professor of economics at Tsinghua University. Junsen Zhang is a professor of economics at the Chinese University of Hong Kong.

We would like to thank Janet Currie, Andrew Gelman, Hilary Hoynes, Takatoshi Ito, Robert Kaestner, Ronald Lee, Andrew Rose, Mark Rosenzweig, David St. Clair, Jane Waldfogel, and David Wise for helpful comments. Holly Ho Ming and Hongyan Zhao provided outstanding research assistance. Almond and Edlund thank the Russell Sage Foundation and Almond thanks the Fulbright Program for financial support.

to at least 200 million peasants" since the mid-1960s (Smil 1981). Food rationing, first introduced in 1953, was used as a tool to encourage compliance with the One Child Policy (Li and Cooney 1993).

Even after the precipitous decline in fertility during the late 1970s and 1980s, poor nutrition persisted, especially in rural areas and among girls. Between 1987 and 1992, the height of children in urban areas increased five times as fast as rural areas, attributable in part to "more inequitable distribution of the economic resources for nutrition" (Shen and Chang 1996). Similarly, Hesketh, Ding, and Tomkin (2002) found that diets were less varied and nutritional deprivation was more common in rural areas of eastern China—anemia (Hb $\leq$ 110 gl^{-1}) was 50 percent more common than in the rapidly-developing cities. Moreover, more than three-quarters of those with anemia in rural areas were girls: 19 percent were anemic versus 4.8 percent for rural boys. Fully 55 percent of rural girls were moderately anemic (hemoglobin concentrations below 120 gl^{-1}), versus 21 percent of rural boys.

Our inquiry is motivated by a growing literature finding the pre- and perinatal periods critical to morbidity and lifespan. Pioneered by Barker (1992), the "fetal origins hypothesis" linked cardiovascular mortality to maternal nutritional status. Later research has honed in on maternal stress as triggering biological responses in the growing fetus that programs for a life in a resource-poor environment (Gluckman and Hanson 2005). However, the bulk of empirical evidence derives from animal experiments; evidence for humans is surprisingly scarce (see e.g., Rasmussen [2001]; Walker et al. [2007]). Omitted factors (e.g., parental abilities and attitudes) can generate positive associations between measures of fetal health and adult socioeconomic outcomes in the absence of a controlled experiment. Therefore, the "most compelling examinations of the fetal origins hypothesis look for sharp exogenous shocks in fetal health that are caused by conditions outside the control of the mother" (Currie 2009, 102).

Observing cohorts born during 1956 to 1964 in the 2000 Chinese Population Census (1 percent sample), we find that men were 9 percent more likely to be illiterate, 6 percent less likely to work, and 6.5 percent less likely to be married if exposed to the Famine in utero. Women were 7.5 percent more likely to be illiterate and 3 percent less likely to work, and tended to marry men with less education, if exposed in utero. We also find that fetal exposure to the Famine substantially reduced the cohort's sex ratio (fewer males), suggesting greater male vulnerability to maternal malnutrition. Perhaps most intriguingly, we find an "echo effect" of the Famine on the next generation: children whose mothers were exposed prenatally also register Famine impacts. In particular, Famine-exposed mothers were more likely to give birth to daughters. To our knowledge, ours is the first study to trace the offspring sex ratio to the in utero environment of the parent.

To test the robustness of our findings, we pursue two additional approaches. First, we utilize geographic variation in Famine severity to generate comparisons *within* birth cohorts. Here, estimates of Famine damage will be confounded by events experienced later in life (e.g., the Cultural Revolution 1966 to 1976) insofar as these events replicated the geographic variation in Famine intensity *and* differentially impacted those cohorts in utero during the Famine. Second, while the Famine was endemic in mainland China (affecting both urban and rural areas), Hong Kong, then a British colony, was spared. The Famine resulted in a large inflow of mainland Chinese into Hong Kong. We can therefore observe whether children of mainland immigrants exposed to the Famine register intergenerational damage using Hong Kong's natality data, derived from the universe of Hong Kong birth certificates.[1] Results from these two additional approaches corroborate the findings from across-cohort comparisons in the Census data: damage to a broad spectrum of outcomes persists forty years after the Famine.

In addition to the potential for remedial investments (Heckman 2007), two factors lead us to believe our estimates of long-term damage are conservative (i.e., biased toward zero). First, the selective effects of the Famine are likely to cull the relatively weak. Second, the comparison group was also affected by the Famine: older cohorts experienced it directly and younger cohorts were the children of Famine survivors. Assuming that these adjacent cohorts were also negatively affected by the Famine, our estimated effects are of the incremental effect of acute maternal malnutrition, as opposed to, for example, starvation while an infant or toddler, or from being born to a mother who starved prior to her pregnancy.

China is experiencing rapid economic growth and, perhaps ironically, this rapid transition may exacerbate the health consequences of maternal (or grand-maternal, see following) malnutrition as the "thrifty phenotype" finds itself in a resource-rich environment. One reason for long lasting, even intergenerational effects, is that a girl is born with all her eggs, which means that daughters and the eggs for their children, future grandchildren, share in utero environment. Another reason is that gene expression is affected by the early life environment, and therefore, the mother's status (health and otherwise) has epigenetic effects. Therefore, while rapid economic growth holds the promise of greater access to education and health care, this new-found affluence also poses health challenges akin to those faced by (especially) minority populations in the United States: obesity, type II diabetes, and hypertension.

The remainder of the chapter is organized as follows. Sections 9.1.1 to 9.1.3 describe the background of the Famine and review the related literature. Section 9.2 describes the 2000 Chinese Population Census and the 1984 to 2004 Hong Kong Natality files. Section 9.3 reports descriptive and

---

1. These certificates record country of birth of the mother. Among Hong Kong mothers who immigrated from the mainland, those exposed to the Famine in utero had worse birth outcomes than other mainland emigrants.

regression results, along with a discussion of potential biases. Section 9.4 concludes.

9.1.1   Famine Background

The Famine ranks as the worst in recorded history. Between 18 and 30 million died due to the "systemic failure" of Mao's Great Leap Forward (Li and Yang 2005). The Famine began in the fall of 1959 and impacted all regions of China. Grain output dropped 15 percent in 1959 and another 15 percent in 1960 (Li and Yang 2005, 846). By 1962, birth and death rates had returned to normal levels.

While weather conditions contributed to the Famine, the radical economic policies of the Great Leap Forward were chiefly to blame (Lin 1990; Li and Yang 2005). In a breakneck attempt to overtake Britain and eventually the United States, labor was diverted from agriculture to industry while grain procurement from rural areas was increased. At the same time, collectivization of agricultural production resulted in shirking and falling productivity (Lin 1990). The political climate encouraged provincial leaders to overstate grain production and despite widespread starvation, China was a net grain exporter throughout 1960 (Yao 1999; Lin and Yang 2000).

Famine intensity varied by region (Peng 1987). Rural death rates rose to 2.5 times pre-Famine levels. Urban residents fared better but were not spared, death rates in the peak year 1960 were 80 percent above pre-Famine levels (China Statistical Press 2000). Central provinces such as Anhui, Henan, and Sichuan were the worst hit, while northeastern provinces such as Heilongjiang and Jilin were relatively spared. By 1961, death rates had returned to normal in more than half of the provinces, but remained high in, for instance, the southern provinces Guangxi and Guizhou (close to Hong Kong).

9.1.2   Famine Studies: Epidemiology

The best epidemiological evidence to date linking maternal nutritional deprivation to subsequent adult outcomes derives from the cohort in utero during the 1944 to 1945 Dutch famine. The seminal study found limited effects at age eighteen (Stein et al. 1975). However, at middle age, this cohort exhibited a broad spectrum of damage including: self-reported health (Roseboom, Meulen, and Roseboom et al. 2001); coronary heart disease morbidity (Roseboom, Meulen, Ravelli et al. 2001; Bleker et al. 2005); and adult antisocial personality disorders (Neugebauer, Hoek, and Susser 1999). Moreover, it emerges that poor nutrition in early to mid-pregnancy is the most deleterious to health outcomes (Painter, Roseboom, and Bleker 2005). These, and studies of the 1866 to 1868 Finnish Famine and the Nazi Seige of Leningrad, have focused exclusively on health outcomes.

Epidemiological findings from the Chinese Famine include heightened risk of schizophrenia (St. Clair et al. 2005) and obesity among women (Luo, Mu, and Zhang 2006).

9.1.3   Famine Studies: Economics

A number of recent studies evaluating the Famine's impact on the socio-economic outcomes of survivors have used the China Health and Nutrition Surveys (CHNS) (Chen and Zhou 2007; Meng and Qian 2006; Gorgens, Meng, and Vaithianathan 2005). The CHNS, which began in 1989, is a panel data set of health and economic outcomes of approximately 4,000 Chinese households from nine provinces (out of thirty-one provinces or province-level administrative regions). The small sample size combined with the collapse of fertility during the Famine necessitates the inclusion of ages well after birth as "treated."[2] However, broad "early childhood" hypotheses make it difficult to reject alternative explanations. The possibility that events at other ages—for instance the subsequent Cultural Revolution and the forced "rustification" of students in outlying areas—confounds results is a concern.

Chen and Zhou (2007) considered those up to age six as treated. They proxied Famine intensity by the province-level death rate in 1960 and found the Famine thus measured to have resulted in stunting of those born in 1955, 1957, 1959, 1960, and 1962, with the largest height reductions for the 1959, 1960, and 1962 birth cohorts. Moreover, they found reduced labor supply of those born in 1959 and 1960, and lower wealth as measured by the size of residence for birth cohorts 1958 and 1959.

Meng and Qian (2006) considered the following birth cohorts as potentially affected: 1952 to 1954, 1955 to 1958, 1959 to 1960, with cohorts born 1961 to 1964 as the reference group. Using reductions in cohort size as a proxy for Famine severity (assumed to occur through Famine mortality), their ordinary least squares (OLS) estimation returned mixed results, and little evidence for a particularly strong effect for the 1959 to 1960 cohort. Instrumenting for cohort size, using per capita grain production in 1997, they found a small negative effect on education, but a substantial (25 percent) reduction in hours worked for the 1959 to 1960 cohort.

Gorgens, Meng, and Vaithianathan (2005) studied adult heights of cohorts exposed to the Famine in childhood. They argued both that children who survived the Famine did not show any stunting and that stunting did occur. They reconcile these two arguments by a third: Famine mortality was concentrated among shorter people. The net effect of stunting and selection, the authors argued, made the height of survivors appear unchanged. However, the claim that no stunting is observed among survivors is controversial (Chen and Zhou 2007; Yan 1999; Morgan 2006).

---

2. In 1960, 105 rural CHNS respondents and 62 urban CHNS respondents were born, with sixty-six and forty-five, respectively, in 1961 (Chen and Zhou 2007, table 2).

9.2   Data

Our primary data set is the 2000 Population Census of China.[3] The 1 percent sample includes more than 11 million records and has not (to our knowledge) been used to evaluate long-term effects of the Famine.[4] Outcomes include educational attainment, labor market status, and residence information of respondents. Demographic information includes sex, birth year and month, and marriage and fertility information (see the appendix).

Unlike preceding Census surveys and the CHNS data, the 2000 Census records the province of birth, eliminating the potential for confounding due to internal migration.[5] The 2000 Census captures Famine cohorts near age forty, and therefore near the flat portion of their occupation and earnings profile. Moreover, it is the first Census to capture near-complete fertility histories of women born during the Famine.[6] We restrict the analysis to those born during 1956 to 1964, a subsample that includes three pre-Famine years and three post-Famine years (death rates peaked in 1960 but were elevated in 1959 and 1961 as well, see figure 9.1). Our relatively narrow birth interval is intended to increase the similarity of the unobserved later-life factors and their effects on Census outcomes.

Our second data source is the natality microdata for Hong Kong (1984 to 2004), derived from the universe of birth certificates. These data include information on maternal country of birth. Restricting the sample to mothers of singletons either born in mainland China or Hong Kong in the years 1957 to 1965 yields some 600,000 records, approximately one-third of whom immigrated from the mainland. The Hong Kong data provide an important control group since all of mainland China was afflicted by the Famine (Cai and Feng 2005).

9.2.1   Measuring the Famine

We use two measures of famine intensity: death rates and average month of birth.

Death Rates

We use the all-age death rate (China Statistical Press 2000) by year and province to calculate two (mortality-based) proxies of Famine intensity. We have data for twenty-nine out of the thirty-one provinces (or province-level divisions).

---

3. Conducted by the Chinese National Bureau of Statistics for mainland China.
4. Shi (2006) used a 0.1 percent subsample of the 2000 Census.
5. Of those born during 1956 to 1964, 6 percent reported moving from another province since birth, with another 10 percent relocating to towns within the province of birth.
6. A mere 0.3 percent of women born in 1960 reported having a child between November 1999 and October 2000. For comparison, 14.8 percent for women born in 1976 had a child in the same period.

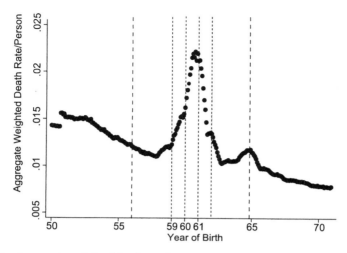

Fig. 9.1   Aggregate weighted death rate by year and month of birth, mainland China
Note: Authors' calculations based on all age death rates by year and province as reported by China Statistical Press (2000).

- First, for every person, we calculate the weighted average of the death rate in the province of birth for the duration of the fetal period, henceforth "weighted death rate" or wdr_{jt}. For example, a person born in January 1960 in Beijing is assigned one-ninth of Beijing's 1960s mortality rate and eight-ninths of Beijing's 1959s mortality rate. This weighted death rate ranged from 0.005 to 0.069 (per person).
- Second, we collapse this weighted death rate by month of birth, thus calculating a population-weighted national average for each month and year, henceforth "aggregate weighted death rate," or $awdr_t$. During the study period, this measure ranged from 0.010 (in 1963) to 0.022 (at the end of 1960), a difference of 0.012. Thus measured, those born toward the end of 1960 and early 1961 were exposed to the greatest Famine intensity in utero (figure 9.1).

Average Month of Birth

In the northern hemisphere, famines tend to be most severe during the winter months. This reduces fertility disproportionately in the latter half of the calendar year, thereby lowering the average month of birth (Stein et al. 1975).[7] This proxy applied to the 2000 Census indicates 1960 as the worst year for mainland China (figure 9.2); that is, consistent with the mortality data. Because immigrants to Hong Kong were a highly selected group, both geographically (the Famine hit bordering provinces later) and due to the

7. Authors' tabulation of appendix table 4 data in Stein et al. (1975).

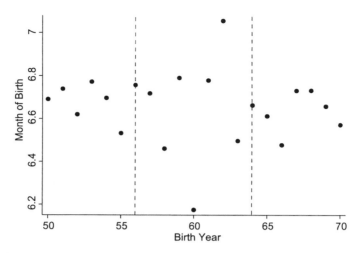

Fig. 9.2   Average month of birth, mainland China
Source: 2000 Census.

particular migration policies in place (further described in section 9.3.5), we cannot rely on mainland mortality data in the Hong Kong analysis.[8] To obtain a proxy for when the Famine peaked for this group of immigrants, we use average month of birth. This proxy indicates 1961 as the worst Famine year for Hong Kong mothers born in the mainland (figure 9.3). As expected of the "control group," there was *no* corresponding change for Hong Kong natives (figure 9.4).

9.3   Results

9.3.1   Descriptive Results

We begin by presenting unadjusted outcomes by quarter of birth (for all Chinese) in the four panels of figure 9.5. These figures indicate that those born around 1960 had worse socioeconomic outcomes than the cohort trend would predict. Recall that this cohort was in utero during the period with the highest death rate, as measured by the weighted death rate (figure 9.1). In 2000, the 1960 birth cohort was more likely to be: (a) not working at the time of the Census; (b) supported by other household members; (c) living in a smaller home and; (d) parents of girls. For some of these outcomes, departures from the cohort trend appear in the adjacent cohorts as well.

---

8. Natality data for Hong Kong identify Mainland immigrants, but not their province of birth (nor province of last residence).

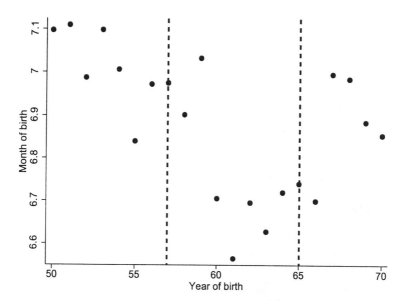

Fig. 9.3   Average month of birth, Hong Kong mothers born in Mainland

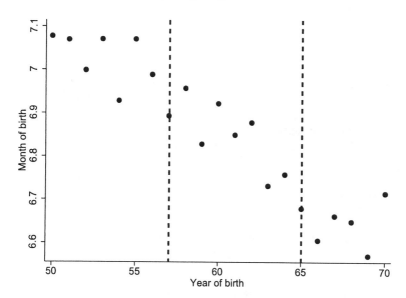

Fig. 9.4   Average month of birth, Hong Kong mothers born in Hong Kong
Source: Hong Kong natality microdata.

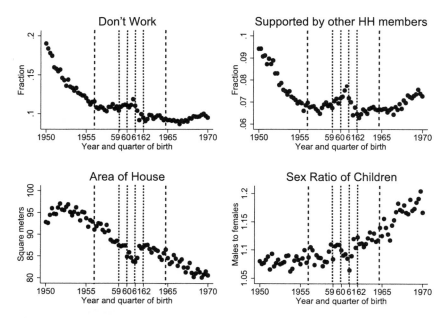

Fig. 9.5   Census outcomes by year and quarter of birth
Source: 2000 Census.

This pattern mirrors the 1959 to 1961 duration of the Famine, with a peak in 1960.

A final descriptive pattern of note is the rise in the sex ratio for the cohorts born up until 1960 and the sharp drop for the cohorts born in 1960 and 1961. The maleness of the late 1950s birth cohorts is in line with the suggestion that infant and toddler girls were disproportionately denied food. That the 1960 and 1961 cohorts are notably female is consistent with maternal malnutrition disproportionately penalizing male offspring, a mechanism that toward the end of the Famine may have dominated post-natal discrimination against daughters.

9.3.2   Regression Results

To investigate systematically how adult outcomes vary with prenatal Famine exposure, we focus on the cohorts born during 1956 to 1964 and estimate by OLS:

$$(1) \qquad y_{it} = \beta_0 + \theta \times awdr_t + \beta_1 \times YOB + \beta_2 \times YOB^2 \\ + \beta_3 \times YOB^3 + \lambda_{province} + \varepsilon_{it},$$

where y_{it} denotes the outcome for individual i born in period t, $awdr_t$ denotes the aggregate weighted death rate by birth year and month of birth t,[9]

9. See section 9.2.1.

and YOB denotes birth year. We enter YOB as a cubic to control for the nonlinear cohort/age effects apparent in the four panels of figure 9.5. Finally, we include a vector of province dummies, $\lambda_{province}$. Thus equation (1) allows for a flexible cohort profile within a narrowly-defined birth interval, and assesses whether the prenatal death rate contributes additional explanatory power, as reflected by $\hat{\theta}$. We estimate equation (1) separately for men and women. We do not include dummies for the month of birth, given its apparent endogeneity in figure 9.2. (However, inclusion of month of birth dummies does not alter the basic results from estimating [1] and [2]; results are available on request.)

Results from estimating equation (1) for the 2000 Census outcomes are reported in tables 9.1 through 9.3. Table 9.1 shows a consistent deleterious effect of prenatal Famine exposure on labor market outcomes. Greater famine intensity is associated with a higher likelihood of being illiterate and not working. During the Famine, awdr increased by 1.2 percentage points, implying, for example, that the most Famine-exposed cohorts were 7.5 percent ($0.5052 \times 0.012/0.081$) [women] and 9 percent ($0.1585 \times 0.012/0.021$) [men] more likely to be illiterate; 3 percent ($0.4714 \times 0.012/0.189$) [women] and 5.9 percent ($0.4017 \times 0.012/0.082$) [men] more likely to not work; and 13 percent ($0.0448 \times 0.012/0.004$) [women] more likely to be disabled. Men in utero during the Famine were 9 percent more likely to be supported financially by other household members ("Dependent"), and the figure for women was 4 percent.

The Census does not have any direct measure of earnings, but there is information on housing, which may serve as a wealth proxy. Thus measured,

Table 9.1   **2000 Census: Labor and housing outcomes for 1956–1964 birth cohorts**

	Illiterate	Don't work	Disabled	Dependent	House area
			Women		
Mean	0.081	0.189	0.004	0.119	87.162
awdr	0.5052**	0.4714***	0.0448*	0.3972***	−220.1528***
	[0.2169]	[0.1530]	[0.0250]	[0.1354]	[48.4753]
N	786,156	786,156	786,156	786,156	772,260
			Men		
Mean	0.021	0.082	0.006	0.019	83.933
awdr	0.1585*	0.4017***	0.0657	0.1399**	−104.7566**
	[0.0784]	[0.1131]	[0.0426]	[0.0674]	[38.3963]
N	818,103	818,103	818,103	818,103	790,342

Notes: awdr = aggregate weighted death rate by birth year and month. Mean = mean of dependent variable. Standard errors clustered at province of birth in square brackets.
***Significant at the 1 percent level.
**Significant at the 5 percent level.
*Significant at the 10 percent level.

Table 9.2   **2000 Census, marriage market outcomes, 1956–1964 birth cohorts**

	Unmarried	Never married	Spousal ed.[a]	Marriage age[b]	Household head[c]
		Women			
Mean	0.061	0.004	9.057	269.237	0.118
awdr	0.2608	−0.0013	−6.3342**	67.4994**	−0.0998
	[0.1632]	[0.0249]	[2.4652]	[28.5417]	[0.1633]
N	786,156	786,156	685,989	783,015	786,156
		Men			
Mean	0.090	0.039	8.060	290.898	0.870
awdr	0.4902***	0.2676**	−0.1692	125.1309***	−0.5145**
	[0.1285]	[0.1035]	[2.5349]	[28.5395]	[0.2302]
N	818,103	818,103	683,041	785,927	818,103

Notes: awdr = aggregate weighted death rate by birth year and month. Mean = mean of dependent variable. Standard errors clustered at province of birth in square brackets.
[a]Includes head-spouse couples only. Education is in years.
[b]Marriage age is in months.
[c]Includes those residing in family units (i.e., excludes those residing in collectives).
***Significant at the 1 percent level.
**Significant at the 5 percent level.
*Significant at the 10 percent level.

greater fetal Famine exposure reduced adult economic status (table 9.1, last column).

We also estimate equation (1) for marriage market outcomes (table 9.2). While marriage was nearly universal for women, inspection of who they married reveals that the Famine-exposed women married men with less education. For men, both the extensive and intensive margins were affected. Men were 6.5 percent ($0.4902 \times 0.012/0.09$) more likely to be unmarried and 8.2 percent ($0.2676 \times 0.012/0.039$) more likely to never have married. Moreover, they married at older ages (1.5 months) and were 0.7 percent ($0.5145 \times 0.012/0.87$) less likely to head their households.

The poor marriage market outcomes are unlikely to be driven by conventional supply and demand factors. As cohorts born during the Famine were substantially smaller than adjacent cohorts, the "marriage squeeze" would work in their favor (see also Brandt, Siow, and Vogel [2007] for a discussion and similar evidence from the 1990 China Census).[10]

Prenatal famine exposure also raised male (relative to female) mortality as evidenced by survival around age forty. The most exposed cohort was 1.5 percent age points (1.3147×0.012) more female (table 9.3, column [1]). The most striking finding, however, is that prenatally exposed women bore more girls, the offspring of the most Famine-exposed were 0.4 percentage points

10. For both men and women, the three smallest cohorts 1950 to 1970 were those born 1959 to 1961.

Table 9.3   **2000 Census: Sex ratio outcomes, 1956–1964 birth cohorts**

	Male[a]	Women[b]	
		Sons/kids	No child
Mean	0.51	0.548	0.007
awdr	−1.3147***	−0.3194**	0.0712
	[0.2651]	[0.1368]	[0.0503]
N	1,604,259	773,291	786,156

Notes: awdr = aggregate weighted death rate by birth year and month. Mean = mean of dependent variable. Standard errors clustered at province of birth in square brackets.
[a]Dummy: equals 1 if respondent was male.
[b]Pertains to children borne.
***Significant at the 1 percent level.
**Significant at the 5 percent level.
*Significant at the 10 percent level.

(0.3194 × 0.012) less male (column [2]).[11] To anticipate results, the Hong Kong data (derived from birth certificates) corroborate this pattern.

9.3.3   Geographic Variation in Famine Intensity

The second test of our hypothesis isolates the geographic variation in the Famine and makes comparisons exclusively within (annual) birth cohorts. This approach reduces the potential for confounding from later-life events with age-specific effects (e.g., if the Cultural Revolution, launched in 1966, delayed school entry among six-year-olds). Here, confounding by such later-life events would require their geographic variation to mirror the Famine (while also replicating the Famine's cohort effects).[12] We estimate by OLS:

$$(2) \qquad y_{itj} = \beta_0 + \theta \times \text{wdr}_{tj} + \gamma_{yob} + \lambda_{province} + \varepsilon_{itj},$$

where θ is the parameter of interest, t denotes year and month of birth, and j the province of birth. The mortality rate is the weighted death rate (wdr_{jt}) previously described for the individual's birth date (year and month) and province of birth. As in equation (1), we include vectors of province of birth dummies ($\lambda_{province}$), and, as the goal is to isolate the geographic variation in health induced by the Famine, we absorb the average differences for each birth year by including a vector of year of birth dummies (γ_{yob}).

Results from estimating equation (2) provide distinct evidence of Famine damage: regional differences in outcomes for the Famine cohort line up

11. Similar results are obtained when the logit transform of the proportion of male children is the dependent variable.
12. In contrast to the Famine, urban residents were more affected by the Cultural Revolution than rural residents. In addition, the Cultural Revolution lasted ten years and therefore impacted a broader span of birth cohorts.

Table 9.4   **2000 Census: Cross-sectional variation in famine severity, labor market, and housing outcomes, 1956–1964 birth cohorts**

	Illiterate	Don't work	Disabled	Dependent	House area
		Women			
wdr	0.1659	0.0953	0.0418***	0.0755	−58.9501**
	[0.1269]	[0.1657]	[0.0116]	[0.0917]	[22.0095]
N	764,786	764,786	764,786	764,786	751,352
		Men			
wdr	0.1231*	0.1628**	0.0585***	0.0321	−52.1040*
	[0.0688]	[0.0666]	[0.0170]	[0.0376]	[28.5949]
N	795,408	795,408	795,408	795,408	768,522

Note: Standard errors clustered at province of birth in square brackets.
***Significant at the 1 percent level.
**Significant at the 5 percent level.
*Significant at the 10 percent level.

with regional differences in malnutrition (tables 9.4 through 9.6). Table 9.4 shows that local famine severity indeed corresponds to the magnitude of damage in Census outcomes. Women born in high-Famine areas had larger increases in disability rates and larger reductions in house sizes. For men, differences in literacy, work status, disability, and house size correspond to Famine severity in the expected direction.

The magnitude of damage obtained from estimating equation (2) is generally either similar to that found with equation (1), or somewhat smaller. Famine-exposed women were again about 13 percent (0.0418 × 0.012/0.004) more likely to be disabled, and the corresponding figure for men was 12 percent (0.0582 × 0.012/0.006). As for housing, the Famine is estimated to reduce the residence size by slightly under 1 square meter (58.95 × .012), with a similar effect for men. For men, illiteracy increased 7 percent and the likelihood of not working increased 2.4 percent.

Again, men from high-Famine areas were less likely to be married (3.5 percent), more likely to never have married (5 percent), married older (.8 months), and were less likely to head their households (.7 percent) (table 9.5). For women, the point estimates have the expected signs, but are not statistically significant. Finally, table 9.6 shows that coefficients for the sex ratio are significant in the expected direction, but roughly one-third the size of the corresponding estimates in table 9.3.

Rural Versus Urban

We also estimate the aforementioned models separately for those born in rural versus urban areas. We find a Famine effect on the labor and marriage market outcomes for both areas, although the effects for the rural sample were larger (presumably reflecting the greater severity of the Famine in rural

Table 9.5   **2000 Census: Cross-sectional variation in famine severity, marriage market outcomes, 1956–1964 birth cohorts**

	Unmarried	Never married	Spousal ed.[a]	Marriage age[b]	Household head[c]
			Women		
wdr	0.0505	0.0217	0.0794	14.7224	−0.0701
	[0.0623]	[0.0130]	[1.5906]	[19.9378]	[0.1297]
N	764,786	764,786	668,672	761,879	760,726
			Men		
wdr	0.2666***	0.1555**	1.5938	67.6296***	−0.5089***
	[0.0696]	[0.0634]	[1.3770]	[22.8696]	[0.1183]
N	795,408	795,408	665,857	764,670	779,087

Notes: wdr = Weighted average death rate for the gestation period, assuming nine month gestation. Varies by province and month and year of birth. Standard errors clustered at province of birth in square brackets.

[a]Includes head-spouse couples only. Education is in years.

[b]Marriage age is in months.

[c]Includes those residing in family units (i.e., excludes those residing in collectives).

***Significant at the 1 percent level.

**Significant at the 5 percent level.

*Significant at the 10 percent level.

Table 9.6   **2000 Census: Cross-sectional variation in famine severity, sex ratio outcomes, 1956–1964 birth cohorts**

			Women[b]	
		Male[a]	Sons/kids	No child
	wdr	−0.3264**	−0.1693**	0.0325
		[0.1390]	[0.0797]	[0.0251]
	N	1,560,194	752,418	764,786

Note: Standard errors clustered at province of birth in square brackets.

[a]Dummy: equals 1 if respondent was male.

[b]Pertains to children borne.

***Significant at the 1 percent level.

**Significant at the 5 percent level.

*Significant at the 10 percent level.

areas). For both rural and urban areas, we find that the Famine reduced the sex ratio of the in utero cohort and again in the next generation (results available from authors).

Province of Residence

Finally, we note that estimates reported in tables 9.1 through 9.6 are essentially unchanged when fixed effects for the 2000 province of residence are included along with the province of birth dummies.

9.3.4   Potential Biases

As the Famine both raised mortality and reduced fertility, Famine cohorts were approximately 25 to 50 percent smaller than neighboring cohorts in the 2000 Census. To the extent that Famine-induced mortality was negatively selective, as would seem most plausible (especially insofar as health is concerned), estimates of damage to survivors are downward biased.

Negative selection into fertility is a greater potential concern, since this could generate the appearance of effects absent any true damage (i.e., upward bias). However, historical evidence suggests that the Famine, unlike the subsequent Cultural Revolution, hit poorer individuals the hardest (see, e.g., Cai and Feng [2005]). The Dutch Famine provides further evidence: fathers of children conceived in the winter of 1944 and 1945 were more likely to have nonmanual occupations (Stein et al. 1975).

Direct evidence on selection into fertility is available from the China Fertility surveys (conducted in 1985 and 1988), which include information on the respondent's mother's educational attainment (further information in the appendix). Plotting the share of women whose mothers had no education, primary or less, secondary or more, or who did not know their mother's education, the 1959 to 1961 birth cohorts do not appear any worse than adjacent cohorts (figure 9.6). If anything, maternal education for the 1959 to 1961 birth cohorts was better than for adjacent cohorts.

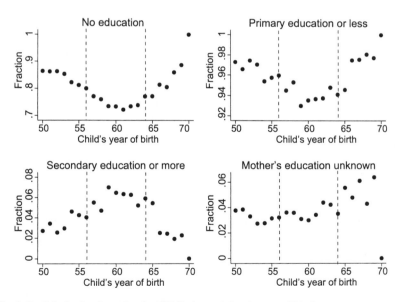

Fig. 9.6   Mother's education by child's (respondent) year of birth

Source: China Fertility surveys 1985/87.

Note: For mother's education unknown, the universe is all respondents. For the remainder, the universe is those who knew their mother's education.

Cohorts born after the Famine may constitute a better control group than those born in the 1950s (who were exposed to higher mortality rates and malnutrition in childhood). Reestimating equations (1) and (2) on the sample restricted to birth cohorts 1959 to 1964, we obtain similar, if not slightly stronger, results (available upon request).

Another possible source of bias is that those born during famines may be born to more fecund women or parents who favor offspring quantity over quality. Whereas we cannot control for parental preferences (other than note, as before, that the maternal education of the Famine cohorts was, if anything, better than that of adjacent cohorts), we can investigate sibship size using a recent survey: the 2005 Urban Chinese Education and Labor Survey conducted by the Ministry of Education in twelve cities in China, covering some 10,000 households.[13] The 1959 to 1961 cohorts do not appear to have more siblings (figure 9.7). Rather, these birth cohorts are on a negative trend (linear and decreasing in year of birth).[14]

However, high infant and juvenile mortality during the Famine years and no effect on sibship size suggests catch-up fertility in the years following the Famine, which would tend to depress the outcomes of those born in the early 1960s. The fact that we found similar, if not stronger, results when we restricted the sample to the 1959 to 1964 cohorts as noted earlier, suggest that cohort-size effects from bunching of fertility had a limited impact on adult outcomes.

9.3.5   Birth Outcomes in Hong Kong

A shortcoming of the analysis using the 2000 (mainland) Census is the want of a truly unexposed control group. Hong Kong Natality data offer a potential solution to this problem. Communist China severely restricted out-migration, a policy that was temporarily and dramatically suspended during a six-week period in the spring of 1962 when a large number of mainlanders entered Hong Kong (Burns 1987). Among the refugees were mainland-born children, who themselves show up as parents in the 1984 to 2004 Hong Kong Natality files. The migration of mainland residents to Hong Kong, during and in the years after the Famine, provides a common environment for those affected by the Famine (mainland immigrants) and those who were not (Hong Kong-born).

The Hong Kong Natality microdata allow us to focus on second-generation birth outcomes, specifically low birth weight and sex. Low birth weight may be a negative outcome because it is a correlate of poor adult health and eco-

---

13. The 2000 Census does not have information on sibship size. Neither can it be inferred from the relationship variable for a household, since most adult siblings live in different households. Finally, the earliest publicly available Chinese census was conducted in 1982, when the 1959 to 1961 cohorts were in their early twenties.

14. This is confirmed by a regression of sibsize on a dummy for birth cohorts 1959 to 1961, controlling for a linear trend in birth year. The coefficient on this dummy is about zero, with a very large standard error (not reported).

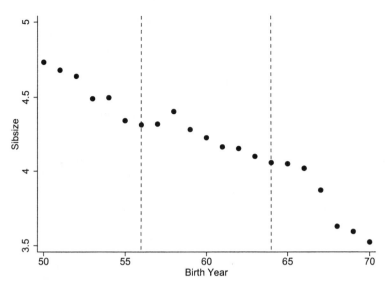

Fig. 9.7   Number of siblings by respondent's year of birth
Source: 2005 Urban Chinese Education and Labor Survey.

nomic performance. As for sex of offspring, a daughter may not be a poor outcome. Still, it may signal poor parental condition; see section 9.4.

We estimate a modified version of equation (1) separately on the subsamples of mainland-born and Hong Kong-born mothers giving birth in Hong Kong during 1984 to 2004. That is, among Hong Kong mothers who immigrated from the mainland, we compare the birth outcomes of mothers exposed to the Famine in utero to other mainland immigrants born before or after the Famine. While migrants are clearly a select group, our identifying assumption here is *not* that migrants are a random sample, but instead that this selection in to migration did not change discontinuously for the cohort of migrants in utero during the Famine.

Dating famine exposure for migrants requires some care. The Hong Kong natality files do not record province of birth for mainland-born mothers, rendering the application of year and province-level mortality rates impossible. Moreover, migrants are likely a selected sample. Therefore, we date Famine exposure by the average month of the immigrant cohorts. Month of birth drops dramatically for mainland-born mothers born in 1961 (figures 9.3 and 9.4). Consequently, we substitute the dummy variable I(1961), which takes on the value 1/100 for those born in 1961, for the death rate (awdr$_t$). A later year for the immigrants to Hong Kong is consistent with the likely geographic selection (more migrants likely from the south, an area that was hit later) and the timing of the migration policy. Again, we do not include month of birth given its apparent endogeneity.

Table 9.7   **1984–2004 Natality outcomes in Hong Kong: Mainland versus Hong Kong-born mothers**

	Mother born			
	Mainland		Hong Kong	
	Low BWT[a]	Son[b]	Low BWT[a]	Son[b]
Mean	0.031	0.52	0.039	0.517
	0.247**	−0.629***	0.014	−0.009
	[0.099]	[0.121]	[0.037]	[0.074]
N	198,452	198,452	393,419	393,419

Notes: Dummy, equals one one-hundredth if mother born in 1961. Mean = mean of dependent variable. Regression results from estimating equation (1) where substitutes for awdr and without the province dummies. The birth weight regressions also include a dummy for the sex of the child. Standard errors clustered by year of birth in square brackets.

[a]Dummy, equals 1 if birth weight was less than 2,500 grams.

[b]Dummy, equals 1 if child male.

***Significant at the 1 percent level.

**Significant at the 5 percent level.

*Significant at the 10 percent level.

A dummy for the sex of the child is also included when the dependent variable is birth weight, since males are on average heavier than females. The birth interval is shifted forward one year from the mainland Census regressions; that is, we focus on births to parents themselves born during 1957 to 1965.[15] Furthermore, we restrict the sample to singleton births. We find that mothers born in 1961 were 8 percent (0.247/0.030) more likely to give birth to a child of low birth weight (less than 2,500 grams), and 1.2 percent (0.00629/0.52) less likely to give birth to a son than mothers born in adjacent years (table 9.7). No significant effects were detected for the Hong Kong-born mothers, despite their greater numbers.

9.4   Summary and Discussion

We use the Chinese Famine 1959 to 1961 as a natural experiment in maternal stress and malnutrition. Despite some forty years of potential catch-up, cohorts exposed in utero registered substantial damage in the 2000 Census. Higher Famine intensity—by virtue of either time or place of birth—was associated with greater risk of being illiterate, out of the labor force, marrying later (men), and marrying spouses with less education (women).

---

15. Clearly, mainland-born mothers born after 1962 could not have been part of the Famine-induced wave of immigration in the spring of 1962. It is reassuring that restricting the sample to 1957 to 1961 strengthens our results (available from authors upon request).

Osmani and Sen (2003) argued that maternal malnutrition "rebounds on the society as a whole in the form of ill-health of their offspring—male and females alike—both as children and as adults" (p. 105). Despite its importance, the nutritional status of pregnant women has been found wanting in developing countries (DeRose, Das, and Millman 2000). Nubé and Van Dem Boom (2003) analyzed seventy-five Demographic and Health Survey (DHS) samples, finding that in South/Southeast Asia, "women's nutritional status relative to men's nutritional status compares unfavorably with results from other developing regions . . ." (p. 520). The prevalence of anemia among pregnant women in South Asia is 78 percent (Osmani and Sen 2003). Our results suggest that male-biased nutritional allocations handicap not only future health outcomes, but also future economic outcomes.

Empirical evidence on the causal effects of fetal nutrition is surprisingly scarce (see, e.g., Rasmussen [2001]; Walker et al. [2007]). Omitted factors (e.g., parental abilities and attitudes) can generate positive associations between measures of fetal health and adult socioeconomic outcomes in the absence of a causal pathway. Therefore, the "most compelling examinations of the fetal origins hypothesis look for sharp exogenous shocks in fetal health that are caused by conditions outside the control of the mother" (Currie 2009, 102). Clearly, such shocks are different from the chronic malnutrition facing women in developing countries. It is, however, difficult to think of an experimental design that could deliver clear evidence on the effect of chronic malnutrition on humans above what can be inferred from nonexperimental data; for instance, babies born in India weigh on average about 25 percent less than babies born in developed countries (Gluckman and Hanson 2005).

Similarly, our findings offer a fresh perspective on current health and socioeconomic outcomes among adults, positively correlated at both the individual and national levels (see, e.g., Case, Lubotsky, and Paxson [2002]; Cutler, Deaton, and Lleras-Muney [2006]). The mechanism behind this "dual relationship" (Smith 1999) has proved difficult to unravel empirically. Our findings suggest that poor fetal health conditions of the past may be at the nexus of the relationship. Indeed, historical nutritional deprivation in *developed* countries may also undermine outcomes in cohorts born prior to major nutrition-assistance programs for the poor.[16]

Perhaps the most intriguing finding is that Famine exposure lowered the sex ratio of not only the first but also the second generation—prenatally exposed women were themselves more likely to bear daughters. This pro-female effect is all the more noteworthy given the well-documented prevalence of son preference in mainland China. Famine-induced reductions in the sex ratio are consistent with empirical work finding lower sex ratios for

16. Almond, Hoynes, and Schanzenbach (2009) found improvements in birth outcomes (including birth weight) with the introduction of the Food Stamps Program in the United States during the 1960s, particularly among black infants. These cohorts also manifest improved health and educational outcomes in adulthood (Almond and Chay 2006).

unmarried or poorly educated mothers (Almond and Edlund 2007). While the magnitude of the Famine's effect on the sex ratio may appear small, it is several times larger than that associated with marital status in U.S. natality data (Almond and Edlund 2007) and is similar to differences found in survey data between mothers living with a partner around the time of conception and those who were not (Norberg 2004). Thus, small changes in the sex ratio can reflect large differences in maternal circumstance.

Trivers and Willard (1973) proposed that evolution would favor parental ability to vary the sex ratio of offspring according to condition: parents in poor condition would favor daughters and parents in good condition would favor sons. Their argument was based on the observation that while the average number of offspring to males and females equalizes, the reproductive success of a male offspring tends to be more resource-sensitive. Maternal malnutrition has been observed to correlate with more female births (see, e.g., Andersson and Bergström [1998]). Pathways include heightened rates of male fetal deaths, as was found to be the case during the Dutch famine (Roseboom, Meulen, Osmond et al. 2001). Another possibility is that starvation affects early cell division of male and female embryos differentially (Cameron 2004). Fetal "predictive adaptive responses" (to use the terminology of Gluckman and Hanson [2005]) set parameters for the adult individual; for instance, her height, which means that maternal constraints affect not only her children, but also her daughters' children.

Yet another pathway is sex selection. As noted, son preference is prevalent in China, and sex ratios at birth (male to female) have trended upwards since the early 1980s. In this case, low sex ratios of those in utero during the Famine may be a reflection of daughters having been actively chosen (or not deselected) by those of low socioeconomic status (Edlund 1999).

To our knowledge, ours is the first large-scale quasi-experimental evidence of a Trivers-Willard effect in human populations. It is also the first evidence (quasi-experimental or otherwise) of an intergenerational "echo-effect" of maternal status on the sex ratio (to our knowledge). Low offspring sex ratios in two generations underscore the long-term impact of maternal health.

Appendix

Variable Definitions

Census 2000

wdr Weighted death rate for the gestation period, assuming nine month gestation, and province of birth. For example, a person born in January 1960 in Beijing is assigned one-ninth of Beijing's 1960 mortality rate and eight-ninths of Beijing's 1959 mortality rate.

awdr Aggregate weighted average death rate, the wdr collapsed by month and birth year. Thus, it is the population weighted mean of wdr by month and year of birth.

mean Mean of dependent variable.

Province The province of birth. Our results are robust to inclusion of dummies for province of residence.

Illiterate Dummy indicating that the respondent was either illiterate or semi-literate.

Don't work Dummy indicating that the person did not work for more than one hour between October 25 and October 31 (in 2000). This includes those who are on leave from a job, as well as nonworkers.

On leave from job Not working because on leave, training, or seasonal lay-off.

Supported by other HH members/Dependent Main income source was support by other household members.

Disabled Dummy indicating that the person does not work because he/she has "lost ability to work."

House area Area of home, in square meters.

Unmarried Dummy indicating that the respondent was unmarried at the time of the census.

Never married Dummy indicating that the respondent had never married.

Spousal education Includes head-spouse couples only. Education is in years.

Marriage age Age in months at time of first marriage.

Household head Dummy indicating that the respondent was household head. Includes only respondents living in "family type" households (as opposed to "collectives").

Male Dummy indicating that the respondent is male.

Sons/Kids Fraction sons among ever-borne children. Excludes women who had not borne any children.

No kid Dummy indicating that the woman had borne no children.

Child mortality Number of children ever borne minus number of surviving children (at the time of the Census), divided by the number of children ever borne, by year and quarter of birth of mother.

Hong Kong Natality Data

I(1961) Dummy indicating that the mother was born in 1961, scaled by one one-hundredth.

Low BWT Low birth weight. Dummy indicating that child weighed less than 2,500 grams at birth.

China Dummy for whether born in mainland China.

China Fertility Surveys

The China Fertility surveys were carried out in 1985 and 1987 in the following provinces: Hebei, Shaangxi, Liaoning, Guangdong, Guizhou, Gansu; and the municipalities of Beijing and Shanghai. (We have not been able to access data for Shandong.) In total, some 46,000 ever-married women between fifteen and forty-nine years of age were interviewed, providing detailed information on pregnancy history. These data are available from the Office of Population Research, Princeton University, http://opr .princeton.edu/Archive/cidfs/.

References

Almond, D., and K. Y. Chay. 2006. The long-run and intergenerational impact of poor infant health: Evidence from cohorts born during the civil rights era. Unpublished Manuscript. University of California, Berkeley Department of Economics, February.

Almond, D., and L. Edlund. 2007. Trivers-Willard at birth and one year: Evidence from U.S. natality data 1983–2001. *Proceedings of the Royal Society B: Biological Sciences* 247 (October): 2491–96.

Almond, D., H. W. Hoynes, and D. W. Schanzenbach. Forthcoming. Inside the war on poverty: The impact of food stamps on birth outcomes. *The Review of Economics and Statistics*.

Andersson, R., and S. Bergström. 1998. Is maternal malnutrition associated with a low sex ratio at birth? *Human Biology* 70 (6): 1101–06.

Barker, D. J. P., ed. 1992. *Fetal and infant origins of adult disease*. London: British Medical Journal.

Bleker, O. P., T. J. Roseboom, A. C. J. Ravelli, G. A. van Montfans, C. Osmond, and D. J. P. Barker. 2005. Cardiovascular disease in survivors of the Dutch famine. In G. Hornstra, R. Uauy, and X. Yang, eds., *The impact of maternal nutrition on the offspring: Nestlé nutrition workshop series pediatric program, vol. 55,* 183–95. Basel, Switzerland: Karger.

Brandt, L., A. Siow, and C. Vogel. 2007. How flexible is the marriage market? Evidence from famine born cohorts in China. Unpublished Manuscript. Department of Economics, University of Toronto.

Burns, J. P. 1987. Immigration from China and the future of Hong Kong. *Asian Survey* 27 (6): 661–82.

Cai, Y., and W. Feng. 2005. Famine, social disruption, and involuntary fetal loss: Evidence from Chinese survey data. *Demography* 42 (2): 301–22.

Cameron, E. Z. 2004. Facultative adjustment of mammalian sex ratios in support of the Trivers-Willard hypothesis: Evidence for a mechanism. *Proceedings of the Royal Society B: Biological Sciences* 271 (1549): 1723–28.

Case, A., D. Lubotsky, and C. Paxson. 2002. Economic status and health in childhood: The origins of the gradient. *American Economic Review* 92 (5): 1308–34.

Chen, Y., and L.-A. Zhou. 2007. The long term health and economic consequences of 1959–1961 famine in China. *Journal of Health Economics* 26 (4): 659–81.

China Statistical Press. 2000. *Comprehensive statistical data and materials on 50 years of new China*. Technical Report. China Statistical Press, Beijing, China.

Currie, J. 2009. Healthy, wealthy, and wise: Socioeconomic status, poor health in childhood, and human capital development. *Journal of Economic Literature* 47 (1): 87–122.

Cutler, D. M., A. S. Deaton, and A. Lleras-Muney. 2006. The determinants of mortality. *The Journal of Economic Perspectives* 20 (3): 97–120.

DeRose, L. F., M. Das, and S. R. Millman. 2000. Does female disadvantage mean lower access to food? *Population and Development Review* 26 (3): 517–47.

Edlund, L. 1999. Son preference, sex ratios, and marriage patterns. *Journal of Political Economy* 107 (6): 1275–1304.

Gluckman, P., and M. Hanson. 2005. *The fetal matrix: Evolution, development and disease,* 1st ed. Cambridge: Cambridge University Press.

Gorgens, T., X. Meng, and R. Vaithianathan. 2005. Stunting and selection effects of famine: A case study of the great Chinese famine. Working Paper, Australian National University, May.

Heckman, J. J. 2007. The economics, technology, and neuroscience of human capability formation. *Proceedings of the National Academy of Sciences* 104 (33): 13250–55.

Hesketh, T., Q. J. Ding, and A. M. Tomkin. 2002. Disparities in economic development in Eastern China: Impact on nutritional status of adolescents. *Public Health Nutrition* 5 (2): 313–18.

Li, J., and R. S. Cooney. 1993. Son preference and the one child policy in China: 1979–1988. *Population Research and Policy Review* 12 (3): 277–96.

Li, W., and D. Tao Yang. 2005. The great leap forward: Anatomy of a central planning disaster. *Journal of Political Economy* 113 (4): 840–77.

Lin, J. Y. 1990. Collectivization and China's agricultural crisis in 1959–1961. *Journal of Political Economy* 98 (6): 1228–52.

Lin, J. Y., and D. Tao Yang. 2000. Food availability, entitlement and the Chinese famine of 1959–61. *Economic Journal* 110 (460): 136–58.

Luo, Z., R. Mu, and X. Zhang. 2006. Famine and overweight in China. *Review of Agricultural Economics* 28 (3): 296–304.

Meng, X., and N. Qian. 2006. The long run impact of childhood malnutrition: Evidence from China's great famine. Working Paper. Brown University, November.

Morgan, Stephen L. 2007. Stature and famine in China: The welfare of the survivors of the great leap forward famine, 1959–61 (February). Available at http://ssrn.com/abstract=1083059.

Neugebauer, R., H. Wijbrand Hoek, and E. Susser. 1999. Prenatal exposure to wartime famine and development of antisocial personality disorder in adulthood. *Journal of the American Medical Association* 281 (5): 455–62.

Norberg, K. 2004. Partnership status and the human sex ratio at birth. *Proceedings of the Royal Society B: Biological Sciences* 271 (1555): 2403–10.

Nubé, M., and G. J. M. Van Den Boom. 2003. Gender and adult undernutrition in developing countries. *Annals of Human Biology* 30 (5): 520–37.

Osmani, S., and A. Sen. 2003. The hidden penalties of gender inequality: Fetal origins of ill-health. *Economics and Human Biology* 1 (1): 105–21.

Painter, R. C., T. J. Roseboom, and O. P. Bleker. 2005. Prenatal exposure to the Dutch famine and disease in later life: An overview. *Reproductive Toxicology* 20 (3): 345–52.

Peng, X. 1987. Demographic consequences of the great leap forward in China's provinces. *Population and Development Review* 13 (4): 639–70.

Rasmussen, K. M. 2001. The 'fetal origins' hypothesis: Challenges and opportunities for maternal and child nutrition. *Annual Review of Nutrition* 21 (July): 73–95.

Roseboom, T. J., J. H. P. Meulen, C. Osmond, D. J. P. Barker, A. C. J. Ravelli, and O. P. Bleker. 2001. Adult survival after prenatal exposure to the Dutch famine. *Paediatric and Perinatal Epidemiology* 15 (3): 220–25.

Roseboom, T. J., J. H. P. Meulen, A. C. J. Ravelli, C. Osmond, D. J. P. Barker, and O. P. Bleker. 2001. Effects of prenatal exposure to the Dutch famine on adult disease in later life: An overview. *Twins Research* 4 (5): 293–98.

Shen, T., and J.-P. H. Y. Chang. 1996. Effect of economic reforms on child growth in urban and rural areas of China. *New England Journal of Medicine* 335 (6): 400–06.

Shi, X. 2006. Does famine have long term effects? Evidence from China. University of Michigan, June.

Smil, V. 1981. China's food: Availability, requirements, composition, and prospects. *Food Policy* 6 (2): 67–77.

Smith, J. P. 1999. Healthy bodies and thick wallets. *Journal of Economic Perspectives* 13 (2): 145–66.

St. Clair, D., M. Xu, P. Wang, Y. Yu, Y. Fang, F. Zhang, X. Zheng, N. Gu, G. Feng, P. Sham, and L. He. 2005. Rates of adult schizophrenia following prenatal exposure to the Chinese famines of 1959–1961. *Journal of the American Medical Association* 294 (5): 557–62.

Stein, Z., M. Susser, G. Saenger, and F. Marolla. 1975. *Famine and human development: The Dutch hunger winter of 1944–1945.* New York: Oxford University Press.

Trivers, R. L., and R. E. Willard. 1973. Natural selection and the ability to vary the sex ratio of offspring. *Science* 179 (4068): 90–92.

Walker, S. P., T. D. Wachs, J. M. Gardner, B. Lozoff, G. A. Wasserman, E. Pollitt, J. A. Carter, and the International Child Development Steering Group. 2007. Child development: Risk factors for adverse outcomes in developing countries. *The Lancet* 369 (January): 145–57.

White, T. 1991. Birth planning between plan and market: The impact of reform on China's one-child policy. In *China's economic dilemmas in the 1990s: The problems of reforms, modernization, and interdependence,* vol. 2, 252–69. Washington, DC: Joint Economic Committee, U.S. Government Printing Office.

Yan, L. 1999. *Height, health, and hazards: Reconstructing secular trends in stature in twentieth century China.* PhD thesis. University of California, Berkeley. (An earlier version presented at the annual meeting of the Population Association of America on March 26, 1999 in New York City.)

Yao, S. 1999. A note on the causal factors of China's famine in 1959–1961. *Journal of Political Economy* 107 (6): 1365–69.

Comment   Ronald Lee

In this excellent chapter, important issues are at stake. How do fetal conditions such as maternal nutrition affect later life health, productivity, and general success? Are childhood conditions a mechanism through which low socioeconomic status is transmitted across generations? Does the Trivers-Willard hypothesis from evolutionary theory apply to human populations? The chapter also addresses an important policy issue about the importance of public assistance for pregnant women or women of reproductive age, which may impact the later development and socioeconomic outcomes for their in utero children.

The identification strategy is to analyze the consequences of a huge exogenous shock: the nutritional deprivation caused by the famine in China during the period of the Great Leap Forward. This shock was limited in time

Ronald Lee is a Professor of Demography and Economics, University of California, Berkeley, and a research associate of the National Bureau of Economic Research.

and to some degree in space. Because it was exogenous, and not the result of choices made by the individuals affected, it provides a quasi-experimental setup for the study of later life outcomes for births that were in utero at the time of the famine.

This chapter contributes to a growing literature on the effects of early life or prenatal circumstances on later life outcomes, including in old age. Some of the authors have already made important contributions to this literature. My role as discussant is to chip away at the analysis, which I will now try to do. I have several points, as follows.

External Validity

Suppose we accept all aspects of the study design and the findings that result. Can we generalize from these findings to reach broader conclusions about the effects of caloric deprivation of pregnant women on the fetuses they carry? The biological response to a sudden and severe shock, as well as to the accompanying stress and anxiety, may be very different than the response to chronic malnutrition. Can we really draw useful lessons about nutritional deprivation as a mechanism for the intergenerational transmission of poverty?

Selectivity of Births

According to some estimates, the Great Leap Forward (GLF) period had around 30 million extra deaths, but also around 30 million fewer births, relative to the numbers that would have been expected based on levels and trends before and after. This leads me to wonder which women gave birth during and right after the GLF and which did not. If births were reduced most strongly in those areas that were most strongly affected by GLF, then the geographic location of those births that did occur would have been atypical. If it was the women who were best able and willing to control their fertility who chose to avoid births during this period, then there may have been negative selection on the mothers of those births that did occur. On the other hand, if the poorest and most disadvantaged females avoided giving birth during GLF then those births that did occur would have been positively selected.

Dynamics of Births during and After Demographic Crises

From many studies of historical and Third World demographic crises, it is well-established that there is a distinct pattern to the response of births to a crisis such as a price shock or health shock (Lee 1997). Births begin to decline around six months after a grain price shock, with this early timing perhaps reflecting abortion, miscarriage, or possibly anticipation of the shock by farmers who may have had better knowledge than was reflected in grain prices. The trough in births comes around twelve months after the shock, and then births rebound, reaching a peak two or three years later that is well above normal levels. Then they decline back toward normal. This pattern reflects biometric aspects of the reproductive cycle and occurs for mechanical rather than behavioral reasons. Ordinarily, some women are pregnant, some have just given birth and are breastfeeding, and some others are ready to become pregnant again. Ordinarily women are distributed across these states. In a reproductive trough, however, women who would normally give birth do not. Rebound occurs because these women who would normally have given birth during the trough are now ready to give birth soon after, because they are not in postpartum amenorrhea induced by breastfeeding. The point is that those born after the shock are also selected, in an opposite way to the selection on births during the trough. For this reason, those born a couple of years after the shock may not be a good control group.

Family Effects

The death of a child in a family would increase the resources available for surviving offspring and to those born next, who would then have better adult outcomes than otherwise. A particular application of this general point is that the death of a child during the GLF would have created a longer interval separating the younger and older sibling, and we know from many studies that longer birth intervals benefit the children at either end of the interval in terms of health, survival, height, weight, and so on.

Heritability of Sex Tilt and the Trivers-Willard Hypothesis

In our evolutionary past, male reproductive success was contingent on competitive success relative to other males, whereas female reproduction was automatic. For this reason, there would have been an evolutionary advantage to females who could tilt the probability of sex of birth toward males when they gave birth in favorable circumstances and toward females when they were in poor circumstances. This study identifies migrant children who came to Hong Kong from the mainland during a brief window of a few months in 1962. These immigrants to Hong Kong gave birth about twenty to twenty-five years later. Using microdata on births, the study examined differences in the characteristics of their births, finding that those affected by the famine had lower birth weight births and a higher proportion of female births, compared to other Chinese immigrants in Hong Kong. This appears to support the Trivers-Willard hypothesis as applied to humans.

This is important new evidence on this point. However, a few points suggest caution. First, it seems likely that the selectivity of migration to Hong Kong would have been different for women and children impacted by the famine. Other women were pulled to Hong Kong by economic advantages, while the Great Leap Forward migrants would have been pushed from their homelands. They would have come from different regions of China. At the period when they gave birth, sex selection by ultrasound became common. Could the famine refugees have resorted to sex selection less readily than economic migrants? Then the sex ratio effect would be behavioral and not biological.

Although I have raised a number of questions about the internal and external validity of this study, I doubt that any of these possible distortions would matter enough to affect the outcome. The evidence in figure 9.5 is quite strong, and overall I actually find the evidence in this excellent study persuasive.

Reference

Lee, R. 1997. Population dynamics: Equilibrium, disequilibrium, and consequences of fluctuations. In *Handbook of population and family economics,* v.1B, ed. M. Rosenzweig and O. Stark, 1063–115. North Holland: Elsevier.

Comment   Naohiro Ogawa

Almond, Edlund, Li, and Zhang have written an intellectually stimulating chapter, estimating the long-term effects of the 1959 to 1961 Chinese famine on those born during that time. By heavily drawing upon a micro-level data set derived from the 2000 China Census (1 percent sample), the authors have successfully shown a major impact of maternal malnutrition upon these cohorts: reduced sex ratio (males to females) at birth in two generations. In addition, they have found that famine survivors, compared with other intact birth cohorts, showed a higher probability of (a) suffering from an impaired literacy; (b) staying out of the workforce; (c) relying upon their family members as dependents; and (d) living in a smaller house.

In their quantitative analysis, Almond and his associates have utilized the following two measures of famine intensity: death rates and average month of birth. In the case of the former, data on the all-age death rate in twenty-nine out of thirty-one provinces was used as a base. The weighted average of the death rate in the province of birth for the duration of the fetal period was calculated for each individual, and this variable was labeled as wdr_{jt}. Then, by collapsing this weighted death rate by month of birth, the authors created another predictor, namely, $awdr_{jt}$, which represents a population-weighted national average for each month and year.

Because of the lack of relevant information representing the level of famine intensity facing each person's household or his or her community, the

Naohiro Ogawa is a professor of economics at the Nihon University and its Population Research Institute.

authors used the crude death rate for the province of his or her birth as a proxy. It should be emphasized, however, that this approximation by the province-level data could present a few statistical difficulties. First of all, the crude death rates are directly affected by age-structural transformations. It is easily conceivable that, owing to regional differences in fertility and mortality, the age structures differed not only between provinces but also between regions within each province to a pronounced extent. In addition, it is also presumable that the famine generated differential impacts upon various age groups in the sampled provinces. For these reasons the age-standardized death rates could be substantially different from the crude death rates employed in the present study. In other words, first, variations in the variable wdr_{jt} are likely to capture changes in various factors other than the incidence of death due to malnutrition. Second, many of China's provinces are quite vast, so that climatic and geographical variations within each province are likely to be considerable, which suggests a high probability that the intensity of malnutrition varied markedly within each province. Third, but not as crucial as the first two points, according to the study by Painter, Roseboom, and Bleker (2005), poor nutrition in early-to mid-pregnancy has the most deleterious effect on health. Following this finding, the authors could have introduced an additional statistical adjustment (e.g., heavy weights in the first half of the pregnancy period and lower weights in the second half) in computing the value of wdr_{jt}. Because of these statistical limitations to the values of wdr_{jt} (and $awdr_{jt}$), caution needs to be exercised in interpreting the computed results presented in this chapter.

This study also indicates that those who managed to survive the risks generated by the 1959 to 1961 famine showed a higher probability of being disadvantaged in terms of education, labor force participation, and wealth accumulation. However, it is plausible that a great proportion of the population belonging to these cohorts who were healthy and well-educated were able to enjoy the economic advantages of their small cohort size, particularly in the form of relative wages at the labor market, just as was the case of baby boomers and baby busters in some industrialized countries such as Japan (Martin and Ogawa 1988). It would be interesting to see if such positive cohort size effects on the majority of these special cohorts born during the period in question could be examined by expanding the scope of the data set the authors have compiled. If such positive cohort size effects proved to be present, the income disparity among the famine-stricken cohorts could be more serious than among cohorts free from the influence of the famine.

The nexus between maternal nutrition and the sex ratio at birth is still important in some parts of the contemporary world. A recent study on Ethiopia, undertaken by Mace and Eardley (2004), is a salient example. In the case of East Asia, judging from its recent serious food shortage, North Korea might be an interesting country for researchers to test the presence of such a linkage. Moreover, in twentieth century East Asia, not only China but other countries as well could provide a number of interesting phenomena to be statistically researched, following a similar line of interest as that found in the study conducted by Almond and his group. In Japan, for instance, the problems of anorexia and bulimia have been serious over the past few decades. Attention should be drawn to the findings derived from one of the recent studies focusing on Norwegian women; this study has shown that maternal eating disorders may influence offspring's sex and that the direction of the effect may vary by eating disorder subtype (Bulik et al. 2008). To date, however, the impact of eating disorders on the sex ratio at birth still remains unexplored in Japan, although Japan's sex ratio at birth has been on a downward trend since 1966, the "year of fire horse."[1] The sex ratio at birth was 107.6 in 1966, but it declined slowly to 105.6 by 1985. Although the effect of the year of fire horse on the sex ratio at birth should have lasted for only one year or its adjacent years, the sex ratio continued decreasing while still remaining at a relatively high level for a long time. Since the mid-1980s, however, the ratio has been oscillating around 105.5—a level observed back in the 1950s. Furthermore, sex selection by ultrasound has never been a common practice in Japan. How, then, can we account for these changes in the sex ratio over time in postwar Japan? It is an academically interesting topic to be investigated by researchers. In any case, the study undertaken by Almond and his associates appears to provide an instructive base for developing proper analytical and statistical approaches to be applied to such future research in Japan.

References

Bulik, C. M., A. Von Holle, K. Gendall, K. Kveim Lie, E. Hoffman, X. Mo, L. Torgersen, and T. Reichborn-Kjennerud. 2008. Maternal eating disorders influence sex ratio at birth. *Acta Obstetricia et Gynecologica Scandinavica* 87 (9): 979–81.

Hodge, R. W., and N. Ogawa. 1991. *Fertility change in contemporary Japan.* Chicago: University of Chicago Press.

Mace, R., and J. Eardley. 2004. Maternal nutrition and sex ratio at birth in Ethiopia. *Research in Economic Anthropology* 23:295–306.

Martin, L. G., and N. Ogawa. 1988. The effect of cohort size on relative wages in Japan. In *Economics of changing age distributions in developed countries, international studies in demography,* ed. R. D. Lee, W. B. Arthur, and G. Rodgers, 59–75. New York: Oxford University Press.

Painter, R. C., T. J. Roseboom, and O. P. Bleker. 2005. Prenatal exposure to the Dutch famine and disease in later life: An overview. *Reproductive Toxicology* 20 (3): 345–52.

---

1. According to a long-standing Japanese superstition, a girl born in this particular year is destined to have an unhappy life and kill her husband if she marries. This (for girls) ominous year comes around every sixty years. For further analysis, see Hodge and Ogawa (1991).

10

Demographic Transition, Childless Families, and Economic Growth

Francis T. Lui

10.1 Introduction

Demographic transition is a well-known phenomenon that has repeatedly taken place in many countries during the last few centuries. Although characterization of this phenomenon may vary among different authors, its main features can conveniently be summarized as follows.[1] Before a society moves from stagnancy to sustained economic growth, there is often a significant improvement in the life expectancy of its population. In the early phase of the development process, population growth rate rises, not only because people live longer, but also because total fertility rate (TFR) may go up. In the more advanced stage of development, there is marked and continuous decline in fertility until it has hit a "minimum" level.[2]

Understanding the mechanics of demographic transition is important both from theoretical and policy perspectives. At the theoretical level, demographic transition is closely linked to the interaction between investments in quantity and quality of children, which is at the core of endogenous growth models. On policy grounds, changes in fertility rates can easily exert profound effects on many socioeconomic issues, such as education, health

Francis T. Lui is a professor of economics at the Hong Kong University of Science and Technology.

Financial support from the Research Grant Council of Hong Kong (Ref. No.: HKUST6466/06H) is gratefully acknowledged. I am indebted to a group of able students for their research assistance. They are Amy Chan, Simon Chan, Steven Chong, Bing Han, Billy Ho, Angela Lam, Chang Liu, John Tian, and Kathy Yu. Lung-fei Lee, Ronald Lee, Siu-fai Leung, Hongbin Li, Roberto Mariano, participants of the nineteenth NBER-EASE, and two anonymous referees have provided valuable comments. They are not responsible for any errors that remain in this chapter.

1. See, for example, Coale (1987); Easterlin (1987); and Dyson and Murphy (1985).
2. See World Bank (1984, chapter 2).

Table 10.1   **Total fertility rates in a sample of economies**

	1965	2008
Asia-Pacific Rim		
Australia	3.0	1.76
China	6.4	1.77
Hong Kong	4.5	0.98
Japan	2.0	1.22
South Korea	4.9	1.29
Taiwan		1.13
Thailand	6.3	1.64
Singapore	4.7	1.08
Developed economies		
European Union	2.7[a]	1.5
United States	2.9	2.1
World	5.1	2.58

Sources: Data for 2008 are from Central Intelligence Agency (2008). Data for 1965 are from World Bank (1992).
[a]The 1965 TFR figure of 2.7 is for Organization for Economic Cooperation and Development (OECD) countries.

care, housing, immigration, retirement protection, business opportunities, saving behavior, and even international balance of payments. These effects are more prominent in economies where fertility rates deviate significantly from the population replacement ratio, which is roughly equal to 2.1. Table 10.1 shows that in 2008, average TFR in the world is 2.58, which is well above the replacement ratio.[3] The European Union, consisting of well-developed economies, expectedly, has a low TFR of 1.5. The United States, with a TFR as high as 2.1, is more an exception rather than a rule. On the other hand, the low TFRs in many economies in the Asia-Pacific Rim seem to indicate that they have already reached some advanced stages of demographic transition, even though the per capita income levels in some are still much lower than those in the United States or Europe. Comparisons with the 1965 figures readily show that these Asia-Pacific economies have undergone major declines in TFR in recent decades. In view of the possibility that low and declining TFRs can upset prevailing social and economic equilibria, it is useful for us to investigate the causes behind the demographic transitions in this region.

The low TFRs in East Asian countries indicate that the women there, on average, bear very few children. However, they do not explicitly tell us how many women choose *not* to bear any children at all. The importance of this matter is often overlooked. Parents can invest in their children's human capi-

---

3. The source for table 10.2 is CIA (2008). There are minor discrepancies between the data there and those from official government statistics. Since the errors are minor, we ignore them.

tal only if they have children. If an adult chooses not to have any children; that is, the optimal quantity of children has a corner solution, the investment vehicle disappears. Endogenous growth models built upon such investment would lose much of their relevance. This problem would not be too important if only a small percentage of families choose to remain childless. However, as the evidence in the next section shows, up to 30 percent of the women in Hong Kong—an economy having one of the lowest TFRs in the world—will never have any children, and this percentage is rising rapidly! Similar situations also occur in many other economies. Thus, the issue of childless families is not a trivial issue that can be ignored by model-builders.

The purpose of this chapter, which is part of a larger study on the demographic transition, is to identify the factors that have significant effects on fertility choices. The theoretical framework is a variant of the Ehrlich-Lui (1991) model. The empirical evidence is mainly based on the data collected in a survey that I conducted.

In the next section, I shall present the evidence to support the argument that zero fertility is a matter that we must reckon with. Section 10.3 briefly discusses a theoretical framework that can generate both the demographic transition and corner solution for fertility. Some testable hypotheses are stated. Section 10.4 outlines the approach for testing the hypotheses, and presents and discusses the empirical results. Concluding remarks are in section 10.5. Finally, some details of the survey are discussed in the appendix.

10.2   The Prevalence of Childless Families

In this section, I shall argue that the experiences of Hong Kong can serve as a "leading indicator" for the demographic transitions in East Asia and possibly other developed economies as well. I shall also provide estimates for the proportion of Hong Kong women who will remain childless throughout their lives.

There is now an extensive literature on the relationship between longevity and fertility,[4] some of them showing that an increase in longevity can initiate the onset of the demographic transition. Life expectancy at birth in Hong Kong in 2006 was 85.6 years for women and 79.5 for men.[5] Not only are these among the highest in the world, they also indicate substantial increases since 1981, when the corresponding figures were 78.5 and 72.3, respectively. As such, it is not surprising to see that the median age of the Hong Kong population has risen from thirty-four in 1996 to thirty-nine in 2006. More importantly, the total fertility rate in Hong Kong, as evidenced in table 10.2, has also experienced a long and rapid decline episode. Table

4. Some examples, in chronological order, are Ehrlich and Lui (1991, 1997); Blackburn and Cipriani (2002); Boldrin and Jones (2002); Kalemli-Ozcan (2003); Doepke (2004, 2005); Zhang and Zhang (2005); and Soares (2006).
5. See table 1.4 of Census and Statistics Department (2007).

Table 10.2   Total fertility rate in Hong Kong

	1965	1970	1981	1991	1996	2001	2006
	4.5	3.3	1.95	1.30	1.20	0.93	0.98

Sources: The 1965 and 1970 figures are from World Bank (1992, 1993). The 1981 to 2006 figures are derived from the age-specific fertility rates reported in table 2.6 of Census and Statistics Department (2007).

10.2 also shows that Hong Kong's TFR has fallen below one only in recent years. Back in 1965, it was as high as 4.5.

The slight increase in TFR in the last few years should not be interpreted as a reversal in trend. From 1998 to 2003, Hong Kong suffered from a prolonged deflationary recession. The fertility rate in that period, as recorded in the 2001 Census, was likely depressed to below trend level because of the unfavorable economic environment. Using arguments similar to Becker and Barro (1988), we expect that parents would try to make up for the "losses" of children when the economy improved again after 2003.

Given the low TFR in Hong Kong, we want to estimate the proportion of women who will have zero fertility in their entire lifetimes. The estimates are based on official census data of various years. These data also allow us to make some simple projections of what will happen in the near future.

Census data can provide information on the number of children that have already been born, but there is no direct information on what would happen to women's fertility decisions in the future. However, if a woman aged forty-five does not have any children, we can reasonably expect that the chance for her to bear children in the future is negligibly small. Figure 10.1 plots the percentages of women at each age group from twenty to forty-five who have never borne any children for the years 1996, 2001, and 2006.

In 2006, the proportion of childless forty-five-year-old women is 29.22 percent. While this is already a very large proportion, we should note from figure 10.1 that the childless rates of women in *every* age group have been increasing from 1996 to 2006. Table 10.3 provides further information on how these proportions change over time. For the forty-one to forty-five age group, the percentage of women having no children rises from 20.9 percent in 1996 to 31.81 percent in 2006, representing roughly an 11 percentage point increase for the ten-year period. Judging from the high proportion of younger women who do not have any children, a proportion that has also been increasing over time, we can safely project that in the next decade, the percentage of Hong Kong women who will remain childless throughout their lives can easily exceed one-third or even 40 percent of the adult female population.

As a robustness test for the estimate that in 2006, 31.81 percent of the women in the forty-one to forty-five years old age group do not have any children, we perform another estimate using a completely different data set; namely, data from a survey that we have conducted. Details of that survey

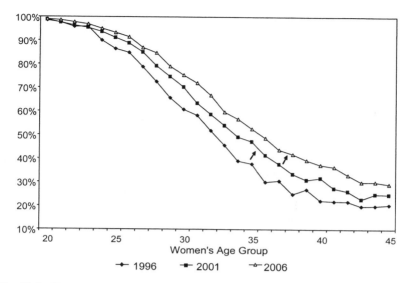

Fig. 10.1   Percentage of women who have no children

Table 10.3   Proportion of women at different age groups who do not have any children

	Age group	
Year	20–40 (%)	41–45 (%)
1996	58.22	20.90
2001	63.83	25.31
2006	69.75	31.81

Sources: Figures for 2001 and 2006 are derived from the 5 percent samples of the 2001 and 2006 Hong Kong Census microdata. Figures for 1996 are derived from the 1 percent sample of the 1996 Hong Kong Census microdata. See Census and Statistics Department (1996, 2001, 2006).

are discussed in the appendix. The survey provides information, among others, on the number of children that the respondents currently have, and the number of children they plan to have *in the future*. The estimate based on these details indicate that 27.5 percent of the women within the forty to forty-four age group do not have *and* do not plan to have any children in the future. Since this additional estimate generates a result that is of the same order of magnitude as the earlier one, we can reasonably believe that indeed a very high percentage of the women in Hong Kong will never have any children.[6]

6. Another robustness test is to look at the proportion of childless men in the population. By using a methodology similar to that which we have applied to women, we estimate that 36.85 to 38.5 percent of the men in the forty-one to forty-five age group in 2006 do not have children. This confirms the notion that many families in Hong Kong will remain childless. The reason why there is a range for the estimate is that the census database only reports the number

The prevalence of childless families is a common phenomenon that goes far beyond Hong Kong's borders. Based on data from China's 2005 1 percent population census, my preliminary estimate indicates that 25.7 percent of women in Chinese cities will remain childless when they reach the age of fifty. This ratio is likely to be much higher in major cities such as Beijing and Shanghai.[7] From table 10.1 the TFRs for Japan and the four Asian dragons are close to one. Since many women in these economies have more than one child, but the average number of children per woman is around one, the proportion of those who are childless cannot be negligible.

Childlessness is prevalent not only in Asia, but also in the West. Even the United States, which has an exceptionally high TFR compared with other advanced economies, has a moderate, but nevertheless significant, voluntarily childless rate of 7 percent in 2002 (Abma and Martinez 2006). In Germany, 21 percent of the women of birth cohort 1960 do not have children. The childless rate for the birth cohort 1966 is estimated to be 29 percent. For university-educated women born in 1965, the rate is much higher at 38.5 percent (Dorbritz 2008). In Italy, it has been estimated that about one-fifth of the women born in 1965 will remain childless (Mencarini and Tanturri 2006). Among British women who have received university education, 25 percent of those born in 1970 will likely remain childless (Kneale and Joshi 2008). In fact, the European baby bust has attracted so much attention that the *New York Times Magazine* finds it newsworthy to publish an investigative cover story with the sensational title of "No Babies" (Shorto 2008).

Thus, the emergence of childless families is not an isolated event, nor can this be regarded as quantitatively trivial. The analysis of Hong Kong's experience is valuable because this can be regarded as a leading indicator for other economies whose TFRs have not yet reached the low levels of Hong Kong. In this chapter, I shall confine myself only to the causes of low or zero fertility rates, but not to their implications.

10.3   Theoretical Framework

In this section, I shall briefly outline a theoretical model that is able to generate the demographic transition. The model is adapted from Ehrlich and

---

of children living in the household. It is well-known that some Hong Kong men have married women in the Chinese mainland, and their children have not migrated to Hong Kong yet. Thus, in our estimation, we have to take into account the number of men who are married, but whose wives and children are not in the household in Hong Kong. Since husbands tend to be older than wives, it is no surprise that the proportion of childless men is larger than that of childless women in the same age group. The corresponding estimate for the proportion of childless men in 2001 is between 27.83 to 29.02 percent.

7. See tables 8.2a and 8.3a of China National Bureau of Statistics (2007). According to the 2005 1 percent population Census in China, the TFRs of Beijing and Shanghai are 0.617 and 0.643, respectively. Although some underreporting might have occurred because of the one-child policy in China, these extremely low TFRs imply that childless rates in these two cities could be higher than 35 percent.

Lui (1991), modified in such a way that it can accommodate zero fertility. It is presented here to provide a theoretical foundation for the main hypotheses to be tested in the next section.

Consider an overlapping-generations economy where all the agents live for three periods: 0, 1, and 2. In period 0, the person is a child and does not make any decisions. In period 1, the person is a young working adult who has to decide how many children she should bear, how much time she should invest in the human capital of each of her children, and how much she should save for retirement. She is obligated to support her parent if still alive. She also acts as a "companion" for her parent, in the sense that her being around would give psychological pleasure to the parent. Even though each person lives for at most three periods, the economy can last forever because some agents are born in each period. In period 2, the agent does not work anymore. She gets material support from her children and her own savings. In addition, she can derive utility both from the quantity and quality of her children.

Let the production function of human capital be[8]

$$(1) \qquad\qquad H_{t+1} = A(H_t + H^*)h_t,$$

where H_t = human capital of a representative working adult at time t; H_{t+1} = human capital of a representative working adult in the next generation at time $t + 1$; H^* = raw labor (which implies that even if $H_t = 0$, H_{t+1} can still be bigger than zero); h_t = the proportion of time that a representative parent at time t invests in the human capital of each child; and A = technology parameter in the production of human capital.

Consumption of a young adult at time t and the consumption when she is old at time $t + 1$ are given by

$$(2) \qquad c_1(t) = (H_t + H^*)(1 - vn_t - h_t n_t - s_t) - \pi_2 w H_t$$

$$(3) \qquad c_2(t + 1) = [\pi_1 n_t \, wH_{t+1} + B(H_t + H^*) \, s_t^m] + \mu(\pi_1 n_t) \, H_{t+1}^\alpha.$$

Each young adult has 1 unit of time. If he or she uses the entire unit to produce the consumption good, output is $H_t + H^*$. Even when $H_t = 0$, raw labor H^* can make output bigger than 0. The number of children borne by a young parent at time t is n_t. The proportion of time spent on raising a child is v. Thus, vn_t is the proportion of time spent on the n_t children. In addition, educating n_t of them requires $h_t n_t$ units of time. Saving rate as a proportion of his or her maximum possible income is represented by s_t. The amount of consumption good provided by a representative young adult to support his parent at time t is given by wH_t. The rate committed by the young adult to support his parent, w, is treated as exogenous here.[9] The probability that a

---

8. This setup is similar to that in Becker, Murphy, and Tamura (1990).

9. This assumption is made for convenience and tractability only. It is possible to model it as the endogenous outcome of an implicit contract.

young adult can survive to old age is π_2. The larger is π_2, the longer is the life expectancy of people. The reason why π_2 is included in the term $\pi_2 w H_t$ is that a young adult does not have to pay for the old-age support of his parent if they have not survived. Hence, $\pi_2 w H_t$ can be interpreted as the expected support for the parent.

The expression for $c_2(t + 1)$ in equation (3) can be interpreted as a composite consumption good consisting of the material part (the terms within the square brackets), and the psychological "companionship" function. When an adult has turned old, each of his children will provide support equal to $w H_{t+1}$. Even though an adult has given birth to n_t children, some of them cannot survive to adulthood. The probability that a child can survive to adulthood and has the chance to work is given by π_1. The second term inside the square brackets is total returns from the agent's savings, where $B > 0$ and $0 < m < 1$. The last term in equation (3) is meant to capture the assumption that the quantity and human capital of his or her children can be treated as a utility-generating consumption good. The parameter μ can vary across different people. A large μ means that the person likes children very much.[10] We also impose the restrictions that $0 < \alpha < 1$.

The utility function of a young adult at time t is given by

$$(4) \qquad u_t = \frac{(c_1(t)^{1-\sigma} - 1)}{(1 - \alpha)} + \delta\pi_2 \frac{(c_2(t+1)^{1-\sigma} - 1)}{(1 - \sigma)},$$

where δ represents the discount rate for future consumption. Since the chance for an adult to survive to old age is π_2, we have to multiply old-age utility by $\delta\pi_2$. We impose the restriction that $0 < \sigma < 1$.

A representative young adult maximizes equation (4) subject to equations (1), (2), (3), and nonnegativity constraints for the choice variables s_t, h_t, and n_t. The first-order conditions are given by the following:

$$(5) \qquad \left(\frac{c_2}{c_1}\right)^{\sigma} = \frac{\delta\pi_2 m B}{s_t^{1-m}} \equiv \delta R_s$$

$$(6) \qquad \left(\frac{c_2}{c_1}\right)^{\sigma} \geq \delta A \pi_1 \pi_2 w[1 + \alpha N] \equiv \delta R_h$$

$$(7) \qquad \left(\frac{c_2}{c_1}\right)^{\sigma} \geq \delta A \pi_1 \pi_2 w[1 + N]\left[\frac{h_t}{(v + h_t)}\right] \equiv \delta R_n,$$

$$(8) \qquad \text{where } N \equiv \mu w^{-1} H_{t+1}^{\alpha-1}.$$

The left-hand sides of equations (5) to (7) can be interpreted as the marginal rate of substitution between period 1 and period 2 consumptions. The notations R_s, R_h, and R_n represent the rates of return to savings, investment

---

10. We assume that μ is positive in the analysis. If a person dislikes children, we can actually treat μ as negative.

in human capital, and investment in quantity of children, respectively. There are some useful properties of this model that can help us to understand the process of economic development and demographic transition. Suppose that in the beginning, life expectancy is low; that is, π_1 and π_2 are relatively small. From equations (6) and (7), the rates of return to investment in quantity and quality of children are low. The economy could be trapped in a zero-growth stagnant equilibrium with no change in human capital over time. Now assume that π_1 and π_2 go up sufficiently. Since both R_h and R_n increase as a result, parents tend to invest more in both quantity and quality of children. Consequently, both n_t and H_{t+1} rise. However, as the human capital stock for the next generation has gone up, its opportunity cost of having children increases as well.[11] In that generation, the parent would reduce the quantity of children, but continue to invest in human capital. As the level of human capital of the parents in each subsequent generation rises, the economy continues to grow, but fertility rate declines. This is the demographic transition.

It should be noted that as H_{t+1} increases during the process of economic development, the term N defined in equation (8) will converge to zero because $0 < \alpha < 1$. From equations (6) and (7), it can be shown that $R_h > R_n$ if and only if $N^{-1} > (1 - \alpha)[(h_t/v) - \alpha/(1 - \alpha)]$. Since the left-hand side of this inequality goes up without bound, at some stage of economic development, R_h must exceed R_n. This means that equality for equations (6) and (7) cannot hold simultaneously. There is an interior solution for h_t, but n_t has a corner solution, in the sense that it should attain the smallest admissible value.[12]

This immediately poses a problem. What is the lowest admissible value for n_t? The first candidate is that it is equal to one, and the second is zero. We should note that if the number of children is zero, it will be futile for the adult to invest in human capital of the children because they do not exist. Consumptions defined in equations (2) and (3) collapse to simpler terms. The person does not have to spend any resources in raising and educating children. During retirement, his or her consumption comes from savings only. There is no financial support from the children and no utility from companionship. On the other hand, if the person chooses to have one child, he or she can continue to invest in the human capital of that child. Equations (5) and (6) are still the laws of motion determining the dynamics of the variables in the model. The decision of whether to choose zero or one can be made by directly computing the utility after substituting the relevant values of n_t and other variables into equation (4). Assume that an agent has chosen

11. Actually the opportunity time cost of investing in human capital also rises, but from equation (1), the higher human capital stock of the parent will make him or her more effective in producing human capital. This mitigates the rise in time cost.

12. From equation (5), since a sufficiently small saving rate can cause the rate of return to savings to go up to some large value, the saving rate always has an interior solution.

to have one child. We can demonstrate by simulation exercises that as the human capital of his or her descendants grows over time, the latter may find it more advantageous to shift over to zero children. The timing of the shift depends on the parameters of the model. In particular, if companionship is viewed as important; that is, μ is relatively big, it will be less likely for the family to arrive at either the corner solution of one or zero. After the shift to the new corner solution, this dynastic family will terminate.

The model discussed previously provides a coherent framework that generates a number of testable hypotheses. The most important of these is the *Demographic Transition Hypothesis: In an economy that has entered a perpetual growth equilibrium, total fertility rate of the potential parent is negatively related to his or her human capital.*

To test the demographic transition hypothesis, we have to introduce a number of control variables, some of which are interesting on their own. The model can guide us in identifying the proper controls. From equation (7), an increase in v will lower the return to the quantity of children. This leads us to the *Opportunity Cost Hypothesis: When a parent finds it more costly to raise children, he or she will have fewer of them.*

From equations (6) and (7), an increase in the educational technology parameter A will raise not only the return to investment in human capital, but also the return to the quantity of children. Hence, we have the *Educational Technology Hypothesis: The more effective a parent is in educating his or her children, the greater is the quantity of children she wants to raise.*

Equation (7) includes an old-age support parameter w. It follows from the equation that when w goes up, the return to quantity of children will also rise. We can state the *Old-Age Security Hypothesis* as follows: *If a person's old-age security motive is stronger, he or she will raise more children.*

Both equations (6) and (7) contain a parameter, μ, which is a measure of people's preference for children. This is another control variable that has to be included in our empirical analysis in the next section. It is beyond the scope of this chapter to explicitly model the factors affecting taste, since there is already an extensive literature on this issue in different branches of social science. For example, Koropeckyj-Cox and Pendell (2007) find that religiosity and attitudes about marriage and gender equality can affect women's acceptance of childlessness. Barber and Axinn (2004) reports that exposure to mass media influences can change people's childbearing behaviors and preferences for smaller families. Schmidt (2008) provides evidence showing that attitudes toward risks can also affect a woman's fertility decision. Thus, the literature and the theoretical model of this chapter both indicate that we should incorporate preference variables as controls in our regressions. Another advantage of including preference variables is that we can quantitatively assess their relative importance in determining a woman's fertility.

10.4   Empirical Results

This section presents and discusses the main empirical findings. I shall first explain the choice of the data set used and provide summary statistics of the data. Then empirical tests based on a Tobit model and a generalized Poisson model are presented and the economic interpretations discussed. I shall then use a Probit model to focus more sharply on the choice of whether or not to have children at all. For reasons to be explained later, despite the fact that the Probit estimator is less efficient than the Tobit, the results generated by the former can still provide us with additional insights. Finally, a number of dummy variables have been used in all the regressions. The meanings of the estimated results on these dummies are discussed.

10.4.1   Choice of Data Set and Summary Statistics

To test the basic hypotheses outlined in the previous section and to generate additional results, the official census (or by-census) data conducted in Hong Kong once every five years would be a good data source. The 5 percent sample contains microdata for more than 110,000 households and 340,000 individuals. Although the large number of observations can give us greater flexibility in the estimations, there are also important shortcomings. Since it only tells us how many children a parent has already had, but not the number of children he or she wants to raise in the future, we have to rely on more indirect methods of estimation such as survival analysis. Moreover, there are many possible determinants of fertility that are simply not included in the census database.[13]

In this chapter, I have chosen to estimate the results using a data set generated from a randomized survey I conducted. Details of the survey are provided in the appendix. In addition to having more specific information on fertility behaviors, the survey contains an important new variable, the number of additional children the respondent plans to have. We can add up the value of this variable with the number of children that the respondent has already had. This would generate the total number of desired total fertility rate, which is the main dependent variable to be explained in this chapter. Given this information, we can also easily construct a dichotomous variable (FERTDUMMY) on whether the respondent wants to have zero, or a positive number, of children.

Table 10.4 contains summary statistics of some key variables from the survey data set. It should be noted that we had set constraints on two variables; namely, approximately three-quarters of the respondents should be women and the targeted age group twenty to forty-five years old (child-bearing

---

13. It does not mean that empirical estimations using census data are of no value. A separate project with similar objectives using census data has been conducted by the author.

Table 10.4   **Summary statistics of the survey data**

Number of respondents	1,017
Ratio of female to male respondents	794: 223
Number of never married respondents	622
Median age of respondents	28
Number of respondents who do not want anymore children	409
Number of respondents who have no children	705
Median number of total desired children	2
Median number of years of schooling	14
Median years of working experience	5
Median years of experience for those currently employed	7
Median monthly income of all respondents in HK$	8,750
Median monthly income of employed respondents in HK$	13,750
Number of homeowners	590
Median size of home in square feet	600
Number of respondents having domestic helpers	152
Number of siblings of respondents	Minimum 0, median 2, maximum 8

age).[14] Other than these, the respondents were chosen randomly. Because of the constraints, the respondents were on average considerably younger than the median age of the Hong Kong population, thirty-nine. Other summary statistics in table 10.4 appear to be consistent with the general profiles of these types of people in Hong Kong. For example, the number of years of schooling for these people is higher than the average person in the population, which consists of many less educated older people. Similarly, the low number of years of working experience also reflects the young age of the targeted group. It can also be seen that the majority of the respondents do not have children, and many of them do not want to have children in the future.

10.4.2   Verification of the Demographic Transition

According to the model of demographic transition discussed in the previous section, total fertility rate, which is represented here by the variable TFR and defined as the actual number of children plus expected number of children in the future, should go down over time when parents become more and more educated. This longitudinal phenomenon can be captured here by cross-sectional data, if we assume that adults having different levels of human capital at a given point in time are similar to those who belong to different stages of economic development over time. Moreover, the pos-

14. A small portion of the respondents fell outside of the targeted group because their actual ages were not always recognizable to members of the research team.

sibility of having corner solutions for fertility; that is, TFR equals to zero, means that the fertility data are censored at zero. A convenient approach to deal with this phenomenon is to use a Tobit model where the dependent variable, desired TFR, is censored at zero. The general formulation for Tobit is given by

(9)
$$y_t^* = x_i'\beta + \varepsilon_i$$
$$y_i = 0 \qquad if\ y_i^* \le 0,$$
$$y_i = y_i^* \qquad if\ y_i^* > 0,$$

where y_i is the dependent variable, x_i is a vector of the explanatory variables, β is the vector of coefficients of the variables, and ε_i is an error term with standard normal distribution.

Table 10.5 presents the summary of several regressions aimed at identifying the determinants of fertility in Hong Kong.[15] The benchmark regression is the Tobit model in regression (1), where the standard errors are obtained by using the robust estimators of Huber (1967) and White (1980). The error term in this regression does not have to be identically distributed.[16]

Two measures of human capital, years of schooling (SCHOOLING) and years of working experience (EXPERIENCE), are used. I have also added the square of these two variables into the regression to capture possible non-linearity in these variables. The estimated coefficients for these four variables are all statistically significant. Moreover, despite the positive signs of the coefficients for the squared variables, within the value ranges of SCHOOLING and EXPERIENCE, desired TFR is always negatively related to these measures of human capital. This result supports the *Demographic Transition Hypothesis* discussed in section 10.3. As the human capital of the potential parent increases, they tend to have fewer or even no children. We should note that the negative effect of SCHOOLING on desired TFR is quantitatively much larger than that of EXPERIENCE. Other things equal, an adult who has fourteen years of schooling would have 1.24 fewer children compared to one who has no education at all.[17]

The positive effect of marriage on desired TFR is consistent with the *Opportunity Cost Hypothesis*. Because of economy of scale, married people would be more efficient in raising children. This is similar to the effect of lowering v modeled in section 10.3. We expect that the desired TFRs of

15. To mitigate possible endogeneity problems, I have also tried various instrumental variable estimators in the regressions. However, the Wald exogeneity tests applied to these regressions indicate that endogeneity is not a problem. In fact, the results reported in tables 10.5 and 10.6 generally remain robust when instrumental variables are used.

16. If we do not use the robust estimator for the standard errors, as expected, the results are more significant.

17. To compute marginal effects in the censored regression model, we need the ratio of the uncensored observations to the total number of observations. In this case, it is equal to 0.841. See Greene (2003, 765).

Table 10.5 **Factors affecting the demographic transition**

	(I) Tobit Dependent Variable = Desired TFR	(II) Generalized Poisson Dependent Variable = Desired TFR	(III) Probit Dependent Variable = FERTDUMMY	(IV) OLS Dependent Variable = Desired TFR
Constant	2.95582****	1.60520****	2.07478*	2.78667****
	(0.73271)	(0.38530)	(1.29690)	(0.64604)
INCOME	0.0000043	0.000008****	0.0000072	0.000003
	(0.0000047)	(0.000002)	(0.0000089)	(0.000004)
MARRIED DUMMY	0.46078****	0.24701****	1.07197****	0.35063****
	(0.09089)	(0.04714)	(0.20328)	(0.07555)
AGE	−0.02126****	−0.01470****	−0.05604****	−0.01432***
	(0.00757)	(0.00397)	(0.01573)	(0.00652)
SCHOOLING	−0.20422***	−0.14388****	0.00997	−0.18473***
	(0.10287)	(0.05214)	(0.17742)	(0.09141))
SCHOOLING^2	0.00709**	0.00462****	−0.00014	0.00642**
	(0.00370)	(0.00190)	(0.00623)	(0.00329)
EXPERIENCE	−0.02758****	−0.01235****	−0.03329**	−0.0239****
	(0.00752)	(0.00400)	(0.01866)	(0.00647)
EXPERIENCE^2	0.000108****	0.000046***	0.00033	0.00009****
	(0.000038)	(0.000021)	(0.00038)	(0.00003)
SIBLINGS	0.06384****	0.00730	0.13163****	0.05039****
	(0.01993)	(0.01039)	(0.04434)	(0.01724)
TRAFFIC TIME	−0.05215*	−0.03168**	−0.14216***	−0.04056*
	(0.03723)	(0.01849)	(0.06857)	(0.03197)
HOUSE SIZE	0.000216***	0.00017****	−0.0000028	0.000199***
	(0.000103)	(0.000048)	(0.00021)	(0.00009)
9 DUMMIES (Results presented in table 10.6)				
Number of observations	929	929	929	929
Wald χ^2	235.11	288.77	153.02	
Prob > χ^2	0.0000	0.0000	0.0000	
ln σ	−0.12738****			
	(0.03920)			
δ		−0.42616****		
		(0.03149)		
Pseudo R^2		0.0852	0.2963	
R^2				0.2324

Notes: Terms inside brackets are standard errors estimated by the method of White (1980) and Huber (1967).

****Significant at the 1 percent level for one-tail test.

***Significant at the 2.5 percent level.

**Significant at the 5 percent level.

*Significant at the 10 percent level.

married people are higher. The negative effect of age on desired TFR may be due to the nature of the dependent variable. Young adults may not fully realize the high cost of bearing, nurturing, and educating children and therefore may plan to have too many children. However, as they get older, they become more realistic about the cost.[18] The time it takes to travel to work competes for resources that can be provided to the children. The negative effect on TRAFFIC TIME again provides support to the *Opportunity Cost Hypothesis.*

The positive impact of the number of siblings of the parent may be due to economy of scale. Siblings themselves sometimes can help out in babysitting and their children can be convenient playmates of one's own children. The result again supports the *Opportunity Cost Hypothesis.*[19] This phenomenon may cause long-term effect for future generations. As the average size of the core family is decreasing due to the low TFR, future parents will have fewer siblings of their own. That will in turn weaken their intent to bear children.

It is well known that population density in Hong Kong is among the highest in the world, with the result that its residents have to live in relatively small quarters. According to the results in table 10.5, the small size of Hong Kong's residential quarters is likely one of the factors causing the low TFR there. This is consistent with the findings in a recent paper by Murphy, Simon, and Tamura (2008), which provides evidence indicating that population density, or price of space, is negatively correlated with fertility rate in the United States. Given the likely scenario that housing in Hong Kong will continue to be expensive, the marginal cost of raising children will remain high.

Assuming that children are normal goods, we should expect some positive effect of income on fertility rate. However, the results of the Tobit regression in table 10.5 indicate the income effect is quantitatively rather small and statistically insignificant.[20] One may suspect that the apparent absence of significant income effect is due to problems inherent in the Tobit estimation, which presupposes that the error term is normally distributed. However, the dependent variable—desired total fertility rate—consists of discrete integers. An alternative approach is to rely on a count model. By doing so, we can also check the robustness of the other results obtained by the Tobit model.

---

18. Heaton, Jacobson, and Holland (1999) study how intended childlessness changes over time. Our finding that intended fertility declines as age goes up is consistent with this early study. If we use the actual number of children as the dependent variable, then the evidence indicates that this is positively related to age.

19. Parr (2005) also finds that the number of siblings of a parent is positively related to her own fertility rate.

20. Income data from the survey has been modified to reduce possible biases in the estimation of income effect. For married respondents whose reported personal income is zero (most of them being housewives), we use the income of spouse instead of the person's own income.

A convenient count model that can be used is the Poisson model. However, this has the restrictive property that the expected number of children would be equal to the variance of the number of children. To mitigate this problem, we employ a generalized Poisson model, which is more flexible. The probability mass function of this model is[21]

$$(10) \qquad f(y_i; \lambda_i, \delta) = \frac{[\lambda_i(\lambda_i + \delta y_i)^{y_i-1}e^{-\lambda_i-\delta y_i}]}{y_i!}$$

for $y_i = 0, 1, 2, \ldots$, and $\ln \lambda_i = x_i'\beta$. If the parameter $\delta = 0$, then equation (10) reduces exactly to the probability mass function of the usual Poisson model. It can be shown that

$$(11) \qquad E[y_i \mid x_i] = \frac{\lambda_i}{(1 - \delta)},$$

$$(12) \qquad Var[y_i \mid x_i] = \frac{E[y_i \mid x_i]}{(1 - \delta)^2}.$$

Results of the generalized Poisson estimation are presented in regression (II) of table 10.5.[22] It can readily be seen that the coefficient for the income variable, though very small, is statistically significant and positive, thus supporting the hypothesis that children are normal goods.[23] All other results are similar to those in the Tobit estimation, with the exception that the coefficient for the size of living quarters is not significant. The core story for demographic transition remains clear and valid. Thus, the results in the benchmark regression (I) appear to be robust. In (IV) of table 10.5, we also report results from an ordinary least squares (OLS) estimation. Again, we find results similar to the Tobit estimation.

If we substitute the median values of all the relevant variables into regression (I), we can readily show that quantitatively, the most powerful factor causing the decline in desired TFR is SCHOOLING. But the median years of schooling of the Hong Kong population is considerably below those in highly developed economies. What are the other factors that contribute to the low or zero fertility in Hong Kong? In all the regressions in table 10.5, I have added nine dummy variables, each representing the respondent's subjective assessment of different factors that may affect fertility. These variables, acting as controls, considerably sharpen the estimations for the

21. See Hardin and Hilbe (2007) and Wang and Famoye (1997).

22. Since the estimated δ in regression (III) is negative, there is "underdispersion" in the data.

23. The marginal effect of an increase in income on fertility rate in the generalized Poisson model can be estimated by making use of the incidence rate ratio. To induce a person having one child to have another one, his or her monthly income has to be increased by more than HK\$85,000. In the survey conducted, there is a question asking the respondents to reveal how much government subsidy they would have to be paid in order that they were willing to bear one child more than what they wanted. The answer for most respondents was several million Hong Kong dollars. This seems to be consistent with the very small income effect estimated here.

objective variables included in table 10.5. The results for these dummies also provide additional opportunities for us to test the hypotheses discussed earlier. Discussion of these dummies will be postponed to subsection 10.4.3, which follows.

10.4.3   Childless Families

The last subsection provides explanations for the occurrence of the demographic transition in Hong Kong. We now focus on the choice for zero fertility. The aforementioned Tobit and generalized Poisson models are appropriate tools for predicting fertility rates of different values, including zero. However, one can argue that the factors determining the choice between zero and positive fertility could be different from the decision on whether one should have even more children. The Tobit or generalized Poisson model does not recognize that the margin between zero and one could be different from, say, the margin between three and four children. Hence, there is some value in using a binary model to explicitly deal with the choice between zero and positive fertility.

A convenient approach is to construct a binary variable, FERTDUMMY, whose value is defined to be equal to one for a person who plans to have at least one child, and zero if he or she chooses not to have any children. The probability of the occurrence of childless families can be estimated by a Probit model, which can be represented by the following:

(13) $Prob\,(Y = 1|x) = \Phi(x'\beta),$

where Y is a dichotomous dependent variable that assumes the value of either 0 or 1, $\Phi(.)$ is the standard normal distribution function, x is a vector of explanatory variables, and β is the vector of the corresponding coefficients. Estimation results of the Probit model are presented in regression (III) in table 10.5.

Before interpreting the results from the Probit estimation, we should note three things. First, the variables included in the two regressions are the same, which make comparisons between the two easier. Second, the error terms of both regressions are normally distributed. Third, by using a single value of one to represent different quantities of children, the Probit method loses some information that is available to the Tobit estimator. This makes Probit a less efficient estimator. Despite this, comparison of regressions (I) and (III) readily indicates that most of the results obtained in the Tobit model remain intact in Probit.[24] The exceptions are SCHOOLING, SCHOOLING^2, and HOUSE SIZE, which do not have significant results.

At this stage of economic development in Hong Kong, years of schooling seem to have stronger effects on the number of children beyond one than on

---

24. We have also tried a Logit model. The results are very similar to those in Probit and therefore not reported here.

the decision of whether to have children at all.[25] The average size of living quarters in Hong Kong seems to be able to accommodate a small family with one child. The cost of space for the first child may be low enough for it not to be an important concern. However, marginal cost of space for additional children may be much higher. That is why HOUSE SIZE is an important variable in the Tobit model, but much less so in Probit, which deals only with positive or zero fertility decisions.

10.4.4   Subjective Assessment Variables

In the regressions reported previously, I have included nine dummy variables as controls, but their results have been suppressed. This subsection discusses them. In the original survey, twenty questions related to the respondents' subjective views of the determinants of fertility were asked, and the answers were recorded as dummy variables. These answers provide nontrivial information on what the respondents regarded as important in affecting their own personal fertility decisions. The twenty dummies were all tried out, but finally I have included into the regressions only those that are statistically significant. Although some respondents had claimed that the other eleven factors were important, the statistical evidence does not support the claim and so they are excluded.

Table 10.6 reports the results on the nine included dummies. Some respondents believed that these were important factors and some did not. Among those who did, the statistical evidence shows that these factors would indeed make a difference in their decisions. Although I have only reported the estimations for regressions (I) to (III), the results are similar in the OLS regression (IV).

Quantitatively, the factor that seems to have the most powerful effect on fertility is whether the respondent liked children or not. This indicates that the preference parameter, μ, which we discussed in section 10.3, is indeed a useful control. However, we should note that only 4.5 percent of the respondents claimed that they did not like children. This percentage is not big enough to explain the very low fertility rate in Hong Kong.

Estimations for other variables in table 10.6 can shed more light on fertility decisions. Variable (a)—negative impact on job and career—can be interpreted as part of the opportunity cost of having children. About one-third of the respondents regard this as an important factor. The negative sign of the parameter estimated again supports the *Opportunity Cost Hypothesis.*

Variables (b), (c), and (e) are related to the respondents' subjective evaluations of how efficient or confident they would be in meeting the obligations of raising and educating children. Apparently, a sizable proportion of people did not feel that they were prepared. These results support both

---

25. The theoretical explanation behind this phenomenon is being explored in another paper by this author.

Table 10.6   **Results for the dummy variables on subjective assessment**

	From (I) Tobit	From (II) Generalized Poisson	From (III) Probit	Percentage of answers with dummy = 1
Factors that negatively affect my fertility decision: Yes = 1; No = 0				
(a) Negative impact on my job and career	−0.18370**** (0.06793)	−0.06121** (0.03527)	−0.28677*** (0.12576)	32.6
(b) No confidence in educational system	−0.14572*** (0.06863)	−0.06128** (0.03545)	−0.22817** (0.12287)	27.0
(c) Don't know how to raise children	−0.26491**** (0.08241)	−0.17184**** (0.04219)	−0.41467**** (0.13671)	21.1
(d) Don't like children	−1.07425**** (0.23034)	−0.46225**** (0.08297)	−0.97074**** (0.24338)	4.5
(e) No confidence in marriage	−0.24085** (0.1256)	−0.12819*** (0.06291)	−0.41780*** (0.18717)	9.5
Factors that positively affect my fertility decision: Yes = 1; No = 0				
(f) Like children	0.46071**** (0.07692)	0.12010**** (0.04214)	0.77030**** (0.12632)	69.9
(g) Having children is part of my social responsibility	0.23870**** (0.08258)	0.11025**** (0.04018)	0.34071** (0.18914)	16.0
(h) Raise children to secure old-age support	0.14859* (0.09992)	0.19844**** (0.04588)	0.15119 (0.18264)	14.6
If you don't have children, what will you do to protect your retirement?				
(i) Don't know what to do = 1; otherwise = 0.	0.32013*** (0.15618)	0.13867** (0.07107)	0.15278 (0.30129)	6.0

****Significant at the 1 percent level for one-tail test.
***Significant at the 2.5 percent level.
**Significant at the 5 percent level.
*Significant at the 10 percent level.

the *Opportunity Cost Hypothesis* and *Educational Technology Hypothesis.* Variable (g) indicates that some respondents' decisions were dependent on the views of others. It is interesting to note that in the spring of 2005, the Chief Secretary of the Hong Kong government at that time, Donald Tsang, made a casual, but widely reported, public remark that women in Hong Kong should bear three children because too low a fertility rate could have negative social consequences.[26] In a city where information dissemination by the media is rapid, many people would have remembered this well-known remark, and some (16 percent in our sample) would believe that giving birth to children was part of their social responsibility. Finally, Tobit and Poisson estimations for variables (h) and (i) indicate that for those people who have

26. Mr. Tsang told the author of this chapter, in an informal occasion subsequent to his remark, that the remark was indeed casual and that the government of Hong Kong would not adopt any policy to encourage higher fertility.

strong old-age security motives, it is more likely for them to increase the quantity of children. This supports the *Old-Age Security Hypothesis.*

Although the primary purpose of including these dummies as control variables is to sharpen the estimations for other variables, we have also obtained more evidence to support the hypotheses discussed in section 10.3.

10.5 Concluding Remarks

In this chapter, I have used Hong Kong's experience to demonstrate that economies undergoing rapid demographic transition may end up having large percentages of women who choose not to bear any children. The serious implications of this possible outcome should be studied carefully.

I have shown that an extension of the Ehrlich-Lui (1991) model can naturally generate not only the demographic transition, but also zero fertility rates for some families. Based on this model, I have proposed several testable hypotheses related to the determinants of demographic transition. These hypotheses are tested by a Tobit model, a generalized Poisson model, and a Probit model, using data from a survey that I conducted. The empirical results make a lot of sense. The quantity-quality of children trade-off, which drives the demographic transition, clearly exists. Other variables, such as different measures of the cost of educating and raising children, number of siblings of the parents, preferences for children, sizes of residential quarters, and social responsibilities also play significant roles in determining total fertility rate.

A number of puzzles remain unexplained in this chapter. For example, the speed of the emergence of childless families in Hong Kong, and possibly in some Chinese cities and several other East Asian economies as well, seems to defy any form of culture-based explanations. Confucian values, which heavily influence East Asian countries, attach the highest importance to making dynastic families sustainable. Why is it that we find some of the world's lowest fertility rates in these economies? The findings in this chapter also suggest that heterogeneous preferences for children may be an important variable that should be explicitly modeled in future research.

Appendix

In this appendix, I shall present details of the survey, upon which the empirical results of this chapter are based.

The survey was conducted over a three-month period spanning from November 2007 to February 2008. Each respondent was requested to answer forty questions, but some of these could be broken down into several sub-questions. Some questions were similar to those asked in the Census conducted once every five years by the Hong Kong government, but there were also new questions introduced. Most of the questions were related to the socioeconomic and educational backgrounds of the respondents and their spouses. There were also specific categorical questions on the factors that the respondents deemed important in affecting their fertility decisions. A key question, not available in the Census, was the additional number of children the respondent would like to have. Before formally conducting the survey, the questions were tested on a small sample of respondents to identify potential problems and to make improvements. This chapter has not fully made use of the answers to all the questions.

The respondents were chosen randomly according to the following procedure. The research teams were sent to each of the eighteen official districts in Hong Kong. The number of respondents chosen in each district was proportional to the population distribution in that district. The research teams were instructed to focus on people who appeared to fall within the age range of twenty to forty-five. The research teams regularly reviewed the age distribution of the respondents to make sure that they were compatible with that of the general population in Hong Kong. We also decided that about three-quarters of the respondents should be women. The survey was conducted at different hours of the day and different days of the week in public areas of these eighteen districts. To enhance randomness, the research teams chose the nth person on sight in the area after finishing with a respondent. A cash coupon equivalent to HK$50 was given to every correspondent who completed the questionnaires. The sample size of the survey is 1,017 observations.

After all the answers had been coded, the distributions of many socioeconomic variables were compared to those from the census data. We have not spotted major discrepancies.

References

Abma, J., and G. M. Martinez. 2006. Childlessness among older women in the United States: Trends and profiles. *Journal of Marriage and Family* 68 (4): 1045–56.

Barber, J. S., and W. G. Axinn. 2004. New ideas and fertility limitation: The role of mass media. *Journal of Marriage and Family* 66 (5): 1180–1200.

Becker, G. S., and R. J. Barro. 1988. A reformulation of the economic theory of fertility. *Quarterly Journal of Economics* 103 (1): 1–25.

Becker, G. S., K. M. Murphy, and R. Tamura. 1990. Human capital, fertility and economic growth. *Journal of Political Economy* 98 (5): S12–S37.

Blackburn, K., and G. P. Cipriani. 2002. A model of longevity, fertility and growth. *Journal of Economic Dynamics and Control* 26 (2): 187–204.

Boldrin, M., and L. E. Jones. 2002. Mortality, fertility, and saving in a Malthusian economy. *Review of Economic Dynamics* 5 (4): 775–814.

Central Intelligence Agency, United States Government. *The world factbook,* 2008. Available at: https://www.cia.gov/library/publications/the-world-factbook/index .html.

Census and Statistics Department, Hong Kong SAR Government. 1996. 1996 Population By-Census 1% sample dataset.

———. 2001. 2001 Population Census 5% sample dataset.

———. 2006. 2006 Population By-Census 5% sample dataset.

———. 2007. *Women and men in Hong Kong: Key statistics.* Available at: http://www .bycensus2006.gov.hk/en/data/data2/index.htm.

China National Bureau of Statistics. 2007. *2005 Nian Quanguo 1% Renkou Chouyang Diaochao Ziliao* (Data from 1% Sample National Population Census of 2005). Beijing: China Statistics Press.

Coale, A. J. 1987. Demographic transition. In *The new Palgrave: A dictionary of economics,* vol. 1, ed. J. Eatwell, M. Milgate, and P. Newman. London: MacMillan: 793–96.

Doepke, M. 2004. Accounting for fertility decline during the transition to growth. *Journal of Economic Growth* 9 (3): 347–83.

———. 2005. Child mortality and fertility decline: Does the Becker-Barro model fit the facts? *Journal of Population Economics* 18 (2): 337–66.

Dorbritz, J. 2008. Germany: Family diversity with low actual and desired fertility. *Demographic Research* 19 (Jul.–Dec.): 557–97.

Dyson, T., and M. Murphy. 1985. The onset of fertility transition. *Population and Development Review* 11 (3): 399–440.

Easterlin, R. A. 1987. Fertility. In *The new Palgrave: A dictionary of economics,* vol. 2, ed. J. Eatwell, M. Milgate, and P. Newman. London: MacMillan: 302–307.

Ehrlich, I., and F. T. Lui. 1991. Intergenerational trade, longevity and economic growth. *Journal of Political Economy* 99 (5): 1029–59.

———. 1997. The problem of population and growth: A review of the literature from Malthus to contemporary models of endogenous population and endogenous growth. *Journal of Economic Dynamics and Control* 21 (1): 205–42.

Greene, W. H. 2003. *Econometric analysis,* 5th ed. Upper Saddle River, NJ: Pearson Education, Inc.

Hardin, J. W., and J. M. Hilbe. 2007. *Generalized linear models and extensions,* 2nd ed. College Station, TX: Stata Press.

Heaton, T. B., C. K. Jacobson, and K. Holland. 1999. Persistence and change in decisions to remain childless. *Journal of Marriage and the Family* 61 (2): 531–39.

Huber, P. J. 1967. The behavior of maximum likelihood estimates under non-standard conditions. In *Proceedings of the fifth Berkeley symposium on mathematical statistics and probability,* ed. L. M. LeCam and J. Neyman, 221–33. Berkeley: University of California Press.

Kalemli-Ozcan, S. 2003. A stochastic model of mortality, fertility, and human capital investment. *Journal of Development Economics* 70 (1): 103–18.

Kneale, D., and H. Joshi. Postponement and childlessness: Evidence from two British Cohorts. *Demographic Research* 19 (Jul.–Dec.): 1935–68.

Koropeckyj-Cox, T., and G. Pendell. 2007. The gender gap in attitudes about childlessness in the United States. *Journal of Marriage and Family* 69 (4): 899–915.

Mencarini, L., and M. L. Tanturri. 2006. High fertility or childlessness: Micro-level determinants of reproductive behaviour in Italy. *Population* 61 (4): 389–415.

Murphy, K. M., C. Simon, and R. Tamura. 2008. Fertility decline, baby boom and economic growth. *Journal of Human Capital* 2 (3): 262–302.

Parr, N. J. 2005. Family background, schooling and childlessness in Australia. *Journal of Biosocial Science* 37 (2): 229–43.

Schmidt, L. 2008. Risk preferences and the timing of marriage and childbearing. *Demography* 45 (2): 439–60.

Shorto, R. 2008. No babies. *New York Times Magazine,* June 29, 34–41, 68.

Soares, R. R. 2006. The effect of longevity on fertility: Evidence from the Brazilian demographic and health survey. *Journal of Population Economics* 19 (1): 71–97.

Wang, W., and F. Famoye. 1997. Modeling household fertility decisions with generalized Poisson regression. *Journal of Population Economics* 10 (3): 273–83.

White, H. 1980. A heteroskedasticity-consistent covariance matrix estimator and a direct test for heteroskedasticity. *Econometrica* 48 (4): 817–30.

World Bank. 1984. *Population change and economic development.* New York: Oxford University Press.

———. 1992 and 1993. *World development report.* New York: Oxford University Press.

Zhang, J., and J. Zhang. 2005. The effect of life expectancy on fertility, saving, schooling and economic growth: Theory and evidence. *Scandinavian Journal of Economics* 107 (1): 45–66.

Comment   Hongbin Li

In this interesting chapter, the author examines demographic transition and growth both theoretically and empirically.

Theoretically, it adapts a *Journal of Political Economy* (JPE) paper by the author and a colleague (Ehrlich and Lui 1991) in a way that allows zero fertility. Its findings can be summarized in the following hypotheses:

- Demographic transition hypothesis: Total fertility rate of a potential parent is negatively related to his or her human capital.
- Opportunity cost hypothesis: When a parent finds it costly to raise children, he or she will have fewer of them.
- Educational technology hypothesis: The parent's fertility rate is positively related to how efficient he or she is educating his or her children.
- Old-age security hypothesis: If a person's old-age security motive is stronger, he or she will raise more children.

Drawing on census and survey data from Hong Kong, the chapter finds empirical evidence that support these hypotheses.

The chapter has many nice contributions. First, it has examined a very important issue in economic development. The theory and empirical evidence can potentially shed light on our understanding of how demographic transition happens and where it will end up for developing countries. Second, low fertility has become a very serious policy issue in Hong Kong. In fact, many people do not even get married, not to speak of having children.

Hongbin Li is a professor of economics in the School of Economics and Management at Tsinghua University.

The following are some comments. As the theory is simple, only serving the purposes of generating some testable hypotheses, I will focus on the empirical work.

1. A nice thing is that the author uses four different models in table 10.5—Tobit, Poisson, Probit, and OLS—all of which generate similar results.

2. The chapter uses several variables to examine the efficiency hypothesis. Some are better than others. Using the fact that married people have more children to support the efficiency hypothesis does not seem to be very good. The exact mechanism of how the traffic time affects fertility also deserves more explanations.

3. While education can be a good right-hand side variable, experience may not be. Having an additional child will affect labor supply of a woman in most economies, including Hong Kong. Also, the number of siblings seems to be a left-hand side variable rather than an explanatory variable.

4. House size is a very interesting variable. If the author can prove that housing price increases with house size in a convex way, then it is an interesting experiment to examine its impact on fertility.

Comment   Roberto S. Mariano

This chapter seeks to identify significant factors affecting fertility choices; in particular, studying the causes of low fertility and childless families in Hong Kong. The theoretical framework is a variation of the Ehrlich-Lui model that accommodates zero fertility. The empirical evidence is based on the author's survey data. The chapter presents reasons to expect zero fertility, discusses a theoretical framework generating both demographic transition and corner solution for fertility, and performs an empirical analysis to verify the following testable hypotheses arising from the model:

- Total fertility rate (TFR) of the potential parent is negatively related to his or her human capital.
- If an adult likes children, it is less likely that he or she will have very few or no children.
- The parent's fertility rate is positively related to how efficient he or she is in educating his or her children.
- When a parent finds it costly to raise children, she will have fewer of them.

Roberto S. Mariano is a professor of economics and statistics, and dean of the School of Economics at Singapore Management University, and Professor Emeritus of Economics and Statistics of the University of Pennsylvania.

In the chapter's empirical analysis, the main dependent variable is TFR, defined as actual number of children + expected number of future children. A Tobit model for TFR is estimated, based on HK survey data described in the appendix. Tobit is the appropriate model here since TFR is censored at zero. The explanatory variables used in the Tobit regression are:

- Years of schooling (squared schooling)
- Years of work experience (squared experience)
- Marital status
- Income
- Age
- Siblings
- Traffic time
- House size
- Eight dummy variables

In this empirical analysis, the author brings up the potential endogeneity of income. In the context of this study, it should be pointed out that income would be endogenous in the model not because of its correlation with other explanatory variables (e.g., schooling and experience), but rather because of its correlation with the error term in the Tobit model.

Furthermore, the explanatory variable SCHOOLING is a prime candidate to be endogenous—TFR affects SCHOOLING—and such endogeneity should be accounted for in the estimation of the Tobit model.

The chapter also studies a logit model for childless families. In a way, there is no need to do this. The estimated Tobit model delivers a more efficient estimate of the probability of the occurrence of childless families:

$$\Pr(y_i = 0) = \Pr(y_i^* < 0) = \Pr(e_i < -x_i'\beta).$$

Contributors

Douglas Almond
Department of Economics
Columbia University
International Affairs Building, MC
  3308
420 West 118th Street
New York, NY 10027

David E. Bloom
Department of Global Health and
  Population
Harvard School of Public Health
665 Huntington Avenue
Boston, MA 02115

David Canning
Department of Global Health and
  Population
Harvard School of Public Health
665 Huntington Avenue
Boston, MA 02115

Worawan Chandoevwit
Thailand Development Research
  Institute (TDRI)
565 Ramkhamhaeng Soi 39
Ramkhamhaeng Rd, Wanthonglang
Bangkok 10310 Thailand

Jiyeun Chang
Korea Labor Institute
35, Eunhaenggil, Yeongdeungpo-gu
Seoul 150-740 Korea

Amonthep Chawla
Thailand Development Research
  Institute (TDRI)
565 Ramkhamhaeng Soi 39
Ramkhamhaeng Rd, Wanthonglang
Bangkok 10310 Thailand

Kyungsoo Choi
Korea Development Institute
PO Box 113, Cheongnyang
Seoul 130-868 Korea

Lena Edlund
Economics Department
Columbia University
1002A International Affairs Building,
  MC 3308
420 West 118th Street
New York, NY 10027

Jocelyn E. Finlay
Department of Global Health and
  Population
Harvard School of Public Health
9 Bow Street
Cambridge, MA 02138

Chin Hee Hahn
Korea Development Institute
PO Box 113, Cheongnyang
Seoul 130-868 Korea

Alejandro N. Herrin
Philippine Institute for Development
    Studies
NEDA sa Makati Building
106 Amorsolo Street
Legaspi Village, Makati City
Philippines

Takatoshi Ito
Graduate School of Economics
University of Tokyo
7-3-1 Hongo, Bunkyo-ku
Tokyo 113-0033 Japan

Dae Il Kim
School of Economics
Seoul National University
Seoul 151-742 Korea

Hisam Kim
Korea Development Institute
PO Box 113, Chongnyang
Seoul 130-012, Korea

Chulhee Lee
School of Economics
Seoul National University
San 56-1, Sillim 9 dong, Gwanak-gu
Seoul 151-742 Korea

Jong-Wha Lee
Asian Development Bank
PO Box 789
0980 Manila, Philippines

Ronald Lee
Departments of Demography and
    Economics
University of California, Berkeley
2232 Piedmont Avenue
Berkeley, CA 94720

Sang-Hyop Lee
University of Hawaii at Manoa
Saunders 542
2424 Maile Way
Honolulu, HI 96822

Hongbin Li
Department of Economics
Tsinghua University
Beijing, 100084 China

Meng-chun Liu
Chung-Hua Institution for Economic
    Research
75 Chang-Hsing Street
Taipei, 106, Taiwan

Francis T. Lui
Department of Economics
Hong Kong University of Science and
    Technology
Clear Water Bay
Kowloon, Hong Kong

Roberto S. Mariano
School of Economics
Singapore Management University
90 Stamford Road
Singapore 178903

Andrew Mason
Department of Economics
University of Hawaii at Manoa
2424 Maile Way
Honolulu, HI 96822

Rikiya Matsukura
Population Research Institute
Nihon University
1-3-2, Misaki-cho, Chiyoda-ku
Tokyo 101-8360, Japan

Hyungpyo Moon
Korea Development Institute
PO Box 113, Chongnyang
Seoul 130-012, Korea

Naohiro Ogawa
Population Research Institute
Nihon University
1-3-2 Misaki-cho, Chiyoda-ku
Tokyo 101-8360, Japan

Fumio Ohtake
Institute of Social and Economic
    Research
Osaka University
6-1, Mihogaoka, Ibaraki
Osaka 567-0047, Japan

Chang-Gyun Park
College of Business Administration
Chung-Ang University
Seoul, Korea

Andrew K. Rose
Haas School of Business
    Administration
University of California, Berkeley
Berkeley, CA 94720-1900

Shinpei Sano
Graduate School of Economics
Kobe University
2-1 Rokko-dai, Nada
Kobe 657-8501, Japan

Kwanho Shin
Department of Economics
Korea University
5-1 Anam-Dong, Sungbuk-Ku
Seoul 136-701, Korea

Noriyuki Takayama
Institute of Economic Research
Hitotsubashi University
2-1 Naka, Kunitachi
Tokyo 186-8603 Japan

Junsen Zhang
Department of Economics
Chinese University of Hong Kong
Shatin, N.T., Hong Kong

Author Index

Subject Index